PAT COLLINS
KING OF SHOWMEN

FREDA ALLEN & NED WILLIAMS

URALIA PRESS
23 WESTLAND ROAD WOLVERHAMPTON WV3 9NZ

Pat Collins - King of Showmen
by Freda Allen & Ned Williams
Uralia Press, Wolverhampton, 1991
ISBN: 0 9511223 8 X

Word processing	MSB LTD
Photo processing	Jan Endean
	& Galata Print
Design	John Revill
Cover	John Revill
Printing & binding	William Gibbons & Sons Ltd
	Wolverhampton

| POST YOUR LETTER EARLY IN THE WEEK |

THE WORLD'S FAIR

| Subscriptions For the time being we regret we cannot accept any new subscribers. A waiting list is being compiled and notification will be sent when vacancies occur. |

No. 2049. Registered at the General Post Office as a Newspaper SATURDAY, DECEMBER 18, 1943. Postage: Inland, 1½d.; Foreign, 1½d PRICE 3d.

PAT
By JAMES R. STYLES.

You never really knew, Pat, how many friends you had made through the long and interesting 85 years that were yours, and that so successfully contributed to the welfare of your people and their business, until you were called to a well-earned rest from labours whose results will never fade from the annals of the show world.

It was only on the day that you were parting for a little time from those who knew you best, Pat, that the overwhelming evidence of their love and high regard for you was so plainly seen. They came from all over Britain to say a sorrowful "au revoir" to a great pal—a pal that the passing years had made ever dearer—and they only represented a tiny few, Pat, whose thoughts and prayers were with you, but who were unable through present conditions to be with you in person. The hundreds that did come represented every shade and class in the world of public entertainers and those who shared in and admired their efforts. They were your friends, Pat, tried and tested in the furnace of years through which they had wandered with you. No social, religious or political barriers lessened in any degree the great esteem in which they held one of the grandest personalities that the show world has ever known. Jew and Gentile, rich and poor, the young and the old, the strong and the feeble, were all there, Pat, in that vast gathering drawn by a common desire to stand once more by your side, as they had stood so many times in the past. There were tears in the eyes of the mighty ones in any business, as there were in the eyes of the humble worker, or the owner of a tiny stall, as their lips closed on the sad word, farewell.

Grand Accomplishments.

They were your people, Pat,—the people of the show world that you so dearly loved, and had done so much to make a better one. Other pens more gifted than mine are to-day lifting the veil that hid from the greater world outside many of your grand accomplishments, so that it may realize to some degree the reason for our sorrow and regret at your going.

The civic heads from the district you loved so well were there, Pat, to share in a common grief and your friends the police whose cause you always championed were close beside you, and the streets were filled by thousands of sympathetic workers, shopkeepers and others who knew you so well. It was a grand tribute, Pat, to the work of making friends—a work whose success was testified and proved by such a mighty gathering.

Lover of Children.

And there were tiny groups of children, whom you loved, and who affectionately knew you as Uncle Pat, standing all along the streets, and some had tiny bunches of flowers in hands pinched with cold, and in their eyes was a great wonder as they gazed at the solemn cortege as it bore away their friend. You loved all children, Pat. I knew that well, by scores of incidents that I have personally witnessed. Do you remember Chester, when you gave the usual free rides to the kiddies and they sang to a song being played on the organ in voices that you said sounded like angels singing? I thought of that afternoon, Pat, as the organ played in that beautiful church of St. Patrick's on the morning of our parting, and tiny children were singing for you Pat as they had always sung for their great friend; only this time there were lots of unseen little children joining in that hymn of praise and deep regret, and greater still would be that mighty pæan of welcome to where angels always sing, and where there is no more parting, no more tears, no more death, only joy and love and life everlasting, the eternal reward that God will not withhold from such a good and faithful servant.

There will be Pilgrims.

Your great and loving heart, Pat, rests in a quiet churchyard to which many a showman will make a pilgrimage to whisper thanks for the example of goodness and generosity you have bequeathed to present and future generations; while your understanding spirit will watch over the destiny of your people, whose tears and deep sorrow at your leaving are the grandest payment that any man could earn during a lifetime spent in their company and service.

"We are judged by deeds, and not by words, by years, and not by fleeting breaths."

Au revoir, dear friend Pat. We shall meet again.

James Styles

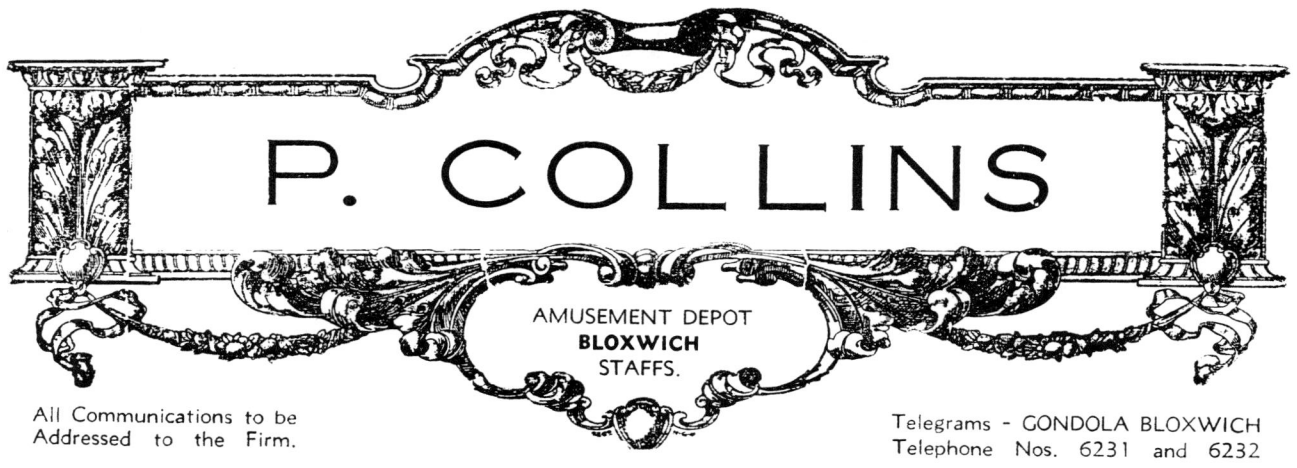

This book has been produced as a limited edition of 2500 copies.

The first thousand copies have been numbered and signed by the authors.

The authors acknowledge the support for this venture given by members of the following societies who ordered their copies in advance of publication:

The Black Country Society

The Fairground Society

The Fairground Association of Great Britain

The text of this book represents the views of the authors, but not necessarily of those who have contributed towards it. The copyright of the photographs belongs to the contributors.

ABOVE: Pat Collins' 1937 Speedway Ark, built by Orton & Spooner and first managed by Billy Watts (Wattie). Note the motorcycles mounted at right angles to the boards of the extension front, the flags, and the overall majesty and grandeur of the machine. By 1937 Pat had presented up to date rides on a grand scale for over forty years. Doing justice to the machine, young Harry Mills (son of Driver Billy Mills) took this photograph at Bloxwich when the ride was new.

FRONTISPIECE;

Pat poses on the steps of the living van, with World's Fair in hand, at Birmingham in 1934 - the period when the "King of Showmen" enjoyed holding court in his van, and sharing his memories with visiting reporters and fans.
Collection of John Pugh)

COVER PICTURES:

LEFT: The centre portion of the Wonderland Organ front as now presented by Bill Hunt, photographed in 1990.
(Photo Ned Williams)

RIGHT: The McLaren engine, "Goliath", in the condition to which it was restored by Rev.F.A.Coley, seen here at Packington Rally, 19/9/1970.
(Photo Brian Yates)

CENTRE: Pat Collins in a photograph believed to have been taken about 1909, at the age of 50.
(Walsall Local History Centre)

BACK COVER:
The Showmen's Guild Testimonial presented to Pat Collins by William Wilson and the London Section on Pat's retirement (1929).
(Collection of Molly Seldon)

CONTENTS

Introduction			9
Chapter 1	The First Thirty Years	1859 - 1889	15
Chapter 2	The Battle of Walsall	1890 - 1894	21
Chapter 3	Pat Collins in the Nineties	1895 - 1899	25
Chapter 4	Edwardian Gentleman	1900 - 1914	31
Chapter 5	Councillor Pat Collins	1918 - 1929	39
Chapter 6	Pat Collins, MP	1922 - 1924	51
Chapter 7	Alderman Pat Collins	1930 - 1939	61
Chapter 8	Mayor of Walsall	1938 - 1939	73
Chapter 9	The Man with a Golden Heart	1939 - 1943	81
Chapter 10	Keep the Flag Flying - 1	1944 - 1962	85
Chapter 11	Keep the Flag Flying - 2	1962 - 1992	93
Chapter 12	Pat and the Showmen's Guild		97
Chapter 13	The Amusement Parks		101
	Sutton Park		
	New Brighton		
	Yarmouth Pleasure Beach		
	Barry Island		
Chapter 14	Bioscopes to Cinemas		117
	Black Country Cinemas		
	Oakengates		
	Chester		
	The Wirral		
	Other Halls		
Chapter 15	Fairground Equipment		131
	New Rides		
	Organ Checklist		
	'Second hand rides'		
	Young Pat's Rides		
	Walsall John's Rides		
	Gravity Rides		
	Death Rides		
Chapter 16	Fairground Transport		165
	Engine List		
	The Showtracs		
	Other transport		
Chapter 17	The Fairs		189
	Birmingham Fairs		
	Coventry		
	Black Country Fairs		
	Cannock Chase		
	Out in Shropshire		
	Chester		
	Out into Wales		
	Heading North West		
	The North West		
	Heading South West		
	Heading North East		
	Heading East		
	Heading South East		
	The Potteries		
APPENDIX 1	WHO's WHO		225
	Biography of the principal characters		
	Managers, tenants, drivers, etc.,		
APPENDIX 2	PERSONAL TESTIMONIES		253

A pre-First World War view of Chester Races in full swing reveals the Jungle Motors in action surrounded by early trucks and a horse-drawn wagon.
(Collection of Joe Chadwick)

COMMENDATION

Many people could lay claim to being an expert in a particular field, but it is rare for anyone to justly be regarded as a 'character'. PAT COLLINS, the Fairground man truly achieved this distinction.

No-one in the Black Country thought about Fairgrounds or Annual Wakes without having Pat Collins in mind. He built a 'push-cart' plaything into a Leisure Empire – A down-at-heel itinerant into a significant philanthropist. An almost illiterate early school leaver into his Town's Mayor and Member of Parliament.

I knew him and recognised he was a 'character'.

I remember helping to 'drum up' trade on the Roll a Penny stalls. I was 'given' a pile of pennies to roll... those watching would then begin to do the same... and other customers would be attracted to the stall. The money 'given' to me went back, of course.... I rolled it, and lost it!

The popular Sunday night Charity Concerts with the Wonderland Organ are also a source of pleasurable recollection to me. As indeed they were to my father, for he owned the Duke of York pub on the corner of Darlaston Fairground, and after the Concerts thirsty folk from the fairground would come over for refreshments.... we did very good business!

Lord Harmar Nicholls Bt., J.P.
Vice President Showmen's Guild.

Looking over Pat Collins' shoulder as he uses a microphone to address the crowd at a sacred music organ concert at Willenhall, presented on the Wonderland Organ - then part of the No.1.Scenic Railway.
(Collection of Joe Chadwick)

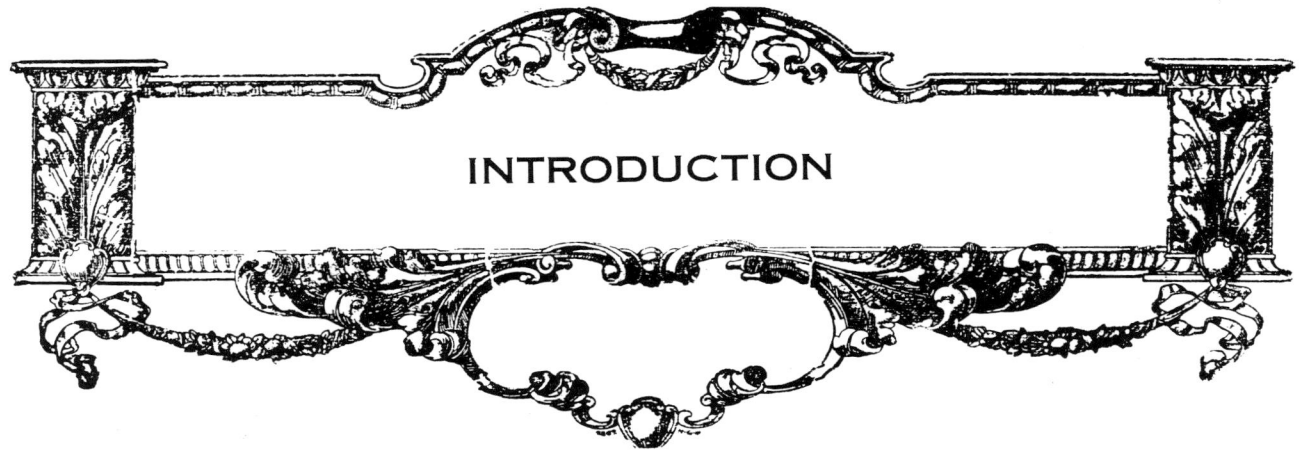

INTRODUCTION

Do you remember the excitement of the fair coming to town? Perhaps it's a childhood memory, or something that aroused your curiosity later in life?

Do you remember the engines and wagons congregating on a dusty patch of ground, or perhaps on the grass of a local common, or even on the cobblestones of a market place?

Do you remember the smell of steam and oil? Did you enjoy the sound of the organ, or if you came from a later generation did you like to hear the latest hits blasted at you from loudspeakers as you tucked into candy floss?

So do we.

Long before the fair opened there was much pleasurable anticipation, and there was the excitement to be had just by watching the fair being built up. If you missed all this, your delight might have been all the greater when stumbling across the completed fair. In the urban areas of Britain the fair must have presented a great contrast to the grey surroundings in which it suddenly appeared.

At night the magic of the fairground was even stronger - where had this vast illuminated maze of colour and movement come from? And how did it disappear again so quickly? Who were the people who sold the ginger snap and the candy floss? Who was the showman who invited us to, "Roll up, Roll up!", to see shows both challenging and mystifying? Who were the chaps who leapt on the back of our dodgems to collect the money and deliver the change? ...or who spun the cars on the Waltzer? Who brought us this strange experience - assaulting our senses, in exchange for our pocket money?

Even in the 1990s, children can respond to the exotic qualities of the travelling fair, and can ask intelligent questions: How does it work? How do they take it to pieces? How does it travel to somewhere else? Where does it go? What is it like to live in a caravan?

The interesting thing is that few adults have the answers. Most seem to be content to keep their memories of the fair in a compartment marked "nostalgia", take the unanswered questions for granted, and assume that fairs are rather like corn circles: they come and go, but they cannot be "explained".

This book has been produced by two adults who have tried to "explain", and where we have not been able to "explain", we hope you will enjoy what we have "explored". We asked ourselves two simple questions. Who was Pat Collins? What was the story of the fair that he established, and which still bears his name today?

We set out with plenty of childlike enthusiasm, not realising just how absorbed we would become, or how we would grow confused as we became swamped with detailed information, as we tried to answer these questions. But before you too plunge in, and read everything we have discovered and assembled in this book, we would like to tell you more about ourselves and the task we have undertaken.

We are both members of the Black Country Society, and believe that the Black Country is an area of outstanding geographical, historical, and social interest. We enjoy exploring the area as it is today, and investigating its' past. We take pleasure in "putting it on the map", i.e. passing on information to others, both inside and outside the region.

Whatever aspect of Black Country life is studied, from fetching the coal to building motorways, the subject soon takes on a human dimension. Every enquiry leads to people, their lives, and their contribution to our heritage.

Just suppose that we thought that the study of local history should focus on the lives of important local figures: local benefactors, civic leaders, or Parliamentary representatives. We should soon encounter the name of Pat Collins, for he was all those things.

Alternatively, we could focus on the lives of ordinary people going about their work, and enjoying their leisure. Once again we would soon come across the name of Pat Collins. Throughout the Black Country, and far beyond it, his name has been synonymous with the pleasure that the travelling fair brought to people's lives.

We became interested in Pat Collins separately, and in different ways. While writing *"Cinemas of the Black Country"* (Uralia Press, 1982). Ned had to sort out Pat's association with several local cinemas, and the role Pat played in bring early travelling cinemas, the "Bioscopes", to local fairgrounds. Freda took up the cause and made Pat Collins the subject of a project for a BA (Hons) Degree in Humanities at Wolverhampton Polytechnic in 1988.

With the help of Marilyn Lewis, then Archivist in the Walsall Library Service, we found the text of E.J.Homeshaw's short biography of Pat Collins produced in 1959. On the basis of this discovery, an article was published in the Black Country Society's journal, *The Blackcountryman* (Vol.19 No.3, summer 1986). The article concluded that Pat deserved a more detailed biography, but the task of producing it would obviously be very demanding and time consuming.

A few other accounts of Pat's life have been produced. For example, Father Greville wrote about Pat in *Merry-go-round* (See below), and Denis Miller wrote an article in *"Three on the Floor"* (No.20, March 1975). Much of this writing covers similar ground, and leaves many questions unanswered.

What obstacles stand in the way of producing a biography of Pat Collins? Firstly, there is the fear that perhaps it's been left too late, and should have been done when there were many more people still alive who could speak of Pat and his fairs from first hand experience. Secondly, it is a subject that requires a variety of expertise - the story of the fair involves the technicalities of fairground rides, engines, transport, organs, and the complex organisation of the business. Thirdly, it is an area where there is a shortage of written documentation, and few records to consult. Fourthly, to make matters worse, many people that we spoke to regarded the history of the Collins family as impossibly complex.

Despite the problems, by the Autumn of 1989, we had taken the plunge and decided to embark on the project. We were encouraged by the response to a request for information that we placed in Walsall's *"Local History News"*, and from the local newspapers, eg the Walsall Observer, Birmingham Evening Mail, Express & Star, Sutton News etc. Most of all we were encouraged by the offer of help from enthusiastic experts who were prepared to come and form a team: Graham Downie and Stephen Smith, of the Fairground Association of Great Britain.

1990 was a very exciting year - our project was underway. We soon had the pleasure of meeting many people who were either related to, or had worked with, Pat Collins, or his family. When we met Anthony Harris we realised that our story could run from Pat's birth in 1859 right up to the present day. The very high standard of presentation adopted by Anthony Harris' Pat Collins Fun Fair provides the book with a happy conclusion.

At the beginning of 1991 we had to face the fact that our project was in danger of getting "out of hand", because our research had opened up so many diverse lines of enquiry. It seemed possible that the material might not add up to a coherent answer to the questions we had originally posed, or, that as a team, we would find it very difficult to know what to include, what to leave out, or what to investigate further. At this stage Graham Downie decided to withdraw from the project. We then took the decision to impose some limits on how much of our lives we could devote to pursuing Pat Collins. In effect, we decided to bring everything together in the book as you now see it. Despite the size of the book, we do not think it will be the last word on the subject. On the contrary, we hope it will stimulate further enquiry, some of which will be of a very specialised nature, and will surface in the fan magazines.

Our research maintained a high level of excitement on every front: meeting interesting and interested people: finding more photographs and documentation than we had dared to believe could exist, and exploring the hitherto unknown world of the fairground, with its very special history, language, and culture. As "mere flatties" we have often been out of our depth, but we have encountered much helpfulness, cheerfulness, kindness, and occasional impatience with our ignorance of fairground matters!

We have been introduced to the world of "showland" through interesting conversations in the paybox, by phone, by visits to fixed and permanent sites, and by visits to living vans. We have tried to produce a book that can be enjoyed by showmen and "flatties" alike. (A "flattie" is someone not born into showland - see Glossary.) Traditionally a showman's way of life is based on "travelling", and we possibly underestimated the difficulty of researching a subject where the targets of our enquiry were, as often as not, on the move.

On the other hand, we were agreeably surprised by the quality of the documentation that does exist in showland. Salvation came in the form of *"World's Fair"* - showland's weeky newspaper produced in Oldham, first produced in 1904, and still "going strong". We are indebted to Andrew Mellor, the Editor of *World's Fair*, for allowing us to quote from its fascinating pages. We have spent many happy hours in the British Library's Newspaper Collection at Colindale, near London, reading the preserved copies of *World's Fair* and *"The Era"*.

When we started we had only limited knowledge of the work of fairground enthusiasts, or "fans", who first shared their interest in the Friendship Circle of Showland Friends (FCSF), and the British Fairground Society (BFS). More recently, fans have united in the Fairground Society (FS) and the Fairground Association of Great Britain (FAGB). All these organisations have produced their own literature, and legendary characters like Father Greville, who ran the FCSF single-handed until his death on 20 July 1966. The enthusiasts, and their associations, represent a vast resource of information on the fairground.

From this vast jigsaw of information, from a huge variety of sources, this book has been compiled, and we wish to thank everyone who supplied us with the pieces. Often the size of the piece was not important ...even the tiniest fragment of information can be vital in completing the overall picture. Our thanks, in equal portions, are extended to all those recorded alphabetically under Acknowledgements. (As they say in World's Fair's reports of funerals - we apologise for omissions!)

We have concluded that Pat was indeed a "King of Showmen". We hope that we have demonstrated that his achievements were remarkable. He showed great optimism and energy in pursuing his endeavours, and inspired affection, loyalty, and respect from those he encountered. He was not necessarily a saintly character, nor was his life one continous round of good fortune, but we think that his story is worth telling.

We hope you enjoy "a good read".

Freda Allen
Ned Williams
Autumn 1991

TIPS, WARNINGS AND ADVICE

Not only does this book tell an interesting story, but it has been carefully designed as an easy to read reference book for showland folk and fairground enthusiasts alike.

The basic story of Pat's life, and the history of Pat Collins' fairs runs from Chapter 1 to Chapter 11. After that the Chapters are devoted to different aspects of his life, and specific aspects of the fairs.

In the later Chapters you will find information on engines, rides and individuals, without having to read your way through the whole book...if that is your choice. Of necessity from time to time there is a little repetition, and it is hoped that this will facilitate easy reference.

One little problem you may have in reading this book is that most of the male descendants of the Collins' family are called either Pat or John. For that reason a Family Tree is included, with dates where known, and where such names as "Young Pat" or "Walsall John" are shown as a matter of simplification and aid to further geneological research.

Not very much fairground history exists in written form, and any research is bound to produce results which have to be treated with a degree of caution. People's opinions and interpretations of findings will differ widely

ACKNOWLEDGEMENTS and SOURCES

From the vast jig-saw of information collected, this book has been compiled and we wish to thank everyone who supplied us with the pieces. Often the size of each 'piece' is not important – but even the tiniest fragment of information can be vital in completing the overall picture.

We offer our thanks, in equal portions, to everyone listed below (as far as possible in alphabetical order).

Don Allen, Frank Allen, Violetta Allen, Harry Alcock, Harry T. Allsopp, Ann Andrews, Fr. Bernard Anwyl, Mick Archer, Joe Ashmore, Roger Austin.

Norman H. Beech, Jory Bennett, Mrs Janet M. Bent, Vera Bishop, Jim Boulton, Paul Braithwaite, Brian Bull, Ernest Burdett, Steve Burdett, Fred Van Buren.

Andrew Cash, Estelle Chadwick, Joe Chadwick, John Chambers, Fred Charlton, Geoffrey Coad, Brian Collins, G. Collins, John Collins, Kevin Collins, Norah Collins, Pat Collins (Barry Island), Pat Collins (Birkenhead), Eileen Cook, Harry Cooke, Mrs Cook, George Corbett, Pat Coyne.

Graham Downie, Alan Duke, Mrs Dorothy Dyas.

Flora Eastwood, Tom Evans.

Allan Ford, Ted Ford, Jane Ferrari, Vanessa Forte.

Ernie Genders, Terry Gilder, Mrs Gough, Miss M. M. Gray, Judy Grindley, John Gwinnett.

Herbert Haines, John Hall, Anthony Harris, Fr. Harrington, Clara Harvey, Jack Harvey, Sydney Hawkins, Lisa Haywood, Mr. T. Holmes, G. A. Hodgson, Brian Hornsey, Peter Hough, J. W. Humphreys, Bill Hunt.

Arthur Jones, Joyce Jones, Mrs M. Jones.

Johan Van Leerzem, Clem Lewis, Brian Luxton.

H.J. Macklin, Albert Martin, Pamela Mason, Michael Miles, K. Miller (Showmen's Guild of GB), Harry Mills, Roger Mills, Bernard Morley, Sally Muldowney, Alf Myers.

Connie Newton, Lord Harmer Nicholls.

John Pallett, G. J. Payne, Robert Preedy, John Pugh.

John Ray, George Reohorn, Mrs Reynolds, Harry Richards, Fred Richardson, Mrs E. M. Riley, Ron Roberts, Cyril Rollins, Jimmy Ryan.

John Sale, Rowland Scott, Kevin Scrivens, Molly Seldon, Mike Simkin, Stephen Smith, Rod Spooner, Elena Stokes, George Sutton.

W.H.Taylor, Nora Tedeschi, R.Tierney, John Tidmarsh, Malcolm Timmins, Ray Tunnicliffe, Bill Tweddle, Christopher H.Tyne.

Margaret Wakelam, S.B.Waring, John Ward, Stan Webb, Roy Webster, Flora Williams, John Williams, Willsons Printers (Leicester) Ltd, Tom Wilson, Mary Withers.

Brian Yates.

COUNCILS
Walsall M.B.C. Legal & Admin Services.
Walsall M.B.C. Leisure Services (Anne Eddon & Antonia Pompa).

LIBRARIES
Barry Library, Glam; Birmingham Reference Library (Local Studies Centre); British Newspaper Library, Colindale; Burton on Trent Library; Chester Library; Derby Library; Dudley Library; Nottingham Library; Ruthin Library; Sandwell (Local Studies Centre); Sutton Coldfield Central Library and Local Studies Librarian Marian Baxter; Walsall Local History Centre; Wolverhampton Library (Local Studies); Wolverhampton Polytechnic (Art & Design) Library; Wrexham Library.

NEWSPAPERS
Birmingham Post, Birmingham Evening Mail, Express & Star Wolverhampton, Sutton News, World's Fair, Walsall Observer.

REGISTRIES
Birmingham District Probate Registry; Clwyd County Record Office; Diocesan Registry of Liverpool; Liverpool Registry; London Principal Registry of the Family Division; Neath Registry; Southport General Registry; Wrexham Registry.

SOCIETIES
Members of the Black Country Society; Burton on Trent Dept. of Transport; Members of the Midland Section of the Showmen's Guild; Wrexham Cemetery Superintendent

We approached members of the Fairground Organ Preservation Society, the Fairground Association of Great Britain, and the Road Locomotive Society for their expert help. This they gave without wishing to implicate the organisations of which they are officers, and of course, we accept full responsibility for the interpretation we have put on the information given to us. In this category we would particularly thank Jory Bennett, Paul Braithwaite, Alan Duke, Bill Hunt, Kevin Scrivens and Stephen Smith.

In the production of this book we acknowledge the assistance and expertise of John Revill (Walsall College of Art), Jan Endean Galata Print and the sustained interest (and forbearance!) of our families, friends and colleagues.

Finally, we would like to sign off with Pat's farewell words to the Showmen's Guild members after his twenty-year term in the office of President:
We wish you Many good tobers, Good munjari, Plenty of denarli, and not too much parney!.... and we hope you enjoy the book.

PS...and if you are 'flatties' too.... interpreted it means *"Many good fairs, good grub, plenty of money and not too much rain!"*

There are a number of books about Fairs and Wakes, many of which mention Pat Collins by name, in passing, and illustrate his rides, engines etc. The following books have been found useful for reference:

FAIRGROUND ART
Geoff Weedon & Richard Ward   White Mouse Editions, 1981

FAIRGROUND ARCHITECTURE
David Braithwaite   Hugh Evelyn, 1968

SAVAGES OF KINGS LYNN
David Braithwaite   Patrick Stephens, 1975

THE TRAVELLING PEOPLE
Duncan Dallas   Macmillan, 1971

HISTORIC FAIRGROUND SCENES
Michael Ware   Moorland, 1977

SEVERAL BOOKS by
Peter Wilkes and Malcolm Slater

ALL THE FUN OF THE FAIR
Graham Downie   produced by the Showmen's Guild

ALSO various books on engines, organs etc.

THE EVENT OF THE YEAR!

PAT COLLINS
presents
BLOXWICH WAKES
AT THE WAKES GROUND, HIGH ST. BLOXWICH
OPENING TODAY (Friday), SATURDAY, MONDAY and TUESDAY
AUGUST 15, 16, 18 and 19. Open Daily at 2 p.m.

COME SEE and ENJOY THE WORLD'S BEST ATTRACTIONS including : —
1969 SUPER DODGEMS DE LUXE! THRILLING WALTZER! FABULOUS JET PLANES! BIG ELI WHEEL! SENSATIONAL SKID   GIGANTIC OCTOPUS! OLDE RAG-TIME CAKEWALK! DOUBLE DECKER GHOST TRAIN!
SONYA ALLEN'S NEW SHOWS! etc.

There will be no charge for admission to the Ground this year!
Free — Admission — Free

Don't forget the CHILDREN'S FREE RIDE TICKETS will be issued on MONDAY AUGUST 18th at 2 p.m. These will be available for use on Tuesday, August 19th from 3.30 to 5.30 p.m.

IT'S PAT COLLINS — The household name for Entertainment!

All Buses stop at Entrance!

This advertisement for the 1969 Bloxwich Wakes gives very full details of the attractions. The following year was to be the last occasion the Wakes was held on Pat's ground.

SHOWLANDS SKETCH ALBUM

No.5. COUNCILLOR PAT COLLINS

Pat Collins was born in Chester on 12 May 1859. Left St Wedburgh's School to join his father, travelling the fairs of N.Wales, Cheshire, and South Lancashire with simple rides. Married Flora Ross in 1880, and set up on his own as a roundabout proprietor. Settled at Shaw's Leasure, Walsall, in 1882, and from this base, in the Black Country, built a large showland empire. Became a major master of riding machines, a lessee of numerous fairs and the owner of fairgrounds. Later owned cinemas, theatres, and permanent amusement parks. Represented Birchills Ward on Walsall Council from 1918 to 1930, when elected an Alderman. Became Mayor of Walsall in 1938. He was elected Member of Parliament for Walsall from 1922 to 1924. He died at his home, Limetree House, Bloxwich, 8 December 1943, leaving a widow, his second wife - Clara

Clubs: National Liberal and National Sporting.

Interests: Boxing, Trotting, and Motoring.

Favourite saying: "We only pass this way once;
                Let us do what we can when we can"

The travelling fair that he created still exists today.

(Picture: World's Fair 22/1/27)

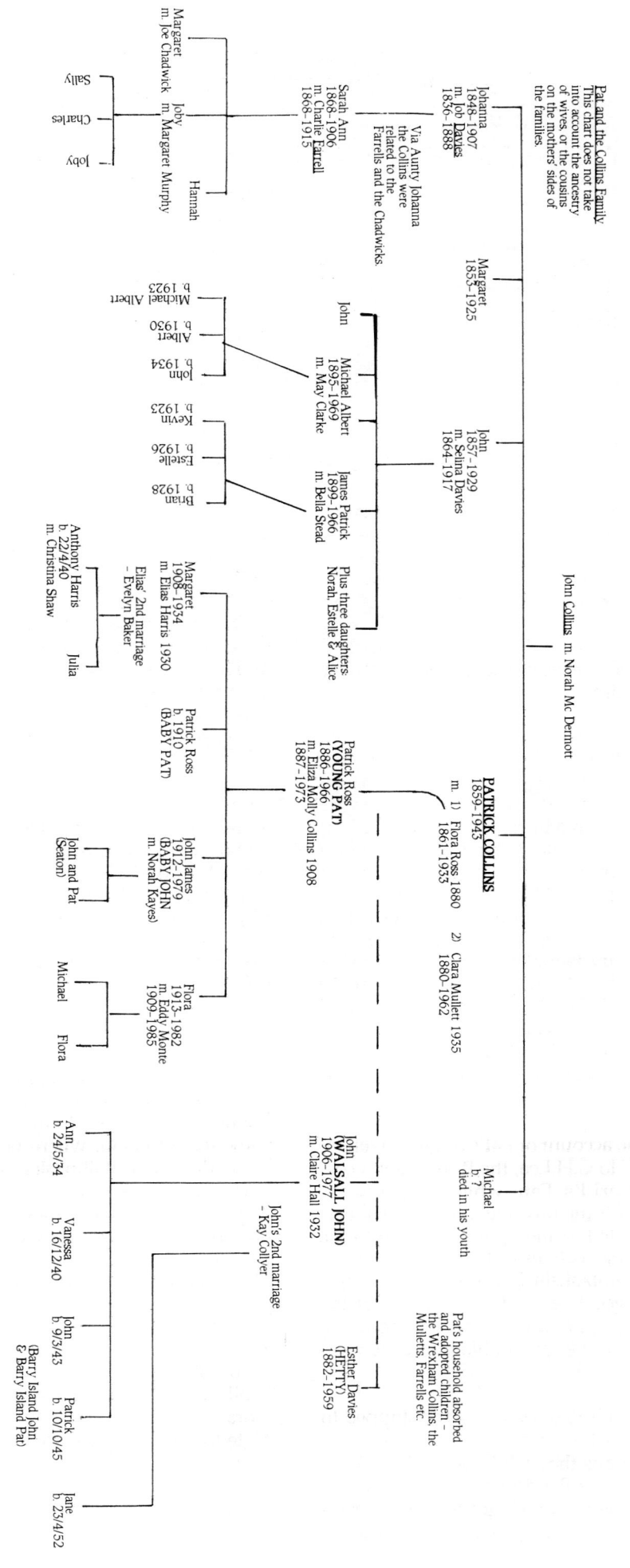

- 14 -

PAT COLLINS-THE FIRST THIRTY YEARS
1859-1889

CHAPTER 1

"Storm clouds gathered over the Irish Sea. A small boat tossed on the restless waves; and among the passengers, one man looked back towards Ireland, and the home he had left to escape political unrest. The storm overtook the boat, and off the coast of England it was wrecked. Only two men survived. One of them, John Collins found his way to Chester and joined the world of horse-dealing, a trade that was already known to him.

Back in Ireland, his wife, Norah, looking after their three sons, decided that she would follow her husband to England. Leaving the boys behind she reached Chester only to find that John had moved on to Whitchurch. At Whitchurch she found he had moved on to Wolverhampton! She finally caught up with him at Kidderminster. Having decided upon their future together, she returned to Ireland to collect the three boys and the reunited family settled in Cheshire. By the age of nine one of the sons, Patrick, was managing a roundabout for his father, and by the time he was 21 he had helped his father earn up to £20,000. Patrick (or Pat as he was known) was eager to start on his own, but his father, John Collins, was not in favour and objected to his family splitting up on this occasion! Pat had to borrow money in order to go his own way"

Well....that was the account of Pat's origins given by Pat Collins himself to C.H.Lea, the Birmingham correspondent of World's Fair when they met at Handsworth Park for the Birmingham Carnival Fair of July 1936, and Mr Lea incorporated this into his account of the Onion Fair in October that year. It seems Pat enjoyed embellishing the facts, especially if it meant telling a good yarn! Large chunks of the story are fictitious, particularly the bit about the boys, because in reality John and Norah's sons were born on this side of the Irish Channel.

Before Pat's death in 1943 it seems no one stopped to establish the 'facts' in the intriguing story of the "King of Showmen". Perhaps they felt it would have been impertinent to try to tie Pat down to separating fact from fiction, so ...if you haven't got the facts, fiction will do and a legend is born. Another reason could have been that Pat rarely stayed still long enough to give in-depth interviews, or ever saw any reason for setting out his life story with any true sense of history.

Half a century later, in attempting to unravel the facts, whatever we manage to find out about the life of 'The King of Showmen', we can never be absolutely certain we have arrived at the truth. For instance, "I was born in 1858", Pat told Mr Lea in 1936. He was nearly right! Read on...

Every biography has to begin with the birth of its hero. In this respect the story of Pat Collins gets off to a fine start, because Pat always celebrated his birthday on the wrong date!.... April 6th. When Harry Allcock came to locate Pat's birth certificate whilst collecting information for the short illustrated biography produced in 1959, he found that Pat was born on May 12th, 1859. (Harry Alcock was a post-war ground manager and an ex-policeman, who helped collect information for E.J.Homeshaw's 1959 biography).

Pat was born in a small house at Boughton Heath, on the outskirts of Chester, and he was christened in St.Wedburgh's Catholic Church in the centre of Chester. His father was John Collins, who had married Norah McDermott. John Collins appears to have come from Ireland, where he and his brother were horse dealers at Ballinasloe on the border between the Counties of Westmeath and Galway. Every year they came to England, via Liverpool or Holyhead, to attend horse fairs, and began their trading in Altrincham at the end of April, continuing to Macclesfield, Congleton, Leek and Derby during May.

John eventually decided to settle in England, and made his first home at Northwich. He bought land at Brook Street which later was used as a fairground. While John and Norah were at a fair in Denbigh, Norah gave birth to a son, John, on 5th April 1857. Note the similarity to the date Pat used as his birthday.

Altogether John and Norah Collins produced five children: John, Patrick, Michael (who died young after being severely kicked by a horse), Margaret and Johanna. When Pat was born in 1859, his father appears to have described himself as an agricultural labourer, but this was not strictly true as it seems that he was also a 'general dealer', interested in trading at fairs and possessing a ride - a 'one boat yacht', which he travelled for much of the year.

Reports of Pat's early life often suggest that he had started from nothing, an impression he himself did nothing to contradict, yet while his background was relatively humble (certainly not affluent in the sense of the word today), he did have a strong family background firmly based in the world of travelling, trading and showmanship. Pat's own progression into the world of the travelling showman was ably assisted by his brother, sisters and their partners. Whether in the beginning Pat's life was a struggle or not, he certainly was not one of the urban or rural dispossessed souls forming part of the nineteenth century poor.

Nor was he completely uneducated. He went to St.Wedburgh's School and his mother greatly encouraged him in learning to read and write, however difficult it was considering the family's somewhat nomadic existence. In 1894, at the age of thirty five, Pat expressed his thanks to St.Wedburgh's by presenting the church with a carved marble pulpit, inscribed "Pray for Pat Collins who gave this pulpit".

Subsequently, and perhaps inevitably, the demands of the family business took precedence over the claims of school attendance, and by the age of ten he was travelling the fairs of Cheshire, Lancashire, Shropshire and North Staffordshire with his father, and brother John (two years his senior). His father's yacht was big enough to hold twenty people, and had to be hauled from fair to fair by two horses. There was also a juvenile hand-turned roundabout hauled by a pony. When the yacht was built up it was swung by Pat and his brother John, alternately pulling on ropes; this was also the time when the boys learnt to fight and to defend their pitch in the rough world of the fairground.

According to the biography prepared by Harry Alcock and E.J.Homeshaw, Pat persuaded his father to sell him the juvenile ride in 1875, when he was sixteen. They claim that Pat paid £80 for it. Another account states that Pat, brother John, Maggie and Joanna's husband jointly owned and presented the yacht. Without a clearer picture of the lives of all the Collins' family it is difficult to be precise as to the order of events, or the extent to which his sisters were already established in the fairground world by the time Pat was entering the business.

One thing that is certain is that Pat married Flora MacDonald Ross on the 20th July 1880 in the Parish Church of Liverpool, according to the Rites and Ceremonies of the Established Church. That church was in fact St.Peter's, Church Street (demolished in 1922) and was known as the Pro-Cathedral (NOT the Cathedral) from the foundation of the Diocese in March 1880 until the emergence of the Anglican Cathedral as a proper entity in 1924. He stated his age as 22 and rank as 'General Dealer'; she incorrectly stated her age as 21, no rank, daughter of a watchmaker. Legend is that Pat was on his favourite pitch in Liverpool and was so poor at the time of his marriage that he had to pawn his suit and attend the wedding in his corduroys. Finding that he had one shilling left in his pocket, he expressed his confidence in himself and his future by throwing this coin into the Mersey! Flora came from Wrexham, but at the time of her marriage she was living in the Toxteth area of Liverpool, while Pat's address was given as Tarbock Street. A more detailed account of Flora's background is presented in a later chapter.

The early 1880's appears to have been the time when the Collins' family began to go their separate ways, establishing themselves in distinct geographical areas. This was not as haphazard as at first appears but was greatly influenced by family backgrounds through marriage. In 1883 brother John married Selina Davies (1860-1914); she was the daughter of William Davies already a well known showman with a base in the North Staffordshire Potteries. Sister Johanna married Peter Davies of the same family; their daughter was Sally who married Charlie Farrell. The links between the Collins, Davies and the Farrells form an important part of the background to the migration of Pat to the Midlands.

Pat and Flora came to Walsall in 1882, two years after their marriage, and when they were both still in their early twenties. He 'rested' his van at Shaw's Leasow (or "Leasure") in that part of Birchills which is just behind Town End Bank. He apparently came only with his pony and a juvenile ride, and some accounts insist that he had no van and slept under the ride, but this seems unlikely as the ride itself must have operated on a fairground pitch near the town centre, on waste ground where the Arcade in Bradford Street now stands. It is also possible that this was not Pat's first visit to Walsall, but certainly 1882 became the date from which he claimed to have 'adopted' the town as his home. He also dated his attendance at the Bloxwich Wake from that year.

While his sister Maggie Collins stayed in Cheshire, his brother John headed for Merseyside and South Lancashire, and Johanna went into Shropshire and the Welsh border. As fairs developed towards the end of the last century their paths may have criss-crossed, particularly at traditional show-business focal points like Chester, Birmingham and Nottingham. It is particularly difficult to chart Pat's progress during the 1880's, or to understand how much was achieved alone, and how much jointly with his brother and sisters, but it is certainly true that the 1880's provided the showman with a major challenge.

Industrial and urban communities were growing fast, particularly in the area now known as the West Midlands, despite periods of considerable economic depression. To be a successful showman it was not only necessary to be able physically to defend one's right to a pitch and to claim that pitch, it was also important to be able to deal with gangs who invaded the fair demanding free amusement and 'protection money'. It is not surprising, therefore, to find that the arrival of fairs and wakes were associated with a considerable increase in the consumption of alcohol, often leading to violence, and the subsequent threat of lawlessness. With this in mind, as Local Government developed, many 'respectable folk' hoped that fairs and wakes would be outlawed. Pat would therefore have found himself engaged in battle on at least three fronts - a) fighting the gangs, b) fighting the growing powers of Local Government, and c) valiantly trying to reform the showman's image by presenting the idea that fairs and wakes could be considered safe entertainment worthy for all the family to enjoy. Much later these causes were adopted by the Showmen's Guild; Pat's part in that story is told in a later chapter.

Pat did not bring the fun of the fair to the Black Country...it already existed... but it was all rather haphazard and little written evidence survives recalling what those days were like. How Pat slipped into the existing local fairgound scene is not recorded, but at that time the business of fairs was sufficiently unregulated that probably anyone could have done so. It appears he simply joined his contemporaries as yet another showman, then rose to outstrip, outshine, and absorb many of them.

In 1935, 'JBT' the Black Country correspondent of the World's Fair, himself a veteran local showman, wrote: *"I vividly remember the theatres and ghost shows that toured around in the 1880's. Local wakes and fairs were situated here and there with no fixed location. Among the popular showmen of the day were Bill Davies, (from Stoke), Shepherd and Russell,(from Brum) and Hayes, (from Dudley)".*

Bill Davies was the father of Pat's sister-in-law, and he may have introduced his son-in-law John, and Pat, to some of the Black Country fairs. In later years, descendants of the Russells, the Shepherds and the Hayes themselves became Pat's tenants. 'JBT' went on to write: *"I was with Johnson's Show and as youngsters we used to be together on the old tobers, and sometimes in opposition, at the old Wakes at Bloxwich, Darlaston, Oldbury, and Bilston. At Dudley and Walsall we used to stand on rough grounds - and we had a rough time very often. Pat had a big struggle when he first came to this area, but soon established his reputation. He had several good employees in his pioneer days. Bill Mullett was a rising Riding Master, and later had charge of various machines which later became very popular."*

During Pat's first decade in Walsall he described himself as a "Swing-boat proprietor of Chester". The land at Shaws Leasow was leased from a David Bird, and Pat first lived at a house at 69 Stafford Street. In the 1890's when he moved into Algernon Street (adjacent to the land in Shaw's Leasow) he called his home "Chester House". The house in Shaw's Leasow was swallowed up in the late Victorian expansion of central Walsall, but the land that he leased,he eventually purchased, and it became his 'yard' and was called "Gondola Works". Pat was thrifty and shrewd and

PAT COLLINS: the proud riding master on the steps of the Mountain Ponies (R4 in our list), built up in a street location. The original of this early photograph was torn and attacked by damp but a copy has survived.
(Collection of Jane Ferrari, nee Collins)

his business began to expand. By the beginning of the 1890's he owned a number of riding machines and sideshows, and with the help of 'tenants' was capable of presenting quite large fairs. The events in 1892, when Pat became engaged in a battle with Walsall Corporation are recorded and described later in Chapter 2. Several claims are made by Walsall folk to the effect that their grandfathers lent Pat 'a few pounds to purchase a ride' or 'to purchase land' about this time but, of course, no written evidence has been found to corroborate these claims.

As the business grew and flourished, so did the family; Pat and Flora's son, Patrick Ross Collins was born on 7th March 1886, in Chester. He was later to be known as "Young Pat".

A new generation of fairground rides also appeared during the 1880's. They were larger and powered by steam; in fact Pat may have acquired his first steam Gallopers as early as 1883. He is said to have made his first visit to Savages of Kings Lynn in 1884, when his father bought 'a fine set of Three-abreast Gallopers'. Pat purchased a second set in 1886. (Pat's set can be identified as the ride powered by Savage's centre engine No.372. but it is not so easy to identify the set bought by his father, or another set that Pat could have bought in 1883, for that matter). However, by the second half of the 1880's Pat was steadily accumulating fairground equipment.

In 1887 he bought an early "Sea on Land" from Savages, powered by their engine No.414, and a second set of Gallopers, built by Allchin & Linnell, with Savage's engine No.420. In 1888 he bought a Switchback Galloper in partnership with his brother John. This was powered by Savage's centre engine No.443, supplied at the same time as engine No.444 which was an organ engine. By the end of the decade Pat not only owned rides, organs and sidestuff, but as the 1890's unrolled he was about to add equipment to generate power for the revolutionary 'electric' lighting.

By 1894 Pat had purchased his first steam road locomotive, a Burrell Showman's engine, "The Emperor". This was followed, two years later by the purchase of "The Empress".

As Pat became 'Riding Master' of several machines, and was steadily acquiring his own engines, en route, it is less clear how quickly the fairs he was attending were becoming truly his own. It was also a time when attendance at a fair was less controlled on a regional basis than it became later, under the rules devised by the Showmen's Guild. Pat, therefore, appeared all over the place and thus acquired quite a national reputation as a showman while at the same time consolidating his position in the Black Country and South Staffordshire. Indeed, in the mid 1890's his four separate 'fairs' were established and were taking part at venues all over England. (See Pat's interview of 1895 with the Newport Advertiser in Chapter 3).

But it was not becoming any easier to acquire a site to present a fair. As Local Government developed new powers, new bureaucracies began asserting their rights to licence fairs and markets. A showman could try to obtain such a license and then, as lessee, let pitches to his fellow showmen. By 1892 Pat was able to call himself "Sole Lessee" of fairs at Bloxwich, Darlaston, Oldbury, Wednesbury, West Bromwich and Smethwick, all in the Black Country. He was also the Lessee of the Birmingham Onion Fair held at the Pleck, Aston, as it had been since the mid 1870's. Even further afield, he was the Lessee at Rotherham Statutes!

In 1893 the Wolverhampton Chronicle published a long article about the Whitsun Bank Holiday Fair in the town, but mentions not a single showman by name. The newspaper reporter however, was much impressed by the new technology of the large, fast-moving steam-powered rides, replacing the previously human-powered rides. The Gallopers and the "Sea on Land" were present; we can assume that they most probably belonged to Pat Collins. The latest 'gimmick' was the arrival of the photographic booth, offering instant photos. It would appear that by this time 'fairs' were regarded as 'respectable'

BELOW: Pat Collins, and his son, Young Pat, photographed in the 1890's by Joe Caddick. Pictures of this vintage are so rare that we have decided to include this faded photograph from the collection of Peter Hough.

since it was also reported that "The Rector and three ladies of St Peter's Church, Wolverhampton, entertained the show people to afternoon tea on Whitsunday 1893"!

During the first thirty years of his life Pat had not only established himself as a showman to be reckoned with in the Black Country; become lessee of a number of fair sites; owner of some sites; proprietor of a number of riding machines, he was also an innovator of renown. His fairs travelled far and wide, and while there remains some surviving documentary evidence relating to the late 1880's and early 1890's it is sketchy, and does not permit a more detailed picture.

However, in the next two chapters, you will see that the 1890's provided more than a few 'memorable moments' when Pat's fairs became the centre of attention of the Press and Public alike!.

BELOW: Although this picture at Oakengates was probably taken early in this century, it gives us a good idea of what the travelling fair looked like in the 1890's. The centre of the ground is occupied by a large riding machine, and the perimeter is defined by side stalls. Across the top of the ground is a wagon-fronted show. (Mr Owen)

ABOVE: Building up the fair in the street produced a rather different layout to that seen at Oakengates. This picture taken at Newport, Salop, is also probably taken in the early 1900's, suggested by the cars on the juvenile roundabout, but it captures the appearance and atmosphere of the early fairs.
(Collection of Michael Miles)

BELOW: The Sea on Land was a good example of applying steam power to the fairground roundabout, and the attempt to produce movement in addition to simply revolving. This picture is reproduced from Frederick Savage's catalogue and must be similar to the machine bought by Pat Collins in 1887.
(Collection of Jim Boulton)

THE BATTLE OF WALSALL
1890-1894

CHAPTER 2

As mentioned in Chapter 1, Pat Collins' rise as a showman was not in isolation. Firstly, it ran parallel with great technological changes in the world of fairground rides and amusements. Secondly, with the rising prosperity of an urban working class having money in their pockets to spend on such pleasures. Thirdly, with the development of Local Government and changing national legislation. All these affected the life of the aspiring showman. If this sounds academic, pause to consider the events leading to two senior Walsall police officers going on a 'mission' that involved buying ice cream and ginger snaps, and filling their notebooks with details of their observations of fairground life in the early 1890's.

Pat, who had been living in Walsall since the early 1880's and called himself the "Swingboat Proprietor of Chester", leased land in Shaw's Leasure from Mr David Bird. At some stage he moved into a house at 69 Stafford Street. He attended the local fairs in the centre of Walsall by The Bridge, and also the Bloxwich Wake. He established his right at such fairs presumably simply by his presence; fighting for a pitch if necessary, and creating a precedent as his reputation grew.

At that time there was no appointed lessee running the fairs because Local Government had not developed to the point where it wished to assume responsibility for such matters. Fairs simply 'happened' where they had always 'happened', many going back to some ancient charter, or they 'happened' wherever an enterprising showman saw an opportunity to create a fair. If they were established by tradition it is likely that they were trading fairs or markets, and that the amusement element of the fair was still in the process of developing. It was but a matter of time before such unregulated anarchy was challenged.

In 1890 the Walsall Corporation Act bestowed new powers upon the Local Council including one which concerned the licensing of "fairs", although there was no definition of this term given at the time. National legislation had already taken into account the changing nature of fairs and an Act of 1868 empowered magistrates to order the closure of a fair if "great rowdiness and immorality was taking place".

Apparently it was assumed that this kind of 'behaviour' was more likely to occur when people went to an amusement fair than when attending a fair simply for the purpose of trading. Whatever the nature of his "fair", Pat now found himself having to apply to the Local Council for a licence. The person who paid for the privilege of organising the fair was the "Lessee". The Lessee could then present his own rides, shows, stalls etc. at the fair, and let ground or pitches to others who would pay him rent as 'Tenants". The Lessee found tenants by advertising in the 'Space to Let' columns of The Era newspaper, and after 1904 also in the columns of the World's Fair newspaper.

In June 1891, Pat's solicitor, John Cotterell applied for a licence for Pat to hold a fair at Bloxwich, on ground behind the house of Richard Thomas, known as 'Tenters Croft'. The application included the comment, *"My Client has for some years past similarly occupied the land without complaint"*, thereby affirming that the application was endorsing an established practice. The licence was granted. In August Pat made a similar application to hold a fair at the end of September on Shaw's Leasure in Walsall, and permission again appears to have been given.

But the next year, in 1892, things began to go wrong.

Walsall Corporation put the leases for fairs out to tender (two fairs held by 'charter' and one that was not). The Bloxwich Wakes was regarded separately and went ahead without any problems, but when it came to the September Fair in Walsall, Pat tendered only £10 for the lease, complaining that he had been charged far too much in 1891. The lease was offered to a Mr Williams of Putney, who was expected to hold the fair on land at Midland Road. Meanwhile, Pat had decided to proceed without the licence and organised a fair on Shaw's Leasure. He provided his own attractions and persuaded others to join him, apparently offering them 'rent free' space on his 'unofficial' fair. It transpired that Mr Williams was left with no paying tenants wishing to join him at Midland Road!

The Corporation were forcibly reminded of Pat's defiant gesture as soon as fly-posted bills announced that Pat was celebrating the Walsall Wakes for three days commencing September 24th. If they had seen and read the small print in an advertisement placed in 'The Era' during August they would have noticed that Walsall was included in the list of fairs Pat was planning to hold at Bloxwich, Darlaston, Oldbury, Wednesbury, West Bromwich and Smethwick, and at Birmingham. In all these places he claimed to be the Lessee. The posters appeared all over Walsall and included adverts for Bostocks Menagerie and Sanger's Wild West Show. It was obvious that the event at Shaw's Leasure was going to be quite a large one.

John Cooper, the Town Clerk, asked the Police to go and collect evidence of what was going on, and also went to see for himself. The two Police Officers and the Town Clerk found one of the largest fairs ever seen in Walsall.....and crowds of people turning out to enjoy it. The outcome of all this was that Pat Collins was charged with 'unlawfully holding a fair, and violating Clause 126 of the Walsall Corporation Act of 1890'. He was duly summoned to appear before the magistrates on October 3rd.

Battle had commenced!

An unprecedented number of people turned up at Court to watch the proceedings, and considerable time was spent in dealing with the case. It caused a lot of interest and for various reasons. At one level, Pat already enjoyed considerable local popularity and many people were ready to enjoy his battle with 'Town Hall Bureaucracy'. At another level, it was an interesting test case and typical of the battles that many showmen all over the country were going to face as Local Government extended its powers. The U.K. Van Dwellers' Protection Society sent their solicitor, Mr Watson-Wright, to observe the event. John Cotterell, Pat's solicitor, had instructed a Mr.Disturnal to conduct his client's defence.

One hundred years later, the detailed record of this case makes fascinating reading, with plenty of drama and comedy as witnesses gave their evidence. However, its chief interest to present day historians is that it gives a detailed picture of the fair organised by Pat, and illustrates the extent of his business, those who were associated with his fairs at that time, and denotes his prestige within that business. As far as the Court was concerned a great deal of time was spent arguing over the definition of the word "fair". The Defence wanted to demonstrate that a "fair" according to the 1890 Act was all about trading and not about providing pleasure and amusement. The Prosecution argued that the definition according to the Act did relate to pleasure fairs, but that trading had taken place anyway. That is why the evidence of the Police Officers who had purchased ice cream and ginger snap was so vital. It also seemed important to prove that Pat had illegally collected rent from his tenants; the 'tenants' themselves denied having paid any rent—despite what they might carelessly have said to the Police Officers.

Inspectors Cliffe and Hamilton, the two Police Officers, did an excellent job in collecting evidence. The handbills they produced in Court have survived to this day becoming valuable historic items; century-old fairground handbills are few and far between! They tell us exactly what rides were being presented at a local fair in 1892: The Mountain Ponies, the "Sea on Land", a Switchback, Gallopers, Steam Swings, etc. The Police also made copious notes about everything they saw, and from them we learn that Pat possessed an engine which was generating current for the electric lighting as well as for the variety of amusements assembled by his 'tenants'.

Mr E.H.Bostock had brought his Wild Beast Show, managed by Sidney Braham, and Parker's Ghost Show had come from West Bromwich. Robert Williams had a 'new unrivalled fine art exhibition'. Shooting galleries were provided by John Lewis, Eliza Tuckley, and R.Delaney (who later managed the Crystal Palace site for Pat). There was a coconut sheet owned by Pat, and two "Whoa Emmas" owned by Thomas Hughes. Joseph Johnson presented a "striker" and two showmen presented rides alongside Pat's rides. One of these was a set of Gallopers belonging to Charlie Farrell (a nephew-in-law) and a set of roundabout cycles belonging to Tom Jervis. Mr Jervis was based in Leicester at the time, but his brother Miles founded a show-business dynasty in South Staffordshire when he established a base near Cannock. In addition to the ice cream and ginger snap, some of which the Police Officers bought, fried fish was also on sale. And someone at the fair was selling whips!

At Court witnesses called by the Prosecution included the Town Clerk, Police, Showmen, Food Vendors and even Pat's bill-poster. Sometimes the cross examination produced interesting asides. For example, the Town Clerk was embarrassed to admit that he could not find the Charter relating to Walsall's Fairs. When it came to the case for the Defence, Mr Disturnal called no witnesses. He concentrated on definitions of the word "fair". After four hours the Magistrates withdrew to consider their verdict, returning within ten minutes to announce that they found Pat "Guilty". He was fined £5, plus costs. An Appeal was lodged immediately, involving more argument this time about who should hear the Appeal. It was eventually agreed that the verdict would be reviewed by the Queen's Bench.

When the High Court heard Pat Collins' Appeal the ruling was delivered by Mr Justice Lawrence. He decided that whether people congregated at the event for the purpose of trade or for pleasure was irrelevant, the fact that they had congregated at all suggested that the event was a fair as defined by the relevant legislation. He gave his verdict in favour of the Corporation, but each party was left to pay their own costs.

It appears that Pat's relationship with Walsall Town Council was not soured by these events and it should

WALSALL WAKES.

LOOK OUT FOR
MR. PAT COLLINS
AND HIS
COLLOSAL COLLECTION
OF
AMUSEMENTS.

SPECIAL!!
COLLIN'S CELEBRATED
MOUNTAIN PONIES,
AND
VENICE IN WALSALL
(First appearance).
HEAPS OF FUN!
STARTLING NOVELTIES!
ELECTRIC LIGHTING!
(By the Walsall Electric Company).
STEAM SWINGS,
NOVELTIES IN ABUNDANCE,
SHOWS OF ALL KINDS,
ALL THE FUN OF THE FAIR.

COME IN THOUSANDS.

WAKE GROUND:
MIDLAND ROAD, WALSALL.

PAT COLLINS, Sole Lessee,

RIGHT: The handbill advertising the "unofficial" Walsall fair of September 1892 - printed in alternate lines of orange and blue - and collected by the police to produce in Court, as evidence in their case against Pat Collins.

ABOVE: The 1893 advertisement printed in the Walsall Observer, announcing Pat's return to "legality", and the introduction of the Gondolas.

BELOW: From the late 1890's onwards the Bloxwich "Wake" was regularly advertised in the Walsall Observer, often listing the riding machines and shows to be seen each year. In this case, Wall's Bioscope show is one of the attractions, the year is 1899, and this show was about to become part of Pat's empire.

COLLINS'S
Grand Fete and Gala,
In commemoration of
THE BLOXWICH WAKES,
Will be held in the PINFOLD FIELD
TO-DAY (SATURDAY),
And MONDAY and TUESDAY NEXT.

Special Engagement of
LAFAYETTE on the high wire.
GALE and LAMB, musical clowns.
BENI ZONG and ZONE.
SISTERS LALLAH, double wire acts.
HAPPY ASHBY, juggler and globe walker.
WALLACE and WARNER, horizontal bars.

Independent of the above Star Artistes
there will be

COLLINS'S { Gondolas,
            Mountain Ponies,
            Electric Jumpers.
WALL'S Cinematograph
PURCHASE'S Menagerie, and other Free Sights.

Admission   ONE PENNY.

LOOK OUT.
GREATEST WAKES EVER HELD IN WALSALL.

WALSALL
WAKES

Will Be Held On

SHAW'S LEASURE

COMMENCING ON
SATURDAY, SEPT. 24,
And Following Monday and Tuesday.

COLLINS' Grand
MOUNTAIN
PONIES,
COLLINS' SEA-ON-LAND.
COLLINS'
SWITCHBACK
Collins' Steam Swings,
Collins' Steeplechase Horses, and
Shooting Saloons.

And a Host of other Attractions too Numerous to Mention.

The Ground will be Illuminated by the
ELECTRIC LIGHT
By the Walsall Electric Light Company.

A. W. BAKER, "Chronicle" Offices, Aston Cross.

therefore come as no surprise to discover that in 1893 Pat Collins had no trouble in becoming the Sole Lessee of Walsall's fairs! It was almost as if the details of the events of 1892 were entirely forgotten because in September of 1893 the Walsall Observer mentioned "the first Switchback railway ever erected in Walsall has been built on vacant land at Midland Road", conveniently ignoring the Switchback built on Shaw's Leasure the year before.

Pat organised the Walsall fairs at the Midland Road site where Mr Williams had only empty pitches the year before, as well as the usual Bloxwich Wake in August. An advert for the September Fair does announce the first appearance of "Venice in Walsall" - with the arrival of the Gondolas. Quarrels with the Council were however overshadowed by an outbreak of smallpox, and the effects of a bitter coal dispute, after which colliers were gradually compelled to return to work accepting a cut in wages.

Pat's success in the Black Country has to be seen against a background of epidemics, disputes and industrial depressions. It should not be assumed that the urban working classes ever had so much surplus cash to spend that being a showman and taking their money was easy. Folk were just as likely to be queuing up outside the pawnbrokers, as they were to be found enjoying railway excursions to the bracing air of the seaside or spending money on the fairground. Sometimes a smallpox epidemic led to the cancellation of the fair altogether. An example of this being in 1894 when the Minutes of the Local Board in Darlaston record that the Board had requested Pat to cancel his fairs; and "their gratitude to him for doing so".

LEFT: Another illustration from Frederick Savage's catalogue shows a Razzle Dazzle. Pat Collins purchased one in 1906, and it was presented under a variety of names.

LEFT: The Rolling Gondolas - this is believed to be the machine that began life in 1891 as a Switchback, but was rebuilt in 1894 as a set of Rolling Gondolas for Pat Collins (R 29). The same machine is illustrated in Weedon & Ward's "Fairground Art", page 150, but is carrying different gondolas.
(Collection of Kevin Scrivens)

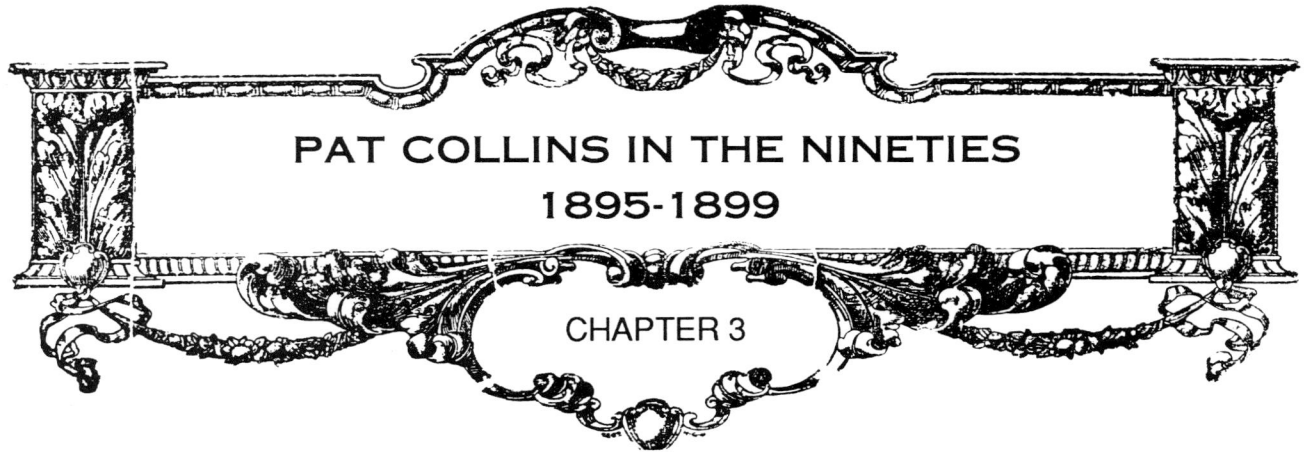

PAT COLLINS IN THE NINETIES
1895-1899
CHAPTER 3

After the Battle of Walsall, what then?

By the early 1890's Pat was a well-known showman of considerable standing. His flamboyant style merited wide newspaper coverage of the battle with Walsall Council which, a century later provides us with descriptions of rides, attractions, and venues that might otherwise not be known. The reports also give us an insight into the way the showmen were frequently having to engage in legal fights against the ever widening powers of Local Government, simply in order to preserve their livelihoods and establish their rights.

In 1893 a newspaper description of the fair in Wolverhampton coyly mentions no showman by name; however, two years later, the local press not only names Pat Collins as the organiser of the fair but recognises his importance in the field of entertainment, and proceeds to entertain readers with a detailed interview!

In Shropshire, the neighbouring county, the town of Newport had traditionally enjoyed two annual fairs, one at the end of May, and one at Christmas - the "Gawby Fair". Both had apparently declined in the 1870's but were revived in the 1880's by Pat Collins' interest. The fair was held in the main street; this caused the town to feel a little apprehensive towards the fair, the arrival of which caused much local debate. The local newspaper, the Newport Advertiser, took an interest in the issue and devoted much space to reporting the May fair. On June 1st, 1895 the paper published a comprehensive account together with a long and detailed interview with Pat. It is worth quoting at length as it really creates the flavour and atmosphere of the old time fairground.

"The fair was, "larger than usual.... the street was literally alive with attractions. By the Vaults, Pat Collins had his Venetian Gondolas and Gotheimer was not far off with his roundabouts. Some of the various proprietors erect their plants with a sort of 'birth-right' vigour. One gent informed the Police Sergeant that he, the proprietor, came for the benefit of the town. Possibly; only it requires a generous turn of mind to admit it'."

The reporter noted the usual coconut stalls, vendors of confectionery, and a boxing booth, as well as two "musical engines" but on Tuesday night when the fair was at its most lively..."*the chief attraction was Pat Collins' Venetian Gondolas, lit by electricity...the track being ellipse shaped, the devolutions caused the riders no sickly feeling, whereas circular motions would probably cause it".*

On Wednesday morning, when only the departed spirit of the fair remained, our reporter sought Mr Collins' private carriage, which was stationed by the Town Hall, just as Mr Collins was breakfasting. We arranged an interview, and before long were both seated in the adjoining hostelry. Mr Collins is still a young man, being only 36, possessing a pair of clear eyes, is of Anglo-Irish birth, and was born in Chester.

HOW DID YOU START ?
"I started for myself in 1851, with £5. two doll stalls and a set of swings. My first pitch was at Wavertree, Lancashire - there were just two men, one boy, my wife and myself. In three days we took £30, and I then bought a set of roundabouts. From there we went to Lynn, where we took £50. From then on, we were continually successful".

HOW DO YOU ARRANGE YOUR PROGRAMME ?
"We begin in February in Oswestry. We have four lots now travelling England: in fact, I claim to be the largest proprietor travelling in the United Kingdom. Our headquarters is in Walsall, where we have our machines repainted and brightened for the Spring."

HOW DO YOUR DIFFERENT LOTS DIVIDE ?
"One takes N.Wales, the Black Country, Shropshire and Herefordshire. Another goes round London and Kent way, another to Lancashire and Yorkshire, and the other to the North of England"

WHICH ARE YOUR BEST BUSINESS PLACES ?
"Wolverhampton, Coventry, the Black Country towns, Newcastle on Tyne, York, Liverpool, Birmingham, Manchester, Crewe, Chester and Shrewsbury. We have a Menagerie and a Pavilion at New Brighton, which we call the "World's Fair". Last Easter Monday 22,000 people passed through our turnstiles there. I employ about 150 men. I

have been coming to Newport on and off for twenty years. I used to come with my father - but this is the largest fair at Newport I have ever presented".

DO YOU LIKE THE FAIR BEING HELD IN THE STREET AT NEWPORT?
"Personally, I would prefer our plant in a field. We could then erect our machinery beforehand, and not have to rush it. We have £1,000 worth of stuff unloaded here at Newport, out of a total of £5,000 worth of equipment....I am the patentee of the Gondolas used in England. My wife and I took a three months' tour of the Continent. We were in Venice - when I saw the Gondolas..I decided 'there was a grand line of business'. We had the ride built, and it opened at the Nottingham Goose Fair last year. There are only two Gondolas of a Switchback nature in England, and they both belong to me. I first supplied electricity to my equipment five years ago. We have our first Burrell traction engine here at Newport - we've had it about six months, and I have six portable engines here"

At this point, Pat was about to show the reporter round his £300 luxurious living "carriage", but the fair manager interrupted the interview to warn Pat that he had only ten minutes to the departure of his train. Pat hurriedly left saying..."*If I had time, I could tell you some of our travelling experiences*"

BELOW: The Rolling Gondolas partially built-up. This is believed to be the machine that began life as a Savage-built set of Mountain Ponies.
(Collection of Molly Seldon)

The interview could almost have been conducted for the benefit of twentieth century historians, such is the detail covered! Pat's account of his early career and his description of the four areas that he visited show just how far he had expanded by the mid 1890's. It is difficult to imagine that his rides travelled so far afield and into areas now associated with other showmen - but as late as 1899 there is evidence of his Venetian Gondolas and his "Ostriches" attending the famous London Easter fair at Wanstead Flats. He makes no mention of his brother or sister Maggie, so, once again it is not clear whether he acted alone in reaching all these places or whether he speaks for the family.

There is no questioning the value and variety of his equipment by this time, or the pride in his innovations such as the Gondolas, and adoption of electric lighting, as observed at Walsall in September 1892. But could he afford the time for a three-month-long tour of the Continent, or was he romanticising about the invention of the Gondola Switchback? The ride, was in fact, second-hand; it was built in 1890 or 1891 for J.Hancock. (Savage's centre engine No.499.) When acquired by Pat in 1894 it was rebuilt as a "Rolling" Gondola Switchback, containing the means of pitching the gondolas as they revolved. It went through several further transformations in the twentieth century. When Pat states that he 'owns two Gondola Switchbacks', the second would appear to be another second-hand machine - originally built for John Murphy in 1888 as a set of Mountain Ponies (Savage centre engine No.438). Obviously by 1895 they had become Gondolas.

Any fairground enthusiast or historian coming across this Newport Advertiser feature of 1895 desperately hopes that this intense interest in the fair will continue through subsequent years, and will possibly include further interviews with Pat. Unfortunately this did not happen and although the paper did follow the fortunes of the fair every now and again, it was never with quite the same zeal. By 1896 only a junior reporter was sent to cover the fair. He came back with a long story, mainly focussing on interesting social observations. He noted that many 'respectable folk' came to the fair during the evening when they could enjoy its pleasures more discreetly in the darkness! He was led to conclude that the days of the travelling fair were numbered as the spread of universal education would make such simple pleasures redundant.

However, this 1896 portrait of the Newport Fair does include mention of performing birds, a mermaid, a Zulu who could walk on fire, the fat woman, and some really "disgusting" freaks, plus the boxing booth and the regular stalls. Caddick's photographic studio gains a mention, and one ride is singled out for attention. On the pitch previously occupied by the Venetian Gondolas, outside the Vaults, Pat was presenting some new "Hobby Horses" - 80 Fox-hunters..."What a sight was presented in the evening when the said fox-hunters were mounted by ladies and gentlemen of mature age", and he noticed that the horses, "instead of being suspended from the top, ran on wheels, and swayed backwards and forwards as they were borne round".

Two rides were acquired by Pat Collins during the mid 1890's; the Tunnel Railway and the Four-abreast Bicycles. The Tunnel Railway was just what its name implied and a narrow gauge locomotive, Savages engine No.641, of 1895, pulled its train round a fifty foot diameter circular track, half of which was in a tunnel, which allegedly made it very popular with young couples who were prepared to brave the smoke for a moment of privacy in the darkness. Steam bicycles, or Velocipedes, powered by Savages engine No.675, of 1896, invited customers to sit on cycles and pedal away like mad as they revolved.

In 1897 it appears Pat paused once more to talk at length to the press. He was interviewed by a reporter for the Nottingham Daily Guardian while attending the Goose Fair, and seems even more self-assured, and possibly 'extravagant' in his claims:

"I was not many years old when I followed in my Father's footsteps as a showman, I claim to be the pioneer of all the roundabouts, bar the rolypoly, which is not my patent. I started in a small way on my own sixteen years ago, and at that time had a little set of roundabouts, some swings and a shooting saloon. I now have two sets of Gondolas, one lot of bicycles, one lot of switchback ponies, two lots of jumping horses, two menageries, and two whole fairs of smaller amusements. I have two very large traction engines, one of which cost £1,400 with decorations and brasses. As regards the electric light, I have twelve dynamos. The patent of carrying the electric light around my roundabouts is my own...

I employ between 400 and 500 workmen, and have a very large works at Walsall. On the ground floor there is a large cleaning shop, where wagons are taken to pieces and dipped in large tanks containing a composition which, in a very short time, removes all of the old paint. I employ my own joiners, carpenters, painters, blacksmiths and electricians. I don't build my own wagons, but merely do all the necessary painting, gilding and decorating. We use as much as 400 lbs of gold leaf during the winter in re-gilding our vans etc. In Nottingham at the present fair I have some 400 tons of

BELOW: Nottingham Goose Fair, 1897. On the extreme left is Pat Collins' Mountain Ponies, and in the centre of the picture is the Channel Tunnel Railway, built by Savage's of Kings Lynn in the mid 1890's.
(Collection of Kevin Scrivens)

equipment. The largest amount of money that I ever took was at Edinburgh it amounted to £300, but sometimes I have taken only five shillings. After travelling from Nantwich to Holmes Chapel in Cheshire some time ago, I erected the whole of my shows and did not take a farthing! It rained torrents hard, and the trippers spent the whole of their time in the local pubs.

In some places we are treated very badly indeed, but that is not the case in Nottingham. As will doubtless be known to many Nottingham people, I bought two sets of roundabouts from the Boston Riding School Company about two years ago, for which I gave about £1,000. The cost of these machines when new would be upwards of £5,000.

Perhaps Pat overstated his right to be regarded as a "pioneer". Manufacturer's lists such as those of Savages of Kings Lynn, seem to suggest that other showmen had been buying their products for almost a decade by the time Pat bought his first steam powered dobbies in the mid 1880's, but even so, his progress from that time to the end of the century was remarkable, and the geographical spread of his operations was formidable.

While Savage's of Kings Lynn were the major builders and suppliers of fairground equipment it was possible for a showman like Pat Collins to buy the latest machine, perhaps built-up for the first time at Lynn Mart in the February of each year, and then travel it far and wide before returning to the "home-base". Some of Savage's records survive, and when these have been studied and interpreted by enthusiastic experts we may have a clearer picture of the relationship between Pat Collins and Savage's.

In the absence of facts, legends abound. One describes Pat arriving at Kings Lynn where he saw an almost completed ride which took his fancy. *"Who owns that ride?...and have they paid for it?"* he asked. He was told another well-known showman was about to pay a deposit on the machine. Pat hurriedly produced the cash and shortly afterwards the ride opened with Pat Collins' name on the rounding boards! Several details make this story improbable, but it does portray the style of an ambitious young showman.

Owning riding machines is prestigious to a showman; having somewhere to put them is just as important. The 1892 "battle" in Walsall would have been followed by others, and there is evidence of another conflict with the authorities concerning the Bloxwich Wake.

In 1896 and 1897 it is reported that Pat was providing the fair at Bloxwich Wake, each August, and had moved it from the park land in the centre of the village, to the field known as Tenters Croft. The Council was ruthlessly trying to abolish the Wake and focus people's attention on the August Bank Holiday instead. The Wake, in mid-August, was becoming a nightmare of drunkenness and lawlessness, though much enjoyed by local colliers. By 1898 Walsall Corporation announced that the Wake was abolished..... but Pat opened his fair on Saturday August 13th just the same!

BELOW: Pat Collins' Four-abreast, of the late 1890's. (R7) The ride is photographed at an indoor location - probably at Islington Agricultural Hall. Some of the horses were later replaced with motor cars.
(Collection of Flora Williams)

- 28 -

There was nothing anonymous about this - it was "Pat Collins Fair" and Pat was taking it upon himself to preserve the Bloxwich Wake. He was not so naive as to blatantly flout the law. A compromise was reached; the event was called *"Collins' Grand Fete and Gala (in commemoration of Bloxwich Wakes)"*. It thus became something rather special. Those attending had to pay for admission, which rarely happened elsewhere, and free entertainment was offered alongside the normal provisions of the travelling fair. It was held on ground 'adjoining the tram terminus' at the Pinfold. It could be said that as early as the late 1890's Bloxwich was coming to play a significant part in Pat's life.

In 1899 Pat advertised the rides that he was presenting at Bloxwich: the Gondolas, the Mountain Ponies, and the Electric Jumpers. Wall's Cinematograph was presenting 'film entertainment' - the Bioscope had arrived on Pat's fair.

In 1899 there is another opportunity to look at Pat's 'empire'. A Notice in the columns of the Walsall Observer announced the Prospectus of P.Collins Ltd - a company being formed at the beginning of that year to *"acquire, carry on, extend and improve"* the established business of Pat Collins, *"Public Amusement Caterer, Traction Engine, and Travelling Roundabout Proprietor"*.

It is not clear what motives existed for creating this company; possibly it was simply a way of raising money by selling everything to shareholders in order to use that money to pay for further expansion. Perhaps it was just a necessary step in regulating the affairs of his sprawling business.

Mr Affleck, the works manager, and a director of Savages of Kings Lynn, valued Pat's assets at £39,000, including property, machines, traction engines and a menagerie. The Company hoped to raise £40,000 to take over the business in October 1899, with Pat agreeing to stay on as Managing Director for at least three years. The other directors named in the Prospectus in January 1899 were Richard Hindle, a 'gentleman' of Blackpool, Thomas Whitehead, an accountant from Manchester, and James Sandon Turner of Birmingham.

By coincidence....the Walsall Theatres Company was being launched at the same time, with a capital of £27,000. The Walsall Observer commented on this coincidence and added...*"As to Mr Collins' business, it has to deal with the whole kingdom, and we expect from the whole kingdom will come the susbcribers, whose applications will probably exceed the number of shares to be allocated"*.

BELOW LEFT: The brass plate from the office of the Gondola Works, Walsall, preserved at the Black Country Museum by David Jones.

BELOW RIGHT: An advertisement in the Walsall Observer for 28 May 1898 indicating that Pat had time for his "hobby" - trotting horses.
(Walsall Local History Centre)

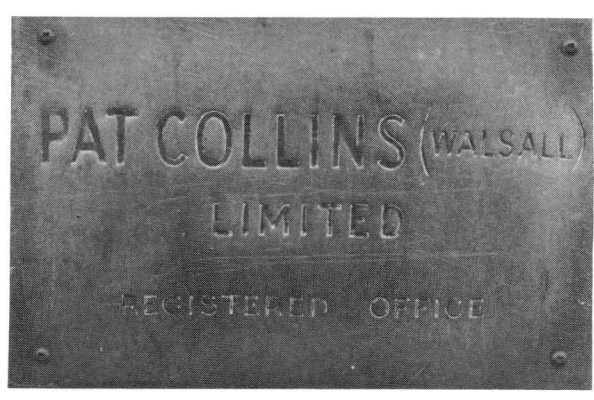

ABOVE: A much enlarged fragment of an aerial photograph of Walsall, looking down onto Shaw Street, at the junction with Algernon Street. This is the only known photograph in existence of the Gondola Works and Pat Collins' yard. Living vans and one engine can be seen in the yard plus the sheds erected for painting, repairing and maintaining Pat Collins' equipment.
(Walsall Local History Centre)

PAT COLLINS-EDWARDIAN GENTLEMAN
1900-1914

CHAPTER 4

Pat began the twentieth century as a man of substance.

He lived at "Chester House" in Algernon Street, Walsall, almost next door to the Gondola Works, the headquarters of his showman's empire, and he was the Managing Director of P.Collins Ltd.; the company owned rides, engines and equipment.

It was unusual for a showman to find time for anything other than the business of the fair, but as the century dawned Pat had the resources to indulge, and time to develop, his interest in trotting. When Bloxwich Wakes came round in 1901 he had to absent himself on the Monday to attend a trotting match in Blackpool where, with his mare "Lady D R", he won the chief prize.

This interest in trotting became part of another local legend concerning a stretch of road between two mile-posts much favoured for local trotting races. These tales feature not only wagers but the surreptitious movements of a mile post!

Pat was forty years old at the turn of the century, but too busy to sit back and contemplate such issues as the 'Mid Life Crisis'. As already mentioned he was not struggling to reach the top of his profession - he was already there! However, he may have paused to consider what to do next, and Homeshaw's 1959 Biography states that Pat experimented with 'retirement' when he was forty one years old. It then adds, *"Within a few days he was back again in the fairground"*. Pat himself is quoted as saying *"I can't stand still, if they tied me down, I should go mad."*

Pat's view of himself as a restless spirit seems a realistic one, and it was a characteristic passed on to future generations of the Collinses. He liked to see himself as an 'optimist', but his optimism needed the stimulus of new challenges that were absorbing enough to overcome moments of doubt, indecision and even bleak despair. Pat occasionally admitted to such feelings of despair, and there is a mention of an attempted suicide. Around 1920 Pat pointed out to Joe Ashmore the spot where he had attempted to take his own life. Some were told that he had tried to cut his throat with a knife, others believed he had tried to hang himself...and it was even suggested that he wore high collars to conceal the scar.

Pat survived these feelings of depression and, undaunted by the pace of technological and social change, played an important part maintaining and enhancing the twentieth century fairground. The arrival of the steam-powered roundabout, the steam road locomotive, and the wonders of internal combustion and electric light brought the fairground into the new century, but many other new innovations were to be introduced to the tobers, and it was not long before Pat was caught up in this, and was fostering and maintaining a reputation for always having something 'new' for the punters.

It is interesting to note that rides purchased in 1902 and 1903, also a show, and at least one of the engines, were purchased in the name of Flora Collins. After her death, comment was made on the way in which Flora herself emerged as an independent showman. This independence may have developed initially as a result of Pat's heavy commitment to the 1899 formation of the company.

In August 1903 there appeared in the Walsall Observer an advertisement announcing that Pat Collins had resigned as Managing Director of P.Collins Ltd., but was remaining on the board. No indication has so far been found as to whether this was upon a technicality, a short-lived change of heart, or an important step in reorganising his affairs. Even with the benefit of hindsight it is not easy to assess what rides were either owned by the company or by separate individuals, or whether at some point they all merged financially. Another question remains unanswered.. "Did Young Pat enter the scene as a riding master in his own right, or as a manager of his father's equipment, or both?"

Pat's household had always "adopted" the orphans of showland friends and relations. The best known example of this being the Mulletts, Clara and William, but there were others. Pat had taken Nellie and

- 31 -

Johannah Collins under his wing, after the death of his cousin - another Pat Collins. On 16 June 1906 Johanna Collins gave birth, at Neath, Glamorgan, to a son - John Collins. He too was absorbed into the Collins' household, and from then on was regarded as Pat's "adopted son". He later became known, and is remembered still by many, as "Walsall John"; he played an important part in the Collins' story. Pat did not grant Young Pat or Walsall John any special favours, insisting they establish themselves by their own efforts, though he did of course provide the opportunities for them to do so.

The Spring of 1907 saw the delivery of the Wonderland organ and showfront, and as this coincided with Young Pat's coming of age some reports claim it was presented to him at Wrexham as a combined 21st birthday/wedding present. The legend seems to have grown out of the confusion surrounding two separate events. Firstly on 7th March a great party was held at Oswestry to celebrate Young Pat's Coming of Age, when he was showered with expensive presents - but nothing quite so expensive as a Marenghi organ and Bioscope show! The second event was the inauguration of "Wonderland" which happened in the middle of April, when the fair was in Wrexham.

BELOW: Young Pat and his wife, Eliza, sitting in front of the Marenghi organ of the No.1.Wonderland Bioscope Show in 1908, in the centre of the picture. On the right:'Little Titch' (Bob Jones)
(Collection of Kevin Scrivens)

Later in life, Young Pat often said he had made his own way in showland, and he talked of 'going into partnership' with his father during the mid 1920's as if it was about to happen for the first time, but other reports would appear to contradict this. For instance, in a 1907 picture of Nottingham Goose fair the rounding boards of the Royal Ragtime Cockerels bears the name "P.Collins & Son", and one of the shows also bore the same name. In 1907 the lessees of some of the fairs are described as "P.Collins & Son", which confuses the issue even more! It is difficult to be precise about who owned what, and the degree of independence attributed to individuals, or even if such distinctions were valid.

With the arrival of "Wonderland" with its magnificent organ another institution was established...The Pat Collins Sunday Organ Concerts. Usually playing sacred music, these concerts attracted large crowds and collections were taken and the money given to charity - usually hospitals. The fact that the concerts were so popular served to draw attention to the fair and those who came on the Sunday no doubt resolved to come back when the rides were open on other days; but they also showed the public that showmen could play a part in the life of the local community, rather than only being interested in taking money on the rides before passing on to the next gaff. The Sunday Concerts enhanced Pat's charitable image as benefactor, and were a public display of his piety. On some occasions money was raised on other days or evenings, and passed on to local charities. For example, the Tuesday evening of the Bloxwich Gala was regarded as a "benefit night".

At some fairs there was quite an "ecumenical" quality to these concerts and clergy and ministers from a variety of chapels and churches gave the events their support. This was important in some areas where the non-conformist chapels had often opposed the fair or preached wariness of the fair's "moral dangers". In Bloxwich, an annual "Camp Meeting" was held at the same time as the Gala and competed for people's allegiance. It is interesting to note that Pat usually invited Protestant churchmen to be associated with the organ concerts; he was himself a devout Catholic but obviously had no time in his life for bigotry.

The sacred music concerts usually ended with the playing of the National Anthem, and later, during the First World War they took on a patriotic flavour. In many cases Pat put in an appearance at the concerts, but the person who had no option in this matter was the 'engine driver', who regarded the concerts perhaps not so 'charitably', as to him it was unpaid work on what should have been his day off.

When the second Wonderland was presented at the Olympia Fun City in January 1908, along with four other Pat Collins attractions, a service was held in the show on behalf of the Showmen's Guild, by Rev.Horne. Five attractions at Fun City would have involved about 50 staff, under the management of Bill Mullett. When Pat talked during interviews of employing so many people, the figures begin to make sense when it is realised how labour intensive fairs were at the beginning of the century. And of course a lot of casual labour was always used.

The first few years of the twentieth century saw the further development of the Showmen's Guild, of which Pat and his brother John had been founder members. By 1907 there was a need for District Representation and Pat joined the Birmingham Committee. Two years later, in January 1909, he became the President of the Showmen's Guild, and held the post for twenty years. His son, Young Pat, was made a member on the occasion of his 21st Birthday. The story of Pat's association with the Guild is told in a separate chapter in order to preserve chronology.

Even in the 1900's, Pat's rides travelled far and wide and appeared alongside those of other showmen at major events like the Nottingham Goose Fair, as well as on his own "runs". As the business was still expanding, the 'season' was virtually becoming 'all the year round'. An enterprising showman could find sites for Christmas/New Year fairs, and fairs held in January and February under cover, such as in Islington Agricultural Hall, or at Olympia, could become a showcase for new rides and create the trends that would dominate the travelling fairs in the ensuing year.

For example, a picture taken in the winter of 1906 shows Pat Collins' Gallopers in the Agricultural Hall, Islington, attended by staff in uniform. The rides were becoming bigger than ever and the showman's

BELOW: Oldham Wakes: The Tommyfield in 1905. On the left are Pat Collins' Rolling Gondolas (R29), on the right are Wm.Mitchell's Cockerels.
(Collection of Kevin Scrivens)

engine was providing both haulage and power for the rides and the elaborate lighting sets. The engines often took their trucks to railheads, the riding machines were carried long distances by rail, and the long engine-hauled road train was becoming more popular. The hiring of local horses to pull equipment between rail heads and fairgrounds was becoming a thing of the past.

On 23 March 1906 Pat Collins obtained the lease on the Crystal Palace ground in Sutton Park, and thus began his association with "amusement catering" on a permanent site. A miniature railway was built alongside the grounds by Miniature Railways of Great Britain Ltd, opening as a ten and a quarter inch gauge line in 1907; it was rebuilt as a 15" gauge line in 1908. In 1912 it was taken over by Pat Collins who continued to run it until 1915. After the First World War it had a rather chequered career, described in detail in John Tidmarsh's book: 'The Sutton Coldfield 15" Gauge Railway" (Plateway 1990).

It is difficult to imagine that Pat could ever have contemplated early retirement at such an exciting time. The Helter Skelter, or 'slip' arrived on the fairgrounds, and motor cars appeared on the switchbacks in 1907, and large double-crank compound steam road locomotives were introduced. The showmen's engines were making their presence felt in showland, and the large switchbacks and organ fronted Bioscope shows with elaborate facades were beginning to dominate fairs.

1908 was just as significant a year. Pat purchased a Brooklyn Cake Walk and stole the show at the Goose Fair with his "Revolving Pigs" on the Galloper. It was the year that Prince Samouda introduced his "Houp-La" at Kings Lynn Mart, and these round stalls appeared to spread very quickly amidst great controversy as to whether it was a 'game of skill' or a 'game of chance' - which ought therefore to be covered by betting and gaming legislation. 'Riding masters' themselves invested in such round stalls, as well as allowing their tenants to do likewise.

Very early in 1908, Pat became involved in issues that in today's 'open' society may seem rather amusing. In World's Fair of 22 February 1908 a letter from Pat told readers...."*Some stallholders, mostly of Emmas, are distributing postcards of a very obnoxious nature, that are not fit for publication. We must put a stop to this disposal of indecent literature. If it is not stopped, it will make it hard for us to keep our grounds and positions respectable and under proper control.*" Although Pat sent a sample to World's Fair they were not allowed to reproduce such offensive material! Once again we are reminded of Pat's determination to clean-up the fairground and to impose respectability and order upon it; indeed some of Pat's fair advertisements in the 1900's stated that "Police are in attendance to enforce order". A visit to the fair was after all often the only escape from routine and repressive drudgery and had to be seen in terms of its glittering spectacular riding machines

BELOW: A motor-car switchback - Pat Collins' Looping the Loop Motors, built in 1907 (R11). Pat Collins is standing on the right, Mr Varello on the left:Photograph believed to be taken in 1909.
(*Collection of Vanessa Forte*)

ABOVE: The Nottingham Goose Fair enjoying a "heatwave" in 1908. Pat's "Looping-the-Loop Motors" on the left, tram pole rising through the platform, and the "hill" level with the engine roof. To the right; John Collins' Razzle Dazzle, Pat's Gordon Bennett Motors and Pat's Platform Gallopers (R9)...blurred by their own movement!
(Nottingham Library Collection).

and shows, not in 'naughty' postcards displaying females in semi-nudity. (One particularly rude card apparently also mentioned the word 'divorce' in the caption!)

It is difficult for us today to imagine that the objection to the sale of risque postcards was such a serious issue, but as 1908 progressed, letters of support for Pat's stand poured into the offices at World's Fair. Only a few letters regarded the crusade scornfully and felt the pictures were harmless.

Fighting crusades, or organising fairs, Pat was certainly kept very busy.

In fact, when his son "Young Pat" married Eliza Fossett at Chester, on 22 January 1908 it appears that Pat was too busy at Olympia to attend. When William Mullett's ten-year old daughter Elizabeth died at – Olympia in February, Pat was again too busy to attend the funeral, although both Flora and Clara were there. (Elizabeth Mullett had had one leg amputated at Wolverhampton in 1905, but was working at Olympia as part of Pat's staff when she died). In April 1908 Wrexham Carnival Committee held a supper in honour of Mr & Mrs Collins and their staff, to say thank you for raising money for the local hospital. Once again it looked as if Pat was not going to put in an appearance, but he arrived just as the meal was over, though as the local paper reported he was in time for the festivities which went on until "milking time" the next day.

It is possible that Pat was "too busy" because his fairs were now being reorganised into a number of "runs" and as well as rostering his own riding machines and making endless arrangements, there was also ground to be let to tenants in order to achieve a reasonable balance of riding machines, shows, stalls and caterers. There was an art in providing the right "mix" and making good use of the ground. Advertisements in World's Fair at this time also indicate that Pat was busy buying and selling rides, or acting as broker or agent. As Easter 1908 approached there were the usual fairs to be presented at Wolverhampton, Walsall and Coventry, but Pat was also planning fairs at London's Alexandra Palace and Oxford.

There are always those who prefer looking back with nostalgia to "good old days" and the World's Fair correspondent reporting on the 1908 Whitsun Fair at Wolverhampton appears to be just such a one. He provides us with a good picture of the fair but his conclusions could be described as 'backward-looking'. Pat was the joint lessee of this fair, with his brother John, and it was often a big fair:

"Again the fine organ of Pat Collins is the outside attraction at his large cinematograph show, and the fit up of the concern, together with his attendants attired in black frock coats and silk hats, offer a completeness so neat and artistic, that, from a monetary point of view also, success is at once ensured. Besides he has full equipments with his racing motor cars, cockerels, horses, aeroplane, looping the loop etc. John Collins has his electric jumping horses, motor cars and airship. William Davies presents his horses, and there is Caddick's American Studio. In North Street is Holland's Palace of Light" - pitched for the first time in Wolverhampton.

"Once in the 1869's and 1870's, Wombell's Menagerie had been the main show, but marionettes, waxworks and acrobatic shows are all things of the past. Our children would be delighted with the old tent amusements if they were brought out once more, but at the rate we are going on wheels, and with steam, no one seems enterprising enough outside the music halls and theatres"

At the Back End of 1908, the Goose Fair was described in the same way. Admiration was expressed for Pat's new "prize porkers" but there was regret for the passing of the horses, ostriches, cockerels etc., they had replaced. The new Cake Walk was also admired, particularly as the proprietors were taking "four shillings a minute". This was described as Pat Collins' Cakewalk, 'the first to visit Nottingham', but Albert Richards' Cakewalk occupied the same position in front of the statue in 1909 and has also been credited with being 'the first'!

At Christmas that year Pat was busy planning fairs in Birkenhead, Wrexham, Birmingham (Soho) and another appearance at Olympia. Rushing headlong into January 1909 (when he was elected President of the Showmen's Guild - see chapter 12), did he have time to notice that Young Pat and Molly were celebrating the birth of their daughter Margaret; his first grandaughter? Years later, Margaret's marriage and early death were to play a part in the complex destiny of the Pat Collins' Fairs.

During 1909 the Bioscopes were enjoying the zenith of their popularity and technical achievement, before handing over their audience to a new phenomena: the permanent "cinema". At the Nottingham Goose Fair in that year were five Bioscope shows, including Pat Collins' No.2. Wonderland. Two months' earlier it had been much admired at Bloxwich Gala, and the Walsall Observer reported: *"A little further on was the cinematograph show with its elaborate front illuminated with thousands of many coloured electric fairy lamps and magnificent organ. It is probably one of the finest pieces of work, in its way, to be seen anywhere in the country. Inside, for the ridiculously small charge of twopence (2d) one saw amongst other things, just how poor old Samson was shorn by the treacherous Delilah, and how he afterwards avenged his sufferings by pulling down the temple about the ears of his enemies. The pictures also included a fine series depicting scenes from the Oberammergau Passion Play.*

Public Notices.

BLOXWICH WAKES WEEK.

P. COLLINS' ANNUAL

FETE AND GALA

AND MAMMOTH FUN CITY,

BLOXWICH WAKE GROUNDS,

SATURDAY, MONDAY, TUESDAY,
August 17th, 19th, and 20th.

Special Engagement—CHEVALIER PONCHABY, Hero of the high rope, in his daring performance 100 feet in mid air, supported by grand array of Variety Artistes, Acrobats, Bar Performers, Gymnasts, High Jumpers, Comedians, Clowns, etc.

A Host of Free Sights.
 The Great Fun City.
  100 h.p. Racing Motor Cars.
   Giant Roosters.
    Japanese Air Ships.
     Ocean Voyages.
      Helter Skelter Lighthouse.

FIRST VISIT—COLLINS' NEW

WORLD'S GREAT SHOW,

The greatest wonder of the present age. The entire 100 feet front of the Great Show is a Marvellous Mechanical Orchestra, equal to a band of 120 performers, magnificently illuminated by 3,000 multi coloured electric lamps. Truly a wonderful sight.

At each performance

THE MEGAPHONE,

The only True, Perfect, Singing, Talking, and Living Pictures.

Circus. Menagerie. Side Shows. Novelty Exhibitions, and all Ye Old English Sports.

Grounds Magnificently Illuminated.

12 Hours Continuous Amusement Each Day.

Admission to Grounds—

1d.   ONE PENNY.   1d.

HER MAJESTY'S THEATRE OF VARIETIES.

MONDAY, August 12th, 1907,
And Twice Nightly During the Week.

LIL HAWTHORNE, Walsall's Favourite Comedienne, in all her latest Successes.
MARCO, Boy Magician and Illusionist.
GERTRUDE BRADSHAW, Soprano Vocalist.
MARTIN HENDERSON, Blind Musical Genius.
FRED CURRAN, Quaint Comedian.
The Struggle for Life on the AMERICAN BIOSCOPE.

WALSALL FREE PRESS: 10 AUGUST 1907

Those who are of a pugnacious disposition, would doubtless visit the next sideshow, attracted by the unlife-like representations of a terrible fight between a semi-naked negro and a white man - one of the combatants was always shown as a coloured man...

....Then there are the Teddy Bears, surely the most grotesque collection of animals ever seen on a roundabout".

When the No.2. Wonderland show came to West Bromwich in September 1909 the usual "Sacred – Music Concert" was advertised on the Sunday night, and this included "The Life of Christ - a Sermon in Pictures". One is left to wonder if this was a show inside the Bioscope booth, or was a film projected so that people in front of the organ could see it.

As the century entered its second decade the fairground riding machine was going through yet another transformation - the arrival of the travelling electric scenic railway. The name was borrowed from a roller-coaster type of ride that had been seen at the White City in 1908, but it was more closely related to the switchback. A major development was the use of electricity to drive the cars round the machine, thus releasing the centre of the machine from the occupation of the steam centre-engine. In its place could be put an organ and the "scenery", including such effects as waterfalls and ornamental lighting effects. One of the first scenics was Farrars, built by Savages, and launched in 1910. Showmen rushed to have their switchbacks rebuilt, but Savages were in financial trouble by the end of 1910, though while in liquidation, they completed some Joy Wheels, and one set was delivered to Pat Collins.

Pat Collins' first new scenic railway (as opposed to a rebuilt switchback), was a Savages machine, and first opened at Wolverhampton Whit Fair, in 1911: it was damaged later in the year, during a storm, and a new three-section extension front had to be built by Orton & Spooner at Burton on Trent (the 'new' ride builder the showmen had found). When Pat's new ride appeared at the Goose Fair with its tropical jungle scenery and decoration it became known as "The Jungle Motors".

Another important acquisition was made at the end of 1911. E.J.Homeshaw, the Bloxwich historian, identifies this as the date when Pat was able to buy "Tenter's Croft" - a field at the Pinfold, at the southern end of the village of Bloxwich, where Pat had been holding his "Fete & Gala" since the late 1890's.

BELOW: Wolverhampton's Fair, in the 1900's. On the right the Rolling Gondolas. Towards the top of the square is Wm.Davies' Four-abreast and in the shadow of St Peter's Church stands the ex-Wall's Bioscope Show. *(Wolverhampton Art Gallery and Museums Service)*

Access from the Walsall road was alongside Limetree House, then occupied by Richard Thomas. Around this time what has become another legendary incident, took place; Pat found the gated access to the ground locked; he instructed his tractor driver to 'drive through' ..and the engine tore the gates from their posts. "Pat paid for the damage", the story goes.

The period from 1912 to 1914 has been described as the most prosperous in fairground history - a kind of golden age for all concerned. The emerging scenic railways, the organs, the fantastic showfronts created by the Bioscopes, the sheer variety of the entertainment, all added up to a spectacular fairground scene. At the Stratford Mop Fair, in the Autumn of 1912, three huge scenic railways stood in a row: Jacob Studt's, Marshall Hill's, and Pat Collins'.

The last two years before the Great War saw Pat Collins trying to add to his network of fairs. It is interesting to consider whether such expansion could have become permanent if the War had not come along, or whether the empire was already about as big as it could possibly be. Would Pat have started buying other family businesses, in the way that Brother John took over J.Whiting's fairs?

What is clear is, that by 1914, Pat had some of the best-looking tackle in the business, and he had established a reputation both for himself and for his fairs that made his "King of Showmen" title difficult to dispute. When Harry Wilding went along to the Onion Fair in 1914 he found it difficult to find words to express all his admiration for Pat and the fair. His report for World's Fair was heavy with superlatives, beginning, *"This year the machines were a deluge and a delight......The Scenic Railway (R15) is a dream of luxury and splendour"*.

Miss Clara Mullett was in charge of this machine, and it was accompanied by the No.1.Scenic Motors (Joby Farrell) and the No.2.Scenic Motors (J.Whyatt), plus Collins' Electric Teddy Bears (Wm.Whyatt), Collins' Three-abreast, and Collins' Wheel. Other machines present were Mrs A.Wier's Three-abreast and Hughes & Martin's Razzle Dazzle. Harry Wilding was shown round the machines by Pat's ground manager, Syd Jeffries.

The shows were headed by the circus, where Harry was met by Flora Collins and handed over to her manager - Walter Kelly. Other shows were Mander's Menagerie, Joe Caddick's Studio and Hughes' Boxing Booth. The only sign of War was that a new stall provided patrons with an opportunity to "Kick the Kaiser's Ass"! The sun shone brilliantly for three days. Pat was already planning his Christmas fairs - after all the War was going to be over by then.

RIGHT: Advertisements in the Dudley Herald, September 1909, for fairs at Blackheath, Brierley Hill and Dudley. Note that the Blackheath advert uses the phrase, "The New Wonderland".

BLACKHEATH WAKES,
MARKET PLACE, BLACKHEATH,
FRIDAY, SEPTEMBER 17th, to TUESDAY, SEPTEMBER 21st

P. COLLINS'
NOVEL ATTRACTIONS
FOR FIVE DAYS ONLY.
THE NEW WONDERLAND
The Grandest Cinematograph Show Travelling, with its magnificent
ORCHESTRAL FRONT
illuminated with thousands of Fairy Coloured Electric Lamps and Sweet Music by all the popular composers. All New Pictures of the world's latest events. Scenes of the Flying Machines by the World's Greatest Aviators at all the Great Trials.

SUNDAY NIGHT, SEPTEMBER 19th.
Commencing 8.15 p.m.,
GRAND SACRED CONCERT
AND A SERMON IN PICTURES,
THE LIFE OF CHRIST.

ON FRIDAY, SATURDAY, MONDAY, AND TUESDAY.
The ever Popular SCENIC MOTOR RAILWAY, RACING BICYCLE TRACK.
With all the other Attractions, will be OPEN NIGHTLY at 6 p.m., except Saturday, which will Open at 2.30.
DON'T FORGET TO VISIT GREAT SHOW.

THE WHOLE OF
P. COLLINS'
GIGANTIC AMALGAMATION OF AMUSEMENTS will visit
BRIERLEY HILL WAKES
And Locate on
THE OLD WAKE GROUND,
COMMENCING FRIDAY, SEPTEMBER 24th to TUESDAY, SEPTEMBER 28th.
WITH ALL NEW ATTRACTIONS.

TO NIGHT! TO NIGHT! TO-NIGHT!
DUDLEY SEPTEMBER FAIR
THE WHITE NOBS FAIR GROUND,
FRIDAY, SEPTEMBER 17th, to
TUESDAY, SEPTEMBER 21st,

P. COLLINS'
FUN FAIR
SCENIC MOTOR RAILWAY
KATZENJAMMER CASTLE AND HAUNTED HOUSE,
SIDE SHOWS, EXHIBITIONS, BAZAARS,
SHOOTING JUNGLES, COKERNUT SHIES,
SWINGS, AERIAL FLIGHTS, &c.,
And all
YE OLDE ENGLISH SPORTS.

COUNCILLOR PAT COLLINS
1918-1929

CHAPTER 5

The end of World War I in 1918 was the start of another period of change in the life of Pat Collins. He moved his base from Shaw Street, Walsall to Bloxwich; he consolidated his interests in permanently sited amusements, e.g. cinemas, theatres, skating rinks; and he took his first formal steps into local civic life.

On 29 April 1918 Pat was co-opted onto Walsall Council as Councillor for Birchills Ward, filling a vacancy created by the election of William Halford to the rank of Alderman. It does not seem that Pat particularly set out with political ambitions but the invitation was given in recognition of his role as public benefactor, and probably because of his generosity to the Liberal cause in Birchills. When they needed a headquarters Pat had provided one; he'd taken part in fund raising activities, and the result of one of these efforts had provided funds to buy the Walsall Ambulance.

Pat's nomination was unanimously supported at two public meetings in Birchills Ward. At the co-option he was described as "the worldwide known veteran showman, and President of the Showmen's Guild". Each member of the Council tried to outdo each other in how long they had known and respected Pat Collins - (this was the man they had taken to Court in 1892 !). If they happily used the term "veteran" on that occasion, what term would be left twenty years later when Pat became Mayor?

At the time of his co-option Pat was described as a resident of Limetree House, Bloxwich. He appears to have acquired a lease on the house about 1915, although he was not able to buy the freehold until 19 October 1926, when Fosters Trust (of the Hatherton Furnaces) disposed of several properties in Bloxwich. Pat had been using the field behind Limetree House, Tenters Croft, for the annual Bloxwich Fete and Gala since 1898, and had bought the field in 1911. Access to the field by the track alongside Limetree House seems to have been somewhat contentious.

The move from Shaw Street/Algernon Street to Bloxwich was therefore gradual in some respects.The first sign of retreat from Shaw Street occurred in 1918 when part of the land was sold on 6 December to the building firm - Deacon and Boardman. Pat continued to appear on the electoral roll for Algernon Street until the early 1930's. The Gondola Works and Pat's office was not transferred to Bloxwich until 3 May 1933, when the remaining land at Shaw Street was sold to the Walsall & District Co-operative Society (Transport Department). The name "Gondola Works" was dropped in favour of "The Amusement Depot", but telegrams went to "Gondola, Bloxwich".

By the end of the First World War Pat had acquired several local cinemas - one of which was only a few yards from Limetree House. This was the Electric Palace in Bloxwich High Street, acquired from Thomas Jackson, the Wolverhampton Baker-turned-Cinema-Magnate. Pat also acquired the Alhambra in Dudley Port, and the Olympia, Darlaston. The 'warmth' of the latter was legendary as the coal seam beneath the cinema was continually smouldering! Pat motored extensively keeping a close eye on the various parts of his 'empire' as he had other similar cinema interests further afield.

During the War, and the post war periods, he continued to purchase engines and equipment, and, as soon as restrictions eased, he began a programme of cinema building. Once again a new chapter was beginning in Pat's life, and once more "expansion" seemed to be the theme. In the early 1920's he built brand new cinemas in Chester, Bloxwich and Oakengates. (All described in more detail in Chapter 14).

These numerous and varied activities coincided with yet another big adventure...his entry into politics as a Liberal Parliamentary candidate. Obviously he did not intend spending his sixties either in retirement or resting on his laurels.

One legacy of the War was the disposal by Government Departments of traction engines, built for potential war service but no longer required. Pat acquired at least four of these engines; three McLarens built in 1917, "The Whale", "Samson", and "Goliath", and the Fowler engine built in 1916, "Dreadnought". They were purchased at an auction at Avonmouth Docks, and young Joe Ashmore did the bidding on

Pat's behalf so that no one knew 'the Guvnor' was after them! Equipment was also purchased at sales at Castle Bromwich, where there had been an aerodrome.

Many showmen had joined the services during the War, and those who survived eventually returned to the fairground. Some, like Harry Weston, sustained injuries which gave them recurring pain for the rest of their lives. Their stoicism is much to be admired. On Monday 1st June 1920, Pat presented certificates and medallions to fifty Midlands showmen who had served with the Armed Forces. His speech referred to the 'missing faces', and his audience sensed that he was genuinely moved. Pat's ability as a public speaker when his life led him into wider circles, is often remarked upon and opinions differ greatly. It appears that his style when facing an audience was not expansive or elaborate, but when he did speak it was with genuine feeling, whether of sorrow, pride or frustration.

In January 1921, at the Showman's Guild Annual Meeting in Islington Agricultural Hall, Pat distributed further medallions to members who had been in the Armed Forces. This was the last mention of such a ceremony and it seems that most showmen had then to focus their attention on the struggle to survive the post war period. They were difficult days, and as the decade unfolded a gloomy saga emerged characterised by economic depression, unemployment, and industrial unrest. The fairground world itself faced a very uncertain future as many other rival 'entertainments' fought for the patronage of the public. Hard times were, according to reports, aggravated by long periods of bad weather.

What was Pat's response to such a situation?

His policy, as always was "to keep the flag flying". Throughout these troubled times, Pat put great energy into maintaining the highest standards of fairground presentation; riding machines were regularly repainted and kept very clean; the grounds were carefully set out, strictly managed and always kept under his watchful eye.

Towards the end of the 1920's the opportunity of a new challenge presented itself. He could not resist. The new fairground "thrill" that arrived just in time to save the decade from dissolving into total gloom very quickly became part of his fairs.

✳✳✳✳

BELOW: Towards the end of the First World War, Pat "raffled" a horse and carriage to raise funds for the treatment of wounded soldiers at Walsall Hospital. He also helped raise money to buy the Walsall Ambulance.
(Collection of R.Deeks)

OPPOSITE PAGE: On the left Flora and Pat Collins join a party at the Cenotaph to place a wreath in memory of servicemen from showland who had lost their lives in the Great War. To the right of the wreath are Mr & Mrs Richard Deeks, and standing behind Flora and Pat is Walsall John.
(Collection of Molly Seldon)

Throughout the war, Crystal Palace Amusements in Sutton Park had been closed, but when the war ended, preparations were started to re-open as soon as possible. The Amusement Park re-opened in June 1919, the attractions advertised were - the Switchback, Joy Wheel, Helter Skelter, Gondolas, Swing Boats, Bicycles, Sideshows, etc. The miniature railway did not re-open until the summer of 1922 operating only until the end of the following season. It was then abandoned for 14 years. The Manager at the Crystal Palace site at the time was R.H.Delaney, and in an interview recorded in World's Fair a reporter confirms the presence of the above attractions and quotes Mr Delaney as saying: *"We have drained the place and built new roadways and approaches, bridges and electric cable. We are putting down the rails for miniature railways. We shall have two Lilliputian trains which will tour round the pleasure park... When the railway is complete we shall then erect a gigantic Figure of Eight, and water caves, and lakes on which to run two or three motor boats."* The re-establishment of Sutton Park Crystal Palace as a popular place of amusement had begun and continued for many years.

Also about this time another permanent site was brought back under the Collins' control, it was the Palace and Palace Grounds at New Brighton.. over the water from Liverpool. Pat had previously been the lessee on this site until outbid by George Wilkie; the latter's success had been costly to Young Pat (who ran the place for his father before the War). Now the situation was reversed. In 1920, the Collins' moved back in, advertised for tenants, and George Wilkie put his equipment on sale...and moved on.

When the travelling season got underway in 1920, a report of the Corwen March fair, illustrated two 'signs of the times'. First of all it was recorded that Walter Hobbs had *"great difficulty steering the engine across the sea of mud bringing the machine into place"*. The bad weather was going to dominate reports of fairs for most of the decade, and the Collins' firm moved many tons of straw and ash trying to make the tober accessible to the punters. Secondly, we learn that the centre of attention at Corwen was Mr Wright's new Foden tractor. The aftermath of the war saw a transport revolution on the fairground as WD vehicles became available, and the steam-wagon builders like Foden and Sentinel fought for showmen customers.

The technology of riding machines was also developing. Steam driven switchbacks had begun to be replaced by the scenic railways before the War, and this trend continued as new machines were produced, or old ones were rebuilt. For example, Pat's first electric scenic, of 1911 vintage, now appeared with dragon cars. At Wrexham in April 1920 this machine, under Clara Mullett's management, stood alongside the Gondolas, looked after by Joby Farrell. By the following year the scenic was replaced altogether, and was sold to his brother, John. Pat was skilful in delivering a good mixture of whatever was new, with rides and shows of well-established popularity. He demonstrated this skill throughout the 1920's.

When Pat Collins appeared at Wrexham in April 1921, his fair was dominated by the new Orton & Spooner Dragon Scenic Railway, and Clara, of course, was in charge of the £2,000 machine. The World's Fair reporter struggled for words...."*it is a gorgeous affair - it's a masterpiece*". It was the centrepiece of the fair for years to come. Sadly, although the fair was well attended, the local population had little or no money to spend. Britain was in the grip of a coal strike. The fair struggled on through Oswestry and up to Chester but the annual races were cancelled. Not only did the colliers have no money, but the shortage of coal brought its own problems...primarily of course, how to maintain fuel supplies to the showmen's engines. Mr & Mrs Fossett, Young Pat's "in-laws" and long established tenants, postponed their purchase of a new Foden lorry until the dispute was over!

Looking around for some good news in 1921 it was noted that the Council in Hanley decided to permit the fair to return to the market place, after an absence of several years. Pat was successful in tendering for the entire lease and opened at the end of July. (He also ran the Shrovetide fair in Longton, and the June fair in Burslem, maintaining his presence in the Potteries.)

October 1921 saw Young Pat elected to the Council in Wallasey...following father's footsteps into civic life; probably a proud moment for his parents. But the year was dominated by low private spending in most mining and industrial towns and was really only 'saved' by the new Scenic; everywhere it went it stole the show. When built up at the Onion Fair in the autumn, Harry Wilder, the World's Fair correspondent could not find words to praise the event highly enough. The Dragon Scenic and the wealth of other attractions *"presenting a wonderful charm and golden glitter"*.

The economic situation seemed no better in 1922, but at the end of the year, showland's attention was turned towards a new struggle - Pat's fight to gain a seat in the House of Commons. We describe his Parliamentary career in a separate chapter, but we pause to mention that showland saw his victory not as a success for the Liberals in Walsall, but as a triumph for showland itself. While offering Pat congratulations in November 1922, World's Fair said, *"His life is a romance, for he has, by hard work, raised himself from a poor lad to the high position he has now attained. Few people would have dreamed twenty years ago that the travelling showman would have one of his own fraternity in Parliament - "Well done Pat Collins - the whole of showland is proud of you."*

BELOW: In September 1921 Burrell 2650 "Mark Twain" (DH 2479) ran away in Perry Park Road, Blackheath. The engine, driven by Jim Morley, and the beast wagon broke away from the other two loads, collided with an oncoming vehicle and left the road. This dramatic scene provides a glimpse of part of the wagon 'front' of Flora Collins' menagerie.
(Collection of Harry Mills)

In 1923 showland's "ambassador" met the King and Queen at a garden party. The exchanges were interesting. Flora told the Queen that she hoped Her Majesty would live to be a great grandmother. The Queen said that she hoped the same would be true for Flora! The King approached Pat by saying, "Who are you?"

"I am Pat Collins, the showman" came the reply.

"And how's business?" asked George V as he shook hands.

"The bottom's knocked out of it, Your Majesty" said Pat (in a moment of honesty inspired by the real situation in showland).

"Well, get the bottom repaired, and carry on!" was the King's advice.

The King's advice was very close to Pat's own philosophy! He was still extending his runs - and in the process of adding Coalville and Market Drayton to his list of destinations. At Easter 1923 he opened at Wolverhampton, Walsall, and Coventry; sent a machine or two to Blackburn, and opened at the Crystal Palace and New Brighton. Just for good measure, the fair in Wolverhampton was described as *"The biggest array for several years"*. A 'new' set of steam yachts were in business, and there was at least one new attraction - the Whip Whop! Later in the year, "Over the Falls" began its popular travels. Pat was among the first showmen to present it.

At the Onion Fair of 1923, not only did Pat have his new "Over the Falls", but also a new American riding device - "the Sheik", although little was ever heard of it again! "Over the Falls" was successful at Evesham and even Stratford, (a fair usually dominated by other well known showmen), and after the Back End run was over it was built up for a long winter run at the Walford Road Rink. The end of 1923 was again dominated by election fever, as Pat had to defend his seat in yet another General Election, after holding his seat as an MP for a mere 12 months. His majority was increased and he was returned to Westminster as Walsall's Liberal MP.

Some of the political events of 1924 were of particular concern to showmen and are described elsewhere.

1924 provided a new prestigious location where Pat could direct his energy - it was the year of the Empire Exhibition at Wembley. In February it was announced that Pat Collins & Son had been granted a concession for providing a section of the amusements in the form of several rides. In March it was announced that Pat had joined others to form companies - "Circular Games (Wembley) Ltd.", and "Carousels Ltd".

The Wembley Exhibition was opened on St George's Day - 23 April 1924, by the King and Queen. Some of the amusements were those usually to be found at permanent amusement parks, for example, the Big Dipper (built by Thompsons), but Pat's job was to

BELOW: Pat Collins' Four-abreast Gallopers at Blackpool in 1921 - note the glass screen to protect the organ from wind-blown sand. In front of the organ stands Harry Weston Snr ("Matey").
(Collection of Kevin Scrivens)

provide "Ye Olde Fair Ground" and he was able to present his Motor Car Scenic, his Razzle Dazzle, the Three-abreast, the menagerie (one of the few 'shows' at Wembley) and a few other amusements.

It may seem strange that Pat's new scenic was not at Wembley, but this can probably be explained by the fact that he was also presenting rides at no fewer than three Easter Fairs... at the same time. The Scenic went to Blackburn (along with Over the Falls), where Clara operated the machine, now fitted with whale cars. Another scenic was at Walsall with Joby Farrell, and Young Pat's Golden Dragons ride was at Wolverhampton. Pat had steam yachts at both Walsall and Wolverhampton and several other machines. A new 'Caterpillar' is mentioned as being presented at Walsall.

Down at Wembley, new fairground rides were being shown to the public, including the Caterpillar, but some were not regarded as suitable for travelling. Innovations included The Frolic, Whirling the Whirl, the Dodgem, and the Witching Waves. An Over the Falls was also at Wembley, but Pat was already travelling such an attraction, and he was the first showman to bring one to the Goose Fair, in October 1924.

To his horror, Pat found he was fighting yet a third General Election in October 1924. Lloyd George came to Walsall in a much publicised gesture of support for Pat, but the campaign was short and concentrated on party politics. Support for the Conservatives and Labour increased, at the expense of the Liberals, and Pat lost the seat to his Conservative opponent. The final twist came in 1925 when the newly elected MP, Billy Preston, was forced to defend a by-election called to right an electoral technicality! By this time Pat had had enough of national politics, was not willing to fight yet again, and withdrew "owing to my continued ill health."

Pat's short Parliamentary career began and ended in his mid sixties over a period of 3 years. His health was not, at that time, too good, but there is no doubt that he found the restraints of party politics in government both irksome and time consuming.

Up in Birkenhead, Young Pat had lost the lease on the New Brighton site which was wanted for 'redevelopment' by the Council. Prospects did not look good. So Pat stirred himself into seeking new energy amd drive by going back to his roots. In March 1925 he returned to personally supervise the North Wales run, which in 1924 had been left in the hands of Young Pat. He enjoyed the fairs at Llangollen, Corwen, Cefn Mawr and Wrexham. At Corwen

BELOW: The Motor Car Scenic presented at Wembley in 1924: Left to right:- Albert Badger, Harry Weston Jnr, Harry "Matey" Weston Snr., and seven uniformed money-takers. The signs on the columns read:- "Decorated by Barnes, of Belper"
(Collection of John Williams)

there was the excitement of opening on the opposite side of the road to some "opposition" (probably Messrs Simon & Greatorex). Bill Croydon set out Pat's fair so well that they won the day!

On Sunday afternoon Pat talked to "DRM" of World's Fair and recalled that he had first come to Corwen at the age of twelve, when the fair was in the market place. He was still at school at Chester at the time, but he remembered coming to help Job Davies - "the great Welsh Showman" (The man who became his brother in law, by marrying his sister Johanna). At Cefn Mawr he met a miner who recalled having a fight with him 50 years' earlier! "DRM" concluded *"There are no cobwebs about Pat. He is Irish and is proud of it - but he loves the Welsh also, and that proves him to be a Celt to the backbone. Pat can understand Welsh and speaks it a little."*

This trip into Celtic nostalgia seemed to put Pat back on his feet, and by May he was making new plans. One involved creating a permanent amusement park at the Lickey Hills, Birmingham but this came to nothing at that time. The other plan was to revive the circus on his fairs, and in this he was successful.

The Lion Show was successfully travelling again as soon as the War was over, under the management of Mr & Mrs Tom Bew, but in the overall control of Mrs Flora Collins. First of all the black lion tamer, Maccomo, (Albert Williams) had been the star of the show, but by 1925 his place had been taken by Captain Clarke and a boxing kangaroo had joined the animals. It was a traditional "show" with a striking frontage formed by the painted wagons. Pat decided to return to these traditions to present his circus and employed Gus Howlett to paint brand new banners. He also bought a new tent. He was ready in time to appear at the Leicester May fair. When it appeared at the Whit-week fair in Birmingham, Harry Wilder wrote in World's Fair: *"Pat has revived the circus at his fair, and the front of the show is chock full of movement, colour, music, and merriment. I must say that the conduct of Mr Collins' ground seems to me to have reached a higher place than that of others. Mr Collins depends on public goodwill and he sees that every tenant and employee reflects this spirit. They have been taught to be courteous under the most trying circumstances. I visited the ground in most brilliant sunshine and found everyone in the happiest frame of mind."*

Three months later when the fair returned to the Serpentine Ground for the Onion Fair, it was still the circus which was the centre of attention. However, it is the 1925 Onion Fair that gives us a very clear picture of just how much equipment was being presented by Pat during these troubled times, as most machines were duplicated or triplicated: for a start there were three scenics - the Whales (Clara Mullett), the No.1. Dragons (Joby Farrell), and the No.2 Dragons (Young Pat). There were also three Three-abreast, and three Helter Skelters, two Razzle Dazzles, two Chairoplanes, and two sets of Steam Yachts, and a Cake Walk. Then, of course, there were riding machines presented by other local showmen, many shows, and umpteen round stalls and sidestuff. Harry Wilding's report on the event covered two pages of World's Fair! Incidentally, the oldest veteran of the Onion Fair that Harry was able to find in 1925, was the Iron-faced Lady, who had been attending since 1872 - - three or four years longer than Pat himself!

Although Pat had recovered from the ill-health which followed his third electoral battle, and subsequent defeat, and he had thrown himself back into the travelling fair with a vengeance, 1925 delivered a reminder that not even showmen are immortal. On 10th September his sister, Maggie Collins, died in her caravan at Pant Asaph, near Holywell, North Wales, aged 72. She had suffered from ill health for some time, and had moved from her home in Chester to be near the convent she supported at Pant Asaph. Pat had fitted out her caravan to make her life as comfortable as possible. World's Fair and the Chester Chronicle both paid tribute to her (see notes in the Who's Who section) and the historian is left to wonder, once more, what part the various members of Pat's family played in helping him along his showland path. "Aunty Maggie's" will was very generous to many people; including her brother Pat.

BELOW: Pat pauses at Wright & Rogers Shooting Gallery at Wolverhampton Whit Fair, 1925. (Nellie Rogers on right) Pat's companion is thought to be Harry Humphreys.
(Collection of John Ray)

Pat's career over so long a period meant he knew very many people, and so he must have become accustomed to the loss through death of family and friends, as age or illhealth took its toll; these losses would have become more numerous as Pat himself grew older. On 1st January 1926 Joe Caddick died at Wallasey, where he had 'retired'. Joe had been the great literary contributor to the birth of the Showmen's Guild, and he travelled his Photographic Studio from his base in Brownhills with most of Pat's major fairs, starting each season at Wrexham and ending at the big Back End fairs. The World's Fair reprinted Joe's letters of 1890, written in Brownhills, in which he had roused showmen and urged them to rally to the Guild, and Pat called for members to observe a minute's silence in memory of Joe, when the Guild met for its annual January meeting at Islington Agricultural Hall.

1926 saw two transitions in the Guild. It was registered as a Trade Union, and in June 1926 William Savage, Pat's close friend and neighbour, took on the post of Secretary full-time instead of on a part-time basis. Pat was still very much concerned with Guild affairs and with any Parliamentary activity that might affect the showmen; this was evident by the article he submitted to World's Fair warning its readers of the implications of the Road Traffic Act in February that year.

The Easter fairs of 1926 came and went in good weather, but unemployment and industrial unrest still threatened the showman's livelihood. As is well known, matters came to a head in May with the General Strike. On the surface things returned to normal after two weeks, but Collins' fairs travelled the mining districts, and the miners remained on strike long after everyone else had returned to work. Even as late as the August of 1926, at Bloxwich Wake, it was still having its effect, Pat offered as a consequence an hour of free rides on the Monday to the children of striking miners. After their rides the children went to Limetree House to meet Pat, and the Trades Council expressed their gratitude.

In a slightly less "political" gesture, Pat joined Councillor Danny Cartwright, and Bert Proverbs from his office, in organising a raffle to try and raise £1,000 for Walsall Hospital. The first prize was a Morris Cowley four-seater car provided by Mr Birch who ran a garage in Stafford Street, and the second prize was a Triumph Motor Cycle. Time had moved on since the days when Pat was able to raffle his pony and trap, during the First World War, for the same cause. £1,000 was duly raised and handed over to Mr Slater, of the Hospital Committee on 5th June.

On the fairground of 1926 there were one or two innovations. The circus, which had proved so popular in 1925, disappeared, although other people still sometimes presented a circus as part of Pat's fair. At the Whit-week fair in Birmingham Mrs Collins introduced a new novelty - the "Bird Cage" which was some kind of maze, but little was heard of it again. By August, however, a genuine new riding device had made an appearance in the form of "The Swish". When it was observed at Crewe in August, World's Fair noted that it was *"very similar to George Green's Whip which has been at Blackpool for a few seasons"*, and a month later, at Wednesbury, it was described as *"very noisy"*. At the Onion Fair, Harry Wilding, said that, *"the new Swish caused much excitement and attracted much business."* It was not taken to the Goose Fair, immediately after the Onion Fair, but did appear at Hull, the following week, where folk must have noted that Pat Collins was still keen to introduce innovations to the fairground.

MEANWHILE.... BACK AT THE COUNCIL HOUSE

The question that must occur to everybody is: did Pat Collins ever have time to attend Council Meetings?

From 1922 to 1924 he was still President of the Showmen's Guild, was Walsall's Member of Parliament, and looked after four travelling fairs, assorted cinemas, theatres etc. The following statistics seem to answer the question above:

YEAR	No.of Council Meetings held:	Pat was "Called" to:	Number Attended:
1924	565	162	42
1925	193	193	63
1926	603	222	80
1927	617	209	89
1928	655	173	67
1929	696	183	58

Most Councillors attended many more meetings, a few attended less.

At various times he served on the following committees: Baths, Park & Cemeteries; Electricity Supply; Gas; Health; Library; Old Age Pensions; Property; Public Assistance; Public Works; Trade Development; Maternity Welfare; Mental Welfare; Transport; Council & Staff Joint Committee; and the Watch Committee.

There was some concern later in the 1920's that showland had not come to terms with the recession, and changes in people's spending patterns. It was reported that the travelling fair had not been innovative enough, and that some of the basic stalls and games had remained unchanged since the beginning of the century. The showmen had to find some razzamatazz or excitement to bring the fair into the jazz age! One of the most promising innovations was the Dodgem..a ride where the punter steered himself towards fellow riders at twice the speed at which riders once sedately sat in glittering gondolas. The problem was to make such rides capable of travelling. The same problem faced the Big Dipper. Not surprisingly, in 1927, Pat again spoke of turning the Crystal Palace Amusement Park into a "second Wembley" complete with Big Dipper.

The quest for the portable Dodgem track, or the search for a satisfactory midget petrol-engined or battery-driven motor car must have exercised the mind of many showmen. At the Islington Agricultural Hall in January 1928, on the floor of what had once been the skating rink, was a giant Custer Motor Track, managed by Mr Wentworth, but under the banner of Pat Collins. Over at Olympia was the Auto-Skooter, made by Lusse Brothers of Philadelphia. Pat told the Annual Meeting of the Showmen's Guild that 1927 had been very depressing and very wet, but he was sure prosperity was just around the corner, and that the new rides would revitalise the fair.

But... still the Dodgem was not quite ready to save the showman's day. At Kings Lynn Mart, in February 1928, Pat presented the Swish as the latest novelty, and thoughts of better weather must have been dashed as the early March fairs were affected by snowfalls. The first sign of the new rides materialising appears to be the "Miniature Brooklyn Motors", introduced at Chester in May, in the care of Bill Mullett. A few weeks later the "Radio Cars" appear at the Birmingham Whit week fair. They did not make an appearance at the Onion Fair of that year, but they did appear at the Nottingham Goose Fair - the first to be held on the Forest Fields site. At the latter fair, Pat not only had his Radio Cars among the thirty riding devices present, he also had another new ride; the "Hit the Deck". They went on to Hull and back to Ilkeston.

One other step taken in late 1928 contributed to Pat's continued progress. In October he learned that he had been successful in bidding for a seven year lease of the ground at Yarmouth Pleasure Beach - at a rental of £3,500 pa. Seaside 'amusement catering' was going to play a larger part in Pat Collins' life in the next few years. He had apparently made an unsuccessful bid to obtain the Sand Hills, Blackpool.

RIGHT: **Limetree House, Bloxwich**
Pat leased the house from about 1915 onwards, and was able to purchase it on 19 October 1926 when the estate to which it belonged was auctioned. The field at the back of the house had been used for the Bloxwich 'Fete and Gala' (the Wake!) since the late 1890's, and had been purchased in 1911. Bloxwich did not completely become the centre of Pat's empire until 1933, when the office and Gondola Works at Shaw Street were closed.
Memories of Limetree House include seeing a signed portrait of the Pope and Pat's trouble-making, long-lived, foul-mouthed parrot.
(Express and Star)

As 1929 dawned, World's Fair still found itself looking back on the previous year with gloom, as it had done throughout the decade. Whether Pat felt more positive we do not know, but his life was nothing if not a tribute to optimism and hard work. His Swish was still 'stealing the show' at the Bolton New year fair, as were his Whales. Over the Falls, and the Lion Show were as popular as they had been in the previous few years. He knew he was in the forefront of bringing the Dodgems to the travelling fair. He also knew that it was time his long presidency of the Showman's Guild should come to an end. He decided not to stand for re-election in January 1929. He was then approaching his seventies.

Pat then once more experienced bereavement. His brother John died in Manchester on 24th January 1929. "Uncle John" as he was generally known, had been based in Liverpool and had much in common with his brother Pat. He too had become an important riding master, and the lessee and organiser of fairs. As we have stated earlier, it is very difficult to establish the measure of support the two brothers gave each other, though we do know that in the early years they were sometimes joint-lessees of fairs and they operated in each other's area. John had a slightly lower 'public profile' than Pat as regards the political arena, but shared his devoutness to Catholicism and benevolence towards organised charities.

H.M.Jay reported in World's Fair *"I am sorry to have to record that Councillor Pat Collins is broken down in health, through the severe mental strain that his brother's death has caused, and has been forbidden to leave his sickbed to attend the funeral."*

In February 1929, Pat wrote to World's Fair: *"The great shock I experienced in the death of my dear brother John, will, I am sure, be appreciated as my reason for not acknowledging through the columns of our official organ, the many letters I have received from friends in regard to my retirement from the Presidency of the Guild. Since my brother's death I have been laid aside with illness...but I am still, and shall always be...a keen and active supporter of our great Guild."*

In fact, not only Pat, but Flora and Young Pat were also ill during the first part of 1929. Of course, business went on as usual; there were even one or two new things to be seen. The "automatics" ..penny slot machines, were becoming part of the sidestuff of the fair, and Joe Fletcher was presenting his "Automatic Saloon" as part of Pat Collins' fair, surviving three very wet weeks at Burslem, then on to Longton for the 'proper' start to the run in February, and so on. Young Pat's son, Boy Pat, introduced a new novelty, the Jolly Tubes; also to be seen in the rain at Burslem! The weather was still bad at Easter and Blackburn was a miserable affair. In Wolverhampton, the Council were mumbling about reducing the three fairs on the Market Patch, to two.

Unexpectedly, Pat was well enough to appear at Wrexham in April, where it was reported that he seemed well and was enjoying the event. As the fair moved to Chester to accompany the races Pat actually attended the Sunday sacred music concert from the organ on the No.1.Scenic - Clara's Whales. It was also noted that the frontage of the Lion Show had been repainted and was looking better than ever, *"the old ghost show front thoroughly re-decorated and the fine organ beautifully lit"*. Pat's spirits revived again when he joined the fair on the Welsh border.

The younger generation were now making their presence felt. The ground managers were still men like Bill Croydon and Pat Tyler, but Young Pat was in overall charge and his children could be seen there too, like Boy Pat and Miss Flora. Walsall John was looking after the Jolly Tubes and occasionally "Over the Falls". When the Pleasure Beach opened at Yarmouth, Walsall John, was to take a part in supervising that part of the empire.

Harry Wilding met Pat at Birmingham Floral Fete in July 1929 and said that Pat looked better than he had looked for years. Could this septuagenarian showman still pull a rabbit from the hat to save the fortunes of the travelling fair before the close of this 'miserable' decade? Of course he could.

In June 1929 an advertisement in World's Fair had quietly announced that a Mr C. More had introduced a new attraction into England and was *"ready to appear at any location"*. The Wall of Death roared into Pat's life. The Patron Saint of Showland is Mercury, the thrill of the fairground ride is mercurial... speed... Salvation had arrived... in the form of a motor bike!

Eventually the columns of World's Fair filled with arguments about who had really first ridden the Wall of Death in Britain, or who had invented it, or who had first travelled it. Arguments aside, Pat recognised a crowd puller when he saw one. Yarmouth Pleasure Beach was presenting The Globe of Death by August 1929, with a team of French riders. Walsall John told the World's Fair that it was a very expensive attraction but was proving to be worth it. In fact, it was rather eclipsing another new ride at Yarmouth... the "Hey Day".

When Pat Collins' fair opened at Dudley in September it caused a sensation featuring a new Wall of Death. The principal rider was an Irish Canadian named Billy Williams (another man who claimed to have introduced the ride to Britain). He was supported by two English riders - Messrs Stanford and

The Nottingham Goose Fair (1927). This was the last fair to be held in the City's market square, and the new Council House, being built, can be seen in these pictures.

LEFT: Pat Collins' Whale Island Scenic (R16) on the left with the Joby Farrell Scenic (R15a) on the right.

RIGHT: A close up of Fowler 14424 "Dreadnought" (DH 2545) alongside the Joby Farrell Scenic.
(Nottingham Libraries)

Todd. The Globe of Death from Yarmouth and the Wall of Death from Dudley then began a spectacular tour of the Back End fairs - the Onion Fair, the Goose Fair, Leicester and Hull.

The man who had been so ill at the beginning of 1929 had a fantastic presence at the Goose Fair in the Autumn, presenting at least eight attractions, making good use of the new site. The amusement park at Yarmouth had been a success and new attractions were planned for 1930. Pat had just acquired the lease on the amusement park at Barry Island, and could look forward to moving in there in the new year. The Palais de Danse under Young Pat's wing had just successfully re-opened in Birmingham...what could there be left to do to round off the decade?

Pat's answer to this question was to hold a huge Christmas fair, Zoo and Circus at the Granby Hall in Leicester, as well as his usual Christmas Fairs in Wolverhampton and Coventry. To make sure the most exciting, and up to the minute, ingredient in this mixture was known to everyone, he made it quite clear that the Globe of Death was going to be at Leicester. In the World's Fair, 'Midlander' complained that the fair was losing its customers to newer, more innovative forms of entertainment, pointing out that over four and a half million Britons had already paid their money to see "The Singing Fool" at cinemas.

Picking up this thread, Pat billed his End-of-Decade Event in Leicester as "THE BRITISH SHOWMAN'S REPLY TO THE TALKIES".

The "Death Defyers" come to Walsall: Easter 1930.

WALSALL
EASTER PLEASURE FAIR
(Fair Ground, Corporation Street West.)

TO-DAY (Saturday), MONDAY AND TUESDAY NEXT.
PAT COLLINS' AMUSEMENTS
INCLUDE:
THE "PEACOCKS,"
GRAND NATIONAL STEEPLECHASES,
CHAIR O' PLANES, GIANT STEAM YACHTS,
LION SHOW MENAGERIE
AND THE LATEST SENSATION, THE
DEATH DEFYERS

WORLD'S FAIR; 16 SEPTEMBER 1929

SPACES TO LET.

Xmas Fair Zoo & Circus

Granby Hall, Junior Training Hall,
LEICESTER.
XMAS SEASON.
BRITISH SHOWMEN'S REPLY TO THE TALKIES.

THE GREATEST FAIR, JUNGLE and CIRCUS Ever attempted in England.
This is a tall statement but here are a few facts—Irrefutable, Truthful, and beyond argument.

A FEW OF THE £1,000 STAR ACTS.

From Berlin, and recently at Blackpool,
COSSMYS MIGHTY GROUP OF MASSIVE LIONS,
in the Arena itself.

From Copenhagen, the Surprise of Circusdom,
THE RIDING TIGER.

THE BUDAPEST RIDING SCHOOL.

THE GREAT ARENA CAGE OF MIXED BROWN & POLAR BEARS

6 Other Great Continental Acts.
Not merely as Bill Matter, but actually from the Greatest Buildings in Europe.

Bailey's GREAT BRITISH CIRCUS.
GLOBE OF DEATH.

I am now **BOOKING SPACES** For This,
The Greatest Show in England

PAT COLLINS,
Gondola Works, WALSALL.

PAT COLLINS, MEMBER OF PARLIAMENT 1922-1924

CHAPTER 6

"I remember my Father coming home after the Selection Meeting saying – "You'll never guess who the Candidate is. It's Pat Collins! "

Miss M.M.Gray, a Walsall Young Liberal in 1922

A surprise choice not only to members of the Liberal Party in Walsall, but also Nationally. In fact, it may have been as much a surprise to Pat himself, for although he was a well known Liberal he was not so well known as an active party worker; he was however, a substantial provider of funds for the local party and he had the substance to maintain status as an MP, if elected.

At the time of his selection each of the three political parties had difficulty in finding a candidate suitable, and willing, to contest the seat, for the financial obligations were onerous, and it is probable that finance played a big part in the final choice in.... all three cases!

The Conservatives, reluctantly, had to agree to put forward a woman candidate, albeit the wife of the retiring Member, Sir R.A.Cooper, who was not seeking re-election due to business commitments. He had held the seat for the Conservatives since 1910, having fought and won three elections (two in 1910) and one in 1918.

In a 95% Poll in Jan 1910, Sir Richard's majority over Maj.E.M.Dunne (Lib) was 545 (Total Electorate 14,713). In Dec. 1910 his majority over J. Morgan (Lib) was 789 in a 92.3% Poll. In 1918, Sir Richard had two opponents, J. Thickett (Lab) and W.H. Brown (Lib), the latter came 3rd in a 63.3% Poll, with a total Electorate now risen to 42,853 because of the inclusion of other districts in the Borough.

Little did Pat realise that in the short space of 3 years he would be called upon to fight 3 Elections! That must have been something of a record in itself.

Pat's majority over his opponents in his first Election in 1922 was 325 in an 84.5% Poll with a total Electorate of 45,009. He had won the seat for the Liberals, the first person to do so since Maj. E.M. Dunne in 1906. When he had to contest his seat the following year, 1923, Pat's majority had increased to 2,163 in a three corner fight, with an 82.9% Poll and a 45,339 Electorate. That time his opponents were S.K.Lewis (Cons) and A.C.Osburn (Lab).

Yet a third Election was called in 1924, considered unnecessary by some but brought about as a result of "hasty indecisions" by a Government divided within itself.

By this time, Pat was getting somewhat tired and frustrated; he fought, but lost in a four cornered fight to the Conservatives who fielded their third candidate in three years, a local man this time, W.Preston, who had no experience of any kind of politics....but he did play Cricket for Walsall!. His majority was 2,434 with an 86.3% Poll, and 46,407 Electorate. However, the local Labour Party was now growing in both numbers and persuasion, and it is suggested that the transfer of more than 4,000 votes from Liberal to Labour caused Pat Collins to lose this third Election.

In the first Election it can truly be said that the personality of Pat played a great part. He was well known both as a local personality and hard worker and also, and not least, for his generosity and human concern for the under-privileged.

Elections at a glance:

Year	Candidate	Party	Votes
1918	Sir R.A.Cooper	Cons.	14,491
	J.Thickett	Lab.	8,336
	W.H.Brown	Lib.	4,914
1922	P.Collins	Lib.	14,674
	Lady Cooper	Cons.	14,349
	R.Dennison	Lab.	8,946
1923	P.Collins	Lib.	16,304
	S.K.Lewis	Cons.	14,141
	A.C.Osburn	Lab.	7,007
1924	W.Preston	Cons.	15,168
	P.Collins	Lib.	12,734
	G.L.R.Small	Lab.	11,474
	J.J.Lynch	Ind.	622

In those days many political meetings were held, and in Walsall usually several hundred people turned up at meetings, with only a few hecklers! Many who remember Pat Collins, say he was not a very good speaker, and particularly not very fluent at public political meetings. However, if, when he was speaking, he became stuck for words, someone in the audience would shout out "Good Old Pat"...then everyone would cheer and applaud...and he would either continue to speak...or the time would have been taken up anyway!

Because of his social work, particularly among the Catholics in the Bloxwich area Pat was well known and had a basis of support outside the ordinary run of political people. The Roman Catholic Priest at that time, Fr.McDonnell, was not only a very good Catholic he was also very active in the Liberal cause... and with a little help from the priest this spurred many to vote Liberal who may not otherwise have done so.

It was possible to walk along any of the streets in the Walsall Constituency and see a picture of Pat Collins in the window, and especially in the poorer quarters of the town. He tried to canvass every house in the Borough; there were more working class districts in Walsall in those days, at Caldmore, and Tantarra Street, and there was a lot of support from those areas, especially from the Irish immigrants, who probably in the main worked in heavy industry. At the first of Pat's Election fights, Labour had no appeal to the voters of Walsall.

At the turn of the century, and again in 1922, Walsall was very definitely Liberally minded; in the three previous Elections it has been suggested that there was very little organisation in the Liberal party and that was why they did badly, but with the selection of Pat Collins as the 1922 candidate, new impetus was given to members, and offers of help for such a local popular figure, simply poured into the Liberal Association offices.

The Showmen's Guild wanted to organise a procession through Walsall to aid the electioneering, but the Liberal Agent, being mindful of the Candidate's expenditure restrictions had to decline the offer.

When Pat 'got in' first time, hundreds of supporters stood outside the Town Hall to hear the results declared, and as soon as they were announced there was much cheering and jubilation, and a rush over to the Temperance Hall, (later to become the Empire Cinema), for more celebrations.

Notable Walsall Liberals were 'at the Count' and recalled that when Pat thanked everyone for their help and support he did so with tears in his eyes. Herbert Lee was the Town Clerk in the 1920's, and the Liberal offices were in Lower Bridge street, where 30/40 people could be accommodated at a Party meeting; there was also another room which could be used, and these offices were over the "Bob Parsons Boxing Academy" at the time of Pat Collins' victory.

People would walk to meetings or use trams; the Town Hall was used for important speakers, the Temperance Hall for those not so important; ordinary meetings were held in school buildings, or, just occasionally perhaps in a church hall. The meetings were usually of a 2 hour duration, with an Introduction, another short speech, then the Speaker, then Questions from the Audience, then a vote of thanks. Some quite important National figures visited Walsall during the three Campaigns, including Lloyd George, and both he and Asquith sent messages to Pat... evidence of Pat's middle of the road Liberalism. Prior to Pat's selection as Liberal Candidate, Walsall had not been considered at all worthy of a visit by such eminent politicians ... but they were not slow to realise the opportunity such a popular candidate provided to further the Liberal cause, nationally.

The local newspaper, the Walsall Observer and Staffs.Chronicle, gave a wide coverage on these Elections, and on 4 November 1922 under Public Notices appears a Letter addressed "To the Electors of Walsall" signed by Patrick Collins, setting out his policies, thus:

" PARLIAMENTARY ELECTION 1922

Ladies and gentlemen, Having been adopted as the Liberal Candidate at the forthcoming Parliamentary Election....... I appreciate this great opportunity to champion the LIBERAL CAUSE for freedom, reform, and progress and, being a Liberal by conviction, I am proud to be associated with this great historic party, which has played so conspicuous a part in the building up of our great Empire.

I am not a stranger to my fellow Townspeople of Walsall, having established my works and business in Walsall some 40 years ago, and during this time lived amongst you, so that I can honestly claim that if I am elected you will have a Walsall man to represent you in Parliament.

This is a great Industrial Town, the needs whereof are varied. My local knowledge and large experience qualify me to represent you as your Borough Member, and should you do me the honour to elect me as your Member of Parliament, I feel sure your best interests would be safe in my hands.

The Coalition Government has died a natural death, and the time honoured party system has been reverted to, which I feel, now the War is over, is the proper thing to do. The voice of the people should be heard, and when the majority pronounces, then that section which it supports should be the governing section.

The Country, needs today, a STRONG AND STABLE GOVERNMENT, and, in my opinion, the Liberal Party, of which I am a humble member, is the party which can best provide such a Government, and this General Election affords an opportunity of electing Liberal Members in such numbers as to be the Governing Party.

*I am convinced that what the Country needs is:-
PEACE, RETRENCHMENT, REFORM.*

I am prepared to give my active support to a policy of this kind, and I believe that the Liberal Party is offering you the surest guarantee of such a policy being carried out.

I will, as briefly as possible, detail the working out of these bulwarks, of Liberalism, which will be my programme if elected, and which I am convinced will bring the dawn of a better day to this old and beloved Land of ours - Peace, Contentment, Prosperity, and Happiness - which we so much need and desire.

PEACE - The Liberal Party stands for peace, real lasting peace. Today there is but the pretence of peace. The Peace Treaty must be revised. Reparations and Allied Debts must be placed upon a reasonable and business-like basis, and thorough and UNIVERSAL DISARMAMENT must be brought about.

Stability abroad is essential to Commerce, and this can only be brought about by the .....and goodwill of the Nations, and towards this end I will honestly strive.

LEAGUE OF NATIONS - Liberal Politics stand for a powerful League of Nations, and not a skeleton or make-believe. The old methods of Diplomacy are antiquated and out of date, must be forgotten, and buried for ever.

To me in these days it is a humiliation and a shame that means should not be adopted to save the rising generations from the nightmare and horrors of War.

War, in these enlightened days should be made impossible; and this can only be done by admitting all Nations into ONE GREAT SUPREME COUNCIL. The League of Nations should be charged with this great responsibility, and its authority should be recognised and its decisions accepted and binding on every Country in the World. To it, International questions should be submitted, and by vesting this authority in a League of All Nations, bent upon maintaining peace, we shall be conferring upon the people of the World, security from the dread horrors of War, establishing better relationships, engendering a spirit of friendliness, and thus making Wars in the future impossible.

I promise, if elected, to serve the best interests of my townspeople and my Country.

Trusting to be favoured with your support, I remain, Your obedient Servant,   PATRICK COLLINS

Lime Tree House, Bloxwich, 1st November 1922 "

This appeared sandwiched between Public Notices. The left hand column announced Lady Cooper's week of meetings for the Unionist cause, commencing on 6 Nov until Monday 13 November. She was addressing 3 meetings per evening, plus an afternoon Women's meeting on the Friday, concluding with Mass meetings in the Town Hall and Temperance Hall. A formidable timetable!

Not to be outdone, the right hand column announced 'Meetings in the furtherance of the candidature of Councillor PAT COLLINS will be held ...'
and listed meetings from Monday, Nov.6. to Monday November 13,.... including TWO Women's Meetings! The notice ended with the words..... "Pat" is "The" Man for Walsall! He has lived with you for 40 years!

It must have been a little difficult for Lady Cooper as she went about making electioneering speeches, for if she deplored some of the conditions she found she had to choose her words carefully lest she implied her husband (the previous Member) had been unconcerned and dilatory.

The Walsall Observer and South Staffordshire Chronicle, on Sat.4.November 1922, reported under the heading LADY COOPER " 'For Empire, Constitution, Economy, and sane Reform' "An appeal to all opponents of the Labour Party's policy to rally to the Conservative Party as the only other crystalised factor in the situation.....
The Liberals of course, have a perfect right to put up a candidate, but I ask you to remember that at the last election their candidate received only 4,000

RIGHT: Pat Collins attends a Liberal Garden Party at the home of Cliff Tibbetts in Aldridge. Along with Pat & Councillor Tibbetts are the Rt. Hon. T. J. MacNamara, Joseph Leckie, and possibly Mr Hawley.
(Collection of Millicent Gray)

odd votes and that it is not very likely their present candidate will be at the head of the poll.." ......A strong believer in the League of Nations, she wanted to build it up and strengthen it, but until it had proved it could do its work she would be no party to weakening Britain's defences....More houses were wanted, but they must not provide them in a way that would ruin the community it was intended to benefit....

Mr Robert Dennison, the Labour Candidate, in his campaigning declared he was " 'Not Ashamed of the Labour Manifesto and Capital Levy'....Labour were in the fight and welcomed the opportunity of contesting the issue, although he thought they were entitled to protest against making the election day other than a Saturday when hundreds of workpeople (including railway workers) would be disenfranchised. .... He believed he was expressing the sentiments of many people, even those who did not agree with his own political views, when he said it was a great pity that Labour was not to be allowed a straight fight with the reactionary candidate..... he did not object to Lady Cooper... whom he described as amiable.... in referring to the Liberal candidate he said he had the greatest respect for his old friend, Mr Pat Collins, but he knew of no more pathetic thing than to see a man or woman jockeyed into a position for which they were obviously unsuited...."

With his renowned enthusiasm and directness, Pat rushed into the campaign "...For Free Trade, Economy, Drink Reform, and No Nationalisation" and the slogan "A Walsall Man for Walsall" ...he was received with loud cheers at his Adoption meeting in the Temperance Hall on Monday, 30 Otober 1922, and said "having been in business in Walsall for forty or more years he was fully alive to the needs of such an industrial community. He was Liberal from conviction, the principles of Liberalism having been born in him and were as 'marrow to his bones'. Liberalism in Walsall was not a lost cause, it was a living reality......Though the Armistice had been signed 4 years ago, there was not that peace at home and abroad which all desired. It was pitiable to see many hundreds of thousands of workers, some of whom were ex-Servicemen walking the streets in idleness trying to find work. I am convinced that the country needs wise statesmanship and leaders and is looking to the Liberal Party to provide this and rescue the country from the terrible morass that it has fallen into owing to the ineptitude and incapacity of the Coalition..... I am a worker and a fighter rather than an orator... and please remember that whatever a Collins promises he will carry out.... the wretched housing conditions in the Birchills district disgusts me.. .if I had the money that Sir Richard Cooper has, it would have been down with these slums years ago and up with some decent houses...... ...although I have merely learned the three R's and talk a simple vernacular, I know what things are... there is only one object in my life, and that is to see that the people have fair play. .... unless there is a move-on in providing better houses for the people there will be the devil to pay when I get to Westminster.... I commenced at the bottom of the ladder but by perseverance have worked my way to the top, although it has been a struggle...."

The candidate's son, Councillor Pat Collins Jnr of Wallasey, said that if his father were sent to the House, he himself would take over the business, lock, stock and barrel.

As might be expected, the electioneering was lively, and the candidates did not take their critics remarks lightly! Sir Richard, canvassing on behalf of his wife, complained "that the Liberal Candidate appeared to spend most of his time at meetings attacking me... and I'm just a plain citizen, except that I happen to be the husband of the Unionist candidate...."

At one meeting, where, as usual he was accorded a rousing reception, it was recorded that Councillor Collins began by saying *"I am not a carpet bagger... I am not a professional politician...but a businessman, of large experience and endowed with a fair amount of intelligence and commonsense. We want more businessmen in the Commons who can touch the spot regarding the waste of public money. It is true that I am not a born orator, my whole life having been devoted to building up a business, but I have reached where many of the 'carpet baggers' will never get. Cut down waste and extravagance by all means, but not at the expense of our ex-servicemen nor the widows and children of the brave men who have fallen...."*

A Women's afternoon Meeting at Caldmore Liberal Club is reported on at length, and a Mrs Pearce, said, amidst laughter "We should all have liked a woman Liberal candidate, but a man Liberal is the next best thing. People who go against the Liberals, go against themselves."...... a resolution pledging support for Mr Collins was carried unanimously.

At one meeting, a Mr James of the Musicians' Union challenged the statement that Mr Collins paid good wages; he quoted the standard rate for a 24 hour week and said Mr Collins did not pay this. To which the reply by Pat was that in the case in question, the worker was only employed for 18 hours a week! Someone else, at a Chuckery meeting, asked if it was true Pat had offered a man a job at 25/- a week. "No", said Pat, "that would be ridiculous because a man could not live on such a wage".

Whereupon another man in the audience shouted that "it would be a good job for Walsall Hospital if there were more Pats, many folk who have more money never gave the Hospital a farthing". Yet another voice said "He gets his money out of the working classes"... and someone else replied "But he need not give it away unless he chooses"..... ... Councillor Collins then intervened and said he did not wish matters of his charitable donations mentioned in his presence... and 'that he never let one hand know what the other did'.

On November 18, 1922 in the Walsall Observer there was a letter thanking the Electors of Walsall, for rallying in support in such a magnificent manner.... *"I have endeavoured to fight a clean fight...and I trust we shall settle down and work with a will to bring to this old Borough that peace and prosperity that all of us so much desire...."*

Also in that issue of the paper, under 'Some Local Reflections' the Reporter queried who received the greater shock...the Unionists for losing, or the Liberals for winning, while Labour were sore at the Liberals for standing in the first place.

After the counting of the votes, and the magnificent victory there were a number of boisterous receptions, and many more speeches. Councillor J A Leckie expressed thanks to all who had assisted in the campaign, including the work of Young Pat...(Mr Collins son). In his turn, Councillor Patrick Collins, Jnr. of Wallasey, said it was the proudest moment of his life to see his 'dad' finish his business career and start a new one at Westminster. He had never known him to do anything to injure a man in his life, but he always tried to help the man who was down. "I am now taking over my father's business", added Mr Collins, "while my father goes and does his duty at Westminster." He expressed thanks to members of the Showmen's Guild and to Walsall people generally for their help and kindness.

Mr S F Hawley said the flag of Liberalism had been kept flying in Walsall for the last four years by Mr Leckie, they had now wiped out the depressing defeat of 1918.... he was sure no other gentleman in Walsall could have polled anything like the number of votes that Councillor Collins had obtained.... at first he had declined to stand, but when a deputation waited on him he could not, out of his big heart, resist their request.

Mr Orton, of Burton on Trent, described as one of the largest builders of roundabouts in the world, voiced the appreciation of the showmen of their president. He said he had never known Mr Collins do a mean or dirty action during the forty years he had been acquainted with him.

And what memories did the ordinary voters of Walsall have ? A young mother in 1922, Mrs Myrtle Gough, recalls putting her son (wearing his hand knitted 'liberal blue' suit) in his pram outside her mother's General shop in Whitehouse Street. "We all rushed outside, when we saw someone stop to look and speak to him", she said, "It was Pat Collins, he was campaigning through the streets for the Liberals; he said, 'What a nice little boy' and gave him half a crown... which of course bought him one or two things in those days because 2/6d was a lot of money then. Each time he passed after that he used to stop and speak to us; he was a very friendly man, always formally dressed in one of those hard-type hats." (Bowler!).

She also recalled the time about three years later, (by which time she had 2 girls, one boy and another on the way "you had children quickly in those days") when they were desperate for somewhere permanent to live. She knew they didn't have enough points to be considered for a council property, but nevertheless went along for interview. She answered all the questions put to her, at the end of which, Pat Collins (who was on the Committee) said..."Oh dear, we will have to see what we can do for you". Mrs Gough filled in a form, and Pat marked it 'Recommended'. Her husband worked for Joseph Leckie, and he also supported the application. The Gough family moved into their Council house within three months... in Lord Street; there were no roads, no paths, and mud everywhere, and it was difficult to push a pram, but it was a roomy home. Rent was 10/6d a week (later reduced to 9/6d!)...her husband's wages were around £2, and her new neighbours, who hailed from Birmingham way, also worked for Joseph Leckie.

Talking about fairs, Mrs Gough remembered Pat Collins was always walking around the Midland Road, Walsall fairground when the Fair or Wake was there... "just as if he was 'ordinary'"! She could also remember the donkey and horse sales and auctions.

Before moving on to Pat's career in Parliament , (somewhat brief though it may have been) it seems appropriate to record yet another instance of his generosity. To express his thanks to showmen for their support during his election campaign, in November 1922, Pat asked them to join him in raising money to "help the poor" in Walsall. His brother, John, started the ball rolling with a donation of £50; Marshall Hill followed with £5; the third donation was a half crown. At Christmas, William Savage (Secretary of the Showmen's Guild) wrote to World's fair to say the fund had been a great success (!) and he published a list of contributors and their donations showing about 15 showmen who had contributed. The Liberal Party office in Walsall had been asked to draw up a list of deserving cases, and according to Savage, 500 of them had been given a rabbit and 2.cwt. of coal, costing 5/- per recipient. (Remember in those days there was no battery farming, producing cheap poultry).

At the January 1923 Showmen's Guild Annual General Meeting held in Islington, the mood was euphoric when dealing with the President's success in becoming a member of Parliament. Pat brought along a handful of speakers to meet the showmen, fellow MP's and Mr Hawley (Tentmaker and JP from Walsall). As Pat rose to speak, the members cheered and sang *"For He's a jolly good fellow'* ... and Pat told them *"Although I have been elected by the voters of Walsall, I have been elected as what I am - a Showman"*. APPLAUSE. Pat assured them that he had already made many valuable friends in the House of Commons and there was no snobbery in the House. (!) Mr Hawley said *"It was not a political victory but a popular victory. Their member was beloved by the working classes of Walsall, and he was with them in trying to forge a link between the Showmen's Guild and the Workers of Walsall"*.

Of course, all was not sweetness and light. By February 1923, letters to the Walsall Observer were expressing Tory bitterness about their defeat, and were generally full of prejudice about Pat. One Tory (a lady?) had told readers that Pat was simply 'an emissary of the Pope' (obviously not a RC, but perhaps she was also disgruntled because all the clergy, both protestant and catholic in the Borough appeared to favour Pat, and a number of them had actually canvassed and spoken in favour of Pat and the Liberal cause at public rallies). A 'Mr Smith' claimed that Pat had bribed his way into Parliament with his acts of charity; and a Mrs Fraser Wood wrote to say that she was ASHAMED of the Walsall elector's choice! (Why?, we might be permitted to ask!).

What of Pat's time in the House of Commons? He had not long been in the house when he made his Maiden speech on the Home Rule Bill.

He posed quite a number of written questions during his time, and was closely associated with - The Fairs Bill; Moveable Dwellings Bill; Performing Animals Bill; Shop Hours Act; Mechanical Games Act (1917 Scotland). It has been recorded in the 'History of the Showmen's Guild' by Thomas Murphy that "the Friends Pat made in the house... proved of immense value to the Guild and its members". And it is believed that those initial contacts in the House have been maintained and continue right to the present day.

A study of Hansard produced Written Questions posed by Pat Collins MP for Walsall, on the following issues:

1683.	Agriculture, Board of Admin and Activities.
1677.	British Museum - Duplicates-loan to Provincial Museums
1203	Election, Local - Walsall. Polling arrangements complaint, (60 women voters at Elmore Green not able to vote at last minute...it was said they came too late. No further action)
1118	Entertainments Duty Repeal-Finance Bill Debate
213	Estate Duty - Aggregation -Finance Bill Debate
1243	Old Age Pensions - Amendment of Act - Economy of Administration (Oral answer given on Pensions plus a list of Members & Govt)
2995	Performing Animals Bill
492	Post Office, Walsall Accommodation (Agreed inadequate, but not in the Budget that year, so no funds available)
1329	Telegraph Service - Telegram - Delay (Dissatisfactory? Baldwin, "NO")
262	Tobacco, Travelling Traders' Tobacco Licences
58	Trade and Commerce Taxation on Industry, GB & the USA, comparison
1778	Transport - Coton Hill Bridge, Shrewsbury, - Heavy Traffic.

Regarding the Question on Transport and Coton Hill Bridge, the following is recorded: Mr Collins asked the Parliamentary Secretary to the Ministry

Mr PATRICK COLLINS, MP

made his Maiden speech in the House of Commons on 29 November 1922, during the Third Reading of the Irish Constitution Bill when he said:

"As an Irishman, this is the happiest day of my life. The House has given us what we have been looking for for 700 years. Five generations of our family have fought for this freedom and, thank God, I have seen the day on which it has come. The hon.Member opposite is very doleful about the Irish question. He may rest assured that Irishmen will do the very best for the country. It is a great act of justice done to them and they will never forget it. You have given them this freedom and you can rest assured that when they take the Oath of Allegiance they will hold to it and will never go back. Irishmen have never had a chance. Now we will give them a chance, and you will never regret it. The Government in Ireland has not had an opportunity. Really the Irish people are moral and peaceable when they get a chance to do what is right. This is the greatest thing that has ever happened to us and there is not an Irishman in England who does not glorify what is done for her. As an Irishman speaking for my people in England, we are thankful for what is done for us, and I am sure you will never regret what you have done."

of Transport whether he is aware that the LNWR Bridge at Shrewsbury, on the main road to Wrexham can be used for traction engines and ordinary heavy traffic ONLY by giving two days' notice to the railway company; and if he will take steps to have the bridge, if necessary, permanently strengthened so that it may be used without this serious delay to traffic being incurred? Colonel Ashley replied, "I assume that this question relates to the Coton Hill Bridge, Ellesmere Road, Shrewsbury, crossing over the Gt Western Railway. The initiative in such matters rests with the local highway authorities, any application from whom to my Department will receive careful consideration.. I am having a Communication on the subject addressed to the County Surveyor of Salop".

Just a quick glance at the questions informs the reader that Pat Collins continued even in Parliament to apply himself to matters which most nearly affected his work and those he represented. Nor is it surprising to read of his interest in a Repeal of the Entertainments Duty; his memory was long, and no doubt the Prosecution and Fine he received in 1917 still rankled. The episode was quoted in the Pioneer Newspaper of 17.November 1917, see below:

THE "RED TAPE" PROSECUTION... Sequel to Proceedings against Mr Pat Collins... Hospital Committee's Sympathy

"The "Red Tape" prosecution instituted by the Excise Authorities against Mr Pat Collins in connection with the Hospital "Benefit" at Bloxwich Wakes - when, through a misunderstanding, the necessary certificate of exemption from the entertainment tax was not obtained - has had a sequel this week. The Hospital General Committee, at their meeting on Monday passed a Resolution expressing sympathy with Mr Collins, and subsequently on the instructions of the Executive Committee, a cheque was sent to him for the amount of the fine imposed by the Bench 15, but, with his well-known generosity, Mr Collins has declined to allow the Hospital funds to be depleted of that amount.

In his letter of reply, Pat thanked the Hospital Executive Committee for their Resolution and cheque and went on to add.... *'had the bench grasped the full facts of the case this fine would never have been imposed. All Charities are exempt from the payment of this tax. You were good enough to inform the Custom Authorities that this 'Benefit' was to take place, and had their acknowledgement. If it was necessary for anything else to be done, to put this matter in order, they, or the police, should have acquainted you, which they did not do; therefore it was only right to assume that everything was in order. The red tape associated with this business is such as to prevent many well-disposed persons from assisting such valuable institutions as yours. I cannot allow your funds to be imposed upon...and enclose my personal cheque for £15...I regret very much all this trouble, and can assure you that this will not in any way prevent me from doing my best for your Hospital and kindred institutions, so far as the future is concerned,* *and, as the general public are now acquainted with the whole circumstances and would rally round to your support, this will be my compensation, Yours very truly, Patrick Collins.*

Back to the 1922/23/24 Elections!

Kenneth Dean MA, in his book "Town and Westminster, A Political History of Walsall from 1906 - 1945, declares that Pat Collins was useful to the Liberal cause..... Nationally, when the 'top brass' realised his popularity could have a spin off effect, and, Locally to keep Labour out. He went on to add that Pat's political views could have led him into either Party, but that probably because he was of Irish descent and a Catholic he aligned with the Liberals since they had pledged themselves to do something about the Irish problem.

"Pat was not radical enough to be Labour" said Kenneth Dean, "in the sense that they were always planning a strategy but were disrupted by internal factions - no unity either between members themselves or between Trades Council". (Some things never change in Walsall!) "They didn't always put up members themselves, but backed, for example, the President of Walsall & District Co-operative, though they didn't back Danny Cartwright, that colourful Independent Labour Candidate, as he had clashed with Pelsall & Dist.Miners' Association; he remained an embarrassment to the local Labour Party for the next two decades". Danny was a friend, employee and colleague of Pat Collins on the Council for many years. (See also our Chapter on Crystal Palace).

Not many politicians, aspiring or elected, have to face three Elections in three years as Pat did. He barely had time to settle in the House of commons when Parliament was dissolved, and electioneering began again. The disruption to his business life can only be imagined; (even if his son Young Pat, vowed to take over the business after the first election.... would Pat really have handed over the reins completely, in his lifetime to anyone...even his son?); and the expense of three Elections to Pat personally would have been astronomical, and coupled with his legendary generosity, probably almost ruinous. To a man of action who had spent his life making 'instant' decisions without recourse to others and who was used to working round the clock to achieve results, the slow grinding of the working of Government must have been exceedingly tedious. But he entered into Election number two with few signs of slowing down or boredom as the following shows:

There were three Candidates again. The Unionists adopted Sydney K.Lewis, and Labour adopted Lieut.Col.A.C.Osburn. Pat Collins again represented the Liberals.

" Speaking in support of Pat's adoption as candidate, Mr S F Hawley said Mr Collins had already done remarkably well in the House of Commons and has surprised even his most sanguine friends. He had not been a silent member, but had not wasted time by asking a lot of silly questions. Mr Collins was largely responsible for securing an order for tubes for battleships for a Walsall firm, thus providing employment for a large number of men in the town for some months. Mr Collins had a magnetic power which made him popular with all parties..." (W.O. 24.11.1923)

The Labour candidate was reported as being 'a doctor with a distinguished military career', and the Unionist candidate said he was "not sorry in any way that he was a working man...in fact he was proud of it because he found better pals amongst the working classes than anywhere else" (W.O. 24.11.1923)

The electioneering this time was more pertinent, and personal. In another W.O. newspaper report in November 1923, the following was recorded: "Continuing, Mr Collins said he did not desire to introduce personalities, but he must reply to Mr.H.G.Williams the Conservative Candidate for Wednesbury (!) who had spoken about his (Mr Collins') 'elephants and fat women'. *"I don't own any elephants"* said Mr Collins, *"although they are very useful animals; neither have I any fat women. But I can tell you this, if Mr Williams and Mr Lewis and the Conservatives have their way, there will be few but thin women in this country. There had been plenty of gibes from the other side about showmen, but the showmen had done their duty to humanity. During the war they gave twenty ambulances to the War Office"*, and, added Mr Collins, *"I saw that our good old Borough had one. Furthermore, the showmen collected £65,000 in three years for hospitals and charitable institutions. It's all very well to talk about politics, but we must consider the huamnity side as well. I have done my best to help the bottom dog, and I want to know what Williams and Lewis have done for humanity"* (Loud cries of "Nothing", and, "Rub it in Pat" came from the audience)

He hotly denied accusations that he could only speak if provided with a typewritten script! And challenged 'that intellectual gentleman' (Mr Hurst) "to make a better speech than I have tonight". There was much applause and a voice saying, 'Go it Pat, give it him'. One thing is certain, Pat was never without vocal support from his large audiences. There was also added excitement at this meeting, when a lockmaker tried to climb onto the platform shouting that he was anti Free Trade, as foreign locks were putting him out of work.

When Pat addressed an audience in his own Grosvenor Cinema, Bloxwich, on Wednesday November 28, he astonished his audience by telling them: *"I was talking with Joseph Thickett at the procession last Sunday week and he told me: 'Pat, I am going to vote for you, and my old woman and son - I don't see why Labour should be putting up against you'"*.

Joe Thicket - a veteran Labour party man from the ranks of Walsall's railwaymen, was currently Mayor - and, as Returning officer, had no vote in the election (!). The Walsall Observer rushed round to see him and JT denied saying any such thing, and said he never referred to his wife as "My old Woman"!

Pat caused embarrassment all round!!

The second Election was scheduled for December 6, 1923, and in the Staffordshire Chronicle on December 1, 1923 appeared the following:

The truth about my visit to Germany:

It has come to my knowledge that the Conservative Party are endeavouring to mislead the public respecting my visit to Germany, with the object of making Political Capital out of it, and I am wishful to warn the Electors against being taken in by tactics of this kind.

THE TRUTH IS THIS:-

In August of this year, I went to Germany to see the Country and its conditions for myself. I went to the Luna park, which is an Amusement park, and saw some new and novel Riding Devices, one being a portable Figure of 8, and the other a portable Water Chute, which are only made in Germany and patented in England. I thought these novel devices would do well in England, and arranged for the purchase of a Figure of 8, also to acquire the Patent Rights.

This would enable me to manufacture these, sell them to the Pleasure Parks and Showmen in England, thus creating a New Industry for Walsall.
(Signed) PATRICK COLLINS
Gondola Works, Walsall. November 30, 1923.

ALSO:

Copy of Letter sent to -

Mr.A.E.Fellows, Chairman Finance committee, Walsall Football Club,

Dear Sir,
WALSALL FOOTBALL CLUB LTD
Referring to the promise I have made to take 250 Shares in your Football Company, I have never made a promise that I have not carried out, and have intended to carry out the same as arranged with you.

It has come to my knowledge that certain rumours are being circulated in the town by the Conservative party that I do not intend taking up these Shares, ostensibly for the purpose of damaging my Candidature. You will know that I have been interested in your Club and the various sports of the Town, hence I am prepared to take up these Shares and thus redeem my promise, but I most certainly object that an attempt should be made to make political capital out of a promise of this kind which was made in all good faith in the interest of your football Club and to encourage sport of this kind in the Town.

I must now ask you to disown any responsibility for such lying statements and that you and your committee have all along been satisfied of the sincerity of my promise and the interest I have taken in your Club.

Yours faithfully,   P.COLLINS.

The 1923 Election was an 'Earnest, but orderly fight' according to the W.O. Dec.8.1923, and the expectations of a close finish were upset. The Walsall Liberals' majority was increased to over 2,000.

The Mayor (Joe Thickett) after the Declaration of the result, first acknowledged the Vote of thanks and then greeted Mr Collins as the MP and congratulated him on a splendid victory, then went on to say he hoped it would be celebrated with "proprietary and decorum". He thanked the unsuccessful candidates and congratulated them on the way they had fought for the faith within them and the sportsmanlike way they had taken the result, and in conclusion he remarked on the absence of hooliganism and rowdyism in connection with the election.

Pat thanked the voters 'from the bottom of my heart' ...cheers...and more cheers when the Rev.Fr.McDonnell appeared on the platform and warmly shook the new Member by the hand....

Continuing his speech, Pat said that his wife was lying seriously ill (sounds of sympathy from all parts) but she had said to him *"Go on and fight, Pat. Keep on fighting for the people." Well, I did fight, and we have won"* .. he went on to thank the press, who he said, had given them a fair crack of the whip, a square deal, this time. He concluded by asking his supporters to go home like law-abiding citizens, to show the other side that we can *'win like gentlemen'*.

Young Pat, had appeared again, and spoke at some meetings and asked the electorate to "support his dear old dad" who was anxious to do all he could for Walsall.

On the eve of poll, telegrams were read from Mr Asquith and Mr Lloyd George wishing Mr Collins success, they read "Our warmest wishes for your return to the House of Commons, where you rendered such excellent service in the last Parliament....."

He was returned, resoundingly for his second stint in Parliament.

However, after the results of the 1924 Election were announced, a tired Pat declared that "The fight in Walsall was not a defeat," he told his liberal supporters, "we were betrayed".

It seems almost with relief after his defeat that he spoke to the Showmen's Guild Members at their AGM in January and said that 'the Labour Government will have the showman's cause at heart.

When, on a technicality, yet a fourth Election was called in 1925, Pat declared himself 'too ill' to stand and fight again.

When the noise and fanfare of electioneering had died down, he recalled that during his time in the House he had found a true friend in the socialist and veteran Labour leader, Ben Tillet.

- 59 -

However, it is good to see that his famous wit survived even his austere surroundings, as he recalls that once, by mistake, he sat at a table reserved for the Conservative Cabinet, but didn't realise his mistake until Stanley Baldwin joined the table. Sir John Simon came and had a word in Pat's ear, and moved him to a table occupied by Liberal backbenchers. Pat said, "That was the closest I ever got to being in the Cabinet".

The brief sojourn in Parliament did nothing to change Pat's philosophy, he once declared, "I am a showman first and a politician second. I am a worker and a fighter rather than an Orator. There is only one object in my life and that is to see that people have fair play". It is frequently recorded that Pat Collins didn't like Parliament. "There are too many brakes on the wheel. I like to get on with the job", he said. Nevertheless he claimed to have done something for Walsall while in the House, by 'getting navy orders for Walsall's Talbot Stead Tubes; reducing the entertainment tax; starting negotiations re compulsory fitting of rubber tyres to tractors, etc.'

During electioneering (and Pat was never short of helpers to take people to the Polls) there was the usual badinage between the candidates; the Conservative candidate for Wednesbury speaking in support of S K Lewis (1923) had particularly annoyed Pat by his 'elephants and fat women speech'... to which Pat Collins replied that after the Election was over he would pay £10 a week to 'show' that candidate around the country as the only conservative-Labour man he had ever seen. The offer was not taken up, but the following jingle set to a well-known music hall tune was echoed round the Borough:

"We've lived together nigh on 40 years
And it hasn't been too long at that;
There's not a fellow in the whole wide land
We'd swop for our dear old Pat'

Kenneth Dean, in his book writes "that thousands of electorate regarded Pat as a kind of Santa Claus, who provided the thrills which made life a little more bearable".

The story is told in the 1922 Election of the old man who went to the polls and was asked by the political canvassers for whom he wanted to vote.
"Lady Cooper?"... "NO" ...
"Dennison?" ... "NO" ...
"Collins?" ... "NO" ...
"Then who do you want to vote for?
Said the old man, "Ah dunna want ter vote for any o' them. I want ter vote for Pat".

GWR

BIRMINGHAM ONION FAIR

DAY AND HALF-DAY EXCURSION
TO
BIRMINGHAM
ON
Monday, August 24th

From	At a.m.	p.m.	Return Fares THIRD CLASS s.	d.
W'hampton (Low Level) -	9.40	9.12	3	6
Stourbridge Junction -	10.50	9.30	4	6
Stourbridge Town -	12. 5	12.30	5	3

RETURN ARRANGEMENTS—SAME DAY
For Stourbridge Town and Junction at 10.30 and 10.45 p.m.
For Wolverhampton (Low Level) at 1.15 p.m.

For full particulars see small folder.

PADDINGTON. STATION. JUNE. 1932
[4]
JAMES MILNE, General Manager.

A curious GWR handbill advertising trips to the Onion Fair, dated 1932. The date appears to relate to the Bank Holiday, not the Onion Fair and the train times do not make sense! Explanations on a post card please!

ALDERMAN PAT COLLINS
1930-1939

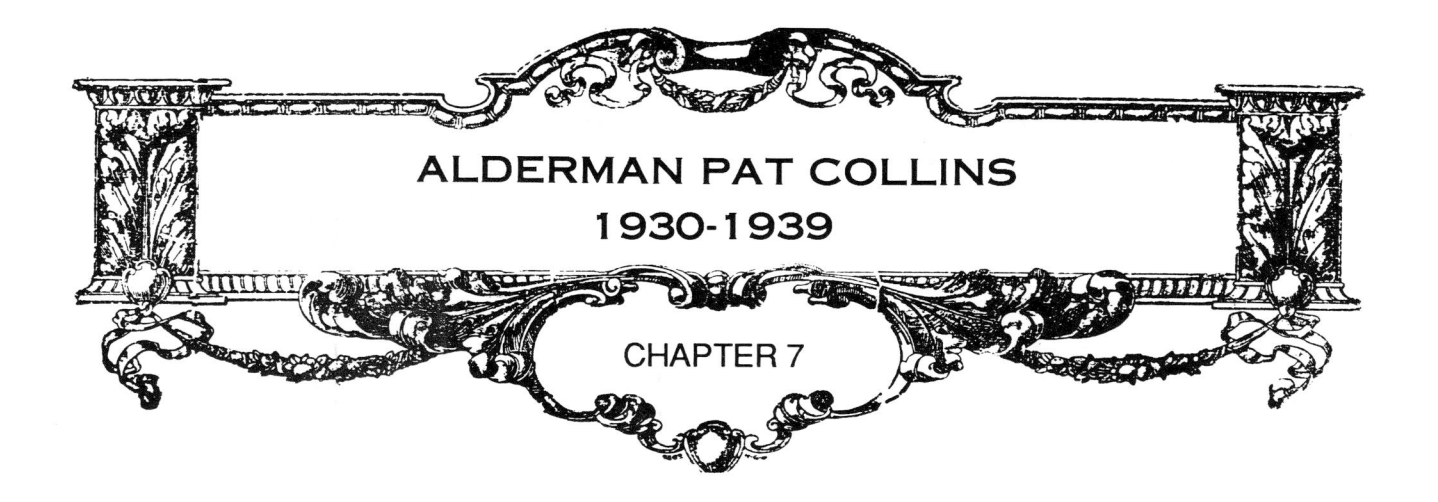

CHAPTER 7

Throughout the 1920's, World's Fair expressed the hope that each new year would be better than the last. Even Pat Collins, given to wishful thinking and optimism, admitted to George V that the bottom had been knocked out of the business! The King of England advised the King of Showland *"To repair the bottom and carry on"*. This was close to Pat's own philosophy of *"Keep the flag flying"*.

For a short time Pat had flown the flag in Parliament. He then redirected his energy to the fairground and the Guild. There were still many battles to be fought, and his personal quest for innovation and presenting the biggest and the best on the fairground never ceased. The 1920's roared into the past, drowned in the noise, speed, and excitement of the Wall of Death.

Pat, now over 70 years of age, was still observing his empire expanding, and he could still find the energy to direct his army from the front line when the occasion demanded. During the first half of the 1930's, reporters from World's Fair would often find Pat marking out his grounds, or solving the day to day problems of running the fairs. He began the new decade by taking on another permanent amusement park - at Barry Island.

At the beginning of 1930, the Showmen's Guild took the opportunity to express their appreciation of Pat's long term as President; they had been denied the opportunity to do so in 1929 through Pat's bereavement and illness. Pat's successor, William Wilson, presented him with a diamond ring, and it was reported that Pat was so emotionally overwhelmed, he was unable to reply.

By February 1930 Pat was moving equipment onto the site at Barry Island, which was christened "Evesham Park" (to embarrass the former occupants - the White Brothers, who moved across the road to the Cosy Corner). This tale of showland "opposition" is told in Chapter 13. "Space to Let" was advertised at both Barry Island and at Gt Yarmouth, Young Pat taking some part in administering the former, and Walsall John still finding his feet at the latter.

Although he had retired from the Presidency of the Guild, Pat still maintained many of his other activities. For example, he was still a local Councillor, and served on a number of Council committees. He had never had the time to become a committee chairman, but his seniority and experience were recognised in 1930 when, on 16th June, he became an Alderman of the Borough of Walsall.

The fair that went on the road as the 1930 season unfolded featured Pat's rides of proven popularity: Clara's Whale Island, the Swish, (then managed by Harry Weston Snr), the Chairoplanes, (then managed by Walter Hobbs), and the Lion Show (William Dutton), and Walter Kelly's Yachts. Switchbacks and machines like the Razzle Dazzle were 'retired' to the permanent amusement parks. Young Pat's children were growing up, and the first generation of grandchildren entered the family business. For example, Margaret was sometimes in charge of the Yachts.

To the already proven attractions was added the new ingredients - the Wall of Death, featuring Jack Todd and his wife as riders, followed by other "teams". Elias Harris, the athletic young son of a tenant - Elias Harris Snr - also rode the Wall at times and during 1930 a friendship developed between young Elias Harris and Margaret Collins, granddaughter of Pat.

The popularity of the Wall of Death led numerous showmen to invest in the attraction, and squabbles broke out concerning the legitimate use of its name, as well as academic debate in the columns of World's Fair about who was the first to ride the 'Wall' in Britain. By the time Pat's fair reached Chester, in May, the advertising had to be very cautiously worded in naming the new attraction. Two separate shows were travelling within the Collins' empire, and they were brought together for the first time at Chester, advertised as *"The Death Defiers in the Globe of Terror, and the Death Defiers in the Drome of Satan"*. 'Satan' was obviously not pleased and exacted his revenge on Jack Todd - as described in Chapter 17.

Just how many 'Globes' or 'Walls' were owned by Pat Collins is not clear. Some were operated by tenants under the Pat Collins' banner. There are also confusing references to Young Pat's Wall, and to

Walsall John's Globe. Both shows travelled extensively, put in extended appearances at the amusement parks (The Wall to Barry, the Globe to Yarmouth), and travelled again during the Back End. They were joined by others; personnel changed, names changed, legends were created, but come what may, there were "Death Defiers" riding Globes or Walls at most of Pat's fairs in 1930. At Bedworth, in September, Margaret Collins, the Guvnor's granddaughter, caused a furore by riding the Wall.

One happy outcome of all this 'death-defying' was the fact that two showland families were united by marriage. On Thursday 27 November 1930, at St Chad's Catholic Cathedral in Birmingham, Margaret Collins married Elias Harris. The reception was held at the firm's Palais de Danse, and the couple enjoyed a honeymoon on the Continent. When they returned to the fair, Margaret assisted Elias in presenting a Wall of Death show, and legend has it that the couple were presented with it as a wedding present.

As the new decade began, the Walls and Globes of Death were not the only new attractions invading the fairground world, the "Dodgem" was also now making its presence felt as part of the travelling fair. It had taken a long time to materialise, having been around for most of the twenties as a potential attraction at permanent sites, but the portable electric Dodgem was now fast becoming a reality, and in 1930, Pat's fairs sometimes featured "Auto-Skooters" and "The Radio Cars". (Most Police Forces in Britain did not have 'Radio Cars' until the 1940's, so the name was probably imported from America!). Both names were used during 1929, and by 1930 the term "Dodgem" was being used - for example when the ride was presented at Worcester Races, under the management of Albert Badger.

Arks were also making an appearance during 1930. They were a further development of the Switchback, segments rotated on a circular rising and falling track, but they were much less ornate than scenic railways, and therefore less heavy and difficult to transport and build up. The first Arks were imported from Germany and patrons sat on carved animals as they revolved - hence the term "Ark" but these 'seats' could be swopped for horses or motorcycles, as on "Speedway Arks" as fashion dictated. Pat imported a German Ark sometime in 1930, and then bought an Orton & Spooner built machine in 1931.

1931 was quite a year of transition. At the Goose Fair there were still four scenics present, including Pat's Peacocks and Dragons, but there were also four new Arks and five sets of Dodgems (Pat had one of each there). It was also the last year that Bostock & Wombell's Menagerie appeared, and several reports commented on the antiquity of Miles Jervis' Channel Tunnel Railway! The excitement of riding a "train" in the dark was about to be experienced . Pat had purchased an Orton & Spooner 'Ghost Train' and presented this in 1932.

The quest for new rides among showmen is well illustrated by the invention of the Water Dodgem. In permanent amusement parks it was probably quite feasible to provide this "marine equivalent" to the electrically powered conventional dodgem, but the thought of travelling a water-tight pool around the country, and having to fill it with gallons of water everytime it was built up, would appeal to no-one but a showman determined to have a ride that no one else did. Sure enough Pat travelled a Water Dodgem to Hull Fair in 1932!

The general picture emerging of the early 1930's is one of Pat in his seventies, elevated to the Aldermanic Bench, still firmly committed to the fair, and still very keen to find new rides and attractions. Many of his managers, staff and tenants, had been with him for a lifetime, and, of course, he had outlived many of them. Young Pat, Young Pat's children, and Walsall John, were all part of the business. By 1933 the centre

Uniting showland families.

1) Left: Margaret Collins, Pat's granddaughter, married Elias Harris on 27 November 1930 at St Chad's Roman Catholic Cathedral, Birmingham.
NOTE that Pat gave the bride away - not her father; and doesn't Elias look like Anthony?
(*Walsall Observer*)

- 62 -

of this busy empire made the final part of its move to Bloxwich. The last parcel of land, and some buildings at Shaw Street, Walsall, were sold to the Walsall & District Co-operative Society on 3 May 1933. Telegrams no longer winged to and from the "Gondola Works", everything now centred on the "Amusement Depot, Bloxwich"....conveniently next door to the Guvnor's home at Limetree House.

The season opened in 1933 with the usual fairs at Lichfield and Longton, and the Welsh run was underway. It was rumoured that Pat might become Mayor of Walsall by the end of the year. There was no visible warning that the old order might gradually begin to change. But personal tragedy was about to strike. After a long and very active life Flora was struck down by a kind of paralysis. In the early hours of Saturday morning, 8 April 1933, at Limetree House, Flora died.

As in many areas of history, the achievements of women on the fairground are less well recorded than those of the men. This is particularly so in the case of Flora Collins. She was quite obviously a "showman" in her own right, and not just a shadowy figure supporting and encouraging her well-known husband. This begins to emerge, in retrospect.

After Flora's death, the Walsall Times wrote:

"During the early hours of Saturday morning, one of the town's noblest women passed away. I mean, of course, Mrs Collins. As soon as it became known, Alderman Collins received hundreds of messages expressing sincere sympathy with him in his great loss.

Mrs Collins, like her husband, was kind, loving and generous, and hundreds will miss her great benevolence. She was a devout Christian, and her motto in life was always 'Do unto others as ye would have them do unto you'. She loved little children and was always a good friend to them. Often she was seen taking little children, who were poorly clothed, into the shops, where she re-clothed them from head to foot. Her sympathy for the wives of unemployed men was always extended in a practical manner.

She was a fine business woman, and once she started a project she never neglected it until its success was assured. The pattern she set to the women in the amusement industry had its effect, and showmen's wives are living in a different atmosphere and have a better outlook on life at the present time than they had many years ago."

The Walsall Observer wrote: *"Her amiable disposition made her many friends, and there can be few Midlands towns in which she could not claim many sincere friendships. She had almost as much experience in the show world as the Alderman himself, for she had helped him in his work practically continuously since they were married over fifty years' ago."*

Such tributes to a loyal wife who had devoted her life and energy to her husband's career were obviously well deserved, but we have to look to World's Fair to find a comment that suggests a little more of Flora's real individuality as a great showman's wife:

"Mrs Collins was always of a restless and energetic turn of mind. Not a born show-woman, it is true, but borne into the life until she revelled in it. Often, in their more prosperous moments, leaving her husband to manage and control his own business, she would venture to embark on her own, managing and controlling her own shows. She grew as her husband grew, and carried their prosperous days with dignity. She had a personality and persuasiveness that were irresistible. In their early days, when ground was wanted and difficult to get, she would meet officials and committees and talk them into what she wanted."

As "JBT", the World's Fair's Black Country correspondent, travelled the area in the week following Flora's death, he was able to report: *"The death of Mrs P Collins has come as a deep shock to showpeople in the district. I had to visit, during the weekend, in the course of*

2) Right: "Walsall John" married Claire Hall at St Mary's Church, Derby on 8 November 1932. (Full details in Appendix 1, "Who's Who".) November was a popular month for showland marriages.
(Collection of Vanessa Forte)

my duties, Birmingham, Oldbury, and Brierley Hill, and in all these places, the older folk, who, like myself, had known Mrs Collins, spoke in high terms of her many admirable qualities and her many kindnesses.

She was a strict, albeit warm-hearted person, and would never tolerate rowdiness or vulgarity on the showground. It was only recently that she gave up being 'on the spot' with the grand showfront which was purchased from Hammersley, known as 'Wall's Phantoscope'. My wife and I worked on that showfront prior to it being taken over by Mrs Collins at the end of the 1890's. Recently the front has been used for the great Lion Show - which has been so well known throughout the Black Country."

Before she died Flora had let it be known that she wished to be buried at Wrexham, her home town, alongside the grave of her late sister, Annie, (Mrs Walter Hobbs). When the funeral took place, on 12 April, large crowds turned out in both Walsall and Wrexham. The funeral coaches of the "official" party were followed from Walsall to Wrexham by about one hundred cars, and people came from all over the country to pay their respects. St Patrick's Church, Birchills, had been packed all night while a Dirge had been sung on receiving the casket, and a Requiem had been sung by local school children in the morning. Father McDonnell officiated.

In the fairground world the copious recording of deaths and funerals often provides information for future historians as to "who was who?" and supplies an oblique comment on relationships. As Flora was carried to her grave in Wrexham, the bearers were Young Pat, John Collins ('Baby' John), William Dutton (her nephew and a ride manager), Elias Harris, Mr Clarke (the lion tamer), and J B Cooper (Pat's accountant and secretary at that time). Young Pat was instrumental in providing monuments to both his parents' graves.

It is difficult to assess the effect of Flora's death on Pat - he made no public statement as he had when his brother died in 1929. Those alive today who remember Pat in his mid-seventies testify that he did lose some of his "flair", and his grip on the reins of his business was perhaps not quite so tight as before. Whether this was just the process of ageing, or the effect of losing his partner of more than fifty years, we have no way of knowing. He still gave no sign of retiring, and as late as 1938 was only admitting, very begrudgingly, that others had come along who could share the burden of running the business. Yet even if his leadership was becoming symbolic, or a workaholic's fantasy, in which his family and managers allowed him to indulge, no one can deny that he still showed great energy, and ability to "bounce back" whatever setbacks fate delivered.

BELOW: Pat and Flora had been married over fifty years when this picture was taken in the early 1930's. Moments of "resting" in the shade of the living van were rare - the precise details of this location and occasion are not known.
(Collection of Molly Seldon)

If anything, the fairs of the 1930's seemed to grow bigger and better than ever, preserving the best traditions with endless new innovations. Only a month after Flora's death, the Leicester May Fair came in for special mention in World's Fair for its, *"...large crowds, excellent layout...the atmosphere of the old fair combined with modern attractions...It was a real treat to see a scenic again, and the machine was riding to capacity every time, and the steam gallopers were also doing their share at a penny a ride"*

At the same fair there were a dozen steam engines, Joby Farrell's living van that had once travelled with Taylor's Bioscope, the Lion Show, alongside the new Ark, and a travelling "Big Dipper". Sam Naishtad and his team were riding the Globe of Death before going on to spend the summer with Walsall John at Gt Yarmouth. The old Cakewalk and Steam Yachts stood alongside Green's modern Caterpillar.

At all the permanent amusements parks there was intense activity.

At Yarmouth the Water Dodgems had found a home, and Pat was about to invent the "Bowling Alley" concept with his new "Flash-o-Ball". At Barry Island, Father Greville, a famous fair enthusiast, came across Young Pat installing an organ in the electric gallopers. The organ was apparently the one that had once formed part of the Randall Williams' showfront. Another fair enthusiast, Jack Wilkinson lamented that 1933 was the year that the scenics virtually disappeared - with the exception of Pat's. Joby Farrell was touring the Dragons & Peacocks while the Whale Island, and Young Pat's Dragons were busy at work in the crystal Palace Amusement Park.

Pat was also promoting new gaffs, such as in August 1933 the venture at the Edgbaston Reservoir, advertised as "Birmingham's Blackpool Week". At Christmas 1933 Pat staged a fair at the City's Bingley Hall.

When death struck again early in 1934, it first took the life of one of the younger generation. Pat's granddaughter, Margaret Harris died in Walsall General Hospital on January 10, following an operation. She was only 25 but was a popular figure in showland and well-known as Elias's partner on the Wall of Death. After a funeral service in Walsall, she was buried in Wrexham, not far from Flora's grave. Young Elias left the Midlands Section, and took the Wall of Death with him. (He returns to the Pat Collins' Fair in a later chapter).

In February, George Bailey died. He was one of Pat's managers, and had worked for Pat for thirty years. The following month Elias Harris Senior died, and in April, William Savage died. Mr Savage was two years older than Pat and was Secretary of the Showmen's Guild. Earlier he had been Pat's secretary, and they had dabbled together in Walsall's Liberal politics. His home had been opposite Pat's in Bloxwich, but he had moved to Harrow in 1926 when his secretarial duties in the Guild became full time.

BELOW: Although quick to invest in Arks, Dodgems, etc., Pat also "preserved" older rides of proven popularity to create the right blend of machines on his tobers. Here is the Joby Farrell Scenic Dragons, complete with organ from the No.1.Wonderland, at Birmingham in 1933.
(Collection of John Ward)

COLLINS
Nap Hand for Hull Fair

THE GREATEST ATTRACTIONS
EVER STAGED IN HULL!

Water Dodgem.

The Original Mont Blanc. What a Thrill!

THE ONLY ONE IN ENGLAND
THE YO YO RIDE.

Speed, Thrills, and Laughter all the Way. The Rage of Nottingham Goose Fair.

INDIAN THEATRE.

12 Royal Entertainers from the Palace of Cawnpore, Hindu Fakirs, Conjurers, Wire Walkers, Nautch Girls & the

GREAT INDIAN ROPE TRICK.

Don't Fail to Visit THE GHOST TRAIN which stops at Spoofy Town.

You Must See THE DEATH RIDERS,

Motor Racing Lions.

One of England's Most Exciting Shows.

GOOD! IT'S COLLINS

DID YOU SEE THE FLEET OF
SUPERCRAFT AUTORACERS
WORKING TO FULL CAPACITY AT BIRMINGHAM ONION FAIR?

Part of the fleet of 9 Supercraft Autoracers delivered to Mr. John Collins

IF NOT, COME AND SEE THEM AT HULL FAIR.

SUPERCRAFT, LTD.,
Woodman Yard, Westow Hill, Upper Norwood, S.E.19.
Telephone: Livingstone 2180

LEFT: The Water-Dodgems appear at Hull in 1932 - along with the Yo Yo, Ghost Train and the Rowliers racing with lions in their Globe of Death!
ABOVE: The Supercraft cars delivered to John Collins in 1935, and BELOW: the Rytecroft Scooter-cars working on John Collins new track at Great Yarmouth in 1934. The cars, operated by a single pedal, could reach 12mph.
(World's Fair)

The 'special event' of 1934 was the Royal opening of the Mersey Tunnel, and fairs were held on every available space on both sides of the Mersey to mark the occasion. Pat took the ground at Sefton Park, and although Bill Croydon was the Ground Manager, Pat and Young Pat were there in person to supervise the event. Pat also had ground at Central Park in Birkenhead, and this was managed by Gilbert Dixon. These major fairs used so much of the firm's resources that Tipton Wakes, which was being held at the same time, was the smallest ever!

On the other hand, developments at the amusement parks extended the firm's collective resources. During this period the pattern became more firmly established of bringing equipment out of the amusement parks to travel the Back End, so the Onion Fair became bigger than ever, and the new Collins' rides continued to make their appearance at Nottingham and Hull, and at Collins' own fairs at Ashby, Burton, Ilkeston etc., Walsall John took his new petro-scooter track to Hull, and 1934 saw Young Pat's son, "Baby Pat", presenting the new Airways a "Mont Blanc" type of ride.

At the beginning of 1935 Pat's life took an unexpected turn. On 11th January, he quietly married Clara Mullett. He was 75 and she was 54, and the Walsall Observer described Clara as his treasurer and secretary for the past thirty years. Clara had been orphaned at the age of 11 and Pat had taken responsibility for the Mullett children. She had grown up in the heart of the fair as part of the Collins' family, and shown herself thoroughly capable of executive status. She managed the Jungle Scenic that was sold to Pat's brother, and took over its replacement - the No.1.Scenic of 1921, later known as the Whale Island. Because this was the "No.1." machine in every way, it travelled the most important fairs and, in effect, Clara was therefore the senior machine manager on the ground.

Usually news of most showland weddings was broadcast well in advance, and were very well attended occasions, but Pat and Clara kept out of the limelight, and few people were at St Patrick's Church, Birchills, on the misty Wednesday morning they had chosen to marry. Fr McDonnell, Pat's longstanding friend, conducted the ceremony, Bill McCarthy one of Pat's managers was the Best Man, and the bride was 'given away' by Hetty Davies. Only one photograph is known to exist of the wedding. The honeymoon, which included a trip to the Continent, started a week later.

By the evening of January 11th, news of the wedding had leaked, and Pat's friend Alderman Joseph Leckie MP told the members of Walsall Women's Liberal Association at their meeting that night. They all loved Pat, and were glad to know that in the new Mrs Collins he would once again have someone to take care of him, knowing that Alderman Collins was

BELOW: Pat and Clara, photographed after their wedding on 11th January 1935 at St Patrick's Church, Walsall.
(Walsall Local History Centre)

inclined to be rather reckless of himself, and worked too hard! When World's Fair passed on the news to the rest of showland "JBT" in his Black Country report added his approval and congratulations on behalf of their fairground friends.

As well as the usual fairs that started the season, there seemed an added impatience to get started in 1935, and Harry Weston's Ark and Dennis Shipley's Dodgems (The Radio Cars) were sent out to brave the February frost in Bilston, prior to commencing the usual run that began with the Dudley fair. In fact, after the Dudley fair, Harry took the Ark out onto the Welsh run. Gilbert Dixon had replaced the late George Baisley in managing the run, but Clara came out to Corwen to see that all was going well. Pat was ill as Spring advanced, and Clara found herself very much in overall charge, with the experienced ground managers taking care of the day to day progress of the fairs.

At the Birmingham Whit Week fair, C.H.Lea of the World's Fair, was most concerned about Pat's health and reported, "*Pat told me that he had not been well, but the old-time fire which made him the greatest of modern showmen is still to be discerned in his eyes and in his speech.*" This 'illness' appears to have been the time when Pat had a throat operation performed on the kitchen table at Lime Tree House. Many must have wondered if Pat's active life was about to change.

C.H.Lea returned to the subject in a long report of the 1935 Onion Fair at the end of September 1935:

"I sat with Pat Collins in his carriage while, with all the fire and force of a young man, this 77 year old stalwart chuckled as he relived the comical side of fair life, and thundered as he told of his struggles.

Pat laughed with glee as he explained how he can lay out a fairground while the architects are still preparing their plans and polishing their theodolites. He had started work at 8am and had not gone to bed until 2am the following day in preparing this, the 59th Onion Fair he has attended.

The Onion Fair this year has staggered everyone by its size....and the problem of parking nearly stumped Pat himself. He told me of one tenant of a "Wheel-'em In" who had a large bus, a long living van, and a car - all of which occupied more space than his joint - and there were something like 200 joints, 2,000ft of sidestuff and 28 rides.

There is something about these veterans which raises them above ordinary men. What ordinary man could have undergone a painful operation as has Pat during the past few weeks, and yet refused an anaesthetic. Mrs Collins told me that Pat underwent the operation, although warned it would be painful, and merely clenched his teeth and let the surgeons use the knife. He told me proudly to tell all his friends through World's Fair, that he feels ten years younger than when I last met him!"

Perhaps Pat was sustained by his own legendary status - no wonder that Mr Lea, and the other reporters who sat in Pat's van, were ready to believe anything that Pat told them, and the stories of his own past gradually became embellished. (See the beginning of Chapter 1).

During the middle of October "P.A.T" of World's Fair, visited Pat and Clara at the Leicester October Fair. He found them personally supervising the dumping of tons of ash onto the muddy ground in pouring rain. He suggested to Pat that the job be left to younger men, but Pat shouted, "It's my duty!". Clara also showed no sign of wanting to sit quietly at home at Lime Tree House. As the No.1.Scenic was gradually phased into retirement, in the care of Clara's foreman, Ted Sherwood, she became manager of The Waltzer - another 1930's refinement of the switchback principle that quickly followed on the heels of the Arks, and which achieved greater enduring popularity.

Many innovations now added to Pat Collins fairs were introduced by Walsall John. His restless roving quest (a family characteristic!) for new thrills to present at the fair ensured that many new novelty rides appeared under the Collins' flag. For example, in 1936, he introduced the Loop-o-Plane, travelling the machine during the Spring, taking it to Yarmouth during the Summer, and then travelling it again during the Back End. From an exhibition in Chicago, John introduced "The Whirlwind Racer" and this was built up at Barry. Some popular old traditional rides did not die, they were simply re-vamped. The No.1.Scenic was re-decorated from top to bottom during the early months of 1936, and when it re-appeared at Wolverhampton at Whitsun, it seemed as magnificent and as busy as ever.

The theme of many World's Fair reports was that Pat was back on his feet, he had overcome bereavements, ill health, operations on the kitchen table, and with Clara at his side, all was well. C.H.Lea, the World's

BLOXWICH WAKES WEEK.

P. COLLINS'

Grand FETE & GALA

The Wakes Ground, Bloxwich.

To-day (Saturday), Monday & Tuesday, Next.

GIGANTIC AMALGAMATION OF AMUSEMENTS.
STAGE & AERIAL PERFORMANCES.   GRAND FREE SIGHTS.

Special Engagement of

Professor BERT POWSEY

The World Famous High Diver, in his marvellous 70 foot dive into a small tank containing only 4 feet of water.

| SPOLDI AND PARIL | PROFESSOR R. CADMAN'S |
| Comedy Aerial Gymnasts and Burlesque Artists, from the London Palladium. | Punch and Judy Show. |

SUNDAY EVENING, AUGUST 14th,

Grand Sacred Organ Recital

In aid of the Hospital. Commence at 8-15 p.m. Admission by Programme, 2d.

TUESDAY, AUGUST 16th.

BENEFIT FOR THE WALSALL GENERAL HOSPITAL.

Roll up in your thousands and support this noble Institution.

2d. - - - ADMISSION EACH DAY - - - 2d.

All Trams and buses stop at entrance.

1932

Fair Birmingham correspondent, seemed to take more and more interest in the survival of Alderman Collins.

For example, from the Whit-week fair in Birmingham at the beginning of June 1936, he reported, *"I was glad to find Pat Collins looking better than he has for some time, and he told me, that despite an attack of bronchitis, he has been fairly well. So far as energy and activity are concerned, he can give an example to many younger men, for even as we talked, he was constantly called into consultation about a thousand and one matters....*

Mrs Collins also looks bright and happy, and Mr Collins confessed that he did not know what he would do without her."

Mr Lea was then given a conducted tour of the ground by Pat Tyler, and admired the repainting of the No.1.Scenic, and the Airways. The latter were in the care of Molly Collins, as her divorce from Young Pat was now completed and Young Pat was now abandoning his place on his father's fairs, and focusing his attention on Colwyn Bay. On the other hand, Walsall John's presence was stronger than ever, and the Loop-o-Plane was stealing the show. Mr Lea noted that Walsall John was operating it and enjoying himself as huge queues of potential riders built up in front of the machine. The number of rides, stalls and shows was impressive, and is described in more detail in Chapter 17. A month later C.H.Lea and Pat met again at the Carnival Fair held in Handsworth Park, and it was here that Pat sat down for two hours and told Mr Lea the story of his life, starting with his father's "escape" from Ireland, the shipwreck in the Irish Sea, and Norah's epic pursuit of her husband!

Following R.H.Delaney's death, the management of the Crystal Palace Amusement park was entrusted to Pat's friend and fellow local politician, Danny Cartwright. Once again there was talk of great redevelopment, and renewed interest in the site. There was talk of reviving the miniature railway, and Walsall John found a new opportunity to develop his interest in the Big Dipper concept. An older gravity ride at the Crystal Palace was taken down, and early in 1937, construction of a new Big Dipper began. Although Walsall John had contributed to Pat's fairs for some time, by introducing new rides, and had managed Yarmouth Pleasure Beach, and looked after various Walls and Globes of Death, it was the Big Dipper that seemed to symbolise his "arrival" as a showman in his own right, and a man in search of his own fortune. Retrospectively it also seems significant that Walsall John became Pat's "right-hand-man" during this period, as Young Pat tended to fade from the scene, by withdrawing to Colwyn Bay.

The Big Dipper at Barry was also being refurbished at the same time - to make its debut for the 1937 season clothed in "scenery". In this form the Big Dippers became known as "Scenic Railways" - a very confusing term, as it had already been used to describe the electrified switchbacks of the 1910's and 1920's.

BELOW: General view of the fair at Aston in 1936. "Goliath" and Clara's van in the foreground. There is plenty to argue about in this picture! Which Wall of Death is by the railway embankment? (Is it Jack Todd's?) Whose swings can we see? What is the ride behind "Goliath"? (Is it the track from the Whirlwind Racer?)
(Collection of Bernard Morley)

Once again Royalty seemed to inspire events in Liverpool, and in 1937, Pat organised a Coronation Fair at Sefton Park. Some thought he was unwise to run this fair for almost two weeks, but both weekends, Coronation Day and the Whit Monday all enjoyed good weather and the event was a great success. While at Sefton Park, Pat sent a telegram to the new King and Queen conveying "loyal congratulations from himself and the assembled show people". If anyone had thought that Edward's abdication had "knocked the bottom out of the Royalty business", no doubt Pat could have given George VI some royal advice about repairing the bottom and carrying on!

In 1937 both Young Pat and Walsall John added something new to the fair.

Young Pat had purchased an Eli Wheel - a twelve-car 50ft Big Wheel, produced by Lusse Brothers of Coney Island, and one of two that they built up at Blackpool Pleasure Beach. The other, a slightly larger wheel was designed for use at permanent amusement parks, but Young Pat had scooped the first "travelling" machine. It was supposed to take pride of place in his Colwyn Bay site, but he travelled it to Wrexham and Chester Races, to Sefton Park, and to a number of fairs in the Black Country.

Not to be outdone, John launched his new attraction at Newcastle Town Moor in June; - the Mississippi Showboat. This was an eighty foot long showfront for a travelling theatre. John had it built at Yarmouth during the winter of 1936/37, directing the operation himself, and using his own staff to assemble parts fabricated by Orton & Spooner. Although associated with novelty rides and the Dippers, John also had an interest in "shows" - an interest that manifested itself on several occasions.

The second half of the 1930's also saw other "innovations" creeping into showland life. The fairground organ was in the process of disappearing, and new methods of delivering music to the fair were being installed. For example, the report of Darlaston Wakes in August 1937 stated, *"The outstanding event at Darlaston was the delivery to Pat Collins of a new Panatrope. A new type of fourway speaker finished in stainless steel, makes a marvellous flash on the Jungle Ride,*

STILL AT THE HELM.

ALDERMAN PAT COLLINS AT BIRMINGHAM FAIR.

Our photograph shows Mr. and Mrs. Pat Collins and Mr. and Mrs. John Collins at Birmingham Fair last week-end. The "Guv'nor," as Alderman Pat Collins is affectionately known among showmen, particularly the tenants on his numerous grounds, is as active as ever and takes a personal interest in all the fairs under his control.

Front Page Story: World's Fair 13/6/1936

and the patrons are very appreciative of the music provided."

At Wrexham in March 1938, three engines were present, but the reporter noticed, *"The proprietor's new Fowler-Sanders diesel generating plant"*. Recorded music and the diesel generator were beginning to modify the traditional role of steam engine and organ music on the fairground. The success of the diesel engine in providing power for municipal passenger transport was also releasing many surplus 'early' buses to fairground use - also changing the visual environment of the fairground. The No.1.Scenic ceased to travel at the end of 1937 season, and the 1938 fairs no longer had the services of its organ. (But this was not to be the end of the story).

One great event of 1938 was the Empire Exhibition, held in Glasgow. Billy Butlin and Walsall John were given joint responsibility for providing the amusements, and, at the beginning of 1938 John began supervising building a huge Big Dipper. Pat himself believed that John would lose all his money on the venture, but the ride turned out to be a great success. Fore-runner of many.

The £25,000 'railway' took three months to build, was 500ft long, 150ft wide, and 100ft high. Five trains, each holding thirty passengers, paying one shilling each for the privilege, travelled along about one mile of track including a 72ft precipitious drop and passage through a tunnel. Somewhere buried among the towering trestles of best Colombian pine was a small office with a red door. This was the office of thirty-year old John Collins, who was about to make a fortune when the park opened for its six-month run.

If Walsall John was about to steal the show in Glasgow, Pat himself was about the steal the show in Walsall. By the summer of 1938 it was obvious that at last, Pat was to become Mayor. Early in May he had been ill, again, and was unable to attend a fair being presented at Stanley Park, Liverpool in honour of a Royal visit, but it was hoped that all would be well for Pat to become Mayor in the Autumn. The story of his year as Mayor is told in the next chapter.

So.... what of the fair itself at the end of the decade, and as Pat was about to fulfil the summit of his local civic life?

The organisation was still vast, operating on three or four circuits, and still finding new grounds if the possibility arose. For example, in August 1938 Pat managed to open a fair on the corner of Kings Road and Shady Lane, Kingstanding, on land that was about to be swallowed up in the expansion of Birmingham's suburbia! Although the organisation was still using engines, many fairs featured no "old" rides at all, and Pat had not played an organ since 1937. The fair was in the hands of the now ageing ground managers (Pat Tyler, Bill Croydon, Bill McCarthy, Gilbert Dixon, George Strickland, and the "family").

"I shall remain in control during my Mayoralty," Pat told the Walsall Observer in September 1938, *"but I have some very able lieutenants among members of my family... and it will be more convenient than it was a few years ago to leave things a little more in their hands."* The Observer then explained who the family were: Clara (his adopted daughter who had become his wife), Patrick Ross (his son), John (his adopted son), his two grandsons (Baby Pat and Baby John) and his grand-daughter Flora (Monte).

At Bloxwich Wakes in 1938 the flags of all nations were hanging over the entrance. The Walsall Observer noticed that the Swastika was absent. The Spanish Civil War had produced refugees, and Alderman Collins was raising money for looking after Basque children living in Birmingham. As the King of Showmen donned his Mayoral robes in November 1938, it is difficult to know whether Pat could have guessed that he would never be a full-time showman, ... in peacetime, ... again.

RIGHT: "Walsall John" has a word with the Guvnor, during the build-up of the 1937 Birmingham Onion Fair. The angle at which John's hat was worn was an indication of his composure! In the background is the No.1.Scenic, but what is the ride in the foreground?
(Collection of Jack Harvey)

The ladies of the Showmen's Guild Midland Section "Forces Comforts Fund" Committee. Standing; left to right: Lottie Deeks, Caroline Deeks, Bertha Sherwood, Lydia Hickman, Lucy Deeks and Beatty Roberts. Seated: Frances Watson, Flora Monte (nee Collins, Pat's granddaughter), Clara Collins, Mrs Deeks, Margaret Chadwick and Harriet Swann. The Committee held garden parties in Bloxwich to raise funds, while the men served in the Armed Forces.

(Collection of Joe Chadwick)

WALSALL AUGUST BANK
Holiday Pleasure Fair
CORPORATION STREET WEST

TO-DAY (Saturday), MONDAY, & TUESDAY.

PAT COLLINS' AMUSEMENTS

1932 (Walsall Holiday Fair)

AUGUST BANK-HOLIDAY ATTRACTION!

CRYSTAL PALACE AMUSEMENT PARK
SUTTON COLDFIELD.

Proprietor - - Mr. PAT COLLINS.

NOW OPEN DAILY
UNTIL SEPTEMBER.

Many New Novelties and Thrillers, including he

GIANT SCENIC COASTER RAILWAY
It's a GEE of a Ride. The Greatest Thriller yet.

NEW MINATURE RAILWAY.
FIRST-CLASS CATERING.

Special Terms for Parties. Seating Accommodation for over 1,500 under cover.

NOW THE MOST-UP-TO-DATE AMUSEMENT PARK IN THE MIDLANDS.

Telephone : Sutton Coldfield 2192.

1939

PAT COLLINS Presents
WOLVERHAMPTON GREAT WHIT FAIR (MARKET PLACE)
Commencing To-morrow (Sat.) Mon., Tues. & Wed. Next

SEE

THE DRAGON AND PEACOCK SCENIC RAILWAY
With its Magnificent Organ
AUTO SCOOTER DE LUXE
Ride 'Em and Douge 'Em
THE JUNGLE STAMPEDE
60 Miles an hour, 60 thrills a minute.
The Very Latest Sensation, The
WALTZER
It's a GEE of a Ride.
THE ATLANTIC LINERS

HOSTS OF SIDE SHOWS, CHILDREN'S RIDES, EXHIBITIONS, &c., &c.
WALSALL GREAT FAIR (Corporation Street West)
TO-MORROW (SATURDAY), MONDAY AND TUESDAY NEXT.
Magnificent Attractions. Spectacular Sights.

1937

PAT COLLINS-MAYOR OF WALSALL
1938-1939

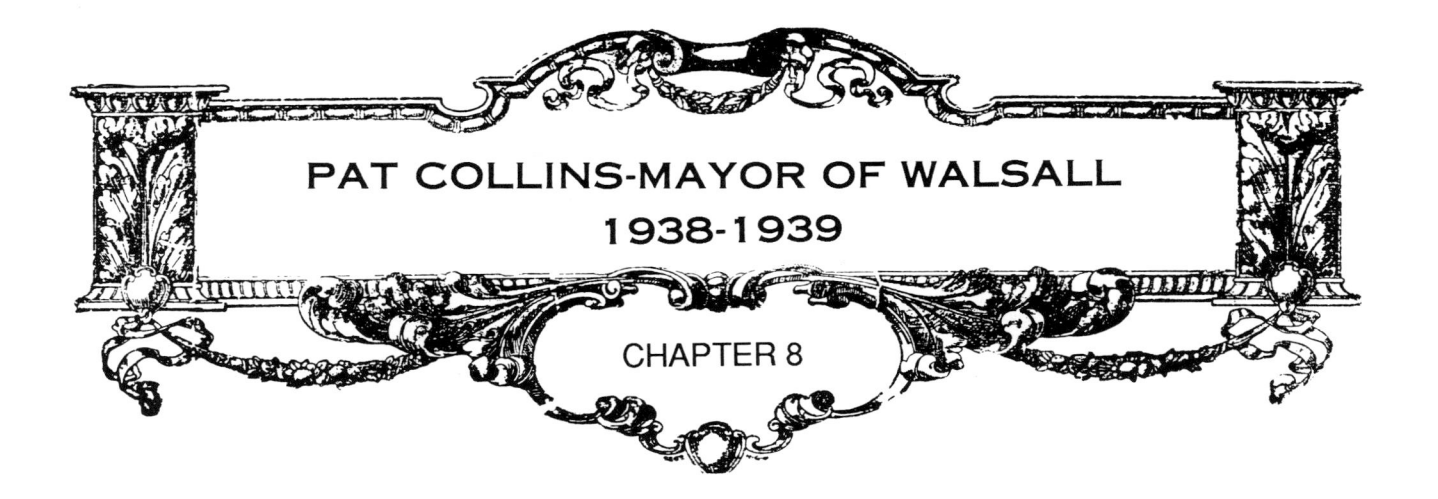

CHAPTER 8

As the previous chapters have shown, Pat was never afraid to grasp new challenges or adapt to changing circumstances. He did not set himself some peak which he should reach to enable himself to coast downhill into a restful old age. His drive and energy could not be explained as a quest for wealth or success, because that same drive was to be found in his life as a public benefactor, local councillor, Member of Parliament, and finally as Mayor.

In his eightieth year he was offered the chance of becoming the Mayor of Walsall, his adopted hometown. It was not the first time the offer had been made. It appears that he had previously been approached a couple of years earlier, in the mid 1930's, when he had been experiencing some illhealth, and had declined the offer. However, in 1938, he seemed fit and well once more, and was happy to become "Mayor elect".

At the end of August he was photographed opening a Children's Corner at the King George V Playing Fields at Bloxwich, and a month later the Walsall Observer was commenting on his "sturdy frame" and "well bronzed countenance". The outgoing Mayor was Dr Drabble, and as his year of office drew to a close the Walsall Observer reporter interviewed Pat about his forthcoming year as Mayor and gave an unusually full account of his life and circumstances.

Pat's comments on his involvement with the Fair at that time are remarkable considering his age and the period of ill-health that he had recently survived. *"I shall remain in control during my Mayoralty,"* he exclaimed. *"But I have some very able lieutenants among members of my family, and during the coming twelve months it will be more convenient than it was a few years ago to leave things a little more in their hands.... So, I think we will manage alright!"*

This statement was followed by a description of Pat's family, making it clear that the position of each person was public knowledge, and relationships within the Collins family were not private in any sense. First of all, acknowledgement is made of Flora's contribution to the success of Pat's business ventures, and then Clara (his second wife) is described as an *"equally valuable helpmate"*. Clara is described as *"formerly Pat's adopted daughter who had given forty years service to the business"*. Pat's other lieutenants are identified as his son, Patrick Ross, and his *"adopted son"* - John Collins, plus two grandsons and a grand-daughter. This indicates the extent to which the family were still seen locally as part of the business as late as 1938, even though both Walsall John and Patrick Ross (Young Pat) were by then businessmen in their own right, and when it was Patrick Ross junior rather than Young Pat who was to be seen on Pat's fairs.

Before becoming Mayor, Pat entertained his colleagues from the Council at an ox-roast at the September fair on the Corporation street ground. He then invited them to take a ride on a machine while he stood at the controls himself. He took great delight in "letting it rip".

As "Mayor-elect" he went along to the opening of the Avion cinema, Aldridge, on Monday 26th September 1938, where George Formby handed the Mayor (Dr Drabble) a cheque for the local hospital fund, of which Pat was such a loyal supporter. Both Pat and Dr Drabble spoke but George Formby stole the show and virtually started a riot among his own ardent fans.

Pat was no stranger to the opening of local cinemas, even if he had missed the opening of his own two Grosvenors! Film still exists of Pat among the guests at the opening of the Rosum, Leamore, and he went along to the Savoy in Walsall when that opened on 3rd October 1938. At the Savoy he later organised a Sunday Concert to raise funds for Spanish refugees, but the interesting twist to the story is that Associated British Cinemas (ABC) had preserved their "rights" in Walsall while the Savoy was being built, by showing films at the Grand in Park Street. As the Savoy opened, the Grand closed. A month later ABC sold a lease on the Grand to Baby Pat, who reopened it with twice-nightly variety on 5th December 1938. But he didn't manage to persuade his Grandfather to come along to give it a Mayoral re-opening!

Pat formally became Mayor of Walsall on 9 November 1938, unanimously elected after being proposed

KING GEORGE V PLAYING FIELDS, BLOXWICH 1938.
"He could walk along the avenue.... which he, and his close friend Will Wiggin had done so much to promote, and he could feel he had improved upon nature for the common good".   (E.J.Homeshaw)

ABOVE: At the opening of Children's Corner, September 1938. In the centre is Miss Windle J.P. and on her left is Pat, on her right is Miss Holloway. The gentlemen on the left are Mr W.Benton, Mr Parry, Will Wiggin and Councillor S.Wiggin. Pat sits on a "roundabout" and contemplates becoming Mayor of Walsall.
(Collection of Ernest Welch)

by Councillor Whiston. It was a time when Walsall Council was dominated by "elder statesmen" such as Sir William Pearman Smith; Dr E.P.Drabble, the retiring Mayor; Alderman Ingram, and Pat himself, (who had first joined the Council in 1918 and had become an Alderman in 1930). No-one could remember when a Roman Catholic had last held the office, and Mayor's Sunday was going to be a little different this time from former occasions as the ceremony was to be held at the RC church of St Mary-on-the Mount, Walsall. Canon Yeo accepted the office of Mayor's Chaplain.

The Vicar of Bloxwich devoted space in his Parish Magazine to the significance of the Mayor's Roman Catholicism - regretting that for the first time for 20 years the Mayor of Walsall did not attend Bloxwich Parish Church! Despite this, he concluded, "... *What Alderman Collins earns he does not keep, and that is his chief glory...The name of Pat Collins is known and rejoiced over far beyond our borders... associated with many a good cause. We admire his courage in accepting office when most men would have chosen to sit in the shade...* ". The Vicar also cryptically refers to Pat's success in *"inducing a large portion of Scotland's population to spend a good deal of money at his counters."* This implies that Pat's business activities had made one of their periodic forays north of the border during the summer of 1938.

During the meeting concerned with Pat's election to office, his colleagues competed to sing his praises, but their remarks also included a frank assessment of his character and qualities, which nowadays people would probably conceal rather than declare. Councillor Tibbetts proclaimed that the new Mayor was a "National figure" known by thousands, known even as far afield as Spain because of his interest in raising funds to alleviate the distress of children orphaned by the Spanish Civil War. Councillor Whiston stated with frankness, "*We will not get any gems of oratory from the new Mayor, but his actions are gems of generosity, and he is a gem himself - a rough diamond refined in the fire of life.*"

Alderman Ingram doubted whether a town could ever have a mayor who was such a "picturesque and romantic figure". If all this sounded rather fanciful, Alderman Ingram was quick to restore a sense of reality. He recalled, fifty four years earlier at the age of twelve, he had first encountered Pat Collins at Bloxwich Wakes. In those days he had admired the process by which Pat had established himself - and his ability to give a "thick ear" to those who opposed him, without permanently incurring their animosity. As Pat took the chair, wearing his scarlet robes, and chain of office, there were those present who still felt he might despatch the opposition with a "thick ear". Pat said that he felt overwhelmed by the occasion, and promised never to let the "*dear old town*" down.

LEFT (opposite page): Tree planting in the George V Park, Bloxwich, 1938. Pat looks on as Wee Georgie Wood clutches a dog, behind him is Arthur Tolcher and Dorothy Harmar. The event was organised by the Water Rats, the dog was called "Ratty", and its owner (to the left of Ratty) was Vera *Ratc*liffe!
(Collection of Vera Bishop)

BELOW: The Mayor and Mayoress of Walsall, November 1938: Pat and Clara Collins, in one of the nicest photographs taken of them.
(Collection of Jane Ferrari, nee Collins)

That evening Pat and Clara welcomed over six hundred guests to the Mayor's Reception at Walsall Town Hall; the event was well attended by his friends from the show business world, as well as representatives from all walks of life in Walsall, and civic dignitaries from surrounding communities. Everyone looked forward to the procession that was to take place on Mayor's Sunday. Large crowds were expected as Pat was such a popular figure and the procession was going to be spectacular, led by the Walsall LMS Silver Band, and including contingents from every quarter of the Borough's life.

As it turned out, Sunday 13th November 1938 was literally a "washout". Heavy rain destroyed all possibility of the procession taking place, and Pat was driven to St Mary's in a car, and everyone else followed in buses! The ceremony was dramatic and colourful in the church, but the public were denied the spectacle they had hoped to see. Consequently everyone turned their attention to another church ceremony due to take place at the church of St Peter, two weeks later, in Bloxwich.

Unfortunately, once again, it was wet. Pat led a procession to the church, but after the ceremony the rain was so heavy that cars had to be used once more to ferry everyone concerned to the Baths Hall. Pat tried to brighten the proceedings by emerging from the church to tell the crowd outside, *"I feel eighty years young!"* but there was some disappointment that the weather had spoilt the historic occasion - the first Mayoral parade in Bloxwich to make its way to the Catholic church. The sermon was given by the youngest Bishop in England - Dr.Bernard Griffin, of Birmingham. His address, and Pat's conduct, convinced everyone that a showman could be as dignified a mayor as anyone else, and this provided the positive start to Pat's mayoralty that the inclement weather had twice denied.

On Monday evening, after Sunday's service in Bloxwich, Pat and Clara were host and hostess at the Mayoral dinner at the George Hotel. The event was largely devoted to an appreciation of the work done by Dr Drabble and his wife during the previous year, but there was also a toast to the new Mayor and Mayoress, and this was proposed by Sir William Talbot - proprietor of the Talbot Stead Tube Works. Sir William paid tribute to Pat's first success in Parliament, in 1922, in securing Admiralty orders for locally made tubes. *"This is what Pat did for a political opponent - what he would have done for a supporter, I don't know!"*. Pat replied by abandoning his prepared speech and spoke spontaneously in his own way. This he could usually do successfully by reminiscing about his career as a showman.

During the first few weeks of his office many congratulatory letters and telegrams were received by Pat. He despatched formal replies to most, but occasionally his showbusiness friends were treated to some candid, and less formal, comments. E.H.Bostock addressed his letter to "Sir Patrick Collins", and after being corrected on this matter, Pat wrote to his old friend, *"... Fancy me at eighty years of age taking upon myself the onerous duties of Mayor of a large County Borough! I have been approached many times during the last ten years, but succumbed to persistent entreaties in a weak moment."*

As Mayor, Pat was invited to many functions, and at these his legendary generosity was often exploited. From this distance of time there is no way of knowing whether he was ever forewarned, but he was constantly being asked for money in public, and, of course, he made an instant response. Every hard-up organisation in Walsall must have tried to invite the Mayor along. He attended many social functions where his skills of oratory were put to the test, but in his role as Mayor he seemed to find a style of public presenta-

LEFT: The Ox Roast at the Walsall Fair of 12 September 1938. Pat inspects the work of Fred Tyler - champion ox-roaster from Stratford-on-Avon.
(Collection of John Pugh)

tion that was totally acceptable. For example, he attended the annual dinner of the Auctioneer's and Estate Agents' Institute, as the guest of Frank Harrison, who later told his son that Pat was a very effective speaker. He told the estate agents, *"I have had much to do with the 'cheapjacks' who frequent our fairs who, after all, are very humble members of your profession, although some of you would not care to recognise them as such."* This caused great amusement.

As Christmas 1938 approached, Pat's health again was not so good, and he cut down on his Mayoral duties. Early in 1939 as he was recovering, he slipped on a step and injured his right leg. On Dr.Drabble's advice he was confined to bed for three weeks and only slowly returned to civic life. The injury occurred while Pat was visiting the Spanish Civil War orphans at their home in Birmingham. Pat was sufficiently recovered however and feeling more like his old self in time to celebrate his eightieth birthday in April. The Spanish children came to present him with a rug they had made, decorated with the Walsall coat of arms. Pat rewarded them with a free trip round the fair, which at the time was in Wolverhampton.

On the day of his 80th Birthday, the Mayor could not be found in Bloxwich - he was away and busy setting up forthcoming fairs.

One week later, at Easter, the fair opened in Walsall. It was an opportunity for Pat to publicly confess his regret that organs no longer provided the music at the fair. He told a local reporter, *"I have little liking for loudspeakers, but we have to keep pace with the times, though, in my opinion, the times are not always right."* Pat felt that the public of 1939 were looking for speed and thrills. He pointed out that the latest Collins's machine was "The Airways", in which patrons whirled around at twice the speed of the old gondolas. Another ride present was "The Flying Fleas", lifting patrons over twenty feet into the air. As another sign of the times the hobby horses and motor cars on the junior hand turned roundabouts were being replaced with models of tanks, bristling with guns.

It was a warm, sunny Easter, and record crowds descended on the Corporation Street fairground. It was the last time that Pat presented a fair in his home town before the outbreak of the Second World War., and he impressed everybody with its sleek modern appearance, but looking back we would perhaps have been more impressed by some of the traditional fairground features, that were soon to fade away in wartime Britain. For example, shows strongly represented were The Continental Cabaret, and the Freak Show. The Fat Lady was a local lass from Walsall itself - only twenty years old but weighing 30 stone!

That Easter Pat was also concerned with other matters. Sir William Pearman Smith - the "Father" of Walsall Council died at the age of seventy five and naturally Pat, as the Mayor, had to lead the civic duties which followed, by making public tributes to Sir William, and representing the Council at the funeral.

Pat also became involved in trying to persuade young men to volunteer for the Territorial Army in the South Staffordshire Regiment.

On a lighter note he was also committed to finding female penfriends for soldiers in the regiment who were serving in India. This began as a simple request from two soldiers who wished to correspond with working class girls who could cook! A national newspaper heard of the quest and Pat found himself mentioned in the headlines as a "matchmaker". Over five hundred girls wrote to Pat from all over the country, wishing to be put in touch with the soldiers. Pat

RIGHT: Pat in his Mayoral Robes pauses to discuss matters with veteran fairground enthusiast - Cedric Conway.
(Collection of John Pugh)

invited half a dozen to meet him in the Mayor's Parlour, and afterwards he told the press, he was impressed that they were all "very decent girls".

Pat was less successful in recruiting soldiers.

In May 1939 parades were organised in Walsall and Bloxwich and Pat joined the platform of figures asking for volunteers. Pat did not mince words. He told the crowd, "*Conscription is coming, and if you don't come voluntarily, you will have to come by law. In a town like this young people should come forward of their own accord.*" The crowd seemed unimpressed. Pat offered the "Mayor's Pound" to any man who volunteered. Eighteen year old Simon Perry, a cabinet maker, of Long Street suddenly volunteered, turned down Pat's offer of a pound, and grabbed the microphone to exhort the crowd to follow his example. But no one else rushed forward.

Pat's off the cuff speeches sometimes provoked controversy, and by May 1939, the girls writing to the soldiers were getting Pat into trouble again. First of all Pat revealed that he had only acted on the replies from Walsall girls - he had ignored the letters from the rest of the country. Pat explained to the press, "The soldiers didn't ask for foreigners... it is remarkable to me how many girls want men." Pat was able to get away with this as every Black Country reader shared his view that folk in the rest of Britain were "foreigners". Unfortunately Pat then went on to say that the trouble with modern girls was that they could not cook.

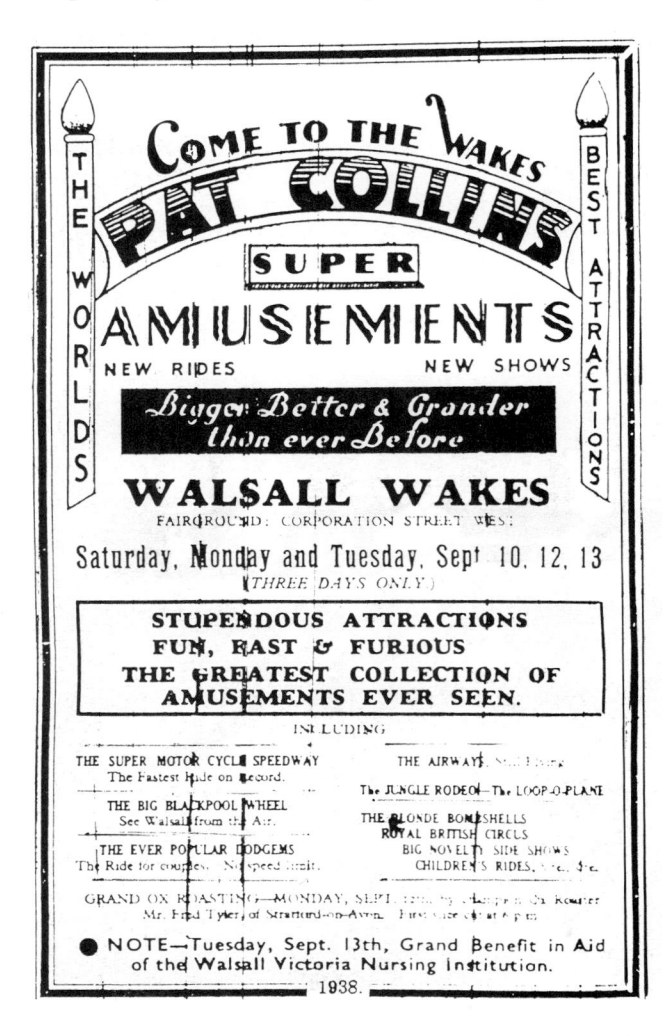

This comment caused quite a stir, and the Palfrey Women's Liberal Committee challenged Pat to join them for afternoon tea on May 18th. The cooking on that occasion was outstanding and Pat and Clara had to defend their position by saying they had meant girls of fourteen, not the ladies of the Liberal Party. Pat entered quite a debate on the subject with Mrs Winterson, and finally concluded that if fourteen year old girls could not cook - it was not their fault, it was the fault of school teachers. This incurred the wrath of Councillor Mrs Brockhurst, a former school teacher. Such were the perils of being Mayor. An interesting detail of this is that Clara had to travel all the way from Crewe to Walsall to be beside Pat on official occasions. Obviously Clara continued to manage and travel with the Fair during Pat's term of office.

At the end of May, Pat took the chair at the Central Allotment Holders Association, and faced angry allotment holders complaining that the Council had failed to provide adequate access roads to their plots. Councillors and officials made excuses, but Pat took the side of the allotment holders. He offered £50 towards a fund to provide annual prizes to growers and said that he was astounded by their complaints. He told them, "*It is wrong to treat these allotments as a joke. The nation needs food. You fellows work hard to grow vegetables...I will do my utmost to see that you get justice..... I don't care what they think or say about me in the Council. I will stand up for what I think is right.... If the Corporation does not put the roads right I'll do it myself,*" Councillor Greystone and the Borough Surveyor pleaded that there were no materials available to do the job. Pat replied, "Nonsense!" The Mayor was then elected as President of the Society.

On 5th June a fire destroyed the Grand Theatre in Walsall. Patrick Ross Collins was leasing the theatre from Associated British Cinemas, but local reports of the event did not include any comments from the Collins, and, from this point in time, it is difficult to know what the loss of the theatre meant to them.

Running the Fair was never far from the Mayor's mind, even when it was left in Clara's capable hands. In the middle of June 1939, he was opening a fete organised by the Electrical Association for Women, in aid of the Walsall General Hospital Appeal; he received a telephone call from Kidderminster and had to make a hurried departure to the fair because there was trouble with some electrical equipment! Maybe he did not even have time to appreciate the irony.

A month later the dispute caused by blaming schoolteachers for the lack of young girls' cooking skills was coming to a head. Pat was invited to Wolverhampton Road Senior School to eat a herring that they were cooking for him. He was called away by business commitments and therefore the paper had to content itself with looking forward to another day; *"Then he will get his herring... and peace will reign once more. Walsall girls will not be satisfied until that day arrives."*

Pat was determined to put on a good show at Bloxwich Wakes during August 1939, despite the impending international situation. Almost symbolically a thunderstorm emptied the fairground on the Monday evening; the weather improved on the Tuesday when Pat preserved the tradition of giving the takings to the Walsall Hospital Fund. It was also noted that there was no Sunday evening concert provided by the organ. Despite such "omens" the Wake was a success and was well attended. As usual there were many entertainers, as well as the rides, but the limelight was stolen by Violo Myllerinne, a 22 year old Swiss giant who was 9.ft.10.ins tall.

At the beginning of September Pat was anticipating crowning the Carnival Queen at the Walsall Hospital Carnival Fair, on Friday and Saturday, 8th and 9th September. The Fair was to be in the Arboretum Extension and the big riding machines were scheduled to be there, but with the declaration of war on September 3rd, the event was cancelled. The showmen returned to the yard at Bloxwich and waited to see what would happen. As Mayor, Pat issued a patriotic message to the people of Walsall. The last few lines of this statement read *"I would urge you all to comply willingly with the regulations and restrictions which have been prescribed for our safety and welfare."* He must have wondered how those restrictions, and other factors, were going to affect both himself and his business.

Pat continued as Mayor of Walsall for the first two months of the War, but by October some attention was being given to his successor, Councillor Cliff Tibbetts, and one of Pat's last duties as Mayor took place on the morning that Councillor Tibbetts was elected to office. On November 10th, Pat unveiled two medallions placed on the main staircase of the Town Hall. These were in memory of the late Sir William Pearman Smith, and the late Joseph Leckie whom Pat had known well. During the same week Pat himself received a fitting honour to mark the end of his Mayoralty; in recognition of his long contribution to local civic life and role as a public benefactor - he was granted the Freedom of the Borough.

On Monday 7th November 1939, a special meeting took place in the Town Hall, which had been decorated by the Parks Department on a grand scale. The Council and Town Hall officials had been joined by other important local citizens, and by a unanimous vote the Council undertook to grant the Freedom of the Borough of Walsall to Pat Collins, an honour which Councillor Tibbetts called, "the coping stone

BELOW: Pat Collins receives the Freedom of the Borough of Walsall on 7 November 1939 in the Council Chamber. He signed this photograph in the top left hand corner. Note the casket which has been presented to him - featuring enamelled pictures of various aspects of his career. Where is it today?
(Collection of R.Hood)

of a wonderful career". Pat was presented with a scroll prepared by the local College of Art, contained in a silver casket featuring enamelled panels illustrating aspects of Pat's life and career. Clara, seated in front of the Mayoral dais, was presented with a bouquet of pink carnations.

Alderman Ingram proposed the presentation and spoke about Pat's life, which he recalled he had first encountered as a child enjoying the gingerbread on sale at the fair. "Showmanship" he said, had been Pat's life, and when he entered it, it was a somewhat rough and tumble business. With the advent of Mr Collins however, the situation was radically altered. He carried out reforms in various manners. He had great ideas about how shows should be conducted, and "*I am told that if people did not do as he wanted he had a fairly useful 'right' and a very formidable 'left'. Be that as it may, reforms in the show business of this country... must be considered the greatest achievement in Pat Collins' business life.*"

Alderman Ingram identified two qualities of Pat's career on the Council. One was Pat's "*Commonsense*" approach to everything, and the second was Pat's concern "*for the well-being of the working class*". Finally, Pat's generosity towards hospitals was detailed.

Councillor Tibbetts also spoke, referring to Pat as a longstanding friend, and commenting on his Parliamentary career. He concluded, "*When he comes out of the Mayoral chair, he ought to take very good care to see that his life story is written. I am sure it would make a best seller.*" As well as receiving praise from his fellow Liberals, the leader of the Labour Group, Councillor Whiston, added his praise and included reference to Pat's concern for the Spanish refugees, some of whom were in the gallery.

Pat responded to the honour bestowed upon him with great emotion. It seems that he stuck to the wording of a sensitively prepared speech, covering his career in Walsall from the 1880's to the Second World War. "*As a young showman, sixty years ago, just after my marriage, I came to Walsall, and pitched my caravan in Shaw's Leasowe. From that day to this, I have never regretted doing so.*"

It was a grand finale to the public life of a most respected Octagenarian, but there was no time to retire into obscurity. He was a showman first and foremost, and he had now to turn his attention to finding a way for his business to survive in Wartime Britain.

BELOW: The times are changing: Wolverhampton Whit Fair, June 1938 - on its new site at Brick Kiln Street. Up until a year before this, it had still been held on the Market Patch (St Peter's Square). A few "traditional" attractions can be seen - the Slip and Mrs Swann's Brandy Snap stall, but new rides are making their presence felt - the Big Wheel and the Waltzer.
(Express and Star)

THE MAN WITH THE GOLDEN HEART
1939-1943

CHAPTER 9

At the outbreak of War, theatres, cinemas and fairs closed. No-one knew quite what to expect, what effect new regulations might have, or if enemy air raids would soon become a reality. But as early as mid September cinemas and theatres were returning to life... though without the neon lighting on their facades. Imagine a fair operating in the evening without its lights! Almost unbelievably the Government appeared to favour a "life as normal" approach in an endeavour to maintain morale as the war machine gained momentum. Restrictions and air raid precautions had to be carefully taken into consideration, and the departure for military service or war work, of many of the showmen and women, allowed for.

As Pat vacated the Mayoral chair he had all these problems confronting him. The Yard at Bloxwich was filled with living vans, and the electoral register of the period reads like a "Who's Who" of Pat Collins employees and tenants. Some were expecting conscription and others waited to be directed to War work in munitions factories. At Lime Tree House Pat had installed a large air-raid shelter in the vegetable garden, and there are several people alive today who remember the early years of the War, and nights spent in the shelter when the air-raid sirens sounded. Pat's temper was sometimes short, and he was taking snuff in ever greater quantities, but his greatest concern was the safety of his great-grandchildren.

Pat and John Collins concentrated on beating the blackout regulations. They went to Hawleys, the Walsall tent makers and ordered a huge canvas roof that could be extended over the top of the fair, or at least could be stretched from the rides to the sidestalls creating an enclosed environment. It is believed that parts of the Brooklyn Speedway, formerly managed by Charlie Hayes, were cut up to help create the structure of the black-out.

Work proceeded quickly enough to be able to present fairs at Christmas 1939 and to demonstrate the "Blacked-out fair" to local councils. Some of the correspondence relating to this has survived. For example, on 22nd November 1939 Joe Proverbs typed out a letter to Wolverhampton Council on Pat's behalf, asking for a reduction in the usual £250 rent:

"In view of the present lighting restrictions, and in an effort to keep the Showman's flag flying, I have devised and constructed a small enclosed fairground, the whole being completely blacked out by means of a dark waterproof canvas. The size of the framework being 155ft by 70ft.

This fairground, entirely under cover, has been open at Oakengates, and for the last two weeks at West Bromwich Wakes, and everything appertaining to the running of same has been carried out to the complete satisfaction of the Police and the ARP authorities, remaining open each day until 11pm. We are opening at Tipton with this fairground commencing Friday this week..."

Wolverhampton Council responded by sending P.C. Jack Aston off to Tipton to investigate, and he filed the following report:

"The amusements consist of about 20 sideshows surrounding two large roundabouts, with a gangway about 6 to 10 feet wide between the sideshows and the roundabouts....There are two entrances, one at either end, and these serve as exits also, there being no additional provision for leaving the shows in the case of an air-raid, except by these two exits. The sideshows are so arranged that they are side by side but in numerous places there are spaces in the joining canvas through which naked lights are to be seen.

In other places only a thin type of canvas has been used and light shows through it... The great danger appears to be the lack of exits for leaving in the event of an air raid."

Whether modifications were made is not clear, but the fair opened on the Brickiln Street site as usual. The fair may have been enlarged because at Easter 1940, when it opened in Walsall, it was possible to enclose the Dodgems, the Motor Cycle Speedway and the Atlantic Airways. Those with memories of the Blackout Fair tend to recall water coming in rather than light escaping! If the canvas sagged it was possible for large pools of rainwater to collect in the roof. When poked with a pole the water came through in a great cascade.

At Easter 1940 it was also possible to re-open the Crystal Palace Amusement Park in Sutton Park, and this site opened every summer throughout the War.

During the late 1930's Pat's fair had often included a small circus, but the outbreak of War seriously curtailed circus activities. Richard Kaye's circus was with Pat Collins' Fair at Nuneaton on the day War broke out. They packed up and returned to their quarters at Brownhills, and, like their colleagues at Bloxwich, they waited to see what would happen. Eventually, their lorries were converted to enable them to undertake a contract to deliver air-raid shelters. Richard's son, Billy, joined a circus that appeared on the stage of variety theatres - he became one of the Roberto Brothers, a triple jockey act, and made his debut at the Theatre Royal, West Bromwich, at Christmas 1939.

At Pat's Easter fair, 1940, in Walsall, a small circus tent did stand alongside the Black-out Fair, but the artistes were part-timers who could only appear when not engaged in War work. One of the artistes was Swami, the knife-thrower, who claimed to have owned his own touring circus in India in the 1930's. He had come to Britain a couple of years before the War, had found a partner for his knife-throwing act and was doing well until the War came along and many circuses closed. He told the Walsall Observer he would have stayed in India if he had known what was going to happen. He was working on the night shift in a wheel factory and knife-throwing in the circus when rare opportunities arose. He sadly felt that he was going to spend his future building wheels rather than throwing knives!

In 1940 the Wartime "Holidays at Home" campaign led Birmingham Corporation to plan a series of fairs in the town's parks. It appears that Young Pat hoped to become the lessee of these fairs, and that his father would supply riding machines. Perhaps this was an indication that Pat's drive and energy were finally running out. Pat himself apparently showed little interest in the venture; perhaps his resources and manpower were consumed by the Blacked-out fair's appearances in the Black Country. In the event, Bob Wilson ran the Birmingham fairs, and they marked the beginning of his rise to become a well-known Midlands showman.

Pat was, as he always claimed to be, an optimist; and the War put this to the test. In August 1940 he made a great show of it being "business as usual" at the Bloxwich Wake. It was well-attended and the message was clear - Pat Collins' Fair was alive and kicking! However, by the end of the year, Pat's health began to decline. Clara nursed him through his long illness while continuing to exercise her managerial grip on the Fair. A serious problem was that many of the older generation of managers and workers were feeling their age; some had died; sons had been conscripted and daughters were in war work. Serious shortages in materials made maintenance and renewal of equipment almost impossible. It was a struggle just to keep going.

On Wednesday morning, 9th December 1943, Pat Collins died, at the age of eighty four. His last words to Clara and John were, "Keep the flag flying." The fair was at Wednesbury at the time, and Clara issued instructions that it was to 'open as usual'. The funeral was arranged for the following Monday, 14th December. The service was to take place at St Patrick's Church, Walsall, and Pat's grave was going to be in a new sector of Bloxwich Cemetery set aside for Roman Catholics.

Before the funeral Patrick Ross Collins went to the cemetery with Father Hanrahan to decide on the site of the grave. Young Pat strode around on the turf in the style of a showman deciding how to set out the fair. Then he dug the heel of his boot into the turf and declared, *"That's it!"* To those who witnessed the scene it recalled the style with which his father completed the survey of a fairground site. As befitted the death of "The King of Showmen", Pat's funeral was to be heavy with symbolism, and something of an epic.

LEFT: A rare picture of the Black Out Fair in operation, Fowler engine, "Dreadnought" attends the Dodgems of Ashton-Under-Lyne in the summer of 1940. The black tilt can just be seen to the right of the engine, as well as the obvious black tarpaulin draped over the firebox end of the engine. *(Collection of Kevin Scrivens)*

On Sunday night the coffin containing his remains was taken from Limetree House, Bloxwich, to St Patrick's Church. Father Hanrahan, of St Peter's Bloxwich, conducted a service of Benediction, and Monday morning began with a solemn Requiem Mass. When the funeral service began, the church was filled to capacity, and of course, there were people from all areas of Pat's life who were anxious to pay their last respects. There were family mourners, and staff and tenants from Pat Collins' Fairs; many other showmen and representatives of the Showmen's Guild. Local councillors, Council officials and business acquaintances came in vast numbers, as well as many local "ordinary folk".

The address was delivered by Provost Yeo, from St Mary-the-Mount, who had known Pat well for many years. Provost Yeo found a striking image with which to open his address concerning "The King of Showmen". He began by revealing that Neville Chamberlain had offered Pat a knighthood in recognition of his public service. Pat had turned down the offer, telling the priest, *"Pat Collins I've always been, and Pat Collins I will remain."* Here was an image that offered an insight into the greatness of the man - he was a humble man who became a "King", without losing the common touch or separating himself from his roots. Provost Yeo surveyed Pat's career comprehensively and paid tribute to his courage, his generosity, his force of character, his business acumen, his forthrightness, and his basic "simplicity" and faith.

The funeral cortege, of some thirty cars, travelled from Walsall to Bloxwich past many sites associated with Pat's life and work. At Bloxwich the burial was officiated by Father Sheeran, who wished to make a point about Pat's love of children. On the way to the grave the coffin was accompanied by six girls in white who had made their first communion on the day of Pat's death. The six coffin bearers were all Pat's employees: Matey Weston, Ted and Frank Sherwood, Ike Bailey, Charlie Hayes, and Joe Proverbs, who at the time was a corporal in the Army. When it came to the mourners, it was difficult to distinguish between relatives, employees and tenants, and the endless list of names include many who have played a part in this biography; the Collins themselves, the Farrells, the Chadwicks, the Montes and Harrises. More than a hundred wreaths surrounded the grave.

At the Council meeting held that same afternoon more tributes were paid to Pat, and many speeches covered familiar ground. Perhaps the most original tribute came from Alderman Ingham, who had known Pat for sixty years:

"We were filled with admiration and affection for Pat Collins. We admired him for the way in which he handled a business that was difficult to manage, and the spirit in which he received the rebuffs, as well as the rewards, of the showman's life, and we esteemed him for his other excellent qualities. He possessed some power that appealed to us all.

What was the secret of it? I have come to the conclusion that it was because he had a golden heart"

IT'S PAT COLLINS'
Again Leading The Way—Presenting ENTIRELY UNDER COVER

DARLASTON April Pleasure **FAIR**

(FAIRGROUND)

COMMENCING FRIDAY, APRIL 5th.

Open Until 11 p.m.

A FAIRGROUND COMPLETELY ENCLOSED.

It's Black Outside—But "Brighter" Inside.

PATRONISE THE FAIR & BANISH THOSE BLACK-OUT BLUES.

N.B.—TO-DAY (SATURDAY) LAST DAY OF WALSALL EASTER PLEASURE FAIR.

LEFT: Making a "feature" of the Black Out Fair - four references to it in one advertisement inviting patrons to the Easter Fair in Walsall and the fair at Darlaston.
(*Walsall Observer 30/4/40*)

ABOVE: Pat's funeral - the coffin is conveyed into Bloxwich Cemetery by Ted Sherwood, Frank Sherwood, Charlie Hayes, Matey Weston, Willie Weston and Joe Proverbs, followed by Young Pat, Clara, Baby Pat, Claire Collins. Also note one of the girls who had made her first Communion!

(Collection of Joe Chadwick)

BELOW: Pat's graves! Young Pat was responsible for both monuments, and he must have chosen the words that led Wrexham folk to believe that Pat was buried with Flora., The truth is that Pat was joined by Clara in Bloxwich! In both Cemeteries the graves are close to the graves of other showland families.

Photograph - Ned Williams)

- 84 -

KEEP THE FLAG FLYING I
1944-1962
CHAPTER 10

Pat Collins died just before the end of 1943.

The previous chapters have primarily been concerned with the life-story of Pat Collins and the history of his fairs. Both inextricably interwoven we think you will agree.

The story after Pat's death to the present day still focuses on the fair itself although the personnel changed. The existence in the 1990's of a travelling fair still using Pat's name, together with permanent sites he started, is in part to do with Births, Marriages and Deaths ("Hatches, Matches & Despatches" in newspaper jargon). Fairground personalities, in this saga are as important as the arrival of new riding machines and transport.

This part of the story is divided into two. The first part ends with Clara's death, and the contraction of the 'empire' and the second part brings our story up to the present day as Anthony Harris takes over the job of "Keeping the flag flying."

In the late 1930's, one of Pat's friends from Bloxwich was talking to him at the fair, and voiced the opinion that Pat must be a millionaire. Pat's response was to wave his hand towards the fair, saying, "It's all just sticks and rags!" Perhaps the real fortunes were made before the First World War. The 1920's and the 1930's had been hard times, but the nature of showmanship was such that to be successful the showman had to be seen to be successful. New innovations and endless investment were a continual drain on resources, especially as some new equipment was of doubtful economic viability or permanence.

Barry Island was home to at least one ex-riding master who had decided to sell his machine rather than battle to maintain payment instalments to the ride builder. The huge scenics proved themselves uneconomic, and showmen soon realised that the biggest and best machine also needed the biggest and best army of workers to transport and operate it... and the biggest and best number of patrons to make it all worthwhile.

Many people must have wondered about the size of Pat Collins' estate, and what was to become of it after the Guvnor's death. When the will was published it was revealed that Pat had left £72,419.4s. Probate was granted to Clara Collins, John Cotterell, Harry Coad and James Cooper. Messrs Cotterell and Coad were Walsall solicitors who had worked for Pat for many years. These trustees had to manage the estate for the benefit of the legatees. In effect, Clara found herself managing the travelling Fairs for the Trustees, while Walsall John was in charge of the permanent sites at Sutton Park, and Great Yarmouth, and was running his own amusement park at Barry Island.

As life returned to normal after the War, Pat Collins' fairs could still find themselves committed to three or four runs - all under Clara's management, and the day to day supervision of the ground managers. If a ride manager needed a new tilt for his machine, he would have to come to Clara to authorise the expenditure, and in some cases, Clara would have to refer the matter to the Trustees. Part of Pat's success had been his ability to maintain his vast sprawling empire and keep it within his grip - "The Guvnor seemed to know everything that was going on!" is a remark heard many times. He could also make very prompt decisions, and had an intuitive sense of how best to resolve a problem. Clara was just as practical and well-versed in showland matters, but her hands were tied, and she too was growing old.

No new fairground rides were built during the War, but, as life returned to normal, showmen had to consider renewing their equipment and transport. The firm of Pat Collins retained the use of steam engines longer than many others, but they were quick to order two new Scammell "Showtrac" vehicles, the first being licensed in September 1946, and the second a year later. They also took delivery of a new "Odeon-fronted" Maxwell Waltzer in the Autumn of 1947. With two arks, two waltzers and two or three dodgem tracks, plus equipment from the amusement parks, it was possible to maintain the "traditional" runs of fairs. (A composite picture of the 1948 and 1949 runs is used to illustrate this in Chapter 17.)

The World's Fair report of the 1949 Onion Fair, by Jack Mellor, gives some idea of the equipment that could still be assembled though not the condition or appearance! There were three Collins' Dodgems, a Brooklyn Speedway, a Moon Rocket; Waltzer, Loop O Plane, two Arks, Ghost train, plus older rides like the Slip, the Cakewalk and the Steam yachts and Three-abreast. Walsall John also presented his "Ducks".

No fewer than six Collins' engines were on the ground, four being used to generate power. A number of rides were supplied by tenants, including Joby Farrell's Chairs, J.J.Collins' Caterpillar, and J.P.Collins' Waltzer. Billy Williams presented two big Wheels, including the one bought by Young pat in 1937. Frank Wilson, of Redditch, brought his Dodgems and Ark and Harry Hall brought a Skid. As well as juvenile rides, round stalls and sidestuff, there were a number of shows - many of which had been associated with Pat's major fairs since before the War, eg Tom Norman's show, Hickman's Boxing Booth, plus two others, Kayes' Circus and Rayner's Show.

Lionel Bennett acted as Ground Manager at the time, and Clara was driven over to Aston from Bloxwich, and would take command from her living van.

BELOW: The "Odeon" Waltzer arrived at the Onion Fair of 1947, the second post-war Onion Fair. As the firm's "Flagship" it was then taken to the Goose Fair.
(Collection of Norman Doone, & Frank Allen)

Walsall John would also usually put in an appearance at the big Birmingham fairs, and was responsible for maintaining another tradition established by Pat - the use of high wire artistes and high divers, acrobats and motor-cycle acts to provide free entertainment for the crowds.

At the 1949 Carnival Fair, a month later, Derick Goodman of the Birmingham Mail called in to see how Pat Collins' fair was surviving without the Guvnor. He found Walsall John, and his wife Claire watching a Swedish balancing act ninety feet above the ground. Claire regretted the noise of the diesel generators, which prompted the reporter to quiz John about the engines. *"We've only got six of them now"* said John, *"The oldest is 42 years, and the youngest is 26. They are wonderful machines, even when you compare them with the latest diesel generators, which need five times the spending when it comes to maintenance. Unfortunately, we've only got three men left who can even drive a traction engine: Cockney Jack, Big Jim Morley, and old Billy Mills, who is still our best driver at 73! When these three drivers go - that's the finish of traction engines as far as I'm concerned."*

It wasn't just the "preservation" of the engines within the Collins empire that attracted attention. John and Clara had also surprised everybody by resurrecting the No.1.Scenic Railway. It was brought out of retirement for the 1946 Onion Fair and caused quite a sensation. In 1948 it appeared again at the Onion Fair, and afterwards made a dash to Hull.

ABOVE: The cold winter of 1947. Snow lies on the steps of the new "Odeon" Waltzer while built up for the Christmas Fair in Wolverhampton, Scammell Showtrac No.2. (KDH 141) in attendance.
(Collection of Rob Webster)

When Walsall John opened the Fun Fair at Battersea Pleasure Gardens in 1951, he effectively turned his back on the Crystal Palace Amusement Park, where he had made a number of innovations in the 1940's. As a consequence he became even further detached from the running of the travelling fairs. By the mid fifties the firm was still running two to three circuits, but the second and third circuits had to use other folks' equipment.

By then the No.1. fair consisted of the Dodgems (Jack Harvey) and the Waltzer (Johnny Cook), the small Ark (Billy Weston, then Jim Clark) and John Collins' "Ducks", augmented by other rides during the Back End. Apart from the round stalls and sidestuff the No.1.fair relied on Eddy Monte's Wall of Death, and Hickman's Boxing Booth to give it more substance. The No.2. fair featured Billy Bagnall's large caterpillar, that travelled under the Pat Collins' name, the Big Ark, Gallopers and a second Dodgem (Arthur Owen).

Harry Alcock was the ground manager on the No.1. run and Lionel Barnett was on No.2., but the fair was more and more under the control of the office, and if repairs were needed, men were sent out from the Yard. The third circuit usually featured rides presented by another showman, such as George Stokes, from Shrewsbury.

The Odeon front of the new Waltzer was damaged by fire in the mid fifties, and while being repaired was replaced by a small Waltzer which had been managed for John Collins by Clifford Croydon. The Maxwell Waltzer returned to use with a flat front and continued in use until taken to Barry Island. After that the No.1. Waltzer position was usually taken by J.P.Collins' Waltzer, managed by Kevin Collins.

It is interesting to consider that by the early sixties, there were really only three Collins' rides still travelling: The Dodgems (Jack Harvey), The Waltzer, now stripped of its "Odeon" features (John Cook) and the Small Ark (Rex Brown). The "new ingredient" in the situation was the return of Elias Harris.

Elias had left Pat Collins' fairs after his wife Margaret's death in 1934. Elias' second marriage was to Evelyn Baker from a family with links in the haulage industry and showland in the Southampton area. Elias worked as an aviation fitter during the War, but afterwards made a return to showland with his Wall of Death. He entered the riding machine business with an Octopus, one of the first post-War novelty rides, and first travelled it in the Eastern Counties with Stanley Thurston & Sons. His travels took him to Luton, Bedford and Northampton, and one year, into Coventry at the invitation of John Collins. By the end of the 1950's, Elias Harris formed a vital part in the presentation of "Pat Collins" fairs.

DARLASTON APRIL PLEASURE FAIR
(FAIR GROUND),
FRIDAY, SATURDAY & MONDAY,
April 26th, 27th & 29th.

PAT COLLINS' WORLD-FAMOUS AMUSEMENTS

FUN! | **FROLIC!**

IT'S PAT COLLINS'
Presents

WALSALL GREAT EASTER FAIR
(FAIRGROUND—CORPORATION STREET WEST)

Today (SATURDAY) MARCH 27th to SATURDAY APRIL 3rd, Inclusive.

OPEN DAILY!

Super Rides include:—Dodgems-de-Luxe, New Autodrome, Jungle Speedway, Big Eli Wheel, Fun House, Juvenile Wheel, New Shows, etc., etc.

SPEED! | ALL FOR YOUR ENJOYMENT! | **THRILLS!**

ABOVE: Some post-War advertisements, like this one from the Walsall Observer (1948) give details of rides and attractions attending the fair.

BELOW: Showtrac No.2. with a road train of three trailers en route to the next gaff at the end of the 1940's. Note some of the "lads" are travelling on the load itself - perched on top of the segments of the Waltzer's platform. *(Collection of Rob Webster)*

- 88 -

In the early 1960's Pat Collins' dwindling equipment was in a poor state, and spending was rigorously controlled by Arthur Rowbottom in the office.

By contrast, Elias Harris' equipment and transport seemed new and immaculate. (The Octopus had been joined by the Hurricane Jets.) Elias' son, Anthony, had left school and was helping his father take on some of the management of the fairs as well as presenting the machines. Lionel Bennett was still Ground Manager, and Jack Harvey was senior ride manager; it was generally felt that the arrival of the Harris family was a good omen for the future destiny of the Pat Collins' fairs.

Clara's death on 7th September 1962, brought down the curtain on the Pat Collins era. She had done her best to keep the flag flying, and died quoting the famous phrase to Jack and Clara Harvey, who looked after her during the last few months of her life. Clara's funeral on 11th September 1962, was every bit as dramatic as Pat's and Flora's had been, and fitting tributes were made to the passing of this remarkable woman. The list of mourners published in World's Fair is one of the most comprehensive lists of people who had crossed the path of Pat Collins' fairs ever assembled. Someone remarked, "*She would have known them all.*" (More is said about Clara's passing in the first section of the Who's Who at the end of this book.)

Before moving on to describe the events of the next thirty years, we should like to record two events appertaining to the fifties, and concerning commemorations.

Firstly, in 1955, the Bloxwich Carnival Committee decided to erect a memorial to Pat Collins. Public subscriptions were collected, and the memorial took the form of a clock, mounted on a fourteen foot high wrought iron framework. It was designed by Frank Greenhough of Bloxwich, and constructed by John Smith & Sons, of Derby.

The clock was placed in the King George V Memorial Playing Fields, and was unveiled on Saturday 29th October 1955, in the presence of representatives from Bloxwich, Walsall Council and Showland. Bert Brittain asked Will Wiggin to pay tribute to the life of Pat Collins. Both men had known him well. Arthur Bates, the President of the Showmen's Guild also spoke, and the clock was duly unveiled and presented to the people of Walsall, represented by the Mayor, Councillor Mrs Brockhurst. Clara attended the ceremony, and joined the party to pose for photographs of the event.

The clock has recently been renovated and Walsall Borough Council Leisure Services Dept arranged its transfer to a site in the Promenade Gardens, Bloxwich, where it was re-dedicated to the memory of Pat Collins on 5th July 1991 by Fr Alwyn. On this date also three wood and wrought iron benches were presented for use in the Gardens, donated by John Collins, Patrick Collins and Anthony Harris.

BELOW: Showtrac No.1. and road train of three trailers. Note the train includes Clara's living van - a slightly less ornate van than one used before the War (see 1936 Onion Fair picture in Chapter 7). At this date (about 1950) the nameplates had not been attached to the Showtracs. (*Collection of Rob Webster*)

ABOVE: Clara Collins (nee Mullett), photographed in 1955 at the time of the first dedication of the Pat Collins' Memorial Clock in Bloxwich. Clara continued Pat's "good works" in Bloxwich and was Chairman of the Carnival Committee for several years.

RIGHT: On 28th May 1959 Clara sits listening to Bert Brittain read E.J.Homeshaw's Biography of Pat Collins. Next to her is the "replica" of the Guvnor, which once stood in Limetree House, and in 1957 was used to decorate the front of the Waltzer!
(Collection of Pat Coyne)

Back in 1959, Clara was once more the centre of attention when it was decided to celebrate, posthumously, the centenary of Pat's birth. The event took place on 28th May during the evening, at the T.P.Riley School, in Bloxwich. Bert Brittain was one of the principal organisers and he had asked E.J.Homeshaw, the noted local historian, to prepare a short Biography of Pat, based on material collected by Harry Alcock. Harry had arrived in the Pat Collins' empire only recently. He was an ex-policeman, and was now expected to use his "authority" as a Ground Manager. It was he who found out that Pat's Birthday was in May, not in April as Pat had claimed!

Calligraphy for the Biography was by a young man named David Barlow, and the finished book comprised 70 pages on finest parchment, bound in scarlet leather embossed in gold. The text was read to the assembled guests on 28th May by Bert Brittain, and the whole evening took the form of a *"This is Your Life"* programme. Clara and Walsall John, plus Billy Bagnall, (Guests of honour) sat on the stage and were introduced to a number of the contributors who added their comments on the written word. These speakers included 86 year old Florence Jones, Jack Perks and Albert Rogers, all of whom had known Pat well, plus others who had hardly known Pat, including Frank Mellor, the Editor of World's Fair, and Thomas Murphy and F.C.Roope of the Showmen's Guild.

The large audience watched the book being handed over to Clara, but she was too overwhelmed to say anything. Walsall John made a brief reply: *"A wonderful thing has happened here tonight, and this book will be cherished by everyone connected with Pat Collins - it will remain in the Collins family for ever and a day"*. Important folk had celebrated together the night before in Lime Tree House. Less important folk held their own gathering immediately after the event,... in The Kings Arms, Pat's old local, a few paces from the entrance to the Yard.

After the unveiling of the clock, in 1955, Clara had granted free rides for children for an hour on the fair at Oldbury, and she did so again on the day after the Centenary ceremony.

RIGHT: In 1957, Walsall John placed the cut-out of Pat on the canopy at the front of the "Odeon" Waltzer - as seen here at the Goose Fair of that year. His placards inform patrons that he is off to build a Big Dipper at the 1958 Brussels World Fair.
(Collection of Kevin Scrivens)

RIGHT: Clara receives the E.J.Homeshaw Biography on 28th May 1959. Walsall John looks on, before saying a few words on Clara's behalf. Behind Clara is David Barlow, the Calligrapher.
Collection of Norman Pearson and Pat Coyne)

A classic example of the stuffiness and intractability of the BBC at that time is typified by a letter Mr Homeshaw received from The Head of Programmes at Broadcasting House, Birmingham..."*After carefully considering the material you have submitted regarding Mr Pat Collins, we regret that we do not feel it is suitable for inclusion in any of our programmes*". More than 30 years later it can surely be said, "how wrong they were!"

The text of Homeshaw's short 1959 Biography has been quoted many times in articles about Pat's life. At the time it was written, the collective knowledge and memories of Pat Collins' friends, workforce and colleagues would have filled a book many times the size of the one you are now reading!   Such is life's irony....but still, ... better late than never.

Within a year or two of the Centenary ceremony it looked doubtful whether anyone would indeed "keep the flag flying" any longer.

ABOVE: Burrell "No.1." leaves Sutton Park on 17th November 1950 with components for the Big Dipper that John Collins was about to build at Battersea Pleasure Gardens for the 1951 Festival of Britain.
(Collection of Bernard Morley)

BELOW: Walsall John and Billy Bagnall are photographed in front of the "No.1." Scenic in the mid 1950's, at the Crystal Palace Amusement Park, Sutton Coldfield.
(Collection of John Ward, via H.Haines)

KEEP THE FLAG FLYING II
1962-1992

CHAPTER 11

When Walsall John came to Bloxwich to attend Clara's funeral he had come "on leave" from a Nursing Home, in London. He was still "The Guvnor", but it was difficult to imagine that he could "Keep the flag flying" other than at Barry Island. The amusement park at the Crystal Palace was closing down with the expiry of its lease. Great Yarmouth Pleasure Beach had already changed hands.

Before she died Clara had spoken of her wish that the No.1.Scenic might be preserved, but, at the time, such a preservation project seemed impossible. Fortunately Tom Hunt was able to rescue the Wonderland Organ, the miniature railway and three showman's engines. ("The Griffin", "The Leader", and "Wait and See".) At some stage it seems that Clara wanted the Burrell "No.l" to be saved locally, but John had agreed to sell it to John Crawley. Albert Martin and George Sutton, assisted by young Barry Island Pat, burned what was left of the Scenic and other "remains" that were to be found at Sutton Park. Billy Bagnall took over other Collins' equipment and some of it went to his amusement park at Chasewater.

The travelling fair struggled on. One problem was that the folks who might have taken it on, were all dispersed. Pat's grand-daughter, Flora, and her husband Eddy Monte, had lost interest in the travelling fair after the death of their 19 year old son Michael, in October 1959, and they had gone into "semi-retirement". Baby Pat had gone to Birkenhead, Baby John and his sons were at Seaton Carew. Walsall John's sons were destined to take on the management of Barry Island and had not grown up on the travelling fair as Young Pat's children had done during the 1930's.

Not long after Clara's death, the Pat Collins' organisation had to swing into top gear to present its major event of the year - the Onion Fair. Ted Cooper, of World's Fair went along to Birmingham to see if the event lived up to the legend, and was very impressed with what he saw, particularly when the thousands of lights created their magical effect as it grew dark. He told the readers of World's Fair that it was felt by many to be "The best Onion Fair ever!" Certainly there were plenty of rides, about fifteen shows, ninety round stalls and a huge range of sidestuff.

He found Lionel Barnett in charge, assisted by Arthur Rowbottom, from the office, and felt that the fair was well-laid out and organised with a thorough attention to detail. He also met John Collins and his second wife Kay, visiting the fair to see that all was well. Unlike Claire his first wife, Kay (Collyer) was not born in showland, but she was able to take a turn in the paybox if the circumstances demanded it!. (Not that there is any suggestion she was required to do so at the 1962 Onion Fair.)

The real sign of the times, however, is to be found in the list of rides present. Only the Super Dodgems (Jack Harvey) and the Waltzer (Johnny Cook) were the real Pat Collins' machines present. The other attractions were provided by Jones Brothers, the Wilsons, Billy Williams, Billy Bagnall, George Stokes, Joby Farrell, Bobby Keeble, and Elias Harris. Within the extended family, Eddy Monte brought his Meteorite and J.P.Collins brought his Waltzer. Walsall John brought his own "Ducks", and the Coaster from Barry Island, presented by his son John.

After the Onion Fair was over, on Saturday night, many of the showmen pulled down quickly and made for Burton Statutes which opened on Monday. The Nottingham Goose Fair opened on the following Thursday. The Pat Collins presence at the latter consisted of the Dodgems (one of ten tracks present!), and Walsall John's Tipping Vampire Jets. (On this occasion Kay Collins did have to take charge.)

Another way in which the Collins empire changed in the 1960's was the acceleration of the sale and disposal of the grounds that Pat had accumulated, and on which much of his success had been based.

Some of the early "casualties" of this policy were on grounds that were also used as Winter quarters, such as Darlaston and Oakengates, but the process became particularly noticeable towards the end of the sixties with the sale of land at Bloxwich and Aston.

The sale of the Yard and "Wakes Ground", plus the sale of the site of the Onion Fair, marked the destruction of two "cornerstones" of the old empire.

The 1970's began with no Onion Fair to look forward to, and Bloxwich Wake, Pat's flagship within the Black Country, suffered an awkward move to Coalpool. The day-to-day management of the fairs had passed from Elias Harris to his son Anthony, with some administration still handled by the Bloxwich Office. The office was working from Lime Tree House itself, and from 1971 onwards the future of the house seemed uncertain.

Walsall John had become the sole proprietor of the Pat Collins' business in 1966, by virtue of being the sole surviving legatee. 1966 was also the year that Walsall John's sons took over the Barry Island Amusement Park from their father. In 1969 they bought the freehold of the Barry site from the Whitmore Bay Syndicate. In the circumstances Walsall John was left with a much diminished travelling fair, in which he had little active interest, and the sale of the grounds must have seemed inevitable.

Walsall John died in Blackpool in 1977, and the travelling fair was inherited by the four children of John's first marriage, plus Jane, John's daughter by his second marriage. Ann, Vanessa, Jane and Barry Island John sold their share in the business to Barry Island Pat, who then ran the travelling fair in a partnership with Anthony Harris.

This partnership ran for about four years, but circumstances changed again when Barry Island John wanted to sell his half-interest in the Barry Island amusement Park to Barry Island Pat. The latter decided to sell his half of the travelling fair to Anthony Harris to raise the money to buy out his brother. The negotiations took about eighteen months, but by the summer of 1983, Anthony Harris became the sole proprietor of Pat Collins Fun Fairs.

ABOVE: Jack Harvey stands by the radiator of Showtrac No.2, having just added the nameplate, "The Major". Jack drove the Showtrac and managed the Dodgems.
(Collection of Jack Harvey)

BELOW: On 29 August 1963, "The Leader" was towed away from Bloxwich to be preserved at Oldbury by Tom Hunt and his son Bill. John Cook drove the Showtrac, and is seen here at Wood Green with Mick Archer, and young Vincent Mills on the engine.
(Photo Stan Webb)

- 94 -

What Anthony Harris had actually acquired was the sole remaining riding machine - Jack Harvey's Dodgems, and a run of forty to fifty fairs - plus the name of the business. Arguably, at this point in time, the name was probably the most valuable surviving asset! Pat Collins' fair was now the property of his late granddaughter's husband's son by his second wife - and Anthony had every intention of keeping the Collins' name on the fairs.

When asked by interested patrons if he is Pat Collins, he usually replies, "Yes, but my name is Anthony Harris." It explains how closely the new Guvnor has assumed the mantle of Pat Collins, his pride in the name of the travelling fair that he owns and his desire to follow in Pat's footsteps, by presenting a first class fair.

Anthony has preserved several of the traditions established by Pat, ranging from his Roman Catholicism and philanthropy, to his dedication to the cause of the Showmen's Guild, of which he is currently Senior Vice-President.

Anthony Harris took full control of Pat Collins Fun Fairs in the summer of 1983, while the fair was at Rowley Regis. Since that time he has "re-grouped" and re-established the reputation of the fair bearing Pat's name. Anthony Harris shows no signs of wishing to re-create the old Pat Collins empire in its entirety, but he shows every sign of "keeping the flag flying", albeit in his own chosen colours.

ANTHONY HARRIS - the present proprietor of Pat Collin's Funfair, photographed at Rowley Regis, June 1990. Anthony's "tackle" is always immaculate and "looks like new" - just as Pat's used to do. His Maxwell Waltzer was first built up at the Longton Shrovetide fair, 18 February 1977 - a traditional 'starting point' from which Pat's fairs have travelled.

ABOVE: Showtrac "The Major", LDH 253, leaves the Netherton Wakes Ground with the Dodgem Truck. The narrow access to the ground was by the Britannia Inn, as seen in this early 1960's photograph.
(Photo Roger Mills)

BELOW: The ERF eight-wheeler "Zo'e" JTO 313 looked splendid in its red livery and white-wall tyres, also photographed in the early 1960's.
(Photo Roger Mills)

PAT AND THE SHOWMEN'S GUILD

CHAPTER 12

The continuity of our narrative would have been broken had we stopped in 1899, or in 1909, to look at Pat's contribution to the history of the Showmen's Guild. This chapter therefore, overlaps some of the information given in chapters 3 - 9, but is perhaps all the clearer for dealing with Pat's association with the Guild as a separate issue.

All the accounts of Pat Collins' life credit him with being a fighter, tempered with a sense of justice and fair play. During the last two decades of the nineteenth century, the period in which Pat established himself, the fairground went through transitions that are reminiscent of the American Wild West. The hero in such a story is not a gunfighter, the hero is the bringer of order and justice, the sheriff who "cleans up the town" and makes it safe for all to go about their business, yet, at the same time embodies some of the virtues of the wilder world that he has vanquished. Pat managed to play this role very well.

In the "unregulated" world of fairs in the 1880's, Pat no doubt had to fight for a pitch, which he then had to defend aggressively. Having got a pitch, the showman then had to defend himself against gangs who descended on the fair to operate protection rackets and to take advantage of the criminal opportunities afforded by the arrival of large numbers of people with money about their person. If these gangs wrecked booths and stalls, or threatened showmen with violence, or intimidated customers, the showmen could rarely expect help from the Police who, generally, sided with the "authorities" in taking a rather suspicious attitude towards the showmen themselves. The battle was therefore threefold: firstly, the aspiring showman had to fight for a place in the business; secondly, he had to fight the gangs; thirdly, he had to set about cleaning up show business in the fight for social justice.

The Onion Fair, held at the Old Pleck, Aston, Birmingham, seemed to attract gangs and their names are now part of history: the Black Mask Gang, the Peaky Blinders, and the Stool Boys. Similar gangs operated in other large cities like Liverpool and Manchester, and, no doubt, smaller factions existed in every urban community visited by the fair. It is claimed that Pat organised his fellow showmen on the basis of "collective security", and they counter-attacked, armed with knuckle dusters and improvised clubs. Pat's grandchildren liked to hear heroic tales of the past in which Grandfather Collins defeated the gangs.

Sometimes the story would end with the leader of the Gang calling a truce, shaking hands with Pat and making an honourable acknowledgement that they had been taught a lesson. The truth is more likely to be that it took a number of confrontations to rid the business of this nuisance. It is also an aspect of the fair that lingers in people's attitudes towards show business, and successive generations have produced potential trouble-makers who can disrupt the living of the showman - from the Stool Boys to the Teddy Boys and so on...

Some members of the middle classes have always felt threatened by fairs, and become disturbed by such boisterous pursuits of pleasure. Nowadays fairs are usually closed at ten o'clock, their generators and loudspeakers silenced. But in the past fairs often operated until midnight and took a great deal of money from punters who came onto the fairground from the pub. Much of the middle class dismay is found in letters to the press and Minutes of local councils as the elders of church and chapel expressed their concern about drunkenness and rowdiness, sometimes only thinly disguising their disapproval of the working classes out enjoying secular activities.

In the early 1890's we have records of complaints about revellers from Bloxwich Wake, walking home to Walsall (very late) singing the popular songs of the day at the top of their voices. The Council debated what byelaws could be enacted to prevent showmen blowing the steam whistles on their roundabouts at night, and, in Walsall seemed relieved to be able to site the fair "out of the way" at Midland Road. Fair operators have had to continue to fight on two fronts to this day, a) to curb the social nuisance they appear to cause, and b) to prevent abolition by Local Authorities and subsequent loss of their livelihood.

In the 'Wild West' of England, townships gradually became settled and adopted bourgeois values. Established townsfolk in a settled home of their own often expressed their hostility towards those who were still nomadic. We should not be surprised therefore to find that one cause for suspicion of showmen grew out of the fact that they "travelled" in pursuit of their business. Even today many people on the fair prefer the word "showman" to describe their own ancestry, and make only general use of the word "traveller". (This causes confusion to outsiders who often use the word "travellers" to describe an entirely different group of people!). In the mid 1880's, George Smith, the MP for Coalville, promoted Parliamentary bills relating to people whose work was migratory. He first concentrated on canal workers, but by the end of the 1880's had turned his attention to showmen. In 1889 he promoted the "Moveable Dwellings Bill" and the showmen eventually joined forces to counter such threats.

As early as the 1870's there had been attempts to organise showmen collectively, but these attempts failed for one reason or another. The events of 1889 were more productive. It was (to use a modern term) a "civil rights campaigner", who first identified the threat posed by George Smith's bill. He drew it to the attention of Mr Pedgrift, the Editor of the "Era". This newspaper, widely read by members of theatrical and music hall professions was spreading its influence to new fringes and this included the travelling showmen. Mr Pedgrift denounced the bill in the Era and wrote to all the major showmen of the day suggesting they mobilise their opposition. (Among others he wrote to George Sanger, James Bostock, Joe Caddick, William Wilson, Randall Williams, John Whiting, the Studts, the Murphys and the Collinses: John and Pat).

Joe Caddick was a travelling photographer, based in Brownhills. His portrait of Pat Collins and Young Pat is reproduced in this book, and he was almost certainly among the photographers who are described as the "latest thing" in the 1893 account of the Wolverhampton Fair. Joe wrote a Showmen's Manifesto to counter the bill, and became a prolific campaigner for the showmen's cause.

In 1890 a meeting was held at Islington Agricultural Hall, used by showmen for mounting winter fairs, at which George Smith faced the hostility of his opponents. He was not treated with physical violence but he did have to leave by the back door!

The showmen began to have regular meetings, thus creating an organisation and its membership; the Van Dwellers' Association has traced its origins to a meeting that Mr.Pedgrift had held at the Black Lion Hotel, Salford, in 1889. Creating this organisation was very time consuming and progressed slowly, and it was not until 1891 that the first President, J.W.Bostock, took office. A proper Constitution was not worked out until 1892, by which time Pat and his brother, John Collins, were on the Committee. Throughout the prolonged formation process, the Van Dwellers' Protection Society was fighting George Smith's Bill.

One hundred years after these events it is interesting to consider what it was that caused such consternation to the travelling showmen. Basically, George Smith was proposing that "moveable dwellings" should be registered by County Councils, and should be licensed for a period of three years following the satisfactory completion of an inspection by an officer of the County Council. Officials would look into sanitation arrangements, problems of overcrowding (ie too many folks of both sexes sleeping in a small space), and the health and quality of life the inhabitants could expect to enjoy in their "moveable dwelling". The powers that the authorities might need to enforce all this had to be backed by Court action in the event of anyone using an unregistered or uninspected dwelling, and the Police would be given wide-ranging powers to enter and search a "moveable dwelling" at any time, having obtained a warrant to do so.

Nowadays, by and large, we take licensing, inspection and regulation for granted; it is perhaps difficult to imagine how outrageous these proposals seemed at that time. Maybe the authorities were right to be so concerned about travelling people a hundred years ago when the health and welfare of the urban poor left a lot to be desired. However, travellers felt George Smith was attacking their way of life, interfering with their liberty, and showing a disdainful ignorance of the standards that showmen maintained in their domestic lives. They felt he regarded them as "ignorant nomads" and his concern for their morals, their hygiene, and the welfare and education of their children, was misplaced.

George Smith was of course challenged, and invited to see the truth for himself, but he appears to have spurned such invitations. He failed to respond to such requests, and on the few occasions he did meet showmen face to face he was evasive. What he made of the meeting at Islington is not clear, and it seems that he never acknowledged that his proposals insulted many showmen, who were proud of their standard of living and the education of their children. Rev.Thomas Horne wrote that George Smith's assumptions, *"...are based upon no real experience of van life."* Later he added...*"...it is the same old story over and over again: the punishment of the just for the unjust - Mr.Smith seems to have no power of discriminating between the wretched drink-besotten gypsy and the showman proper."* Perhaps in this comment Thomas Horne put his finger on it. What really outraged showmen was that they were to be adversely affected by legislation that was aimed to deal with other folk (with whom they disassociated themselves). This was to happen again and again, and is still happening in the 1990's; showmen suffer because of society's dislike of itinerants.

In 1893 the Moveable Dwellings Bill was defeated. This led to some decline in interest in the Guild on the part of its members, but the Executive Committee (of which Pat was a member) still continued to fight on behalf of showmen. The fight throughout the last decade of the century was mainly with local authorities who were extending their powers and often using them to regulate fairs, abolish them, or make it very difficult for showmen to earn a living - just at a time when the new fairground technology and equipment meant that a showman had to make a much larger financial investment in his business. It was no good investing in an expensive riding machine if you were going to be denied the opportunity of putting it to use at a good fair. Pat's battle in Walsall, in 1892, was repeated in many parts of the country.

In 1900, Lord George Sanger became the third President. For a time the Association survived financially only because of generous donations made by the President, Tom Norman and Pat Collins. The position of Secretary was still an honorary one, yet there was a great deal of work to be done. The Association was reconstituted as a Trade Union, and communication improved with the launch of the newspaper - World's Fair. This paper was not produced by the Guild, but members like John and Pat Collins contributed to establishing it. The title "Showmen's Guild" gradually replaced the earlier name and in 1907 District Committees were formed and both Pat and John Collins were on the Birmingham Committee. John was also on the Manchester and Liverpool Committee.

In 1908 the Moveable Dwellings Bill was resurrected, and referred to an Enquiry, which spent two years looking into the matter. The revival of this contentious issue galvanised showmen back into more vigorous support for their Guild, and in January 1909 Pat Collins took over from Lord George Sanger as President. Pat's Presidency was to run for twenty years which was remarkable considering the diversity of his activities.

In 1950, when Thomas Murphy came to write a history of the first sixty years of the Guild's existence, he had this to say about Pat Collins:

"If ever there was a worthy successor to a brilliant predecessor it was Pat Collins; the fairground never produced a more eminent man - one of the greatest personalities Showland has ever known. Ever in the place where the fight was hottest, never sparing himself time or money in the effort for the betterment and vindication of his fellow showmen...a fighter to his fingertips...together with Rev.Thomas Horne, he wove the Guild into a sound and splendid fabric."

Rev.Thomas Horne was also one of the remarkable characters produced by showland, and in 1914, he became the Guild's first full time secretary, a post which he held until his death in 1918.

Returning to Pat's early years as the Guild's President, we see a change in style. Once he had fought with his fists, but now he had to develop the skills of spokesman, negotiator and diplomat. Whatever his literary limitations, he could absorb and retain information and was not intimidated by organisational complexities. If you found yourself in an argument with Pat, you had to be sure of your facts. On the fairground, men knew that if they "cussed" Pat...they could expect a better "cussing" in return! He enjoyed argument where he was sure of his ground, although he was not so keen on argument in the Council Chamber or the House of Commons where he was frustrated by the lack of plain-speaking and the subtleties of politics.

Guild Meetings were often held at important fairs, in a showman's tent, and some showmen recall Pat setting up arguments and sitting back while others fought - the pleasure of a promoter watching a fight! Most of all, people recall his common sense approach to problems and his willingness to take action when impatient with mere words.

His first few years of office were good years for show business. The new electrically driven scenics were beginning to replace the central engine powered switchbacks. The Bioscopes and Shows were reaching their peak and were suddenly faced with extinction through competition from cinemas and variety - but at just the right moment.....the organs were about to find new homes in the new scenics. 'New' rides and innovations were making the industry more exciting than ever. The years 1912 and 1913 were the most prosperous in fairground history.

The outbreak of the First World War interrupted this "Golden Age" of the fairground and no one seemed to know how the trade ought to react to the new situation. Pat took the view, during both Wars, that it should be "Business as Usual". He seemed to feel that the working population would need the pleasure provided by the fair as an escape from the grim reality of War, and monotony of war work.

He tried to persuade Nottingham Corporation not to cancel the Goose Fair in October 1914, but Urban Councils were worried about possible air raids. Some showmen were able to retire to Winter Quarters, from where they operated as a 'permanent' site, or for short seasons. Other showmen and their labour force volunteered for military service, and some faced the possibility that their engines would be rquisitioned for War Work. The travelling fairs appeared to have come to a standstill by 1916.

The secretary of the Midland Section of the Guild was William Savage (related to the Savages of Kings Lynn, the engine ride manufacturers), and when Rev.Thomas Horne died in 1918, William Savage took over his position as full-time Secretary to the Guild. He lived in Lonsdale House, Bloxwich, next to Limetree House, and so the Headquarters of the Guild for the next eight years was Bloxwich! It is not clear whether Mr Savage worked for Pat's own organisation as well, or solely for the Guild.

The return to Peace saw a big increase in the membership of the Guild and 1919 witnessed record takings at fairs. Against this it had to be admitted that costs had risen dramatically. A scenic railway once costing £3,600 could now cost three times that figure. The Guild had many new problems to face, including the wartime introduction of Entertainment Tax. The Guild's President continued to be kept busy both in his Guild office and in further developing his own business.

In 1922 Pat made history by being the first member of the Guild to be elected to Parliament, his fellow members of the Guild having turned out in force to support and assist in his election campaign. While Pat sat in the House of Commons for two years he was able to represent both the interests of his constituents and of the showmen. For example, in 1923 he tried to introduce a private member's bill to transfer to the House of Commons the Home Secretary's power to abolish fairs!

On losing his seat in the Commons in 1924, then 65 years of age, Pat re-affirmed his commitment to the Guild and to the fairground. There was no talk of 'retirement'.

The administrative work of the Guild continued to increase and, in 1926, the Central Office was moved from Lonsdale House to Imperial Buildings, Bridge Street, Walsall.

The following year Pat was in the news again protesting about the decision to move the Nottingham Goose Fair from the City Centre to Forest Fields. Having lost that particular battle he, as President of the Showmen's Guild, led the members in making the best of the new site.

Pat finally retired as President in January 1929, after twenty years in office. In Chapter 5 we describe how Pat's retirement conincided with his brother's death, and therefore the event was not celebrated until the following year.

He was succeeded in office by William Wilson, the London-based showman, who subsequently moved the Central Office to London.

Pat himself continued his work in the Midland Section of the Guild.

An interesting token of the Guild's gratitude to Pat survives in the form of a giant sized painting of himself, commissioned by the Guild in 1925, and presented to Walsall Corporation. It hangs in Committee Room 2 in the Town Hall, Walsall.

BELOW: Pat Collins sitting next to William Wilson, his successor in the role of President of the Showmen's Guild, at the Guild meeting of 1930. Flora Collins is standing behind Mr Wilson.
(Collection of Barry Island Pat)

THE AMUSEMENT PARKS

CHAPTER 13

In the process of acquiring rides and building up several "runs" of fairs, Pat Collins' name was clearly associated with the travelling fair - the "true" business of the showmen who, consequently also described themselves as "travellers". However, the late nineteenth century development of the seaside resort produced another environment in which showmen could operate - the fixed site amusement park, offering all the 'fun of the fair' to holiday-makers and day-trippers.

Just as the railways played a part in the creation of seaside resorts, urban transport played a part in developing places on the outskirts of conurbations that could be used by the town-dweller in search of a breath of fresh air. Trams and local train services provided the gateway to open countryside, and the showman realised that "all the fun of the fair" could be enjoyed just as much on beautiful landscapes, and in the West Midlands this led to the popularity of places like the Lickey Hills, Clent Hills, Kinver Edge and Sutton Park.

Showmen who provided entertainment at fixed places could lead a more settled existence, and were therefore regarded as "amusement caterers" rather than as "travellers". This sometimes led to conflict between the Showmen's Guild and the Amusement Caterers' Association. Nowadays the same gulf exists between the travelling fair and the world of "theme parks". But, ironically, the distinction between these two worlds has often been difficult to assess.

Nothing is ever quite "permanent" even in an amusement park, and the same families operate in both worlds, and travel or anchor as time and season dictates. Pat Collins' empire eventually embraced both worlds, and that is the concern of this chapter

Sometimes a showman's progress towards acquiring an amusement park was a gradual process - first appearing on the site as a tenant, then making a bid for the lease. Having obtained the lease, the space on the site could be let to others, and therefore not all the attractions in a park had to be provided by the proprietor. This can make the history of amusement parks just as complicated as the history of the travelling fairs, but for the purposes of this book we will simply try to describe the involvement of Pat Collins and Walsall John with such sites.

We begin by looking at the Crystal Palace site, in Sutton Park, in the Royal Borough of Sutton Coldfield, as the site was the nearest to the centre of Pat's empire. Then we proceed to New Brighton on the Wirral Peninsular, where the presence of the Collins' family seems to have been least documented, and then we take a look at the better known amusement parks at Great Yarmouth and Barry Island.

The New Brighton connection was severed by the mid 1920's, but from the early 1930's onwards, the other three sites played a part in the lives of Pat and Walsall John. Young Pat was involved for a short period and then established his own site at Colwyn Bay. Today, the name Pat Collins is still to be found at Barry Island, represented by a grandson and great-grandson still in the business.

THE CRYSTAL PALACE; SUTTON PARK

The Crystal Palace Amusement Park was one of Pat Collins' best known ventures into the world of amusement catering on a permanent site, but was probably his second such venture, having maintained some kind of permanent presence at New Brighton since the 1890's. However, the proximity of the Crystal Palace to Pat's headquarters gave it an important place in his empire. Pat's presence at the Crystal Palace certainly ensured that his name was indelibly linked in people's minds and associated with their trips to the park, and rides on the fair. Pleasurable nostalgia surrounds yesterday's simple pleasures, made all the more memorable because leisure time was most often at a premium.

Sutton Park consists of over two thousand acres of woodland and unspoilt heath, a few miles north east of Birmingham and the Black Country. The working population of the industrial areas travelled in great numbers to this open space at weekends and public holidays, and it became much more accessible with the growth of public transport. Many reached the park on foot, but the ride on the tram, the excursion train, or the charabanc, was part of the pleasure of the trip.

In 1868, a thirty acre site was opened by Job Cole as the Royal Promenade Gardens. He started fairly modestly with refreshment rooms, etc. and over the following decade, he and his sons developed the site considerably. In 1878 they promoted the Sutton Park Crystal Palace Company, and the main task of this company was to build the large glass-roofed pavilion that gave the site its name. It was claimed that it could accommodate two thousand people, and was built over vast cellars for stabling horses.

By the 1880's visitors were welcome to walk in the gardens, refresh themselves at the adjoining hotel, go boating on Wyndley Pool, or exercise themselves on a bicycle track. In the Crystal Palace itself, you were invited to "......*dance, or romp, or gambol....regardless of gloomy clouds and drenching rain outside*".

The Crystal Palace Company eventually went bankrupt, but others took over the lease, and parts of the grounds were sub-let to a variety of enterprises offering the public new attractions. A zoo arrived, making it very clear to its potential customers that it was not to be confused with the travelling menageries! Roundabouts and sideshows such as shooting galleries began to appear in the early years of this century. Some amusements in the grounds at that time could have been provided by Pat Collins.

In 1906 the Crystal Palace was condemned after an accident in which part of the floor collapsed, but the main part of the pavilion was to stand for more than half a century. The precise events of 1906 are not clear, but the lease on the grounds seems to have changed hands again. The "zoo" operated on the site by a Mr King, also closed with financial troubles in 1906 and it would seem that this may again have been a time of re-negotiating leases and sorting out who was going to do what on the site. One recent publication concerning the park states that Pat Collins acquired the lease on 23 March 1906, but it is not clear whether this applied to the whole site or just the part on which he was providing some amusements. It may be that Pat became the leaseholder but that he sublet the amusements to the Russells for the period from then until the Great War. In any case some of the Russells remained as tenants on the Crystal Palace site until 1961.

Sutton Park, Birmingham.

ABSOLUTELY THE "VENICE OF ENGLAND."
WITH AN UP-TO-DATE AMUSEMENT PARK.
SURROUNDED WITH NATURE'S BEAUTY, and within call of
ONE MILLION PEOPLE.

WANTED

ALL KINDS OF NEW RIDES, GAMES, SIDE SHOWS, AUTOMATICS, SPEED BOATS, ICE SKATING RINKS, DANCING, ETC.

This park will be under my personal direction and I will get you the crowds of people if you have the goods.

Apply :- PAT COLLINS JNR.,
c/o Pat Collins, Gondola Works, Walsall.

In 1907 the first miniature railway was laid down at the Crystal Palace. This was a 10 1/4" gauge line built by Miniature Railways of Great Britain Ltd., the brainchild of W.J.Bassett-Lowke and Henry Greenly, "Nipper" hauled the first train in Sutton Park's new line in June 1907. The following winter the railway was re-gauged to 15", and extended. The summer of 1908 saw a new locomotive, the "Mighty Atom", at work in the park.

Despite the success of the line, MRGB Ltd put it up for sale in 1912. It was bought by Pat Collins who continued to operate it right up until the First World War, when the park was put over to military use.

It is unclear what else, if anything, Pat Collins provided at the Crystal Palace in the years just before the war, or whether he left it entirely to the Russells, but if later policies are anything to go on, it seems probable that he 'retired' his older rides to the park as they ceased travelling.

After the First World War, Pat seems to have been quite keen to re-establish the amusement park, and by June 1919 he was able to announce its re-opening. His advertisements list the rides to be found there; A Switchback, the Joy-wheel, the Helter Skelter, Gondolas, Bicycles, Swingboats, sideshows etc.

Because the amusements were being offered on a fixed site, it is tempting to think of the attractions as being permanent, but of course they were changed, and taken in and out of the park when they were required for travelling. For a time the site was managed by R.H.Delaney, who had been associated with Pat Collins for many years. Mr Delaney was interviewed by a visiting correspondent of World's Fair in July 1920, and said,

"*We have well-drained the place, made new roadways and approaches, put in electric cables, and are putting down the rails for miniature railways. We shall have two Lilliputian trains which will tour round the pleasure park. The station will be in keeping with the line, and for picnics and pleasure parties it should provide endless enjoyment. When the railway is complete we shall then erect a gigantic Figure of Eight, and water Caves on the lake on which to run two or three motor boats. The existing amusement devices are the imposing Dragon Railway, the Switchback, the Joy Wheel, Gee Whizz, Swings, Shooters, Emmas, Sheets and sideshows.*"

The miniature railway was slowly revived, probably not re-opening until late in the summer of 1922. (What Mr Delaney meant when he described plans for railways, in the plural, is not clear). By 1924 it appears to have been abandoned again. The fortunes of all the equipment at the Crystal Palace seemed to face such vicissitudes, and at some stage the amusement park began to acquire the reputation of being a "dumping ground". By the 1950's this was institutionalised and part of the grounds became an "official" graveyard of Pat Collins equipment!

(World's Fair 25/1/30)

RIGHT: The Miniature Railway at Sutton Park before the First World War. The line was opened in this form in 1908, and was taken over by Pat Collins in 1912. The locomotive "The Mighty Atom" was built in 1908.
(Collection of John Sale)

RIGHT: The Miniature Railway in the 1950's, enjoying the care and attention of Tom Hunt, and his son Bill. The locomotive, "Sutton Belle" is being driven by John Ward, whose girlfriend, Serena, worked in the "Booking Office".
(Collection of John Tidmarsh)

RIGHT: The Coronation Dipper - the 1937 Scenic Railway seen amongst the trees of Sutton Park.
(Collection of John Sale)

Obviously as rides became difficult to travel, or less profitable, it made sense to "retire" them to an amusement park for a further lease of life. It was also a place where the younger members of the family could "cut their teeth". Pat Collins' grandson Pat (Baby Pat), recalled in an interview in 1990: *"I spent a couple of years at Sutton Coldfield. They used to say, 'If it's had it - put it at Sutton'. When I was there we had a Tunnel of Love, an old Dodgem track that had seen better days, and a set of Dragons that was my father's."* This must have been in the latter half of the 1920's.

Mr Delaney ran the park until his death at the end of 1934. He had given forty eight years' of service to Pat Collins, assisted by his wife for thirty of those years. Pat appointed a fellow Walsall Councillor, Danny Cartwright, to the post of Manager at the Crystal Palace in the Spring of 1935. Danny Cartwright had been at the Crystal Palace for seven years, and ran the children's boating pool. C.H.Lea, the World's Fair Birmingham correspondent, called in to see how Mr Cartwright was doing, and made the following report, published 31.August 1935:

"Pat Collins has, at Crystal Palace, a Switchback, a Scenic Railway, a Helter Skelter, a Dodgem Track, a Three Abreast, a Dragon Grotto, a Yo Yo and a Mirror Show, and there are all the usual attractions, swings, throwing games, arcades etc. Great developments are to take place at Crystal Palace...and all that is needed is the permission of the magisterial bench at Sutton Coldfield.

Mr Cartwright gave me permission to report the plans...These include a hotel, a zoo, a full licence, an extension of the amusements, and a publicity scheme which will bring so many people to Sutton Coldfield that the town will enjoy a prosperity it has never known.

I can remember that one of the great attractions at Crystal Palace was the miniature railway which ran through the wood, and I was glad to hear that this may be re-started in the near future.

I sincerely trust that permission will be granted for Pat Collins to go ahead, for I cannot see how this venture can possibly fail. With Mr Cartwright in command, success is assured."

Eventually, Walsall John took greater interest in Sutton Park, and devoted some of his restless energy to it. John's primary interest in gravity rides, ("Big Dippers") was reflected in the building of a new Dipper in early 1937, in time to open for that season. He also acquired more miniature railway equipment from Gt Yarmouth, and this was moved to Sutton during the winter of 1937/38. (See the Chapter on Gt Yarmouth). A new station was built for the "Pat Collins Express", and the line used part of the cycle track laid out in the days of the Royal Promenade Gardens. The line opened again in 1938 as the "Crystal Palace Railway", and a model engineer named Dudley Priestley was engaged to drive the train, which he did until about 1948. Billy Bagnall was also regarded as competent to drive the engine when required!

Billy Bagnall was a showman with his own equipment who gradually became associated with the Crystal Palace in the late 1930's. By the Second World War he was effectively the Manager, and looked after the site while the War was on. There was much coming and going of vehicles operated by fairground folk on war-work while the War was on, and the amusement park opened for business at some Wartime holiday periods.

The "Coronation Thriller", the gravity 'dipper' ride built in 1937 provides something of a mystery for the historian. Some reports indicate that it closed in 1939 when War broke out, and then fell into disrepair. However, a report of 1943 tells us that workers flocked to the fair as a relief from the long shifts and dislocation of war work, and the dipper was among the attractions they enjoyed. In the early years of the War Walsall John had moved to Sutton Coldfield, and it is possible that he restored the 1937 ride, or built a "new"

LEFT: The Scenic Railway at Sutton Park on 5 August 1950, not long before it was dismantled and taken to Battersea Park. The history of such rides is examined in Chapter 15.
(Collection of Kevin Scrivens)

one from parts obtained from Southport. (The dipper was the chief attraction at the park from 1946 to 1950, when it was moved to Battersea). The 1943 report also mentions the Brookland Speedway, Airways and Dodgems, the Looper and the miniature railway. The list of stall holders present contains the names of the folk who were to be associated with the park until its demise: Billy Bagnall, George Dobson, Mr Russell, George Strickland and Timmy Keyes.

John Collins (Walsall John) lived at Four Winds, Sutton Coldfield, and was well placed to keep an eye on the amusement park in the aftermath of Pat's death. However, it does not seem that there was much money available after the War to re-invest in the site. Clara and John decided, even before the War was over, that a ballroom would be a great attraction if it could be created within the Crystal Palace. Refurbishing the main hall was out of the question so John Collins purchased a Big Top marquee and it was erected in the great hall without using the poles - it was slung from the girders of the Crystal Palace roof! A portable maple dance floor was installed and the Dance Hall opened in 1945, and was a great success. Alec Hooper, a ballroom dancing champion managed the hall, until 1948.

There was still a tendency for some rides to come and go at Crystal Palace, while others came to "retire", and faded away! Ghost trains came and went, sometimes staying at the Park during the summer and then travelling the Back End fairs in the Autumn. In 1948, Walsall John was telling the Sutton News that it was still his intention to greatly expand and improve the Crystal Palace Amusement Park. In the spring of each year, as the park prepared to open to the public, the advertisements in the Sutton News generally stressed that "new" attractions were being provided. In the spring of 1950 the public were told that "new dips" had been added to the Big Dipper, there were new speedboats on the lake, and Pullman coaches on the miniature railway.

When the Crystal Palace was used as a Ballroom with Alex Hooper as Manager during the war years, there were Yanks stationed in Sutton Coldfield. Music was provided every Monday, Wednesday, Friday and Saturday, by Teddy Thomas and His Band, with vocalist, Jannett and trumpeter, Ronnie Hughes. After the war, Alex Hooper moved on to open his own Dance Studios in Birmingham.
The Band also played on the Home service for the BBC under the title "The Teddy Thomas Orchestra"..the dance band of the future. ("Jannett" is now **Mrs J Bent** of Solihull).

Mr Ted Ford (now living in the Isle of Wight) recalls a party he attended to celebrate victory after the 1914-18 War, probably in 1919. "We schoolchildren went to the Palace with 'Free' tickets for rides on the Swings-Roundabouts-Helter Skelter and others, not to mention the Miniature Railway, which ran from the Crystal Palace station through the park and back again to the fun fair. Afterwards we all attended the tea party-bunfight in the Crystal Palace itself, sitting down to lots of "goodies", a rare treat for many of us in those days.

Mr Norman H Beck describes himself as an old Suttonian, with pre-war memories of riding on the Miniature train out to Wyndley Pool and back from the Crystal Palace, in about 1920, when the fare was tuppence. He rode on the Big Dipper and played shove-halfpenny on lots of different stalls. Postwar, after demob from the RAF he and other young

BELOW: The "Tilt-a-Whirl" - a Waltzer-type riding machine at Sutton Park in the 1950's. Note J.J.Collins' Three-Abreast on the right, and the concrete stumps of the Scenic Railway.
(Collection of Arthur Jones)

LEFT: Traditional rides at the Crystal Palace: The Razzle Dazzle bought by John Collins to provide "olde tyme" entertainment for the visitors, photographed on 28 May 1950.
(Collection of Kevin Scrivens)

LEFT: The Steam Yachts at Sutton were little used when photographed in 1952.
(Collection of Rod Spooner)

LEFT: The Jack and Jill Glide seen at Sutton in 1952. The concrete stumps of the Big Dipper can be seen between the Glide and the Brooklyn Race Track.
(Collection of Rod Spooner)

men used to wend their way to the Crystal Palace Dance on Saturday night 'looking for the girls'....until he got married and 'that was that'. Mr Beck was a Gentlemen's Hairdresser in civvies, and about 1950 he recalls going to John Collins' fabulous house in Halloughton Road, Four Oaks, where he met their guest, Freddie Mills, the boxer, who was to give an exhibition fight at Crystal Palace. Occasionally, John Collins would visit the British Legion in Rectory, he would just walk in, and it would be 'drinks all round'.

After the Big Dipper's departure, the Collins' Three-Abreast Gallopers were built up at Sutton, managed by Walter Hobbs. He had been with Collins for forty years, having first worked on the No.2. "Wonderland Bioscope". (His father, Walter Hobbs Senior had married Flora Collins' sister). The Gallopers were taken out to the Onion Fair, across to Hull and back to the Carnival Fair and then returned to Sutton, but that was their last outing with Walter Hobbs, who died in 1947. Mick Green travelled them for a time until their final retirement to the Park, where they stayed until its closure.

After the Hull Fair of 1948, the Crystal Palace became the home of the No.1.Scenic Railway, first the object of some loving attention and restoration, then the subject of neglect and decay! It was brought from Bloxwich to Sutton by the engine "Lord Curzon", and when the ride was built up it was managed by Harry Passey. Early in 1950, the ex-Tuby organ was removed, and a new Chiappa 98 key organ was fitted behind the :"Wonderland" front. During 1951, while still running, much of the ride was repainted and redecorated.

The original Orton style was followed by a talented painter named Phil Ryon Hodnett who had worked for the firm since 1944.

In 1948, a new "Speedway" was built in the centre of the Big Dipper, and the petrol driven cars were maintained by Billy Templeton. John Collins also built an open air theatre at the Wyndley Pool end of the grounds and presented open-air variety shows featuring many artists and the Vernon Adcock Orchestra. The first show was opened by Freddie Mills, who shared John's interest in boxing. Freddie stayed at Sutton for a week and became a good friend of the family and the staff during that time.

After the Big Dipper was taken from Sutton to Battersea, in 1950, it appears that Walsall John virtually turned his back on the place and was never seen in Sutton again. Billy Bagnall was left to administer the park's last decade, generally marked by decline, despite intense periods of activity at bank holiday weekends.

The miniature railway on the other hand, underwent a reversal of its fortunes. In 1948 Clara and John agreed to sell the railway to Tom Hunt, engineer and businessman (of Hunt Brothers (Oldbury) Ltd.), who

BELOW: The No.1.Scenic was the pride of the Crystal Palace site, seen here in 1951 condition with front pillars removed for repainting. Note the portrait of Pat incorporated into the centre of the extension front.
(Collection of Arthur Jones)

was a long time friend of the Collins' family, and a steam enthusiast. As the Sutton Miniature Railway the line enjoyed a successful renaissance. (The full story is told in "The Sutton Coldfield 15" Gauge Railway" by John Tidmarsh, Plateway Press 1990).

By the end of the 1950's the writing was on the wall, despite the variety of rides and amusements still to be found there. A 'lake' was formed by stretching a wall between the concrete foundations of the departed dipper, and motorboats were provided. For one season the lake was left "dry" and some cycles that had been found in tbe Crystal Palace cellar were provided instead. The Dodgems, managed by Tommy Draper, stood opposite the miniature railway station. In the winter the cars were stored in the ballroom, as the Dodgem track space was used to work on repairs to other rides.

In the row of rides behind the Dodgems, was the Dragon Scenic, gradually looking more and more 'the worse for wear'. It was operated by George Corbett, and later, George Sutton ("Tarzan"). There were some "Comets" operated by Jack Mack, the site electrician, or his daughter, and then there was a Waltzer which was also in poor condition. In the corner was a well presented set of Chairoplanes owned by Albert Martin, Billy Bagnall's son-in-law, and a Ghost train. By the side of the Crystal Palace itself stood the old steam yachts, rather infrequently used, and Timmy Keyes' "Shooter". Nothing appeared from Barry, and Gallopers came and went. Rides belonging to Billy Bagnall, were likely to come and go anyway, because he was still travelling rides while managing the Park

Visitors to the park at the end of the fifties remember seeing all kinds of fairground equipment resting in the graveyard. In one place a tree seemed to have grown through the remains of an organ, and the cellars beneath the dance floor in the Crystal Palace probably contained all kinds of relics. A large quantity of organ paper music was salvaged, but the remains of a Bioscope frontage and parts of various rides were destroyed.

The Dragon Scenic was carefully dismantled at the end of the 1960 season and it was rumoured that Clara Collins was keen that it should be preserved as the last surviving Orton & Spooner Scenic Railway. Tom Hunt took the Wonderland organ away for restoration and the components of the ride were stacked to await their fate. The lease on the Crystal Palace site could not be renewed in 1962, because the Council had an alternative use for the land. No-one seems to have expressed a desire to find a new site for the amusements, let alone establish a museum where the Dragon Scenic might be preserved. The 1962 season itself was very wet, and to add to the gloom, Clara died in the September, as the park's season was drawing to a close. Some of the equipment joined Billy Bagnall's rides in being transferred to a site at Chasewater, but much had to be scrapped.

Barry Island Pat, then seventeen years of age, helped Young Tarzan and Albert Martin burn the remains of the Dragon Scenic.

On 7 October 1962, the last train ran on the Sutton Park Miniature Railway, and the railway was promptly dismantled and all the equipment moved into storage...where it has remained to this day.

The only Phoenix to rise from the ashes of the Crystal Palace has been the Wonderland Organ, and it rests today in the care of Tom Hunt's son, Bill (Managing Director of Hunt Brothers (Oldbury)Ltd and is probably in better condition now than when it was new.

The Crystal Palace site was, eventually redeveloped.

NEW BRIGHTON

Pat Collins' association with New Brighton is also something of a mystery. New Brighton is in the northern part of Wallasey...over the Mersey from Liverpool.

In February 1920 Young Pat wrote a letter to the Editor of World's Fair discussing the family's presence at New Brighton: *"I beg to point out that my Grandfather and Father have been coming to New Brighton for the past fifty years, being an old Cheshire family....I am a property owner in New Brighton, and two of my children were born there. My Father was a tenant of the place for twenty five years under the late Mr.Connelly - before the Corporation took over."*

It is not clear whether Young Pat was referring to the complex between Virginia Road and the Marine Promenade, the site of which the Palace/Gaiety cinema was a part, or the amusement complex by the Tower Promenade, where the famous New Brighton Tower was built in 1896/7. The evidence suggests the former, and, if so, it was a site that was developed in the early 1880's. This site did, indeed, become the property of Wallasey Corporation in 1906. It seems that Young Pat may have leased it from the Corporation soon afterwards, ie. the period from 1906 to 1913). But what is interesting is Young Pat's claim that the Collins' family had such a long association with the site. In fact, it is one of the rare and mystifying references to the generation preceding Pat, and a glimpse of Pat's Father, John, as a travelling showman.

Another comment on early days at New Brighton is made by Pat himself, in the Newport Advertiser interview quoted in Chapter 3.

Young Pat goes on, *"...After the Corporation took over, they turned it over to me, and I had it for seven years, until Mr. Wilkie got it by making a higher bid, which meant that I had to clear out at a considerable loss"*

Young Pat is, in fact, writing to World's Fair to explain that he has just acquired a three-year lease on the site by outbidding George Wilkie, and he cannot understand why George Wilkie is complaining about all this, when he, Pat, had been so philosophical about it all when the situation had been reversed on the earlier occasion! The consequences are illustrated in advertisements that appear in following editions of World's Fair. George Wilkie advertises equipment for sale, and Young Pat offers "space to let", stating that his Pavilion, Palace, and Palace Ground will open two weeks' before Easter.

It seems that Young Pat only ran the site for the duration of the three year lease, 1920-1923. An impression of the New Brighton site during this period is given in a report by H.M.Jay in the World's Fair of 18 June 1921.

OPPOSITE: The No.1.Scenic seen at the Crystal Palace in 1954. (Compare with picture on previous page). The Juvenile roundabout has also been repainted, and on the right are the Comets.
(Collection of Arthur Jones)

ABOVE: The site at New Brighton, said to be photographed in 1913. Beyond the Motor Car Switchback and the Yachts is one of the early wagon fronted shows, thought to be presenting a Menagerie.
(Collection of Kevin Scrivens)

"Collins' enterprises are in all their summer glory - waiting for the rush of holidaymakers - a credit to their owners and tenants. The riding machines have all got the Collins' hallmark, and include Dragons, Motor Cars, Three-Abreast, and a new ride built by Albert Barnes of Rhyl: The Dash. There are Cycles, the Slip, and Swings, and the stalls, all branded by Pat Collins Jnr, include Derby Racers, Monkey Climbers, Sailing Yachts and Shooters. George Clowes has his Waxworks and Automatics."

Mr. Jay also admired Joe Caddick's famous veteran living wagon, in which he had 'retired' to the New Brighton site, and the Gaiety Picture House. The building used as a cinema or theatre had been known as the Gaiety for some time, but during Young Pat's second tenure it became "Collins' Palace Cinema". After remaining closed during 1924 and 1925 the cinema had a further short burst of life in 1926, and then remained dormant like the rest of the site during the latter half of the 1920's. The site saw some use as a motor-coach park until about 1933 when it was re-developed as "the New Amusement park".

In conclusion, our suggestion is that Pat presented attractions at New Brighton as a tenant up until 1906. From 1906 to 1913 it was part of the Collins empire, and again from 1920 to 1923. After that time Pat had no further connection with the site, and Young Pat gradually disentangled himself from his interests in the area.

YARMOUTH PLEASURE BEACH

The Collins' association with Great Yarmouth, way out on the East Anglian coast, seems to belong to the same period as his association with Barry Island, a period at the end of the 1920's, when Pat's two sons were able to take on a supervisory role in new areas of business. In particular, Walsall John seems to have found his feet in Gt Yarmouth, enjoying the early years of married life with a home in the town, and having the opportunity in the amusement park to develop his taste for novelty rides and fairground thrills. Walsall John then travelled some of these attractions through the Back End fairs. (On the other hand Young Pat's supervision of the Barry Island park was more short-lived, and was followed by his "retreat" to his own ground at Colwyn Bay).

The first Great Yarmouth Beach Pleasure Park was opened on 24 July 1909 with a limited number of attractions, and was greatly extended in the early 1920's. The land on which it stood was leased from the local council and in late 1928 they accepted an offer of £3,500 per year from Pat Collins for the lease. In moving into Yarmouth for the 1929 season, Pat and his son John were anticipating what the firm would be doing at Barry Island one year later.

BELOW: Pat Collins' Pleasure beach Amusement Park at Great Yarmouth, 1929. The Jackson-built "Hey-Dey" is in the foreground, and in the distance can be seen the Water Chute and Figure of Eight which has the front from the G.T.Tuby Scenic fitted in front of it.
(Collection of Kevin Scrivens)

RIGHT: Burrell "No.1", photographed in June 1952, decorated and prepared for taking part in Bloxwich Carnival.
(Photo Stan Webb)

RIGHT: Foster 14446 "The Leader" as preserved by Bill Hunt, seen here in the early 1980's at Much Marcle. "The Leader" was the last engine to work commercially on the fairground when it retired in 1958. After restoration Bill Hunt took the engine to Nottingham Goose Fair in 1981 to generate power for the Wonderland Organ. In 1985 it powered Anthony Harris' Waltzer for three days non-stop.
(Photo Bill Hunt)

RIGHT: The Wonderland Organ and accompanying Scammell at the Dorset Steam Fair 1990.
(Photo Ned Williams)

During 1929 the park was upgraded with new attractions, including Sam Naishstad's "Globe of death". When Thomas Jackson, of Macclesfield, announced in September 1929 that they would be importing a new ride called the "Hey Dey", one was ordered for Yarmouth Pleasure Beach, thus ensuring that the new innovations would continue in anticipation of the 1930 season.

In the summer of 1930, World's Fair reported the presence of the Auto Speedway and a large Midget Motor Car Track (both as "popular as ever"), the Skid, Toy Taxis and the Globe of Death on the position previously occupied by the Jolly Tubes. The main ride in the centre avenue was Barron's "Whirl-a-Car", and the top end featured Walkers' Water Chute and Collins' Glide. The "Mighty Figure of Eight" was still there, but an ornate frontage that had been in place in 1929 had disappeared, and it was noted that a "Bobsleigh Slip" crossed the front of the Figure of Eight. The "Hey Dey" left Yarmouth towards the end of the season to be "travelled".

Henry Rymer visited Gt Yarmouth in 1931, to keep readers of World's Fair up to date. He told them, *"This season the Pleasure Beach looks a picture of brightness in a red and white colour scheme...On the left there is a galvanised roof-shed, 800.ft. in length, the longest straight stretch in the country. Here ball games predominate. The north side is bounded by a Ghost Train, the caves, variety shows, automatics, skee-ball and American boxball. In the centre we find Lussé cars by General Amusements, and Custer cars by Miller, Autocars, and a few joints for spinners and other games.*

At the west end is a Collins' Figure of Eight, a big slide, and a very fine miniature railway with steam engine, electric signals and a miniature Paddington Station."

The search for new rides led to a desire to replace the "Figure of Eight", and a new gravity ride was found at an exhibition in Paris. It was 580.ft. long and 80.ft. high, and several German workers came over to Yarmouth to assist in its reconstruction. Two English brothers were instructed to learn the trade: Harry and Edward Wadbrook, who thus became the British experts on the construction of the German scenic railways and "Big Dippers". Their expertise was used several times by Walsall John, who was also making this kind of ride his speciality. The Scenic Railway at Yarmouth opened for the summer of 1932, and was a great success.

Another new attraction was the Water Dodgem, which John had taken to Hull fair in October 1932. This was taken to Yarmouth for the 1933 season, where it joined the Auto-skooters, a Skid, a Caterpillar, Ghost Train, Jack & Jill slide, the miniature railway, and a number of juvenile rides. There were plenty of stalls and games, and shows included Marionettes, two Whales, and Sam Naishstad's Globe of Death, ridden by Henri Corbiere and his daughter. In the following years other innovative attractions made their debut at the Pleasure Beach, like the Loop o Plane and the Brooklands Racetrack.

A comment made in World's Fair on 28th March 1936 gives us clear indication that Walsall John's restless spirit could not be contained by the demands of the Pleasure Beach: *"Although John Collins is kept busy in other parts of the country he is in constant touch with what is going on at the Pleasure Beach"*. We learn that Mr J.R.Minns is the manager "on site", and after noting the extensions, alterations and redecoration, credit is given to *"John Collins, and the Wadbrook boys"*.

In 1937 John built a Dipper at Sutton park, followed by the one at the Glasgow Exhibition. While John's life was increasingly spent away from Great Yarmouth, we should not forget that the amusement parks were managed under the watchful eye of the Guvnor. In his seventies he still liked to be seen to be in charge. For example, in early September 1936, Pat and Clara made a "tour of inspection" of Yarmouth Pleasure Beach, and told the World's Fair reporter that all was well.

At the end of the 1930's, Walsall John's family home was moved to Barry Island, presumably in anticipation of becoming the proprietor of the amusement park. However, the progress of the War led to the family settling in Sutton Coldfield. He was then no longer concerned with the day to day supervision of the Yarmouth Pleasure Beach.

When the lease on the Pleasure Beach expired in 1952, it was renewed by John Collins, but he was by then absorbed by his other commitments, and the new fair at Battersea Park. At both parks there were rides presented by the Botton Brothers, and they took over the Yarmouth lease from John. The Botton Brothers did much to update and improve the park until it changed hands again in the mid 1970's.

It is difficult to assess the importance to the Collins' firm that the Great Yarmouth Pleasure Beach made, during the quarter of a century they were associated...it was certainly the most remote part of the empire! One strange contribution that Yarmouth makes to the Collins' story concerns the eventual regeneration of the Miniature Railway at Sutton Park...apparently abandoned by the Collins' in the mid 1920's, after its brief Post-War revival.

The year after Pat and Walsall John took control at Yarmouth, a Richard Parkinson installed a miniature railway at the park. It opened late in the 1929 season, and was then much improved for the 1930 and 1931 seasons. It was well built and well run, but by the second half of the 1930's it was losing money, and it closed at the end of the 1937 season. Mr Parkinson sold all the track, equipment, and locomotives etc. to Pat Collins. Although the Vendor was in his eighties, he then organised the transfer of the railway to Sutton Park and oversaw its rebuilding in the Midlands. It was open, in part, in May 1938! No-one has been able to explain why Pat and John decided to re-open the railway at Sutton yet again. A possible explanation may be that Walsall John having an interest in the railway, and knowing the aged proprietor was losing money at Yarmouth saw an opportunity to acquire it at a good price, and thought it could be used at Sutton Park, as a way of re-invigorating the line.

'Brummies' visiting the Crystal Palace in 1938 and 1939 may have wondered why the little locomotive's tender bore the letters "Y.M.R", but that, at least, can be explained once it is realised that the Collins' empire encompassed such far-off places as Gt Yarmouth!

The other Yarmouth contribution to the Collins' story concerns the German Big Dipper. Young Walsall John had an insatiable desire for new rides and novelties that he could introduce to the amusement business, and "Big Dippers" were something he could make "his own". The ride at Yarmouth provided the inspiration for the massive Dipper he built for the Glasgow Empire Exhibition of 1938. The ride at Glasgow was rebuilt at Barry Island, and by 1940 he was building a Roller Coaster at the Golden Gate Exhibition in San Francisco. In turn, Sutton's second Dipper went to Battersea Park, and rides were built in the lunar Park at Rome, and at the 1958 Brussels Exhibition. And all this sprang from the search for new rides to install at Great Yarmouth!

BARRY ISLAND

The town of Barry, and Barry Island, on the South Wales coast, not far from Cardiff are roughly 150 miles from Bloxwich - the centre of Pat Collins' empire.

Why did Pat Collins build a permanent pleasure park so far from the rest of his operations? The answer is bound to lead to an interesting story.

Barry grew into an industrial town with the arrival of the Barry Railway, and by the beginning of this century it was both a railway town and a major coal exporting port. As in the Black Country, the needs of the large working class population included recreation and leisure. The town's coastal position made it ideally placed to become a "resort" - a place for day excursions to the sea. The railway was extended to Barry Island in 1896, and to the Pier in 1899. The beach at Whitmore Bay, and the dunes behind the beach, connected to the "mainland" by a causeway that carried the road and railway, became a popular destination. A switchback railway was built on the island, and in 1912, a "Figure of Eight" railway. The First World War interrupted the gradual development of the area.

But none of this had anything to do with Pat Collins.

There is one word that explains how Pat came to Barry: "Opposition". Pat had become a successful showman by defeating his competitors. A man who had once had to fight for his pitches did not mellow in his attitude towards opposition, nor did the rules of the Guild cover all situations. Or at least not quickly enough for Pat! For instance, when "opposition" opened once in Wednesbury, Pat summoned rides from far afield and built up overnight on adjoining land. The next day all rides on Pat's fair were free! The "opposition" soon learned that they were not likely to make any money on territory Pat regarded as solely his own.

Pat regularly presented a fair in the park at Evesham, but one year he discovered he had been "gazumped" by the White brothers who had put in a higher bid for the lease of the fair. Pat was not pleased. "Who are these White people?" he asked. The reply was "They come from the sand dunes at a place called Barry Island". He did not forget.

Meanwhile..back at Barry Island...the area had continued to grow and after the War the promenade and sea wall were built and completed in 1923. Whites' fair moved off the beach and onto the ground surrounding the "Figure of Eight". The 1920's were a time of slump in the coal trade, but White brothers ran a successful pleasure park on this land - leased from the Whitmore Bay Pavilion Syndicate Company. Pat probably made his first appearance at Barry Island by being a tenant in Whites' Amusement Park. It seems that about 1927 he brought the Midget Motors to the site, and these were managed for him by Mr Winchester, aided by Nic Walls and Flossie Williams.

When the White Brothers came to renew their lease for the 1930 season, they found they had been "gazumped" by...Patrick Collins of Walsall!

The Whites vacated the site in February 1930, and moved across the road to the "Cosy Corner" site. Pat had arrived in Barry Island.

Although this legend explains Pat's arrival in Barry Island solely in terms of "opposition", it has to be admitted that Pat had been looking for a permanent seaside amusement park during the 1920's. Barry Island and Great Yarmouth might simply have just happened at the right time. There is evidence, for example, that he was just as keen to acquire a site in Blackpool, but he had been outbid.

As in all established railway towns there were some Chapel folk who had no love of the fair, and opposed Sunday opening, but the day excursionists had their way and the amusement caterers prospered as charabanc trips added to the numbers coming by rail. Pat fought a minor battle over "Sunday opening" and eventually "won", but there had been several Sundays when the site had prepared to open, only to remain closed at the last minute.

During the first season Young Pat took control of letting space at Barry Island, but before long a competent manager was found in the person of Mr.C.C.Bertram, a well-known showland figure. Rides and shows were retired to Barry Island, as they were to other fixed sites, one early example being Flora's Menagerie; that went to Barry during the early 1930's, but the pleasure parks also had their share of new and exciting attractions, and novelty rides.

An expansive advertising campaign was started to persuade Day Trippers to come to Pat Collins' Amusement Park...from far afield...and by the mid-thirties the numbers had broken records year after year. Outside the railway station was a huge sign saying, "Pat Collins invites you to Barry Island", and at the back of the site was a car park, and even a car-repair bay where mechanics could carry out repairs to your car, while you went to enjoy the amusement park!

The World's Fair correspondent visited the park in July 1937 and the lengthy report produced, included the following:-

"Riding machines are the most important exhibits, and I was glad to see that Messrs Pat and John Collins' Whirlwind Racer has been positioned in place of honour. Built by Orton & Spooner, it does not take up a lot of space, yet it affords its owners a grand chance to recoup themselves, for each of the lengthy cars holds a dozen passengers. It has become a general favourite with the trippers.

Next on my list was the Water Chute, the first in South Wales, although there is now a second at Porthcawl. With the top platform rising high in the air, it is a landmark for miles around, and a joy to behold when illuminated by hundreds of lights.

New to the Principality, the petrol driven cars of John Collins' Brookland Racing Track, occupies the chief position in the park. No ground is complete without an old-style ride, and it was a happy thought when Mr Collins resolved to erect his Three-Abreast alongside the petrol car track. The beauty of the decorations of this pre-war machine is something to enthuse over, for in those days Showland painters knew how to capture the imagination of the public.

The Figure of Eight, is a massive erection, controlled by the Thompson Scenic Company, and is painted green and white to harmonise with the surrounding scenic effects. Many people consider that such a ride is too risky to participate in, but it is to the credit of the staff that there has never been a single mishap since it was built.

Pat Collins' extra large Dodgem Track replaces the Water Dodgems of a year or two ago. The cars seemed as if they had just left the maker, so smartly were they painted. The final giant of the central section of the ground was the Ghost Train. Positioned above the platform was a flash depicting a ghost-like figure wrecking two trains, which were rushing through the darkness. Arcs are playing on to the picture, and the scene in the evening was really majestic.

BELOW: "Evesham Park" - Barry Island about 1930, while the skyline was still dominated by the Figure of Eight.
(Collection of Brian Luxton)

Novelties and sideshows include Moby Dick, the fifty foot whale, the Ruxton Murder Exhibits, where Mr.Booth-Royd tells the story in a way that gives no cause for complaint, E.A.Smith's House of Laughter, and, paying a welcome return, is the Globe of death, featuring Speedy Hendry and "Cyclone Bill" Hendry."

The report goes on to list the stallholders and arcades of "automatics", the caterers and the palmists, and the rides provided by tenants - the Caterpillar (John Iles), the Whip (George Green) and the Mono Rail (Harry Saunt).

Later in 1937 Barry Island was in the news when Cyclone Bill from the Globe of Death married Rose McArdle on 1st August at Cardiff Registry Office. They were married in their motor-cycling clothes, and newspapers had to keep a straight face as they told their readers that "Speedy Hendry was the Best Man, and Dare Devil Jerry the Bridesmaid"!

In 1938, John Collins organised the building of a huge scenic railway, or "Big Dipper", at the Empire Exhibition at Glasgow. It was 50.ft.long, 150.ft.wide, 100.ft.high, and offered a mile long ride. It was traversed by five trains, each carrying thirty people. After the Glasgow Exhibition, it was dismantled and taken to the World's Fair at Liege, Belgium. It was hurriedly evacuated from Belgium when War broke out and was brought to Barry Island, replacing the old "Figure of Eight". It took three months to build up the six hundred tons of Columbian pine timbers, and it was said that the ride had cost John Collins £25,000. Naturally enough, it became the best known feature of Barry Island. In the 1930's the park also contained a set of Gallopers, the Caterpillar, the Dodgems, and a Whip, and some of these rides travelled the Back End fairs. Nothing is really "permanent" in an amusement park.

At the very end of the 1930's Walsall John moved his family's permanent home from Great Yarmouth to Barry Island, although the term 'permanent home is perhaps a misnomer when describing the life of someone as restless as Walsall John!

Pat then sold the Barry Island Park to Walsall John, but the possibility of the Barry Docks being bombed during the war and again led John to move his family.....this time to Bloxwich, and then to Sutton Coldfield.

The Barry Island site was not therefore part of Pat's estate when he died in 1943 - it already belonged to John. However, the leases on the Crystal Palace site and Great Yarmouth Pleasure Beach were part of the estate, and John took responsibility for them, while Clara managed the travelling fairs. The parks provided a place where showmen could "retire", as well as a place for retiring rides. Therefore there were always senior showmen to be found to assist in the day to day management of the sites. For example, Bill Mullett, (Clara's brother) had 'retired' to Barry, and John had trusted managers in the form of Len Smith and Mr. Collier.

BELOW: The entrance to the park at Barry Island in 1937, decorated for the Jubilee. The new Whirlwind Racer can be seen on the left.
(Collection of Eileen Cook)

Walsall John's family grew up in the world of the fixed site fairs, because their home was at Sutton Coldfield...at one time they just had to go through the gate at the bottom of the garden and they were in the park..and running to the Crystal Palace site which was their playground in the school holidays, and an early introduction to the business.

Today Walsall John's son, Patrick, runs the Barry Island site, and his son, also named Patrick has joined the business, which connects four generations of Collins' with Barry.

When Patrick left school in 1962, he came to look after Barry Island with his older brother John, and to distinguish them from all the other Pats and Johns they are referred to as "Barry Island John" and "Barry Island Pat". They took over the park, from their father, in 1966, just as their father had taken it over from Pat, and in 1969 they were able to buy the freehold of the site from the Whitmore Bay Pavilion Syndicate.

Since then, the contents of the park have changed many times, ensuring the Park is at the forefront of providing the latest and best rides - in the tradition established by their grandfather.

The huge scenic railway was dismantled in 1973. In 1976, a new Log Flume was planned, which took four years to materialise. The tradition of travelling some of the rides at the Back End Fairs has continued, and Barry Island Pat has taken novelty rides to such places as Ashby, the Onion Fair, Burton, the Goose Fair, Hull, Ilkeston, and back to Birmingham for the Carnival Fair.

On Walsall John's death in 1977 the travelling side of the business was left to his children, but the brothers were already the owners of the Park.

Subsequently, Barry Island Pat bought out his brother's interest in the park, and thus sixty years after Pat's arrival there, the park is still owned by a Pat Collins .....his grandson

Barry Island Pat now only travels to the Goose Fair and Hull, but at Barry Island itself a link with the past is maintained by the presence of "The Major", the Scammell "Showtrac", new in 1947, and still owned by the same family nearly half a century later.

BELOW: A 1930 advertisement seeks tenants for the new park at Barry Island, and a 1921 advertisement informs visitors of what is to be found at the Crystal Palace. (*World's Fair, 1930 and Walsall Red Book 1921*)

SPACES TO LET.

The Sensation of 1930.

The New "Evesham" Pleasure Park, Barry Island, South Wales.

The Most Glorious Seaside and Golden Sands in all Wales.

NOW YOU SHOWMEN AND OPERATORS—BRING OUT YOUR NEW STUFF & YOUR LATEST SENSATIONAL STUNTS AS WE HAVE

SPACES TO LET

SHARES OR RENTAL, FOR

New Rides, Games, Automatics, Shows, Death Riders, Ice Skating Rinks, Dancing.

In fact, anything new to South Wales.

KIOSKS FOR SWEETS, TOYS, TOBACCO, & SOFT DRINKS.

The G.W.R. alone carries Forty Thousand Trippers into Barry Island every day of the Season.

OPEN EASTER FOR THREE DAYS, THEN COMMENCING FOR THE SEASON ON WHIT SATURDAY! AND WHAT CROWDS!

All Stall space under cover. Huge covering for the crowds.

THE STATION AND CHARABANCS EMPTY THEM RIGHT ON OUR PARK.

We get them first, last and all the time.

DON'T BE LEFT OUT, GET BUSY AT ONCE AND APPLY.

PAT COLLINS, Junr., c/o PAT COLLINS, GONDOLA WORKS, WALSALL.

CRYSTAL PALACE

Amusement Park.

SUTTON COLDFIELD

Proprietor — — Mr. Pat COLLINS.

Open from Easter to September each year FROM 10 a.m. to 10 p.m. DAILY

This Amusement Park is the only place of its kind in the Midlands, there being nothing like it within 100 miles. Both the London & North-Western & Midland Railway run to it. Also Trams & Motor 'Buses take you almost to the entrance gates.

All the Latest & Most Up-to-date Amusements, including :—

DRAGON SCENIC RAILWAY. SWITCHBACK RAILWAY.
HOUSE OF LAUGHTER.   GREAT AMERICAN JOY WHEEL.
MINIATURE RAILWAY.   JUVENILE ROUNDABOUTS.

Also BOATING ON THE LAKE Adjoining.

Light Refreshments can be obtained in the Palace Grounds. Schools and Parties Catered for

For a thorough day's Healthy Recreation & Enjoyment, one should not fail to visit the above Amusement Park.

For further information and particulars, apply :—

P. COLLINS, GONDOLA WORKS, WALSALL.

BIOSCOPES TO CINEMAS

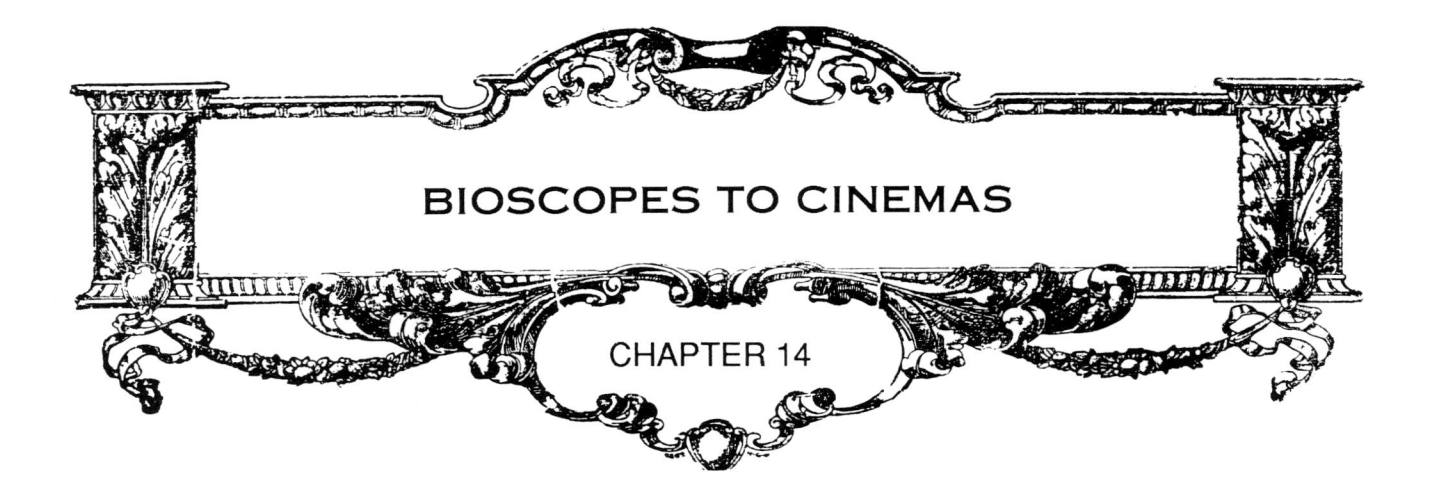

CHAPTER 14

The wonder of 'moving pictures' was quickly exploited on the fairground, through shows known as "Bioscopes".

These are looked at separately since Pat Collins' interest in moving pictures led him later on to invest in Cinemas, and subsequently in theatres, skating rinks and dance halls, seen to be an extension of his involvement in amusement catering on permanent sites.

When cinematography was demonstrated in London in early 1896, the fairground world was already well prepared to exploit the novelty, and wasted no time in doing so. There already existed a number of travelling shows. Some of these were waxworks, freakshows, marionettes, circus acts and animal shows, but others were specialists in various optical illusions and lighting effects - the ghost shows, the myrioramas and dioramas, magic lantern shows etc. It was a fairly natural step for some of the shows to move into cinematography.

Some pictures were shown in booths constructed at ground level, and were fairly small, while others were much larger using the showmen's wagons to form a frontage to the "auditorium", and incorporating refinements like stages, seating etc.,...One or two shows had underfloor heating! The frontage itself incorporated a stage, and steps were provided so that customers could mount the stage, stop at the paybox and pass into the show.

The manager of the show was known as the "Doorsman", and one of his duties was to drum up an audience with his spiel delivered from the stage. He was assisted by a "stepman" who would take part in the rituals of launching each show and regulate access to the paybox via the steps.

The first Bioscopes are seen with the steps in the centre, the organ incorporated into the frontage on the left, and the engine standing on the right. These were called the "wagon-fronted" shows to distinguish them from the subsequent generation of Bioscopes featuring the organ in the centre of the frontage, with steps, payboxes and entrances on either side. The accompanying engine moved to the side of the show, and these were known as the "organ-fronted" shows. The early shows used limelight to project a picture and naptha flares for illumination. Electricity, produced by the engine's dynamo, replaced the flares, and carbon arcs produced improved light output from the projectors on the later shows.

By the summer of 1896 a showman named Randall Williams had a Bioscope on the road, and he was followed by a number of other showmen, sometimes presenting it as the latest fairground attraction, sometimes travelling independently of fairs. This was a period when Pat Collins was rising fast as an important showman, investing in new rides and keen to exploit technological advances and so on, but he does not seem immediately to have joined the rush to own a Bioscope. In fact he may have waited to see if he felt such investment was justified. In 1898 when there were five Bioscopes present at the Nottingham Goose Fair, Pat was content to present a Lion Show, though this may well have been somebody else's show presented in Pat's name.

In November 1898, Randall Williams, pioneer of the travelling Bioscope shows, died, but his adopted sons, Richard Monte and James Monte carried on the business in his name. It seems that about this time Pat acquired his first Bioscope, but the sequence of events is obscure.

Certainly Bioscope shows were being seen in the Black Country and other areas where Pat presented his fairs, well before the turn of the century. For example, in July 1898, Captain Walter Payne was presenting his Bioscope show on land by the Market in Bilston, when there was an 'incident'.

To produce the limelight, a stream of burning hydrogen was directed onto a cone of lime. The projectionist then had to gradually introduce a stream of oxygen, and if he did so too rapidly it caused a slight explosion blowing the rubber hose off the gas jet. These circumstances could be safely handled by a competent operator but were known to alarm the audience!

About 500 people were in Captain Payne's Bioscope

when such an explosion occurred. Someone shouted "FIRE" and the audience panicked. Captain Payne (who was by the projector) could have extinguished the fire immediately but he rushed from the projection booth judging that it was more important to deal with the panic in the audience. Several women were crushed, and some fainted, as there was a stampede to the six emergency exits, but there was no serious injury and Captain Payne restored order.

Afterwards people spoke with great admiration for the way he had quietened the crowd and directed their exit. Meanwhile the fire engulfed his machine, his supply of films, and then burned the canvas roof of his booth. Undaunted by £500 worth of damage Captain Payne told the press he hoped to be back in business by the end of the week.

Whether Pat Collins, only a few miles away in Walsall, took note of such incidents there is no way of knowing.

Pat appears to have been the kind of showman who was primarily more interested in "riding machines" than presenting "shows". At a Pat Collins' fair of the 1890's the shows were usually presented by others, some became very well known, eg. Bostock's Menagerie and Parker's Ghost Show. In 1899, the advertisements for Bloxwich Wakes (or "Fete and Gala", as we ought to call it!) a Bioscope show was being presented by "Professor" Wall.

At the turn of the century Pat 'took the plunge' and purchased Wall's Show. For the next decade he presented his own Bioscopes, but quite how many he presented is a mystery; some interested parties declare he owned six different shows, though probably not all at the same time.

The history of the Bioscope is a badly documented subject, and confusing. In particular it has not been possible to identify the two shows sold to Mr.Bliss and Mr.Irwin mentioned in a "Merry-go-Round" article (Vol.7.No.6), or the show destroyed by fire, according to a Fairground Jottings article (No.16). The two organ-fronted shows of the second half of the 1900's are however more easily identifiable than the early wagon-fronted shows.

Some conclusions reached are set out below as something of a trail blazer awaiting more light to be shed on the subject.

B1 Ex-Wall and Hammersley Ghost Show
The Wall's cinematograph appearing at Bloxwich Wakes in 1899 was not the original Ghost Show frontage. That front had been destroyed by fire, its replacement was converted to Bioscope use in 1897, in the first rush of enthusiasm for the new invention. It was a two-wagon fronted show, with large central entrance and an organ (probably a Gavioli) to the left hand side, protected by a blind ....and to the right of the entrance was a portable electric light engine. (As Wall's Phantascope in the mid 1890's, see picture featured on p.4. of Peter Wilke's book "The Great Nottingham Goose Fair", Trent Valley Publications,1989).

Pat is said to have purchased it upon Henry Hammersley's retirement at the end of 1899, or beginning of 1900. Although the name Collins was added to the frontage above the entrance, very little else was changed at first, and it can be seen in another Goose Fair photograph with the word "Wall's" still visible on the orb of one of the lamps.

So...at the 1900 Bloxwich Wakes, the Cinematograph Show is included in the equipment presented by Pat Collins. The advertisement for the Wakes tells us that the films shown included scenes of the Boer War, and "Local Views of Works in the District". Many early Bioscope pioneers made their own films of local people and events, and this is proof that Pat's show did likewise. Unfortunately, there is no proof that Pat himself handled a cine-camera or developed any personal interest in cinematography. He did not become a member of the Cinema Veterans Association, which consisted of pre-1903 film-makers, and presumably the films and presentation of the Bioscope were entirely in the hands of a manager.

When the riding machines became the property of "P.Collins Ltd.," there are indications that the ex-Walls Bioscope became the property of Flora Collins, or, at least was under her management. Flora appears to have installed an 87 or 89 key Marenghi organ. The portable electric light engine was made redundant in 1904, with the arrival of Burrell road locomotive No.2713, "His Majesty", which was regarded as Flora's engine, and was later associated with moving her living van.

After the First World War the frontage was put to use as Flora's Lion Show and Menagerie. (See Ch. 15)

B2 The Second Wagon-fronted Show
A second Bioscope show was added in 1901 or 1902, and is believed to be the showfront built by Savage of Kings Lynn which was presented at Hull fair in 1898. It was made for travel by rail, and the two front wagons had to be built up on gantries. It was completed by a Gavioli organ (probably an 87 key model), and a Savage portable electric light engine in the usual positions. It appears to have been sold in 1905, to Seager & Scott, when the firm acquired a new wagon-fronted show.

B3 The "New" Wagon-fronted Show
At the Lichfield Shrovetide Fair in 1905 a new Bioscope was presented. The Era reported that Pat Collins had filled the Market Square, and "Their chief attraction was an entirely new cinematograph exhibition - certainly the very best seen in the district". This is possibly the show that appears under various names (eg the Electric Kosmograph) until the arrival of the organ-fronted shows of 1907. In 1906 it appears as presented by P.Collins & Sons, in that short period when Pat and Young Pat were working in partnership. (Young Pat may have also owned his own showfront, used to front a menagerie, as seen in the photograph of the New Brighton Amusement Park, said to have been taken in 1913).

ABOVE: Collins' presenting the ex Wall's show at Nottingham Goose Fair in 1899, with organ on the left, and electric light engine on the right. The globe of the arc lamp above the organ still bears Wall's name, and the pillar supporting the proscenium is built-up through the organ tilt!
(Collection of Jim Boulton)

Wonderland No.1.

The Bioscope Show, generally known as Flora Collins' No.1.Wonderland Show, was presented for the first time at Wrexham Fair in April 1907. The North Wales Guardian of 12 April 1907, told its readers about the fair: "Undoubtedly the one attraction to be remembered is the wonderful show which is being patronised by all visitors. The Living Pictures are the best of the kind that have ever been seen in Wrexham. The electric Orchestron draws countless numbers. The beautiful organ with its magnificent sculptural work and dazzling paintings eclipse anything of the kind ever seen before in Wrexham. The organ being used for the first time, came direct from Paris this week."

The Marenghi 104 key organ, with its fluid art-nouveau carved facade, said to be designed by Zotocornella, was incorporated into the centre of a matching showfront built by Orton & Spooner, leading to endless debate concerning what originated from Paris, and what came from Burton on Trent. The organ was installed by J.Wentworth, which he mentioned as a postscript in his advertisement in World's Fair on May 4th: "PS. I have just completed that elegant concern of Mrs Flora Collins which had its debut with enormous success at Wrexham Fair. It is the only one so far - the second will follow shortly for Mr William Taylor".

Mr Wentworth's comments confirm the often quoted fact that the No.1.Wonderland was similar to William Taylor's show of 1907. (See "Fairground Art", page 125).

The showfront incorporated three thousand multi-coloured electric lamps, and these were used to present the "Electric Firework Display". At a set time, the arc lamps were switched off and the coloured lights presented their "Show", controlled by the organ register using special "lighting books", a concept that Marenghi had just patented. Various costs have been quoted for the Wonderland, at the time (and ever since!) but the variations can be accounted for once an attempt is made to consider what was being included in the figure: just the organ, the organ and showfront, or the complete show and equipment? It was a two to three thousand pound investment, and led to further investment in showmen's engines etc.

The equipment for showing the films had also improved and the Wonderland Show used the latest Gaumont "Chronophone" sound system, which enabled the film being shown to be mechanically synchronised with sound produced from a phonograph. Amplification was still a technical problem and shows probably included both sound and silent pictures, interspersed with short variety acts. However, the advertising was able to exploit the possibility of presenting "Singing, talking, coloured living pictures" some years before these became technicalities that could be taken for granted in the cinema trade.

The "auditorium" behind the showfront was used at Wrexham for a meeting of the Showmen's Guild, and Rev.Horne conducted a service in the Wonderland Show. 1907 saw the launch of Sunday Sacred Music Concerts and "Services" using the Bioscope organs, and these became fund-raising events where the proceeds could be given to a local hospital charity, or Carnival Committee. It is said that Pat Collins seldom, if ever, invited a Roman Catholic priest to conduct these events, regarding his faith as something that still encountered Protestant hostility.

Everywhere the Wonderland Show went in 1907 it became the centre of attention. At Easter it was presented at Birkenhead, and during the summer it returned to Merseyside to appear at the Sefton Park Fair, in Liverpool.

At the latter, it stood alongside Bostock & Wombell's Menagerie, as well as another Collins' Bioscope show. World's Fair reported "The outside appearance of Mrs Flora Collins' Animated Pictures is all that can be desired. The Marenghi organ being admired by all. Inside, the splendid Gaumont Chronophone picture, 'Hannah, Won't You Close that Door?' was especially well received"

Back in the Black Country, at the Bloxwich Gala, the first visit of the "World's Great Show" was presented as the "Greatest Wonder of the Present Age". The Walsall Observer recorded, "On Sunday there was a large attendance at the Wakes Ground to hear a sacred concert on Mr Collins' wonderful mechanical organ. Indeed the most outstanding feature of the Wake has been the organ, an instrument costing no less than £2,000. It is reputed to be the largest of its type ever built. At intervals the organ has been illuminated by hundreds of electric lights of various colours which continually change, and present a beautiful effect." The show went on to Darlaston, and Oldbury, where the great attraction was the film of the Driscoll - Baker fight, and then went on to the Onion show.

There has been some debate concerning the contemporary use of the "Wonderland" name, but the name was used in World's Fair at Easter, and again in describing the Onion Fair when the phrase, "First in the showline was Mrs Flora Collins' grand new enterprise - Wonderland" appeared. At the Onion Fair there was also Sagar's Bioscope. Such was their popularity in 1907, that large fairs often had several Bioscopes lined up next to one another "in opposition". For example at the Goose Fair, Flora Collins' show competed with Bioscopes presented by Arthur Twigdon, Captain Payne, John Proctor, and President Kemp. At Bulwell in November, Wonderland was joined by Arthur Twigdon (again), Relph & Pedley's and James Crighton.

The name "Wonderland" is used more regularly in local advertisements for fairs in the Black Country in 1908. World's Fair starts to talk about No.1.and No.2. Wonderland towards the end of that year, and in 1909 the second show is sometimes locally referred to as the "New" Wonderland. Both shows stood alongside each other in 1910 on the Reservoir Ground at Aston. The Bioscope shows had then reached their zenith. Film-showing was about to become the prerogative of the permanent cinema, and the prime place on the fairground was about to be taken by the Scenic Railway.

After the First World War, the Marenghi organ from the No.1 Wonderland Show was built into the centre of the No.2.Scenic Railway, the "Dragons and Peacocks" managed by Joby Farrell. The machine travelled until 1932, and the organ was probably "retired" to the Crystal Palace site.

Wonderland No.2.
Pat Collins obviously liked the 104 key Marenghi organ, and he must have decided that Bioscopes were a worthwhile investment for he ordered a second show which, if anything, was even more ornate than the first. In this case it was similar to President Kemp's and Charles Thurston's Shows, but as Pat Collins always liked to be that little bit bigger and better than anyone else, it is claimed that the Bandmaster on his organ was bigger than those on the other two! (Thurston's show of this type is illustrated in "Fairground Art" page 124).

The No.2.Wonderland may have made its first appearance at the fair held at Olympia from Christmas 1907 to New Year 1908, and may have been placed under the management of Young Pat, and his new bride. Certainly, in September 1908, the World's Fair featured a photograph of this show, captioned: "Mrs P.Collins Jnr and her staff on the Wonderland Show".

Unfortunately reports of 1908 fairs appearing in local newspapers do not identify which "Wonderland Show" they are describing. World's Fair was often more concerned with other innovations, new rides etc., that were coming on the scene. At Smethwick in October 1908, however, it very specifically stated that it was the No.1 show that was present, and at Christmas the same year, the two Wonderlands can be distinguished because Flora is reported as taking the No.1. to Wrexham, and Young Pat is reported as taking the No.2 to Birmingham (Soho).

Thus we are left to wonder which show was present at Wolverhampton at Whitsun, when the show was much admired and the World's Fair reporter observed its attendants "attired in black frock coats and silk hats". Both shows were very ornately decorated and lit with a multitude of lights, but the entrances of the second Wonderland featured a more obvious arch, rather than the peacock motif used on No.1. The bandmaster on the No.1 stood well to the front of the organ facade, but the No.2 bandmaster's head had to be accommodated in its own arch within the organ front!

Later in 1908, the timber struts supporting the tilt's extension over the frontage, were replaced with elaborately decorated Corinthian style columns, and carved proscenium panels were carried across the front. In this very extravagant form the No.2.Wonderland was photographed at the Nottingham Goose Fair in 1908,

RIGHT: The difficulty of tracing the history of the shows and their fronts is illustrated by this picture of the ex-Wall's show (B1) presenting Flora Collins' menagerie at Barry Island in the early 1930's. An organ is now on the right of the frontage.
(Collection of Jim Boulton)

RIGHT: The 1905 wagon-fronted show apparently photographed at Birmingham in 1906 while bearing the legend "P.Collins & Son" on the portico.
(Collection of Kevin Scrivens)

BELOW: The "No.1" Wonderland Show with the Peacock motif above the entrances, and the Marenghi Organ occupying the centre of the frontage.
Collection of Jim Boulton)

ABOVE: The No.2.Wonderland Show, apparently photographed at Oldbury in 1910. It is interesting to compare the frontage seen here with the Wonderland Organ front as preserved by Bill Hunt today.
(Collection of Kevin Scrivens)

BELOW: The No.2.Wonderland Show as fully built up with its ornate carved and gilded proscenium, seen here at Nottingham Goose Fair in 1908. The Bioscope was at the height of its popoularity at this time and this frontage represents the zenith of its presentation.
(Collection of Kevin Scrivens)

when it looks to have stood in front of a row of other shows occupying the line along the top of the fair.

Perhaps as a sign that cinematography had "moved on", a circus was presented behind the Wonderland front in 1910, and in the remaining years up to the First World War it may have hosted variety shows etc. The frontage slipped into oblivion; but the organ lived on.

After the First World War the No.2 organ front was sent away to Orton & Spooner and was built into the centre of the new No.1 Scenic, and completed by them in 1921. A 98 key Gavioli organ was put behind the front, rebuilt from a 112 key-less instrument. The No.1. Scenic was first presented with Dragon cars, but quite soon these were replaced with Whales, and the ride enjoyed a long decade of popularity as Clara Mullett's "Whale Island".

Thus Whale Island became the centre of Sunday evening Sacred Music Concerts, in the tradition established in Bioscope days. The whales were replaced with Dragons and peacocks about 1933, and the ride was retired in 1937...only to be revived after the Second World War, then retired a second time to Sutton Park. During this post-War revival it was decided to replace the Gavioli organ with an organ more along the lines of the original Marenghi, and this work was undertaken by Mr Chiappa. It appeared at the Onion Fair complete with dummy console imitating a theatre organ, and dummy organist whose hands and feet actually moved on the keys and pedals!

The ride and organ were threatened with destruction in 1962 when the lease at Sutton Park expired. Fortunately, the organ was rescued by Tom Hunt and the task of restoring and presenting the organ has been carried on by his son, Bill Hunt (See Who's Who) The 98 key frame was retained as a large quantity of 98 key music was available, but the front has been lengthened to return it to something of its original Marenghi-style glory. The survival of this front is therefore one of the few tangible links with the vanished era of the Bioscope Show.

CINEMAS AND THEATRES

Pat Collins became interested in acquiring cinemas, variety theatres, skating rinks, etc almost simultaneously. Whether dabbling with Bioscopes had led to an interest in acquiring cinemas, or diversification into fixed-site entertainment made economic sense at the time, we may never know, but by the end of the First World War, Pat was the proprietor of a number of cinemas and theatres. He was not the only showman to move from running Bioscopes to cinemas, but such showmen were in a minority, and Pat was one of an even smaller group who did so while still continuing his involvement with the world of the travelling fair. Generally, Pat seemed to add to his business interests rather than move from one activity to another. After the First World War he told a young employee that he owned fourteen assorted establishments. (See Joe Ashmore's testimony in Appendix 2).

It is impossible to establish what is included in this list of "fourteen", or even if he was accurate in making such a claim. However it is conceivable that the list could have included the Cinema De Luxe (Chester), Electric Theatre (Bloxwich), Olympia (Darlaston), Alhambra (Dudley Port), Hippodrome (Warwick), Hippodrome (Burslem), a 'small hall' near Tunstall, the Tivoli (New Brighton), the Hippodrome (Seacombe/Wallasey), the Waldorf Skating Rink (Birmingham) and the Monument Lane Palais de Danse (Birmingham). To exercise personal supervision over the management of such a scattered empire must have been something of a nightmare, particularly when added to the task of running several travelling fairs, and some permanent amusement parks that needed revitalising after the First World War! Pat was in his fifties as he commanded this empire - and in addition, was soon to begin campaigning for a (short) Parliamentary career.

After the War, building materials were in short supply for projects like new cinema construction, but by the early twenties Pat was building three new cinemas. The period of the early to mid twenties was really the time when Pat was most involved in the fixed site amusement of the cinema. Some accounts of Pat's achievements are vague about when he di-

BELOW: Pat (on the left) on the steps of the Grosvenor Cinema, Bloxwich. This frontage survives, although it is no longer a cinema.
(Collection of Peter Hough)

vested himself of these enterprises; other accounts probably under-estimate the involvement of Young Pat in this side of the business; an exaggerated view of Pat's commitment may therefore emerge.

It is not possible to arrange a survey of the cinemas and theatres in any chronological order, so it seems sensible to deal with them geographically, starting in the Black Country, progressing through Oakengates and Chester to the Wirral, returning ultimately to Birmingham via The Potteries and Warwick!

Black Country Cinemas
Before the end of the First World War, Pat seems to have acquired three cinemas in the Black Country, at Dudley Port, Darlaston and Bloxwich.

At the junction of Groveland Road and Dudley Port stood a timber framed building clad in corrugated iron. It may once have been a Salvation Army Citadel, but in the first decade of this century it had become the Alhambra Skating Rink, during a roller-skating craze that swept the country. Films were occasionally shown at the rink, and after the Cinematograph Act came into force in 1910, it was modified in order to receive a Kinematograph Licence from Tipton UDC.

The hall went through various changes of name, but Pat Collins revived the name Alhambra, and from 1918 onwards the advertisements carried this name and his own name as the new proprietor. He ran it until December 1927 when he sold it to a fellow showman, Miles Jervis, of Chasetown. The building survived until 1935 when it was replaced by a "modern" cinema, which continued to use the name "Alhambra" from 8 April 1935 until closure on 2 August 1963. For the last ten years of its life it was operated by the son of Miles Jervis, also named Miles.

Pat's hall in Darlaston became famous in local cinema history, though not because of its aesthetic programmes! No, the Olympia was notorious for its warmth...an effect created by subterranean spontaneous combustion in the coal measures beneath the cinema! It occupied a site in Blockall, a short way from the centre of Darlaston. As at Dudley Port, the building had Non-conformist ancestry plus tales of conversion to a skating rink. It opened as the Olympia cinema, The "Limp" on 19 October 1912. At the end of the First World War it was acquired by Pat, and was managed for him by Walter Mould. A local newspaper reported that Walter Mould took his staff on an outing to Llangollen by charabanc on 8 August 1920. The report mentioned that Pat Collins was unable to

---

GROSVENOR CINEMA
HIGH STREET, BLOXWICH.

MONDAY AND SATURDAY, TWO DISTINCT SHOWS, at 6 and 8.15.
TUESDAY TO FRIDAY, CONTINUOUS, 6.30 to 10.30.

GRAND OPENING
MONDAY NEXT, DECEMBER 11th, at 5.45.

MONDAY, TUESDAY, AND WEDNESDAY,
DOUGLAS FAIRBANKS in

THE THREE MUSKETEERS
Based on the Immortal Novel, "The Three Musketeers," by Alexandre Dumas.
Supported by Episode 9 of the Serial—**THE FLAMING DISC**.

THE OPENING CEREMONY WILL BE PERFORMED BY
LADY ARTHUR GROSVENOR
(of Chester),
And the First Night's Proceeds given to the WALSALL Y.M.C.A.

THURSDAY, FRIDAY, AND SATURDAY,
NORMA TALMADGE
(The Star Supreme) in Her Greatest Masterpiece—
SMILIN' THROUGH
A Drama of To-day and Yesterday, in Eight Stupendous Reels.
Supported by Episode 4 of the Serial,
BREAKING THROUGH
PATHE GAZETTE, showing all the Latest News.

N.B.—This Cinema has been built upon the original site of the Electric Theatre, and is, without doubt, one of the Finest Halls in the district.

For Pictures, Comfort, and Music, the "GROSVENOR" is IT!

NOTE.—The Central Theatre, Bloxwich, will only now be open for CHILDREN'S MATINEE, SATURDAY AFTERNOON, at 2.30

POPULAR PRICES—5d., 9d., 1/- (including Government Tax).
RESERVED and BOOKED SEATS, 1/- and 1/3 (including Government Tax).
Box Office Open Daily 10 a.m. till 12.30, and 4 to 5.30 p.m.

join the party, but helped pay for the trip! At the end of 1926 the Olympia was sold to Messrs Mortimer Dent and Joseph Cohen, (CD Cinemas). Two years later it was acquired by the ABC Circuit, and remained in their hands until it finally closed on 10 December 1955.

Pat Collins' third cinema venture in the Black Country was more substantial, and provides the only existing monument to this side of Pat's activities - the Grosvenor, Bloxwich, and it is an interesting story

Pat's adoption of Bloxwich as his home and headquarters proceeded in stages. The process began in the 1880's with his attendance at the Bloxwich Wake. By the 1890's he was the official lessee of the Wake, which had moved to Tenters Croft, by the Pinfold, where the trams from Walsall terminated. Then Pat acquired the field, and by 1915, was able to lease Limetree House which stood at the High Street entrance to the field.

A few paces along the High Street, towards the centre of the village stood the Electric Palace, opened at the end of 1912 by Thomas Jackson, a baker and confectioner from Whitmore Reans, Wolverhampton, who was fast establishing himself as a local cinema magnate. Like the Alhambra at Dudley Port, and many other small cinemas of that time, it was a timber building clad in corrugated iron, into which 400 patrons could be crammed. It was "improved" a few months after opening and a balcony was added, but it seems that the front of the building was fairly unpretentious. Why Thomas Jackson sold it to Pat Collins at the end of the First World War is not clear, although Mr Jackson may have needed money to carry out 'improvements' to the Palace, Walsall.

When 16 year old Joe Ashmore joined Pat Collins in 1918 he was not impressed with what he saw at the Electric Palace and did not hesitate to offer Pat some advice!

"...in the evening we returned to the Electric Palace. In those days the films were very inflammable and Pat had a crafty way of approaching the projection room very quietly so that he could open the door quickly to find out what was going on inside. I followed him in, and we found the operator puffing away. Actually, this operator claimed he couldn't care less about Pat Collins because he had a good job as an electrician down the pit, which kept him out of the Army, but he went to pieces when he saw the Gaffer. The fire blankets which were supposed to be wet, were as dry as cork; and the two fire buckets of sand were full of fag ends. Pat Collins instructed me to take control of the machines immediately - they were that old you could hear them a mile away!"

BELOW: The interior of the Grosvenor, Bloxwich looking towards the screen and orchestra pit, photographed by John Maltby when the cinema was acquired by Oscar Deutsch.

"I ran the show until the end, and then reported to Pat in the Manager's office. The manager was Mr Leach who weighed about 24 stone. I said, 'Mr Collins, you'll have to spend some money. You'll have to get a new screen, or send for Malins of West Bromwich. They can drop the screen, open it out flat, put glue all over it, and throw silver sand over it, to make a first class screen'. Pat told the manager to get that organised."

"The theatre was a proper showman's outfit - there were wires hanging out everywhere, so I completely re-wired the place, cleaned the arc lamps and whitewashed the reflectors until I could present a good clear picture. I felt very enthusiastic about it, and there was something exciting about working for Pat Collins...I could still be his slave to-day!"

Sometime in the next twelve months Pat must have decided to demolish the Electric Palace and to replace it with a brand new purpose built cinema. Pat's friend, Thomas Wood, was about to build a new cinema in Bilston, but he also provided full stage facilities perhaps afraid that the future of the cinema business might not be long term. Pat seemingly had more confidence and approached the Walsall Architects, Messrs Hickton & Farmer, requesting them to design a thousand-seat cinema on quite a grand scale. The Electric Palace showed its last film, "The Tatters", on 3 December 1921, and was then demolished.

On the following Monday, 5 December 1921, Pat began presenting films at the Central in Park Road. This building was previously a chapel 'converted' into a cinema in 1913 for the Wilkes' family. Thomas Wood had used it for a year or two early during the First World War, and then shows were resumed by the original owners, although these may have ceased by 1921. Pat needed the Central to maintain his presence in Bloxwich while his new cinema was being built. Shows ceased at the Central when they began at the new cinema; Pat then used the premises to repair fairground equipment. The building was sold to Bert Brittain in 1937 when it was again 'converted' this time to a garage. Bert had also been a friend of Pat's, and helped in compiling the 1959 Biography.

The Bloxwich building firm, J & F Wootton, built Pat's new cinema, which it is said cost £12,000. (As much as a new scenic railway!) It was to be called the "Grosvenor", a name much better appreciated in Chester than Bloxwich - but perhaps Pat intended opening a whole chain of Grosvenors. Some members of the Grosvenor family were friends of showmen such as the Collinses and the Farrells, and the Collins' family never entirely forgot their associations with the Chester and Wrexham area.

The "Grosvenor" opened on 11 December 1922, and Lady Arthur Grosvenor came along to perform the ceremony. Ironically, Pat could not be present, as he was fulfilling his duties at the House of Commons. In his absence, Lady Grosvenor praised both the new cinema and its proprietor, saying that she had known him for years and that Walsall had shown good sense in sending him to Parliament. The Mayor of Walsall, Councillor Warner and Fr. McDonald also made speeches. The latter expressed the belief that Pat would represent the town for many years to come and might, eventually, take a seat in the House of Lords as "Lord Bloxwich".

The audience settled down to watch "The Three Musketeers" and the proceeds, just over £25 were donated to the YMCA. One interesting detail of this occasion arose from the fact that Pat's loyal 'regulars' at the "Central" had just seen Episode 8 of the serial "The Flaming Disc" and therefore the opening of the "Grosvenor" must have been one of those rare occasions when a new cinema opened showing the ninth episode of a serial!

The cinema's proximity to Pat's home and headquarters gave it a special place in his empire. Families from the fairground looked forward to free admission to Pat's cinema, and, conversely, children at the Matinee looked forward to winning free rides at the fair!

When the 'talkies' arrived, Pat had already sold his other two Black Country cinemas, but the Grosvenor still belonged to him. A sound-on-disc system was installed in July 1930, and a proper Western Electric sound system arrived at the end of 1931. Projection was always from a small room beneath the balcony, almost level with the screen, which was slightly concave.

Eventually Pat sold the Grosvenor to Oscar Deutsch in 1935, and it became one of the latter's Odeons, closing as the Odeon on 2 May 1959, just before the local celebration of the centenary of Pat Collins' birth. It was then almost twenty five years since the building had been part of Pat's empire.

Now, another quarter century on, Limetree House and the Wake Ground have vanished from the landscape of Bloxwich. However, Pat's cinema still stands, and is currently in use as a nightclub.

The Grosvenor, Oakengates
In Oakengates and Burslem, Pat may have developed fixed site entertainment because he already owned ground or leased land on which he held his fairs. In Oakengates, there was Owen's Field, where Pat had presented his fair in the town at least since the 1890's. Facing Market Street, at the eastern end of the town centre, Pat built his second "Grosvenor". It was smaller than the hall at Bloxwich and only provided seating for 700 patrons, but it had one or two architectural similarities with its sister in Bloxwich and, therefore, may well have been designed by Messrs Hickton and Farmer again. (The similarities centred around the "Hathenware" treatment of the entrance).

This Grosvenor opened on 19 November 1923, with the film "Who Are My Parents?". Once again Pat missed the opening ceremony; this time he was heavily committed fighting yet another election campaign. In his absence the ceremony was conducted by Young Pat, who announced that the proceeds from the first show were going to be donated to the Oakengates Town Football Club. The cinema was left in the capable hands of young Joe Proverbs, who had previously been assistant manager, and Musical Director, at Pat's cinema in Chester. (This Joe is believed to have been the Uncle of the Joe Proverbs who ran the Pat Collins' office in Bloxwich, see Whos Who)

The Grosvenor was a victim of Pat's retreat from the cinema business in the mid to late twenties, and was sold to a Mr W.G.Allbritt in 1926. Pat's association with the cinema which he had built in Oakengates was, therefore, only a brief three years, and this has to be borne in mind when grand totals are announced to record the number of cinemas and theatres he owned. The Grosvenor went through further changes of ownership until it closed on 1.April 1967.

The Chester Connection

When Mr Proverbs moved to the Grosvenor, Oakengates, in 1923, he left the Cinema De Luxe, which was at 95 Brook Street, Chester, where he had been Musical Director. Thus he moved from the first of Pat's purpose-built cinemas to the last. It is not clear how early Pat had planned to build and open a cinema in Chester, but he was certainly "quick off the mark" during the period of post-War shortages, and the Cinema de Luxe was built by the Spring of 1920.

It was designed by W.Matthew Jones, and was described by the Chester Chronicle as "up to date and commodious". It was opened on Monday 18 April 1920 by Lady Arthur Grosvenor, who was accompanied, on this occasion by her two daughters. The Chester Chronicle reported that Lady Grosvenor was welcomed by Pat and Flora as she arrived at the cinema, and made a speech to the large audience, in which she stated her admiration for the building, and for Pat's generosity as a public benefactor. She added "I know Mr Collins personally, and am glad to number him among my friends". After her speech, a picture of her Ladyship, in Red Cross uniform, was projected onto the screen and the audience applauded.

Pat did not speak publically himself on this occasion, and it was left to Young Pat to speak on behalf of the family in thanking Lady Grosvenor for opening the cinema. Young Pat thus played an important role in opening all three "new" cinemas, and possibly supervised the management of the Palais de Danse. Young Pat presented the guest with a silver rose bowl, bearing an inscription to mark the occasion. The takings, £56, were donated to the YMCA Fund for the Bishop's Palace Scheme.

The cinema advertised itself as "Collins' Cinema de Luxe", under the management of Mr J Locker, who presumably transferred from the Electric Palace, Bloxwich. The first programme featured "Carnival", which ran for the full six-day week, although the supporting programme and serials changed on the Thursday. Thereafter, there were two 3-day programmes per week. It was then, of course, a silent cinema, with an orchestra under Mr Proverb's direction.

At the end of February 1926 the name "Collins" was dropped from the Cinema's name, and on 26 June that year it closed for 2 weeks, during which time it was refurbished. It re-opened on 12 July 1926 as "The

BELOW: The modest frontage of the Grosvenor, Oakengates. Note some of the fenestration is similar to that found at Bloxwich.

Majestic" under new management. Whether it had been purchased from Pat Collins, or was operated on a lease, is not clear, but the change of name seems to mark the end of Pat Collins' association with it. By the end of the 1930's it was absorbed into the Gaumont British Circuit, along with the brand new Gaumont and the ancient Music Hall. Pat's major business connection with Chester was in providing the fair on the Little Roodee to accompany the Chester Races every May.

The Wirral Connection
Pat once claimed that his father, and even his grandfather, had visited the Wirral as travellers for many years. In the 1890's he told the Newport Advertiser that he had a menagerie at New Brighton. About 1906 he seems to have taken on the Palace Amusement Park, after the local Council had become landlord of the site. By 1910 Young Pat seems to have made New Brighton his home, and from then on it is Young Pat who seems to establish the strongest connection with the Wirral, but, as usual, we cannot be sure to what extent this was achieved independently of Pat.

Young Pat's sons were born in New Brighton; "Baby Pat" in 1910, and John James ("Baby John" in 1912). Baby Pat has been able to confirm that his father controlled at least three premises for cinema or theatrical use at one time or another in the New Brighton area.

The Palace, Virginia Road
The Palace was originally part of an amusement complex that was developed in the early 1880's. Films were first shown in the corrugated iron building in 1906 when it was leased by Wallasey Corporation to Messrs Lievers & Bennet. Changes of use and changes of lessee were fairly frequent, and the lease was acquired by Young Pat in 1920. For a while it was known as "Collins' Picture Palace". Live entertainment returned in 1923 in the form of concert parties, but the theatre remained closed during 1924 and 1925 - a time when Young Pat may have resumed travelling. The lease was sold to Joseph Gabriel who re-opened the place on Whit Monday 1926, but it closed for the last time on 11 December that year. It remained abandoned for several years, until demolished in 1933. The "New Palace Amusement Park" was built on the site.

The Tivoli, The Promenade
The Tivoli was quite a grand building, situated close to New Brighton Pier, and with a long imposing frontage that included six shops. It was built as a 636-seater theatre, with boxes, balcony and well equipped stage and fly tower. It opened on 6 April 1914, and records indicate that it was sold to Pat Collins in September 1921 for £37,500. However, ever since its opening it had been managed by ' F.V.Ross' - and this surname suggests a connection with the Collins' family.

Films were included in variety shows, but on 19 February 1923 it "re-opened" as the Tivoli Super Cinema". By the summer, stage shows were being presented again! In October 1928 it was sold to Provincial Cinematograph Theatres (PCT) for £27,000. The new owners also alternated films with live shows, until "Sound" arrived in 1930. Changes of use and ownership continued until a final closure in 1955. It was demolished in 1976.

The Hippodrome, Victoria Road
This typical late 19thC theatre was a mile away from the Tivoli in Seacombe; it was opened on 18 December 1899 and owned by James Kiernan, seating 900 patrons and enjoying full stage facilities. Films first supplemented live entertainment in 1904. In 1908 it changed its name from the Irving Theatre to the Kings. It became the Hippodrome in 1918, under the management of F.V.Ross (see above). Pat Collins, or Young Pat, may have owned it from the beginning of the First World War. It was sold in 1928 to the Gordon Circuit. The name of Pat Collins is mentioned again when there was an attempt to revive the fortunes of the Hippodrome in 1934, but this could have been Pat, Young Pat or Baby Pat! It was 'reborn' as the Embassy in 1936, presenting cine-variety, and continued to have a chequered career until it finally closed in 1959.

Young Pat seems to have been in business in the New Brighton and Seacombe areas of Wallasey from just before 1910 until the end of the twenties. The Amusement park had also been abandoned by the mid twenties, although Young Pat did make one further bid for the site in the mid 1930's. Young Pat had also presented his own fairs in the Wirral area, but his career is poorly documented. (See his personal statement made to the World's Fair in mid 1927, quoted in Appendix l).

Pat in the Potteries
The Potteries do not yield their secrets easily! Pat Collins' fairs were held at Hanley, Stoke, Burslem, Longton and Tunstall, and some of these may have been on ground acquired by Pat, but no clear picture emerges as to what he may have owned in the area. However, the Hippodrome, Burslem, is listed as part of his empire from the end of the 1920's onwards, and it seems that Pat retained his association with the place longer than most of the others. Several people recall moving the seats out of the Hippodrome, possibly about 1940, and bringing them back to Bloxwich for storage. Baby Pat recalls that his Grandfather also had a "small hall at Tunstall"

Hippodrome, Warwick
This Hippodrome appears in lists of Pat's interests at the end of the First World War. It was a large building and boasted a balcony etc. but the auditorium itself had a corrugated iron roof, and audiences, like those at the Alhambra, Dudley Port, remembered the noise of the rain on the roof long after they had forgotten everything else! Films had been shown since 1912, when it was known as the Picturedrome. Pat may have owned or leased the hall in partnership with Florence Jones. Like other halls he acquired at the end of the First World War, it seems that he wished to sell it by the mid twenties. By 1926 it was sold to the Hockley Picture House Company, and their manager, W.J.Savoury had replaced Pat's manager, C.W.Morgan. It is not listed in Kine Year Books after 1928, and had certainly closed by the beginning of the Second World War, if not at the beginning of the sound era.

Two Halls in 'Brum'

According to Baby Pat, his father, Young Pat, looked after the Palais de Danse, in Monument Lane, Birmingham for a couple of years. Young Pat was responsible for the opening, or "re-opening" in September 1929, at the time of the second partnership with his father. Much more significant, however, as part of Pat's empire was the Walford Skating Rink in Sparkbrook, Birmingham. Joe Ashmore was able to confirm that Pat took him there in 1918, and in the late 1920's Pat was making good use of it to present an indoor fair over the Christmas/New Year period. For example, in 1927, the No.1.Scenic, the Chairoplanes, the Cakewalk, and Over the Falls were all built up inside the hall as well as some sideshows. There is also evidence that the hall was used for film shows and boxing promotions.

Both the Walford Road Rink, and the Palais de Danse, were also used on occasions as a meeting place for the Midlands Region of the Showmen's Guild. Not having found any "hard facts" as to when these halls came into existence, or ceased to exist, it is interesting to note the way they often unexpectedly played a part in Pat Collins' activities. For example, over the New year period at the beginning of 1930, Pat provided a fair to stand alongside Chipperfield's Circus at Dudley. Always wanting to make the most of any opportunity, it seems that Pat organised a flying visit of the Circus acts to the Palais de Danse, where they put on a Friday afternoon matinee, before dashing back to Dudley

The Lichfield Mystery

"JBT" was the Black Country correspondent of World's Fair during the 1930's, and he often made cryptic comments about his own long memory of showbusiness. In the issue of 13/2/37 he mentions a painter named Bob Brown and adds "...he also painted for Pat Collins, and did up the hall which I obtained and opened for Mr Collins at Lichfield - the first permanent "palace" in the Cathedral City".

This is the only reference we have ever come across linking Pat with a cinema in Lichfield. We have substantiated the fact that Pat had no links with the Palladium opened 1912, and owned by John Thornburn of Tamworth. It is clear that he had nothing to do with The Regal (1932). If "JBT's" statement is correct, we assume he may have been referring to some early shows put on at the Minster Hall, Dam Street.

The Grand, Walsall

In late 1938, Pat Collins took a lease on the Grand Theatre, Park Street, Walsall, from Associated British Cinemas (ABC). This was neither Pat Collins or his son, ... but Baby Pat,.... continuing the family tradition. Baby Pat tried to revive "live theatre" in a building that had been used as a cinema for several years. The experiment was brought to an abrupt end when the theatre was destroyed by fire in June 1939.

ELECTRIC THEATRE, HIGH STREET, BLOXWICH.

Proprietor ... ... MR. PAT COLLINS.

MONDAY, TUESDAY, and WEDNESDAY, William Fox presents Virginia Pearson in THE LIAR. Episode 1 of Pathé's Cyclonic Serial, HANDS UP! WINKLE ON THE WARPATH.

THURSDAY, FRIDAY, and SATURDAY, Phillip's Film Co. present THE EMPTY CAB, Five-Part Production. Chapter Three of the Celebrated Pictures, ADVENTURES AMONG THE CANNIBALS. Episode 11 of THE WOMAN IN THE WEB.

MONDAY and SATURDAY, Two Distinct Shows, at 6 and 8.15.
TUESDAY till FRIDAY, Continuous, 6.30 to 10.30.
CHILDREN'S MATINEE, SATURDAY, at 2.30. Price 1d., no Tax.
POPULAR PRICES, 4d., 6d., and 8d. (Including Government Tax).

BLOXWICH WAKES WEEK.

P. COLLINS'

Grand Fete & Gala

THE WAKES GROUND, BLOXWICH,

TO-DAY (Saturday), MONDAY AND TUESDAY NEXT.

Gigantic Amalgamation of New and Novel Attractions.
Grand Free Sights. Stage and Aerial Performances.

N.B.—TUESDAY—Benefit for the Walsall Hospital.

2d. ADMISSION EACH DAY (including Government Tax) 2d.
All Trams Stop at Entrance.

1922

ABOVE: The Grosvenor becomes the Odeon - Pat's cinema in Bloxwich photographed by John Maltby a few days after the completion of the sale to Oscar Deutsch. Although Pat missed the opening in 1922 while working in the House of Commons, he did use the hall for campaigning in the 1923 election, and was known to visit the Saturday matinees. Children who could not afford to go in congregated outside the cinema on Saturdays hoping that Pat would arrive and instruct the manager to let them in free of charge! In the 1990's, the Pat Collins' Memorial Clock stands at one end of the High Street, the cinema, now a nightclub, stands at the other.

FAIRGROUND EQUIPMENT

CHAPTER 15

How many *rides* did Pat Collins own?

A wonderfully simple question...but there is no simple answer!

Obviously, new rides eventually replaced worn out rides, or were sold or were scrapped. Sometimes the same ride re-appeared under a new name, or was constructed by amalgamating parts from former rides. As usual there is very little documentation relating to the subject, and Pat himself was given to exaggeration. For example, his claim that the Rolling Gondolas were painted by Italian craftsmen, probably created the myth that Savage, the ride-builder of Kings Lynn had imported foreign labour!

We also have to take into account that Pat bought and sold riding machines, and sometimes was said to be "presenting" a ride when in fact it was owned by another showman just occupying Pat's "position". Like many famous showmen, Pat developed strong links with the major ride builders: first Frederick Savage, and then Orton & Spooner. The builder usually supplied spares, and carried out some repairs, modifications etc., long after supplying the machine. It is also possible that some of the machines were bought on "hire purchase".

The study of a showman's machines is thus very complex.

In compiling this list we acknowledge the help of Stephen Smith and Kevin Scrivens, but any inadvertent errors the lists may contain, are not theirs. It is hoped that the list will, at least, be a starting point for further study, and of interest to all fairground followers.

Firstly the rides Pat purchased 'new' are listed, then the rides purchased 'second hand'; to create a chronological picture the lists have to be integrated. An attempt has also been made to take into account the rides associated with Young Pat and Walsall John, together with the rides bought after Pat's death. Not listed are the juveniles and stalls Pat may have owned; shows associated with Pat's fairs are dealt with separately.

a) RIDES PURCHASED 'NEW'

R1 The First "Dobbies"
Looking back to when he arrived in Walsall in the early 1880's, Pat claimed that he owned little more than a hand turned roundabout or some swings. In the years that followed he added dramatically to his equipment and claimed that he was a pioneer in all the new technology being applied to such equipment. The truth is that steam had been applied to the task of turning roundabouts since the late 1860's. The firm of Savage's based at Kings Lynn had established their reputation as builders of steam-driven fairground rides by the time Pat bought his first ride from them in 1886. In that year he bought a set of Dobbies powered by Savages centre engine No.372, and an organ engine, No.373. (Various accounts of Pat's life refer to an earlier visit to Savages when his father is said to have bought a ride, this may have been "steam horses" of 1877/78, Savage engine No.172, and organ engine No.173).

A set of "Dobbies" consisted of horses slung from the swifts of a centre-engine roundabout, but unlike the Gallopers, there was no attempt to create any up and down motion to the movement of the horses.

R2 The Sea on Land
The Sea on Land was developed by Frederick Savage and William Sanger, and consisted of six small yachts, complete with sails and rigging. As these revolved they were given a rolling and pitching movement. Savages built at least 20 sets in the 1880's. Pat bought a set in 1887, with centre engine No.414. It appears in most of the advertisements for Pat's fairs during the early 1890's and must have been a well-travelled ride, but it was subsequently sold to Edward Morley and was rebuilt as a switchback.

R3 Gallopers
This set of Gallopers appears to have been built by Messrs Allchin & Linnel, but was powered by Savage centre engine No.420 of 1887.

R4 The Switchback Gallopers
In 1886 Savages introduced the "Mountain Ponies" a ride that combined the straightforward Galloper with

- 131 -

LEFT: A rare view of the "Steam Bicycles" (R6), seen at Hanley Wakes, Fountain Square, 1898. On the left are the Three-Abreast "Fox Hunters". Both machines are typical steam-driven rides of the 1890's. Also note the water cart on the right. *(Collection of Van Buren)*

LEFT: The Platform Galloper (R9) as seen at Crystal Palace, Sutton Coldfield, after the First World War. Pigs and Teddy Bears had been used as mounts on this machine at various times, to add to the difficulty of identifying machines, and the domes and droppers appear to have come from R6 (see above). *(Collection of John Ward)*

the excitement of the Switchback with its hills and vales. Pat's set was supplied by Savages in 1888, with centre engine No.443, along with organ engine No.444. Throughout the 1890's this ride is mentioned in local advertisements for Pat Collins' fairs, but at the turn of the century, the horses must have been removed and replaced by chickens. From 1900 onwards we find the ride mentioned as the "Electric Farmyard", and then the Barn Door Roosters, Farmyard Roosters etc. At some stage the ride might have been jointly owned with brother John, or passed to him and then to D.Davies. It seems to fade from local advertisements about 1908.

R5 The Tunnel Railway

Savage's introduced their new "Channel Tunnel Railway" ride in the mid 1890's, although the idea seems to have been around before that time. A steam engine, specially designed to circumnavigate the tight circle of the ride, hauled its train through a "tunnel", in which riders could enjoy the excitement, or privacy, afforded by darkness, providing they could put up with the smoke and steam! Savages built six such rides and engine in 1895, and Pat Collins had engine No.641. The equipment included an electric light engine, mechanical organ and its engine, and the paybox

R6 The Velocipede, or 4-abreast Bicycles.

Sometimes simply called the "Steam Bikes". The ride was built by Savages in 1896, and was powered by engine No.675. Before the application of steam, rides of this nature had been produced on which the riders provided their own pedal-power, but as each cycle was attached to all the others circulating in the grooved track, riders could only proceed at the speed created by their joint effort. The duration of the ride was controlled by a brakesman. Velocipede rides had been powered by steam centre engines since the 1870's, so Pat was fairly "late" in purchasing this one in 1896. It appears among the rides Pat presented at various fairs the following year, but then disappears rather rapidly, although it was still in use in 1909, when motor cars were dominating the riding machines. At Bloxwich Gala, the Walsall Observer reported, "...*People were dashing from nowhere to nowhere in comfortable-looking motor cars at the rate of twenty miles an hour, whilst on the other side was a cycle track on which the riders pedalled furiously without the least hope of overtaking those in front.*" The ride was sold to J.Harris.

R7 4-abreast Gallopers

The manufacturer of this ride has not been identified, but it was built about 1897. At one stage the horses were replaced with ostriches, but the horses were back in place when the ride spent the 1919 season at Blackpool's South Shore. The ride was sold to W.Hastings at Margate, where it was damaged by fire. However, the domes off the rounding boards survived and passed to J.Beach's Gallopers, on which they are now preserved, presented in the 1980's by Bobby Rawlins.

R8 The Steam Yachts

Sometimes known as the Giant Steam Swings, built in 1902, by Savages, powered by their engine No.797. Supplied to Flora Collins, the yachts enjoyed a long career in the Collins' empire, but, as usual there is a problem of knowing how many yachts were owned by Pat, and which set was which.

At Easter Fairs at Wolverhampton and Walsall, 1924, there was a set of Yachts at each fair, and, for once they are more clearly identified: A "No.1" set was at Walsall, with boats "King" and "Queen", and a "No.2" set was at Wolverhampton, with boats "Lion" and "Tiger". At the Onion Fair of 1925 both sets were present at the same fair. The "King and Queen" set was the machine normally associated with Young Pat's departure from New Brighton and his return to the Midlands.

BELOW: The Four-Abreast (R7) apparently photographed at Earls Court in 1906, when some of the horses had been replaced with motor cars. (Compare this with the picture of the same machine used in Chapter 3). The domes of this machine are now preserved on Bobby Rawlin's set of Gallopers).
(Collection of Jim Boulton)

The Yachts that finally came to rest at the Crystal Palace site after the War, appear to be a different set altogether. This set was purchased by Walsall John as late as 1948 from Percy Cole, who had bought them from Tom Jervis. They appeared at the 1948 Onion Fair, and at Hull, along with the revived No.1.Scenic, and then took up residence in Sutton park, where they were eventually scrapped in the 1960's. At Sutton they were regarded as a poor money-maker, and had been relatively little used. The boats were named "Dreadnought" and "Superb". The nautical flavour was preserved in such names. Even the manager of the Yachts could be affected: in the 1930's Pat's Yachts were managed by Walter Kelly, and as years rolled by he became first "Captain Kelly"...and then "Admiral Kelly"!

R9 The Platform Galloper

This ride was supplied by Savages in 1903, with engine No.800, along with an organ engine No.801. This was the period of "Pat Collins (Walsall) Ltd" and, like the Yachts, it seems to have been supplied to Flora Collins - perhaps to distinguish it from the pre-1899 equipment that Pat sold to his own company. The horses were at some stage replaced with Pigs and Balloons. At the 1908 Goose Fair Pat's ride stole the show. The World's Fair report stated *"The mighty Pat Collins can always be relied upon to show us the latest thing in his line of business, and the gorgeousness of his roundabouts and shows is as stupendous as ever...genuine novelty is provided this year in the "Prize Porkers" - or Revolving Pigs"*.

Yet in 1909 the pigs had been replaced by Teddy Bears on the platforms. In the 1909 advert for the Bloxwich Gala, the public were told, *"First visit, and quite new - the Teddy Bears, the most enchanting riding machine ever invented"*. The reporter from the Walsall Observer saw them rather differently, he told his readers: *"Then there were the Teddy Bears, surely the most grotesque collection of animals ever seen on a roundabout. They lurch forward and jump back when least expected"*. After the First World War this ride, with horses back in place, found its way to the Crystal Palace site

R10 Razzle Dazzle

The Razzle Dazzle introduced a new riding experience to the fairground. The riders sat on radiating bench seats on a rotating platform, but once rotation was underway the whole platform tilted or dipped as it went round. It was supplied by Savages in 1906, with engine No.828. Brother John also invested in a Razzle Dazzle, and it was sometimes John's machine that was seen at fairs at which they were joint lessees. Pat also may have acted as an agent in selling Razzle Dazzles, helping to confuse folks with the idea that he had more than one such machine. Pat's machine was also known as the "Japanese Air Ship" and in 1907 enjoyed a season as "The Wheely Whirly" the Japanese Sensation.

Whether the original Razzle Dazzle survived the First World War is not clear. Pat Collins presented a Razzle Dazzle at the 1924 Wembley Exhibition, and travelled a machine in 1925 and early 1926. At the Onion Fair of 1925 it was described as the "No.2.Razzle Dazzle". A machine survived to be used on various permanent sites into the 1930's.

John Collins purchased a Razzle Dazzle after the Second World War, a Howcroft-built machine with a tortuous history. It was travelled and then installed at the Crystal Palace until the early 1950's.

R11 Switchback
Also known as the "No.3 Motors".

By 1905 Savages had built several motor-car switchbacks, in which the riders swept over the hills and through the vales in motor cars - the latest symbol of technological progress and wealth. Pat's set, known as the "Looping the Loop Motors", was built in 1907, with engine No.838. During 1907 it appears to have been presented by Young Pat. At the Onion Fair in 1907 it appeared alongside the No.1 and No.2 Motors but a World's Fair report made the comment that the No.3 was a *"true motor car ride"* and was a new invention by Pat! The ride is clearly seen in many photographs of Nottingham Goose Fair. It was later much rebuilt when combined with parts from the George Tuby Scenic Railway.

R12 The Aeroflyte

Supplied by Savages in 1909, with centre engine No.851, with organ engine No.852. The ride is described as similar in size to a set of Gallopers, but with large revolving wheels on the platforms, in which seats were hung. Its name is not mentioned in any advertisements seen to date, unless it is the machine listed as attending Dudley Fair in September 1909, when there is mention of " Aerial Flights".

R13 Cake Walk

The Brooklyn Cake Walk might have appeared as early as 1907, but really made its presence felt in 1908, after appearing at The White City, at London's Olympia, at the beginning of the year. World's Fair reports imply that Pat purchased the ride premiered at The White City, but the year saw many other innovations and nobody seemed to have time to catalogue the rapid spread of the Cake Walk. One report of the 1908 Goose Fair credits Pat with bringing the first Cake Walk to Nottingham but the report was more struck by the "Revolving Pigs" (see R9). However, it did add that the Cake Walk was very popular and that the proprietor was taking four shillings per minute. (Ironically, it may have been someone else's Cake Walk using Pat's position).

In 1909 it seems that Pat Collins purchased a Brooklyn Cake Walk, built 1909, by Taylor, Plinston Bros. but there may have been an element of Pat buying and selling such rides. As usual matters can be complicated by both Pat and Young Pat travelling Cake Walks. Certainly in the late 1920's there seems to have been one managed by Harry Swain and another

LEFT: Steam Yachts, "Beatty" and "Nelson", supplied in 1921 as "King and Queen" with Savage's engine No.883 (R37). Probably first used at New Brighton by Young Pat, but seen here at Edgbaston Reservoir in 1933. (The set used at Crystal Palace is illustrated in Chapter 13).
(Collection of Kevin Scrivens)

RIGHT: Pat Collins' Razzle Dazzle (No.2) used at the 1924 Wembley Exhibition Old Tyme Fair. The machine used at the Crystal Palace after the War is illustrated in Chapter 13. *(Collection of Kevin Scrivens)*

RIGHT: A rather poor photograph of Pat Collins' Cakewalk at Birmingham in 1933. It is possible that the figures and carved woodwork may have been transplanted from another attraction.
(Collection of Jim Boulton)

BELOW: The Three-Abreast "Grand National Steeplechase" seen at Birmingham in 1933.
(Collection of Jim Boulton)

looked after by young John James Collins (Young Pat's son). The Cake Walk became one of the rides deliberately kept going to preserve the best of the "old time" fairs in the midst of the latest attractions. Thus, Harry Richards' Cake Walk was presented at some of Pat Collins' fairs long after the Second World War.

R14 The Haunted Castle
Savages built this "Fun House" about 1908, and it is described as "The Haunted Castle" in the Bloxwich Gala advertisement of that year. The following year it has become the "Katzen-jammer Castle". In January 1909, Pat advertised in World's Fair that he was in a position to build Katzenjammer or Haunted Castles for other showmen. Prices ranged from £300 to £1,000. After the First World War it made its way to the Crystal Palace.

R15 Scenic Railway
The first electric scenic railway supplied "new" to Pat Collins, as opposed to being a converted switchback, was built by Savages, and was "opened" at the Wolverhampton Whit Fair in 1911. By the time it was presented at the Nottingham Goose Fair of that year it had tropical scenery on the rounding boards and low extension front. It was, therefore, sometimes known as "The Jungle Motors". It was damaged in a storm at Rotherham Statutes Fair, in 1911, and Orton & Spooner had to build another front for the ride, with a three-section extension front with deep foliage rounding boards and rustic "tree trunk" handrails.

In 1916, a set of Orton Dragon cars were put in place of the Motors, and a waterfall put in the centre behind the organ. It was managed by Clara Mullett, and was attended by the engines, "Emperor" (Burrell 3291), and "Clara" (Foster 13052). Nine trucks were needed to transport the machine, three trucks to a "train". In many instances this meant that "Emperor" made two trips to move the ride from place to place. Sometimes "Jack Whyatt" (Burrell 3447) was used with this ride. A 110 key Gavioli organ, acquired from a French garden cafe, played in the centre of the ride.

In 1920, the ride, organ and engines, were sold to Brother John, who gave it to his son, Michael Albert, as a wedding present. "Clara" had been driven by "Lump Coal" Billy Reohorn and he had to go to Lancashire with his engine, while keeping his family in the Black Country. The ride itself was familiar to Lancashire folk as Pat often sent it to Bolton, Burnley, Ashton, and Oldham.

R15a Scenic Railway
The original standard Savages top of the above scenic was added to the bottom that had originally been the Looping the Loop Motors (R11). It was rebuilt by Orton & Spooner in the early 1920's, the Savages centre engine being replaced with an Orton & Spooner organ/centre truck, and probably originally supplied with Dragon and Peacock cars. The Marenghi organ was taken from the No.1.Wonderland Show. The original cars were replaced with Whales, and, eventually in the 1930's it was used at Barry Island. While travelling it had been managed by Joby Farrell. It was attended by "Dreadnought" (Fowler 14424) and "Goliath" (McLaren 1623). Some of the original rounding boards may still be in existence, but most of the ride was burnt as scrap at the Bloxwich Yard.

R16 The No.1.Scenic Railway
The machine known as the No.1.Scenic was built by Orton & Spooner in 1921, as one of their standard pattern "Tropical Scenic Railways". It was first opened on the Market Place at Burton on Trent (the home town of Orton & Spooner), in the summer of 1921. Burrell engine "No.1" (3865) was supplied new to Pat Collins specifically to travel with this ride, which it did in partnership with "Goliath" (McLaren 1623). The ride was managed by Clara Mullett, released from the first scenic on the sale of that ride to M.A.Collins the previous year.

When new the ride was fitted with dragon cars, but these were replaced with whale cars in 1922, and for the next decade it was known as the "Whale Island". They were removed in the early 1930's and dragon and peacock cars took their place, and survived as the cars used on this ride until the end.

An important feature of this scenic was the organ. The Marenghi organ front from the No.2.Wonderland show was fitted to the Orton organ truck while the ride was being built. Behind this front, a 98 key Gavioli organ was installed that had been taken from a scenic that Pat Collins had purchased from George Tuby. Just as sacred music concerts had been held in front of the Wonderland show, organ concerts could now be held in front of the scenic.

The ride travelled very extensively on Pat's No.1.circuit until 1937, and had made a number of appearances at the Lancashire fairs until 1933. It was then taken into store at Bloxwich. After the War, Clara and John Collins decided that it should make a spectacular re-appearance. Burrell "No.1" once more took charge and the scenic was taken to Hull fair in 1948. Afterwards it was taken to Crystal Palace, Sutton Park, and it was decided that Chiappa would rebuild a suitable organ to go behind the Marenghi front. During 1951 the ride was dismantled in stages, while still in operation, and completely repainted and redecorated in the original style.

Having survived and enjoyed some degree of rejuvenation it was then very sad to see the ride deteriorate during the second half of the 1950's. The interior scenery, and the unused waterfall remained, but parts of the outside of the ride were removed. Even the heads of the dragons and the peacocks were removed. The organ disliked the damp conditions and only remained playable due to the efforts of Tom Hunt, who operated the miniature railway. The ride was dismantled at the end of the 1960 season and stored under sheets at the park. There was talk of the ride and organ being preserved.

In September 1962, Clara died, just as the lease on the Crystal Palace was expiring. Tom Hunt had persuaded Clara to allow him to remove the organ for preservation and, later, had done likewise with the organ front. Albert Martin and George Sutton, assisted by young Barry Island Pat, were instructed to

ABOVE: Notingham Goose Fair: 1909. On the left are the Looping-the-Loop Motors (R11). On the right are the Teddy Bears (R9), on which the "bears" had just replaced the "pigs". Behind this it is possible to glimpse the Gordon Bennett Motors (R29) and John Collins' Razzle Dazzle. No.2.Wonderland is built up behind the Gordon Bennett Motors
(*Nottingham Libraries*)

BELOW: A close up of the front of Pat Collins' "first" brand new electric scenic, as opposed to converted switchback (R15). The pillars illustrate the "jungle" treatment given to the frontage. This picture shows the Orton Dragon cars that replaced the original "motors" about 1916.
(*Collection of Kevin Scrivens*)

- 137 -

THE NO.1.SCENIC

LEFT: The No.1.Scenic (R.16) "as new" in 1921, built-up in Burton on Trent Market Place by Orton & Spooner.
(Collection of Kevin Scrivens)

LEFT: Having spent a decade as the Whale Island, the No.1.Scenic was given Dragon and Peacock cars in the early 1930's, and the machine is seen here at Newport, in front of the Vine Vaults, in 1933.
(Collection of Peter Hough)

LEFT: The No.1.Scenic "revived" and repainted, as seen at Hull Fair, on 16/10/1948, before its Final retirement to the Crystal Palace, Sutton Coldfield.
(Collection of Kevin Scrivens)

Advertisement for "Over the Falls", World's Fair, 8th September 1923.

E. J. Kilpatrick hands you – OVER THE FALLS – the World's Greatest Laugh!

All Enquiries re the above Record-breaking Amusement Riding Device to be made to

Mr. Henry Grattan Finn,

Now Touring with Mr. P. Collins's Concerns,

Who is the Personal Representative of the Patentee and Manufacturer:

E. J. KILPATRICK,

International Amusements,

Chicago, New York, and 446 Strand, London.

burn the remains of the scenic. Had it survived just four or five years' longer, the preservation movement might have saved it; when this was suggested by Captain Stratton in 1962 few believed such things were possible.

Tom Hunt set about restoring the Marenghi 'Chiappa-modified' organ, and was able to build it into a truck behind part of the Wonderland front. It made its return to public life at the White Waltham Steam Fair of 1964. Tom's son, Bill Hunt, continued to improve the organ, extending the front, returning the bandmaster to the position from which he had disappeared in about 1950, and enhancing the quality of the organ's sound, by adding pipes as close as possible to their original positions. The 98 key frame was retained as so much music in this format had been salvaged from the Crystal Palace cellar.

Rl7 The Joy Wheel

Savages went into liquidation in 1911, but were allowed to complete a number of Joy Wheels, and one came to Pat Collins. Riders were invited to try and sit or squat on a slightly conical disc as it spun, and others derived pleasure by watching their discomfort! When it toured the Black Country in 1911, Pat's advertising described it as ":*The Sensation of the season. America's very latest amusement furora - one long shriek of laughter"*. Its popularity as a travelling ride seemed short-lived, and after the First World War it was retired to the Crystal Palace.

R18 Chairoplanes

German ride manufacturers had perfected roundabouts in which customers rode in planes suspended from the spinning frame before the First World War. After the War, simpler versions were made in which seats replaced the planes, and some of these machines were imported into Britain during the 1920's. Pat's Chairoplanes are mentioned in his advertisements for his fairs during the 1925 - 1928 period.

R19 Over the Falls

Over the Falls was imported from America, the result of Walsall John's search for new rides, even in his teens! It seems to have "arrived" in 1923, accompanied by the American engineers who came to demonstrate how it was built-up. The build-up required the erection of a tubular steel frame, and everyone involved, including John, became expert acrobats as they swung from one part of the structure to another. John also drove the AEC, ex-Flying Corps lorry, that provided the ride's transport, along with another 3 ton AEC on solid tyres. The latter was replaced with a Maudslay (driven first by Frank Buck, later by George Messham).

The ride consisted of a long "conveyor-belt" or carpet, and having climbed to the top of the falls, punters sat on this continuous belt for a bumpy ride to the foot of the falls. It was popular, and travelled widely; at some stage managed by W.Brennan.

It seems that Pat also acquired a second "Over the Falls". Possibly built by Walkers of Tewkesbury, this one was delivered to a Mr.Woolf and was managed by George Roberts. George, and the ride, had joined Pat Collins by Easter 1927 when it appeared in Wolverhampton, while the other "Over the Falls" was at Blackburn. One of the "Falls" passed into the hands of Jack Barry, who had known John since his schooldays, and it was eventually put on a permanent site at Walney Island. The transport for this "Falls" was one FWD lorry and Peerless chain drive vehicle. It might be assumed that it was this one that was bought by Jack Barry, as it was advertised "For Sale", with the FWD and Peerless transport in January 1928. However, Jack Barry was presenting an "Over the Falls" for Pat at Hull in the October of 1928. When it appeared a few days later at Ilkeston we are told that it was Walsall John's "Falls". In his January 1928 advertisement Pat had stated *"I have three sets - one too many"*. This may be another example of Pat's tendency to exaggerate, or it may mean that Pat had two "Falls" and John had one.

However, there were definitely two "Over the Falls" travelling in 1928, and they both appeared at the Onion Fair. (Walter Hobbs Jnr was in charge of one, and Norman Goodwin was in charge of the other). Their popularity ensured that they travelled to some prestigious fairs.

The wealth of newer attractions in the 1930's does not seem to have made "Over the Falls" entirely redundant. John Collins took one to the 1938 Glasgow Exhibition, and it seems that, just after the War an "Over the Falls" was reconditioned and sent to the fair at Olympia!

R20 The Dodgems

At the Islington Hall Fair of January 1928, Mr.Wentworth, was demonstrating a Custer Motor Car Track, under the banner of Pat Collins. Although rides on which the patrons drove miniature self-propelled cars had been popular for some time in fixed amusement parks, the problem seemed to be one of manufacturing a travelling version of this ride. Although we associate "Dodgems" with electrically driven cars, picking up their current from an overhead mesh, and returning it via the metal plates of the track, the early experiments with self-propelled cars seemed to rely on producing miniature petrol-engined vehicles - the "Auto-Scooters" or "Radio Cars".

At Chester Races in May 1928, William Mullett was in charge of the "Miniature Brooklyn Motors" and at the Birmingham Whit-week Fair, Tom Taylor was in charge of the "Radio Cars". It is not clear whether these were all one and the same machine. To confuse us further neither terms are used in describing rides at the 1928 Onion Fair. At the Goose Fair, we learn that the "Radio Cars" were presented by Pat Collins, and the term is used again at Bulwell Wakes. Mean-

LEFT: Pat Collins takes a chair in his own "Chair-O-Planes" at Wolverhampton Fair, Whitsun 1925, watched by Albert Badger.
(Collection of John Ray).

- 140 -

while, the "Auto-Scooters" were at Hull and then Ilkeston. Although these were a new ride as far as the travelling fair was concerned, they appear to have received little special attention - the limelight was still occupied by "The Swish".

The World's Fair published a short article on Dodgems on 13th October 1928, indicating that the Lusse cars were the first electric Dodgems, but once again the term "Auto-Scooter" is used ambiguously, and it is not clear whether the distinction between the petrol-driven cars and the electric cars was the crucial difference.

Perhaps the proper "electric" Dodgem did not appear on the travelling fair until the following year. It is usually thought that Pat Collins' first Dodgems set was built by Orton & Spooner in 1929, and made an impressive appearance at the Nottingham Goose Fair of that year. Once again the reports of the fair tended to concentrate on other innovations - in 1929 the great attraction was the arrival of the Wall of Death.

The Dodgems, thereafter

It has been argued that it does not make sense to identify a No.1., No.2., No.3., etc. sets of Dodgems. Having taken a long time to materialise as a feature of the travelling fair, the "Dodgems" suddenly appeared at the very end of the 1920's under a bewildering number of names: the term "Dodgem" not being in widespread use until 1930. From then on it is very difficult to catalogue them. New cars might be placed on old tracks, further new names were invented and so on. In the 1930's and 1940's Pat Collins' fairs may have travelled three Dodgems at any one time, and may have used others at the amusement parks. The Orton & Spooner track identified above may have been sold in 1937, when Pat placed the following advert in World's Fair; *"For Sale - Handy Little Dodgem - complete with 20 cars, 62' x 42', built by Orton & Spooner. Reason for selling - I have too many Dodgems"*.

Generally the tracks grew larger and the cars tried to keep up with styles created by the motor trade. In the summer of 1938 Pat took delivery of a larger "Supercar" track, and the distinctive fretwork and roundings can often be seen in photographs of Pat's fairs. Trying to identify the Dodgems by the names of the managers in charge of them does not seem to work, as they changed frequently before the War. In the 1928/29 period Baby Pat is often credited with looking after the "Auto Scooters"/"Radio Cars". Once the term "Dodgem" is in regular use it is first in the care of Albert Badger. For a time Charlie Hayes looked after the set on the No.1. run , and John Ryan looked after another. Both Dodgems were at the 1936 Onion Fair, and World's Fair noted that John Ryan's set had "new glittering cars". The following year we come across a set of Dodgems presented by J.Crewe.

It was not unknown for Clara Collins to take control of the Dodgems at major fairs like Liverpool Royal Visit fair of 1938, leaving Ted Sherwood, her foreman, to look after the Waltzer, released from the Scenic by that machine's retirement in 1937. After 1937, Ted Sherwood regularly presented the Dodgems.

BELOW: The Dodgems at 'Willenhall Wakes in 1932. Left to Right, Arthur Bate, Billy Beesley, unknown, and Tony "Tich" Robinson in the car. The car is a typical Lusse-built car of the period, and the distinctive Orton & Spooner fretwork can be seen in the background.
(Collection of Jimmy Ryan)

LEFT: The Dodgems, believed to be photographed in 1935, with Saxon cars.
(Collection of Jimmy Ryan)

LEFT: The Dodgems at Chester Races fair in 1938 with Rytecraft cars built to "air flow" design. Note the barley-sugar brass poles fitted to the cars.
(Collection of Jimmy Ryan)

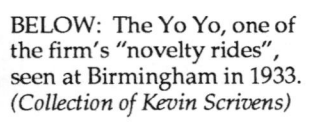

BELOW: The Yo Yo, one of the firm's "novelty rides", seen at Birmingham in 1933.
(Collection of Kevin Scrivens)

R21 Noah's Ark

The large scenic railways were labour-intensive and too grand for their own well-being. The Ark was a new variant on the switchback, segmented platforms travelled up and down the hills and vales of a circular track, the animals on which the punters could ride were mounted on the platforms - hence the name: ARK. The first one was built in Germany in 1929, and the first one to arrive in England was imported by William Wilson for the following year. British manufacturers, Orton & Spooner, and Lakin, quickly produced their own versions. They were smaller and less ornate than the scenics had been, but once proven successful they increased in size and decorative splendour. Pat Collins travelled a German Ark in 1930, and also advertised such rides as "For Sale", implying he was an agent/importer of them. It was probably transferred to one of the permanent sites when the Orton & Spooner Ark arrived the following year.

R22 Noah's Ark

This was a 42.ft diameter Ark built by Orton & Spooner, supplied 1931. It was sold to a London showman (James Watts) about 1943, along with the McLaren, "Samson".

R23 The Ghost Train

This ride was another innovation of the early 1930's, and Pat's Ghost Train was another product of Orton & Spooner. Ghost Trains became an essential feature of the amusement parks, and, as with other popular rides, it is difficult to know exactly how many Pat Collins used.

R24 The Waltzer

"Waltzing" rides had appeared at the fair on and off for many years, but the development of the Ark led to the modern revival of the idea. It was quite possible to replace the animals or motorcycles of an Ark with gyrating "tubs" that could lurch and spin as they circulated the track on their segmented platforms. Pat Collins' first Waltzer was an early Lakin machine, built in 1933, and eventually sold to Frank Codona in 1947, when the firm took delivery of a new Waltzer.

R25 The Swish

The Swish was the name given to Savages version of the Skid or Swirl, rides that traced their ancestry back to the invention of "The Whip" - a track on which riders were propelled and spun while seated in tubs. Pat's Swish is described as "new" in a report of Crewe Fair in the summer of 1926, and the World's Fair writer comments that it was "very similar to George Green's Whip which has been seen at Blackpool for several seasons. At Wednesbury in September 1926 it is described as "noisy", although at the Onion Fair it *"caused much excitement and attracted much business"*. From the Onion Fair it went on to Hull.

It is recorded as appearing at Wolverhampton at Easter 1927, under the management of J.Bailey, but other references to it seem few and far between until it is presented as "new", once again, at the Kings Lynn Mart in 1928. During the 1930's it is often referred to as "the Skid" and for a time was looked after by Baby John.

R26 The Flying Fleas

This was basically a large Chair-o-Plane machine and was probably built in Germany. It was travelled during the early to mid 1930's, and, after the War was built up at the Great Yarmouth amusement park. By the mid 1950's it had joined the scrap heap at Sutton Coldfield.

BELOW: The Orton & Spooner Ghost Train of 1931 (R23) seen at the Birmingham Onion Fair with "The Leader" in attendance. On the right is the front to the Globe of Death.
(Collection of Peter Hough)

R27 The Mont Blanc, The Airways
Built in 1934 by R.J.Lakin, and travelled until the War. It was presented by Baby Pat (Young Pat's son) for a year or two, and was given the name "The Airways". The "up to the minute" image of this ride quickly established its importance. It appeared at the Goose Fair in 1935, where it took the position that had previously been occupied by the No.1.Scenic - a sign of the times! Later managed by Dennis Shipley and others. After the War it was used in the amusement parks, including the Crystal Palace, Sutton Park, where it was eventually scrapped.

R28 Super Speedway Arc
This ride was built in 1937 by Orton & Spooner, with motorcycle mounts, and was one of the firm's largest Arks. After the War, Autodrome car bodies were fitted to the platforms and it travelled in this guise into the 1950's. It was travelled by Billy Bagnall, and when the lease expired at Sutton Park, it was included in the equipment he purchased and took to his short-lived amusement park at Chasewater, where, eventually it was scrapped.

NOVELTY RIDES

Hit the Deck
Briefly mentioned in 1928, when described as a "new" ride at the Goose Fair, and then at Ilkeston.

THE YO YO.
Introduced at Great Yarmouth Pleasure Beach in 1933, and travelled to one or two of the larger Back End fairs. This was another example of the "novelty ride". The patron rode the roundabout in a chair slung from the roof of the ride by elastic ropes - enabling one to bounce up and down while revolving!

The Jolly Tubes
Rarely listed by the World's Fair as an attraction at Pat's fairs, but the 1929 account of the fair at Wrexham, dscribes them as "new", and they were being presented by Walsall John, who, shortly afterwards seems to have taken charge of Over the Falls.

LEFT: Pat Collins' "Airways" (R27) seen at Stratford Mop Fair in Autumn 1935 when presented by Baby Pat.
(World's Fair)

LEFT: The Flying Fleas (R26) when presented as "Up in the Clouds" at the Nottingham Goose Fair of 1936.
(Collection of Kevin Scrivens)

- 144 -

Second Hand Switchbacks

BELOW: Stripped of its extension front and domes, the same machine is seen here with Whale cars at Birmingham in 1928.
(Collection of Bernard Morley)

ABOVE: Young Pat's Scenic Dragons (R29) seen at New Brighton. The manager, Jimmy Harris, is thought to be the man standing on the steps. The 1891 machine had been rebuilt as Gondolas for Pat in 1894, then rebuilt again in 1906 as the Gordon Bennett Motors. Here it is seen with Dragon cars, installed early 1920's.
(Collection of Peter Hough)

b) THE FOLLOWING RIDES WERE PURCHASED 'SECOND HAND' BY PAT COLLINS

R29 Young Pat's Dragons
This ride started life as a switchback, built for J.Hancock in 1891. It was rebuilt by Savages as a set of Rolling Gondolas for Pat Collins in 1894. Thus they "rolled" or pitched as they circulated the switchback track. The ride was rebuilt again in 1906 as the Gordon Bennett Motors, and in 1909 the old centre engine was replaced by a new Savage Traction Centre engine, No.847, "The Wonder". In 1911 the ride was rebuilt as a scenic railway, and was taken over by Young Pat. Dragon cars were installed in 1922, and it was known as the "Mountain Dragons". For a time, Young Pat ran the Mountain Dragons at the Palace Amusement Park at New Brighton, under the management of Jimmy and Lilian Harris. Still later, Whale cars were fitted..

R30 Scenic Railway
This machine was supplied new to George Tuby in 1912, and was sold to Pat Collins in 1920. The front from the Looping the Loop Motors was put on this ride. Probably the "Scenic Motors" referred to as late as 1927/28.

R31 Switchback
This ride began life in 1888 as a Savage-built set of "Mountain Ponies" for John Murphy (Savage engine No.438). Later rebuilt as Gondolas. They were a combination of Gondolas and Motors in Pat's ownership, and it was sold to Hibberts in 1909.

R33 Maggie Collins' Gallopers
Built in 1896 by Savages, (centre engine No.664), described as a small set of 3 Abreast Gallopers. Maggie Collins advertised in World's Fair of 16.5.08 that her 3 Abreast was for sale "the quickest and the best running on the road". She said she was retiring due to ill health, and the ride could be inspected at the Chester Races Fair. It appears that the machine was not sold and that she continued to travel it. Maggie Collins died in 1925, and it seems that Pat absorbed some of her fairs as a Welsh border circuit.

Apparently this set of Gallopers was purchased by Slaters of Carlisle in 1932, and was travelled by them for five years. In later years a set of Gallopers bearing the legend, "Auntie Maggie's Gallopers" was in use at Seaton Carew.

R34 Ex Beach Gallopers
This 3 Abreast set was new to Beach in 1897, built by Savages, centre engine No.697.

YOUNG PAT'S RIDES

Like his father, Young Pat occasionally made exaggerated remarks about the number of rides that he owned, or had owned. (See the profile of Young Pat). This adds to the difficulty of presenting a satisfactory list. Perhaps Young Pat acquired his own equipment as he regained the lease on the New Brighton ground in the early 1920's. H.M.Jay's report in World's Fair visited the ground in early summer 1921, and listed the following equipment as "branded Pat Collins Junior": The Dragon Scenic, a Motor Car Scenic, a Three-Abreast, Cycles, Slip and swings. There was a brand new ride - "The Dash" built by Albert Barnes of Rhyl. Three or four stalls were also regarded as Young Pat's, and the Gaiety Picture Palace.

Some of these attractions did travel before and after their season at New Brighton. For example, The Dash was seen at Wrexham fair in April 1923, along with the Whip Whop!

In addition to R29 listed above.. .. ..

R35 The Jungle Scenic
This was a scenic railway purchased from the sons of Randall Williams. It was managed for Young Pat by Jimmy Crewe.

R36 The Velvet Coaster
This was a Scenic Railway purchased new from Savage's in 1915. It was fitted with a 1909, 112 keyless Gavioli organ. The engines used with this ride were Burrell 2988 "The Mascot" and Burrell 2709 "Mabon", both acquired second-hand. In 1918 the machine, and "The Mascot" were sold to Harness Brothers.

R37 The Steam Yachts
The boats were named "King" and "Queen", and they first appeared in Young Pat's ownership in 1920 or 1921. For the first two years they were managed by Billy Harris, and then by George Studt. George left in 1927 to run his own sidestalls and juveniles, and he was replaced by Walter Coe (Coey). On the road, they were usually pulled by "Helpmate" (Burrell 3183 of 1910), and the Yachts themselves were powered by Savage engine No.883. By the early 1930's, the Yachts were renamed "Nelson" and "Beattie".

R38 The Cake Walk
See R13.

R39 The Big Wheel
In 1937 Mr Thompson, of Blackpool Pleasure Beach, and Lusse Bros.Ltd set out to import Big "Eli" Wheels from America's Coney Island. Two wheels were built up, one to demonstrate the amusement park model, the other, a 50' wheel with 12 cars, to demonstrate the travelling model. Young Pat purchased the latter, to become the first showman travelling a Big Wheel in Britain. He intended using it at his Colwyn Bay ground, but it travelled extensively - to Wrexham, Chester, Liverpool, around the Black Country, the Goose Fair, and back to Birmingham for the Carnival Fair. Young Pat also had his own Dodgem track at Colwyn Bay, and this was sold to his son and daughter-in-law (Baby John and Norah Collins).

UNPOWERED EQUIPMENT

HELTER SKELTER
also known as the Lighthouse Slip
The first Helter Skelter presented in this country is said to be T.Harrison's model, seen at Preston Fair in 1905. Pat seems to have had at least one tower in 1906.

At Bloxwich, in August, the amusements included a "Yankee Helter Skelter", and Young Pat presented a tower at the 1906 Burton Statutes Fair in the Autumn. In March 1907 Pat placed an advertisement in World's Fair: "FOR SALE - Helter Skelter - Slipping the Slip - Having three will sell one"

At the 1925 Onion Fair, where so many rides were "duplicated", Helter Skelters were triplicated. A Helter Skelter was still being travelled in the late 1930's, and one was included in the amusements on offer at the Crystal Palace in 1939.

ABOVE: Young Pat's Scenic Dragons travelling before being built up at the New Brighton site. Seen here on an unidentified grassy fairground.
(Collection of Molly Seldon)

BELOW: The ex Randall Williams Scenic Railway (R35) managed for Young Pat by Jimmy Crewe. Thought to be photographed at the 1924 Wembley Exhibition Old Tyme Fair.
(Collection of John Williams)

ORGAN CHECKLIST

Organs attached to the Bioscope Shows:

1. The ex-Wall & Hammersley Show. (B1)
   This show featured an 87 or 89 key Gavioli Organ.
2. The second wagon-fronted show (B2)
   This show probably featured an 87 key Gavioli Organ.
3. No.1.Wonderland
   Originally featured a 104 key Marenghi Organ. See below.
4. No.2.Wonderland
   Originally featured a 104 key Marenghi Organ. See below.

Organs and Rides:

1. The Joby Farrell Scenic (R15a)
   Used the 104 key Marenghi Organ from the No.1.Wonderland.
2. The Gordon Bennett Motors (R29)
   Used a 98 key sleighbell Marenghi Organ.
3. The 1911 Scenic (R15)
   Used a 110 key Gavioli Organ, originally in a French Cafe.
4. The No.1 Scenic (R16)
   Used the front from the Marenghi featured on the No.2 Wonderland, with an ex-Tuby 112 key-less Gavioli behind (converted to 98 key). After the War this was replaced with a 98 key Chiappa.
   Now restored and preserved by Bill Hunt.
5. The Ex-Randall Williams Scenic (R35)
   The organ originally in this ride was a 110 key Gavioli used on the Randall Monte-Williams Bioscope. Young Pat put this organ into a set of Gallopers, and replaced it with a former 112 keyless Gavioli.
   This probably replaced for a second time before the ride was broken up at Lickey Hills in 1927.
6. The ex George Tuby Scenic (R30)
   The Organ used was a 110 key Gavioli supplied in 1909.
7. Pat Collins bought a 112 key-less Gavioli in 1909.
   In 1915 it was placed in a new Savage-built scenic presented by Young Pat. The machine was sold in 1918 to Harness Brothers who late rebuilt the Organ to 98 keys, after which it was sold to John Green of Preston.

BELOW: The Marenghi organ used on the No.1.Scenic, being towed onto its gantry, around which the ride will be built, at Bolton New Year Fair in the early 1920's.
(Collection of Peter Hough)

THE ARKS

ABOVE: "Over the Sticks", the big ark managed by Billy Weston, seen here at Crystal Palace, Sutton Coldfield, in September 1949.
(Collection of Kevin Scrivens)

RIGHT: The small ark, presented by Harry "Matey" Weston, photographed at the Walsall Arboretum Fair of 1952.
(Collection of Rod Spooner)

RIGHT: The small ark, Motor Cycle Speedway, in its final form, without extension front but with rounding boards and shutters nicely painted, at Birmingham in November 1959.
(Collection of Fred Richardson)

RIDES ASSOCIATED WITH WALSALL JOHN

As stated previously, listing 'who owns what and when' is difficult, and a particularly good example is the Wonderland Show which made its debut at Wrexham in 1907. It is sometimes described as a 21st Birthday present, or 'forthcoming' wedding present to Young Pat. Whatever the case, it is seldom later described as Young Pat's Wonderland Show. On the other hand, the Yachts, and the engine "Little Helpmate" are more consistently described as belonging to Young Pat. So long after the events and in the absence of reliable records, it is impossible to accurately assess the transactions, acquisitions or financial independence of the Collinses in the period of time covered by this book

However, Walsall John's children were always given to understand that their father had been given few special favours by their grandfather, and that he had started his career as a 'tenant', or a manager of his father's ride. Being as restless and progressive as Pat himself, it has been suggested that he saw the opportunity to make money by building a Big Dipper...his father disapproved at the time, but was subsequently proved wrong. It would make an intriguing story! Perhaps some of the rides that John first imported or acquired were purchased on behalf of his father, but they have not been listed as rides and equipment belonging to Pat Collins in our main list. Overlook this possibility therefore, and accept the following as an attempt to list rides associated with Walsall John.

THE HEY DEY
A new ride introduced by the importers, Thomas Jackson of Macclesfield, late 1929. Was built up at Great Yarmouth, but was also travelled. (Possibly this was the ride described as the "Atlantic Roller" seen as a new attraction at the Onion Fair in 1929).

THE TILT-A-WHIRL
Introduced at Yarmouth Pleasure Beach during the summer of 1934, as the latest thrilling ride. Eventually incorporated into the attractions to be found at the Crystal Palace site.

OVER THE TOP
Another new attraction at Great Yarmouth in 1934. Designed by George Openshaw, and built by Messrs Lang Wheels of Uxbridge. It was a 1930's version of the ride now known as Swinging Gyms.

THE WHIRLWIND RACER
This machine was a new attraction to be found at Barry Island when the park re-opened in May 1936. It had a 183' x 85' track built by Orton & Spooner carrying two cars that John had imported from the Chicago Exhibition. The cars traversed the track simultaneously and appeared to race each other. Despite the size of the track it was possible to travel the ride, and it was built up at Aston for the 1936 Onion Fair. The Whirlwind Racer was included in the attractions presented at the Glasgow 1938 Exhibition.

THE LOOP O PLANE
John Collins introduced this as a new ride at the Yarmouth Pleasure Beach in May 1936, and advertisements in World's Fair indicate that he was acting as an agent, able to import such rides and sell them to other showmen. One was brought to the Whit Week fair at Birmingham at the beginning of June 1936, and was described as the "sensation of the fair". John himself was operating it with great glee, and endless queues waited for the ride. The report indicated that the machine travelling was the "original" and that the one at Yarmouth was the second such machine. John Collins told World's Fair that they were being manufactured at the rate of two per month. The Loop o Plane travelled to a number of major fairs in 1936, including Oxford St Giles, where it was reported that Pat and Clara came to see it, and that it went from the Onion Fair to the Goose Fair.

BELOW: The advertisement for the new Loop-o-Plane that appeared in World's Fair, 9 January 1937.

LOOP-O-PLANE
DISTINCTLY DIFFERENT — THIS RIDE IS BREAKING ALL PROFIT RECORDS!

It has stolen the show and created new standards for consistent earnings wherever it has operated. Loop-O-Plane has what it takes— flash, spectacular performance, a new sensation, a real thrill. It turns a dead spot into the centre of attraction. Nothing compares with it for ballyhoo, the ability to draw a crowd.

Since Nottingham Goose Fair Four Machines have been sold. The Loop-O-Plane has been to Birmingham four times in 18 months, and on the last occasion got 9d. per person, the same as the first time, and at Nottingham 1/6 per person.

SPECIAL PRICES FOR MACHINES SUPPLIED IN WINTER MONTHS.

SPECIFICATIONS, PRICES, TERMS:—

JOHN COLLINS,
Pleasure Beach, Great Yarmouth

THE BROOKLAND RACE TRACK
John opened his "petro-scooter" track in 1934 at Yarmouth; Rytecraft, the manufacturers of the "scooter cars", featured its success in their advertising. In the autumn of 1934 it visited the Back End fairs. As with the Loop o Plane, there appears to be at least two of these rides in operation - one that stayed at Yarmouth, and one that travelled and possibly became the track at the Crystal Palace.

THE MOONROCKET
John presented his new Moon Rocket at the Newcastle Town Moor fair in June 1938, and at Oxford St Giles, and the following Goose Fair.

THE SMALL WALTZER
John Collins' small waltzer was a frequent feature of the post-war fair, when it was managed by Clifford Croydon, the son of Pat's ground manager, Bill Croydon. It had illuminated front rounding boards, featuring musical instruments and notes.

JOHN'S DUCKS
Sometimes known as the "Goosey Gander Ride" or "Ducks and Drakes", all of which gave an unflattering picture of the cars in which the patrons rode on this straightforward roundabout. John's aversion to green was illustrated by leaves painted on the rounding boards in turquoise.

THE ROTOR
At the Battersea Pleasure Gardens, in 1951, was a large metal "Rotor", built by Orton & Spooner. Patrons enter a large "silo" and when it revolves they find themselves pinned to the wall, as the floor is withdrawn from beneath them, Walsall John immediately ordered a similar ride, slightly smaller and to be built in wood. Orton & Spooner used the experience they had gained in building Walls of death and the new ride was first built up at the Kelvin Hall, Glasgow, for the following New year. It was used at Barry Island and travelled the Back End fairs.

THE VAMPIRE JETS
Not to be confused with Elias Harris' Hurricane Jets, John imported this ride from the USA, and hauled it from Barry to the Goose Fair behind Showtrac, "The Major" in 1964.

GRAVITY RIDES
As the Collins' moved into the amusement parks at Great Yarmouth and Barry Island, they encountered the gravity rides such as Figure of Eight Railways and Water Chutes. (These rides were generally owned by companies or individuals who were tenants of the owner or lessee of the park The Americans had extended the principle behind such attractions to produce the "Roller Coaster", and some European builders of fairground equipment, like Schippers, of Hamburg, built them between the Wars. Walsall John's quest for thrills and excitement naturally led him to these attractions. First of all a "German" Big Dipper was purchased in Paris and was built at Yarmouth for 1932. This was followed, in 1937 with a similar ride at Sutton Coldfield. (Messrs Schippers assisted John with these projects, and the Wadbrooks, of Yarmouth developed the necessary expertise to do some of the building work).

In 1938 John built the huge Big Dipper at the Glasgow Empire Exhibition, which was a great success with the patrons, and was a financial success for John. Although, at first, offered for sale after the Glasgow Exhibition, John decided to dismantle the ride and rebuild it at Liege in Belgium. In 1939, not long after its completion. It had to be very hurriedly pulled down and shipped out of Belgium as a result of the outbreak of War. It was then rebuilt at Barry Island.

The 1937 ride at Sutton was replaced in 1946 with a Big Dipper that was the chief attraction at the park for four seasons until being moved down to Battersea. Whether this was completely a "replacement" or a "rebuild" is not clear. It appears to have been "replaced", if we take Southdown's words at their face value in a World's Fair report of 27 April 1946: "The new attraction at Collins' Crystal Palace Amusement Park will be the giant Scenic Railway from Southport which is now being erected. It was bought by John Collins, and will cover half an acre of ground".

BELOW: Some idea of the size of the Brookland Race Track can be gained from this picture taken at Hull Fair in 1948.
(Collection of Kevin Scrivens)

LEFT: The Loop-o-Plane in action at the Birmingham Trinity (Whit-Week) fair in 1950, surrounded by swings and Harry Richard's Cake Walk,
(Collection of Kevin Scrivens)

LEFT: The Tilt-a-Whirl, introduced at Yarmouth Pleasure Beach in 1934, seen here in 1948, looking like a rather naked Waltzer.
(Collection of Kevin Scrivens)

LEFT: John Collins' Moon Rocket at Newcastle in Summer 1938 before its travels to the Goose Fair, etc. After the War it was built up at Gt Yarmouth.
(Collection of Kevin Scrivens)

It may have been augmented by parts of dippers that John may have bought and put into store. It was not unknown to rebuild or extend existing dippers. For example, the advertisement in the Sutton News announcing the re-opening of the park for the 1950 season specifically states that two new dips have been added to the Big Dipper! John went on to present such rides at the Brussels World Fair of 1958, and at Rome's Lunar Park. In 1940 he had taken a half share in a roller coaster built at San Francisco.

DEATH RIDES

Walsall John presented Walls and Globes of Death at Great Yarmouth, and then travelled them, during the 1930's. See the separate section on Death Rides associated with the Pat Collins empire.

SHOWS ASSOCIATED WITH WALSALL JOHN

John displayed quite an interest in shows, and theatrical presentations, and is even reputed to have bought and sold a music hall at some stage! In the summer of 1937 he presented his Mississippi Showboat - an elaborate showfront for a travelling variety show. He supervised the building of this at Great Yarmouth during the preceding Winter, from parts fabricated by Orton & Spooner. It was inspired by the popularity of the film, "Showboat". The following year, 1938, he presented his "Ro Lo" which was a new Fun House.

THE WORLD'S FAIR, SATURDAY, OCTOBER 8th, 1938.

FOR SALE
EMPIRE EXHIBITION
SCENIC RAILWAY

Or would consider percentage basis proposition.

John Collins, Scenic Railway, Empire Exhibition, Glasgow.

ABOVE: This advertisement appeared in World's Fair on 8th October 1938, but it seems that John was unsucessful in trying to sell the Glasgow Big Dipper. It eventually reached Barry Island, via Belgium!

ATTRACTION FOR A MIDLANDS AMUSEMENT PARK.

Visitors to the Crystal Palace Pleasure Grounds, Sutton Coldfield, owned by Alderman Pat Collins, should find a ride on the sensational new gravity ride (seen above in course of construction) as enjoyable as those they took on the Switchback which it replaces. Mr. Andrew Vettal, of Cincinnati (Ohio) is responsible for its construction. [Photo: "Birmingham Gazette."]

AFTER THE WAR

ABOVE: Walsall John's small Waltzer, managed by Clifford Croydon. The machine began life as an Orton & Spooner Ark of the mid 30's - rebuilt as a Waltzer with illuminated translucent panels in the frontage. Eventually retired to Seaburn and sold to Billy Murphy.
(Collection of Mrs Croydon)

John's Ducks - the Goosey Gander ride managed by Harry Passey seen here at Wolverhampton, 30/3/59. Johnny Ryan's Dodgems behind.
(Collection of Fred Richardson)

LEFT: The 1937 Speedway Ark, seen at Birmingham Onion Fair 1948, managed by Watty Hayes. The motorcycles have been replaced with "autodrome" cars. It was eventually presented by Billy Bagnall as his "Tunnel of Love".
(Collection of Kevin Scrivens)

ABOVE: The Odeon Waltzer stripped of its Odeon extension front (destroyed by Fire), seen here in 1958 with No.1.Showtrac in attendance.
(Collection of Mick Archer)

RIGHT: By the following year, 1959, the front of the Waltzer had been repainted. Seen here under the management of John Cook, at Wolverhampton on the evening of Boxing Day 1959.
(Collection of Fred Richardson)

RIGHT: Billy Bagnall presented his ex Cadona Autodrome of 1939 as a Caterpillar bearing Pat Collins' name as part of the Birmingham Trinity Fair, 11/6/60.
(Collection of Fred Richardson)

Just as he was interested in novelty rides, he was also always looking for novelty shows. Some of these were shortlived, and many have names that give no indication of what they actually were. (eg the "Boomerang" and "Rollata" of 1951).

Another "Show" that interested Walsall John was the Boxing Booth. He built one at Gt Yarmouth, which opened in the summer of 1934. Harry "Kid" Furness was the principal boxer, and on August Bank Holiday 1934 the ex-world Champion, Jimmy Wilde came along and showed the crowds his Lonsdale Belt. John collected boxing "artefacts" and before leaving Lime Tree House he invited a local paper to photograph the belt won by Owen Moran, a World Bantamweight champion.

THE SHOWS

As Pat began to realise many of his ambitions in his quest to present the biggest and best it was necessary to strike a balance between rides, stalls and shows. It appears that the only shows he himself owned were the Bioscopes, the Lion Shows / Menageries, and the "Death Rides". The other shows that formed part of his fairs were presented by showmen appearing as his tenants, Many of them travelled with him regularly from fair to fair, and returned year after year, so although they did not appear exclusively on Pat's fairs, they became associated with him...

LIFE WITH THE LIONS

Travelling menageries were once as popular as the travelling fair and circus. No-one had clarified the issues of animal rights, and this was the only opportunity afforded the general public to see such exotic animals. We are writing about the days before TV and Safari parks of course.

From the account of Pat's illegal fair in Walsall, in 1892, we know he gave pride of position to E.H.Bostock's Menagerie, and that by the end of the 1890's he was presenting his own lion shows and menageries. In the 1900's the Bioscopes stole the show, but as soon as cinemas took on the business of showing films the bioscope showfronts reverted to the business of presenting animal and circus shows.

Flora became particularly associated with the Lion Show after the First World War, managed by Tom Bew, and later R.Varley, then Norman Goodwin. Lion-tamers became legends only to fade into later obscurity; men like Black Albert, the second "Maccomo" (Albert Williams), Captain Clarke, George Laurance. The Lions were always "Legends" as well, and were nearly always called Nero or Wallace. It was claimed that they were wild "forest bred" creatures, but most were born in captivity, and Pat and Flora were known to entrust the care of lion cubs to their own alsations.

Even so, the Lions did sometimes attack their tamers! George Laurance was badly mauled at Willenhall in 1896. It was also good publicity if the lion could be persuaded to "escape" every now and again, but there appears to have been at least one occasion at Bloxwich in the early 1930's when the escape was not planned.

Towards the end of the 1920's the Lion Show is often credited to Pat rather than Flora, and occasionally it comes in for special comment. For example, in reporting on the fair at Wrexham in April 1929, World's Fair adds 'Pat Collins' Lion show was repainted and was looking better than ever - the old ghost show front thoroughly redecorated and the organ beautifully lit".

It is never quite clear if the Lion Show and Menagerie were two separate shows, although a report of the Birmingham Whit Week Fair of 1925 implies that they were separate and discusses the fronts of both shows - on that occasion Pat's show was a circus and Flora's was the Lion Show. If they were entirely separate shows it seems reasonable to assume that it was Flora's show that became the menagerie that "retired" to Barry Island from 1930 until her death. Pat's Lion Show continued to appear until late 1933 or early 1934. Thereafter lions were presented by other showmen.

PUTTING ON A SHOW

Freaks, Flea Circuses, enormous ladies, gentle midgets, Ashanti Warriors, Gigantic pigs and tiny horses all appeared at the shows on Pat Collins' fairs. Listed below are a few of the showmen, and some of their shows:

The Westwood Children:
giants from New Zealand who travelled with Pat in 1908.
Dot Raynor:
In the early 20's travelled a model coal mine, later developed Flea Circus.
James Stockwell:
The Lobster-clawed girl, bearded ladies, bird-faced man, three-legged man, living skeleton, negro turning white etc.
William Shufflebottom:
a Wild West Show.
Jack Parry:
Travelled for years with Pat. Built up quite a large snake and reptile show in the 2 0's. Presented Big Chief Red Snake in the 30's.
James Styles:
Presented freak and novelty shows with Pat from the mid 1920's onwards, midget eskimo, fat girl, beautiful giantess (Titania) etc.
Jack Headley:
Indian fakirs.
Charles Relph:
Freak shows.
Joe Gardiner:
Billy the giant pig, and Wee Jimmy, the miniature race horse.
Pat Kilbride:
A master of the unusual show, for example at the 1936 Onion Fair, he appeared with 'The Secret of Life of the Chinese Underworld" with a new showfront painted by Barnetts of Oldbury, invoking the mystery of the Triads and Opium Dens.
Tom Norman:
presented variety shows and novelties, carrying on a

RIGHT: George Laurence with Collins' Lion Show about 1907. A "thirty year old photograph" published in World's Fair in May 1927.
(World's Fair)

RIGHT: Dot Rayner's Flea Circus that travelled with Pat Collins' fair during 1934 through to the Onion Fair, and then went to the Goose Fair where it was filmed for a Gaumont British News Reel.
(World's Fair)

RIGHT: Kayes' Circus travelled frequently with Pat Collins in the 1930s. Richard Kayes' daughter, Norah, seen in this picture, married Pat's grandson Baby John (J.J.Collins).
(Collection of Norah Collins)

tradition established by his father, Tom Norman, the "Silver King". In the 1930's he travelled people like Bonita the Rifle Queen, and the Great Carmo, who did a season at Great Yarmouth for Pat. After the War, Tom Norman's 'Palladium Show' maintained the only regular organ presence at the Onion Fairs. The Shows faded from the fairground after the Second World War, although for a time they were to be found at the larger fairs, including the Onion Fair.

THE BOXING BOOTHS

There is a long history of presenting pugilistic 'activities' as an attraction of the fairground, and many famous fighters trace their beginnings back to the boxing 'booths', 'academies' and 'pavilions'. Boxing attractions were welcomed as part of Pat Collins' fairs as Pat and his sons all took quite an interest in the sport. Pat and Walsall John often feature in anecdotes where they lay-out their opponents with skilful use of their fists. It was also an interest of many Black Country patrons of the fair, because the region has its own traditions and heros, such as William Parry, the "Tipton Slasher".

Many local people have vivid memories of the Boxing Booth from the patron's point of view, and the name of Charlie HIckman seems particularly well-known. However, as you will see below, there were several boxing shows that travelled with Pat Collins' fairs.

A typical story runs as follows:

"When I went to the fair in Wolverhampton, I was virtually penniless. I spent the last of my money on visiting the boxing booth, after watching the "show" outside for a long time. The speiler asked for local lads to volunteer to fight one of the boxers for a money prize, and immediately someone volunteered. After being "beaten" the speiler then asked us to throw contributions as a consolation prize for the local volunteer. About £3 was collected, and I immediately decided it was worth being beaten just to receive the cash collected from the audience. I pushed my way to the front to volunteer to take on the next boxer. Three rounds later, when I was thrown out of the ring, no collection was made on my behalf, nor for any of my successors! Later I saw the first "local Volunteer" chatting with the other boxers. Our contributions had simply supplemented the income of a professional! I returned home bruised and broke".

The anecdote tells us something of the aura of the boxing booth. It offered an alluring challenge to many young men out to prove their manhood, but like many aspects of the fairground that tended to give the business a bad name, the odds seemed stacked against the punter. The boxing booth has almost, but not quite entirely, disappeared from the contemporary fairground, and now that it is almost consigned to the world of fading memories, we find that people are divided - some mourn its passing, others are overwhelmed with nostalgia at the thought of it.

Those who have talked to us from the showman's side of the ropes, have spoken about the poor money earned in the boxing booth, and some fairground workers were prepared to be "fodder" in the ring to supplement their income. Even some engine drivers, such as Maurice Pendle, had a cauliflower ear and a flat nose to prove this. Maurice told his friend Ernie Genders in a taped interview, "I've had hell knocked out of me many a time, but I was glad to do it - it earned me a few bob"

Joe Ashmore can recall playing the "stooge" described in the story quoted above: *"As another source of income...I would walk past the boxing booth and they would say "Here's a lad from your home town who is going to fight Jim Slater" I would strip to my shirt and braces, put the gloves on, and fight three rounds with him, which would earn me a drink. Jim Slater had fought three championships and had a cauliflower ear. I had to be very careful not to bump it, but on one occasion I did catch it, and really hurt him. He set about me, and I found myself fighting back. In fact, I put him on the floor, which totally surprised me, and everybody else"*

The boxing booth proprietors were tenants of Pat Collins, he did not run a booth of his own. Therefore they were not tied exclusively to Pat, to some extent they could pick and choose which fairs to attend, but they did travel fairly continuously with Pat along the "runs" of the fairs, and many returned season after season. Some are listed below:

"Professor" Harry Cullis

Born 1856, often joined Pat Collins on the Welsh run, and then travelled into the Midlands. In the early part of this century he often presented a "troupe of athletes" as well as fighters. Young Pat once wrote to World's Fair to extol Harry's skill in finding champions.... *"dear old Harry Cullis could put his head down a pit in Wales and call up champions"* (WF 5.8.33)

Harry's champions included Bob Fitzimmons, Tom Thomas, Freddy Welsh, Owen Mooran, and Harry Mansfield. In later life, Harry Cullis fell on hard times financially and by the 1930's he was a tenant with a round stall at some of Pat's fairs.

Bert Hughes

Born 1851, his boxing booth began travelling in the 1880's. It was still thriving in the 1930's, when travelled by Bert Hughes Jnr. It travelled some of the Lancashire fairs, and often joined Pat Collins at Chester. Like Harry Cullis' show, it then appeared at many of Pat's fairs in the Midlands. The front of the show was decorated with photographs of many of the champions who had appeared in the booth.

Billy Woods

An ex-Scottish feather-weight champion, who came from a family associated with boxing and showland activities in Scotland. When he was seen at Kingstanding in the autumn of 1934 by C.H.Lea the latter provided a detailed picture of the booth in his World's Fair report: *"The front of the show is a gorgeous work of art, depicting in seven panels incidents famous in the fighting world. With the aid of a tannoy, Billy Woods draws a crowd, and then, very skilfully, and without a word, he displays a pound note...and explains that there is a one pound note for any man who can go six rounds with one of his boxers...Immediately there are challengers, the doors are flung open, and the crowd streams in.*

I entered with the stream and very soon the tent was filled, and for nearly an hour the audience was treated to some excellent fighting. It is remarkable value which Billy Woods offers - sixpence to see ten rounds. His boxers were Sam McVie of Jamaica, and Dick Langford of Chicago, both coloured men, and Kid Harris of Worcester."

In 1936 at the Onion Fair, no less than three boxing booths - Hughes', Wood's and Hickman's were present.

Charlie Hickman
Legend is that originally Charlie was a chimney sweep before becoming a fighter and boxing booth proprietor. But his father was Tom (the Gas) Hickman a nineteenth century prize fighter. Quite when Charlie Hickman Snr began to present his boxing booth is not clear.

Old Charlie Hickman had a large family, most of whom became associated with the show. His sons Young Charlie and George were foremost in presenting the show, but sister Annie rang the bell on the showfront and demonstrated her skill with the punch bag. There were also daughters Jennie and Florrie. Annie Hickman married Bernard Hayes, the son of Charlie Hayes, a family that had been based in Dudley before Pat Collins came on the scene. Florrie Hickman married Tommy Roberts, another regular tenant of Pat Collins.

Young Charlie was born in 1910, and he made his professional boxing debut when he was seventeen, at Brierley Hill. He reached the height of his career four years later, in 1931. He won the Crystal Palace Heavyweight "White Hope" Competion, collecting a Gold Belt as he did so. He returned to a hero's welcome at the fair at Dudley. The chance of training as a British "White Hope" never materialised and Charlie's life,

RIGHT: The front of Hickman's Boxing Booth, standing next to the Wall of death, and John's Ducks.
(Collection of Mrs Croydon)

RIGHT: The front of Bert Hughes' Boxing Booth at the Onion Fair in 1925. Hughes' boxers had included Taff Wall, Joe Bowker, Dido Plumb and Len Johnson, the black middleweight champion.
(World's Fair)

in the 1930's centred around the travelling boxing booth. In 1937 he was taken ill at Tamworth, and died after an operation at Walsall General Hospital - at the age of 27.

The Hickman's Booth continued to travel with his widow, Lydia Hickman, at the helm. It survived the War and was still travelling in the 1950's. It was the centre of attention at the 1951 Onion Show when Randy Turpin made an appearance at the show.

In 1936 the boxers appearing at Charlie Hickman's booth at Bloxwich Wake were listed as: Pat Haley of Hanley; Joe Lees of London; Gunner Smith of Stockport; Johnny Hughes from South Wales and Darkie Baker of Stoke. Later regulars included such local men as Ray Steadman, Jackie Fry and Teddy Blackham. Most famous of all was the boxer turned speiler, Barney Tooley from Brierley Hill. His real name was Richard Holloway, a butcher who worked by day at Marsh & Baxter's, but once away from work he spent his time drawing the crowds to Hickman's show.

DEATH RIDES

Correctly ascribing the ownership of various 'death rides' at any given time is extremely difficult. A good example to start with would, perhaps, be Walsall John's "Globe of Death" which opened at Great Yarmouth in the summer of 1929. The globe itself was the property of Sam Naishtad, who then travelled the Globe, with Walsall John, through the Back End fairs. It is consequently then referred to as "John Collins' Globe of Death". The riders were Monsieur Corbiere and his daughter Elizabeth. One novelty feature of their act was to invite volunteers from the audience into a sidecar to experience riding the globe for themselves! Apart from presenters and riders, the "frontman" was just as important, and on John's Globe of Death Frank Hodgson was both "manager" and the man who could drum up trade with sparkling patter. The Corbieres appeared at Great Yarmouth for several seasons.

Perhaps the success of the Globe at Yarmouth encouraged Pat to acquire a Globe of his own. This was built by Orton & Spooner, and handed over to Pat Collins when the firm came to Burton Statutes Fair in September 1929. Once again the team seemed to be French: Paulitt & Henri Abbins, managed by M.Boignet, and "directed" by Victor Fuller. It went on to the Goose Fair, and to Leicester, and returned to Leicester for the Christmas Fair in the Granby Hall.

Meanwhile...the Wall of Death had also arrived on Pat Collins' grounds, appearing at Dudley Carnival Fair in September 1929, then moving on to the Onion Fair. The riders were Messrs Williams, Stanford and Todd. Billy Williams was an Irish Canadian who was one of the people who claimed to have introduced the Wall to Britain. Jack Todd was to become a well-known wall rider.

At the Goose Fair of 1929 Pat Collins presented both a Globe and a Wall, but whether the Wall was really his own seems doubtful. By the following year, Walls and Globes were spreading quickly. An employee of Orton & Spooner, who eventually became the senior foreman joiner, recalls that the firm could have built as many as ten walls! Legal battles were looming over the rights to use the name, and the correspondence column of World's Fair was about to embark on an inconclusive debate on who really introduced the Wall to Britain.

By the Spring of 1930, Pat was presenting his own Wall, with Jack Todd as his principal rider. A great point was made in the advertising for the Chester Races fair that both his Wall and Globe were appearing together on the same ground for the first time, and, in order to avoid legal dispute over names they were being presented as "The Drome of Satan" and "The Globe of Terror"! (see Chapter 17)

Sometime, also in 1930, Jack Todd went his own way, and young Elias Harris was to be found riding on Pat's Wall of Death. Certainly, in describing the marriage of Elias and Margaret Collins in November 1930, the Walsall Observer gives readers the impression that Elias is presenting the Wall, and was going to be assisted in this by his wife. We have not found any documentation to prove that Pat gave Elias and Margaret the Wall as a wedding present. Perhaps they were given the management of the Wall, and Elias later purchased it and took it with him when he left the Midlands after Margaret's death in 1934?

When the Wall of Death is included in the list of attractions presented at Pat's fairs during 1935, it is normally described as John Collins' Wall, and the riders appear to be Bob and Mildred Lee. By the mid 1930's it becomes increasingly difficult to identify which Globes and Walls were at the amusement parks at Yarmouth and Barry, and which ones were travelling...if, indeed, there was any distinction. Towards the end of the 1930's Baby John (John James Collins) was also travelling two Walls, one featuring the Blonde Bombshells, and the other featuring Skid Skinner.

Pat's granddaughter, Flora, had married Eddy Monte, who rode the Wall of Death as 'Speedy Williams'. After the war, Eddy Monte's Wall of Death appeared at many of the Pat Collins fairs. The show never lost its excitement or popularity; it simply became less profitable, with its labour intensive build-up and pull down, in a world of increasing high-tech rides and easy unfolding from trailers. Like many other "shows" associated with the fair it seemed doomed to extinction.

However, one Wall of Death still travels in the 1990's. It is presented by Allan Ford. He purchased the ride from the Cripsey family, and Roy Cripsey bought the Wall from Elias Harris during the last War. It is possible, therefore, that the Wall travelling today is the Pat Collins' Wall of 1930.

RIGHT: Elias Harris, and lion, climb onto the Wall of Death. This is believed to be the Wall that Pat's grandson-in-law sold to Roy Cripsey, and which is now travelled, as the last Wall to still travel in Britain, by Allan Ford.
(Collection of Anthony Harris)

RIGHT: Eddy Monte's Wall of Death which travelled with Pat Collins' fair in the immediate Post War years. This wall was last travelled by Tommy Messham.
(Collection of Molly Seldon)

RIGHT: Eddy Monte riding the Wall with a demonstration of trick riding. The noise and vibration add to the spectacle of seeing these feats performed on a vertical wall. The patrons are looking down into the "silo" from behind the safety wire.
(Collection of Molly Seldon)

'AT BIRMINGHAM FAIR.

[Evening Despatch Photograph.
Mr. PAT COLLINS, the well-known amusement caterer, and his son sample one of their "runabouts" at Birmingham Onion and Pleasure Fair.

LEFT: Pat and his son, young Pat, pose for the Birmingham Despatch at the Whit-Week Fair of 1931.
(Collection of Freda Allen)

BELOW: The Orton & Spencer Ghost Train seen in its "modern" guise at Hull Fair. 14/10/47.
(Collection of Kevin Scrivens)

Fairground Memories

ERNEST BURDETT

I lived the biggest part of my early life in Witton, which is practically adjacent to the Serpentine Ground at the rear of Aston Parish Church, and I have some recollections of Pat Collins' Onion Fair from say 1922 to 1938.

Each year people used to look forward to the annual visit, and as children it was an exciting sight to see the various vehicles, such as huge traction engines drawing shows along the main road from Walsall for assembling on arrival at the fairground by staff in a very short time. The fair stayed for 3 days. The people used to walk to the fairground from various directions, except where the No.3. and No.3X trams travelled from the City Centre to Witton, as we had no buses in those days. They came in droves, whatever the weather. Some people might have travelled by train, of course, and the trains came from Walsall either to Witton Station or to Aston Station,; or they came from Birmingham. There was a lot of talking and jollification as people walked along to the fairground, and when they were returning happily they often had balloons etc.

There were two entrances, one at Witton end and one at the church end, with no admittance fee. Charges were made for the rides on the Cake Walk, Waltzers, Horses, Helter Skelter, Big Bertha, and Roundabouts etc. There were many side shows, such as Coconut shies, shooting alley, tombola, boxing booths...the Fattest Lady in the World..or the Smallest Horse. From time to time new items appeared, such as the Chair o Planes and Dodgems. While some looked dangerous I cannot remember any serious accidents occurring.

Huge crowds attended and it was midnight before departure...and one can imagine that with the ground covering being of ash and with the dust created...when you got home you were covered from head to foot...though it was another story when it rained! But everyone seemed to enjoy themselves. The lighting and power was produced by large generators run off the power of the traction engines; one of the sights people used to like to see and listen to was the mammoth organ, which is still in existence..and I have recently seen this in operation at the May Fair in the village of Kinver (where I now live).

On the Sunday before the Onion Fair closed, there was usually a Service given by the Vicar of Aston Parish Church, for the fair people. The fair was finally dismantled, packed and moved on to Nottingham 55 miles away, which fair was known as The Goose Fair. The Serpentine Ground now belongs to Aston Villa Football Club...Asda had one of their large Supermarkets on part of the land.....and had to close when the FC had a Home Match...but now even they have moved.... to One Stop at Perry Barr....and the site will probably be reclaimed for other leisure pursuits or as additional car parking.

Mrs Sydney Hawkins (nee Boys)

"My father James Boys owned the New Mills at Pleck and because he was regarded as a friend by Pat Collins we children were always given free rides etc on the fair. About 1926/27 I remember the first fairs at the Walsall Flower Show, and a new Chair o Plane ride...there was no one going on it, so Pat Collins let us have a long free ride to give others the confidence to come and use it!. I remember Pat Collins as a very strict disciplinarian with a kind side to him. He was "rough - like a farmer" and I remember seeing him 'lash out' at a man who had wronged him. The man was flattened. He was very territorial, and disliked competition."

Gerald Pee

When I was 12 years old I used to collect and deliver laundry for a neighbour who owned a Grocer's Shop and also took in washing. On one occasion, just as I arrived at Lime Tree House Pat came storming out cursing violently and sent me flying! Pat picked up the clean washing, disappeared into the house and tossed out the dirty washing. I turned to leave, Pat called me back and gave me a note. I returned to the shop and handed in the note thinking it was a complaint...but it turned out to be a note...signed by Pat Collins... granting free admittance to the Wakes Ground and free admission to the shows...including the Lion Show.

Kenneth Waterhouse

I am a retired dental surgeon. Before the war I used to practise dentistry in a place called Bloxwich, with my partner Berwyn Hughes; we started the practice from scratch and it was hard going. Pat Collins' fairs had their winter quarters at Bloxwich, where they repaired all their machinery, and painted the horses and did everything needed for the summer season. Well Pat Collins was very good to me; he used to send me patients; he came himself. He was a very gracious man, a very nice fellow.....he was particularly amiable...if he could do you a good turn he would. In the end, either Mr Hughes or myself had almost the whole of the fair people as patients, and Pat always paid for the treatment...I seem to remember that. In those days it was vastly different from what it is today. An extraction with a local anaesthetic was half a crown; a filling I think was 7/6d. A compound filling would probably have been 10/6d....I forget how much dentures were...oh..about 4 or 5 quid..no more than that. The show people were just ordinary people like you and I, always seemed to be well dressed. Always seemed to have money. They were always polite..."

To Showmen and Stallholders.

P. Collins'
Back End Wakes and Fairs
All Sure Winners till Xmas and New Year over.

NORTHWICH & WITTON WAKES,	Commencing Friday, Sept	10th.
OVER FAIR	,, ,, ,,	17th.
SANDBACH	,, ,, ,,	24th.
NEWCASTLE, (STAFFS.)	Commencing Friday, Sept.	10th.
WILLENHALL	,, ,, ,,	10th.
BLACK HEATH	,, ,, ,,	10th.
BEDWORTH	,, ,, ,,	10th.
ATHERSTONE	Commencing Friday, Sept.	17th.
BRIERLEY HILL	,, ,, ,,	17th.
WORCESTER HOP FAIR	,, ,, ,,	17th.
POLESWORTH	,, ,, ,,	17th.
HANDSWORTH	Commencing Friday, Sept.	24th.
ASHBY	,, ,, ,,	24th.
UTTOXETER	,, ,, ,,	24th.

Birmingham Great Onion Fair,
Commencing September 30th.

BURTON STATUTES	October 5th.
EVESHAM	Commencing October 7th.
LEICESTER	,, ,, 14th.
ILKESTON	,, ,, 21st.
BULWELL	,, ,, 28th.

CANNOCK, WEST BROMWICH, SMETHWICK, BROWNHILLS, HEDNESFORD, and Fairs right up to

Xmas and New Year Fairs
WOLVERHAMPTON, BIRKENHEAD, CHESTER,
WALFORD ROAD RINK, BIRMINGHAM,
Right in the Heart of Birmingham.

Send your application in at once, stating the nature and size of your Show or Stall, to—

P. Collins, Gondola Works, Walsall
Telegrams: "Gondola, Walsall."
Telephone Nos.: 701—702.

Guild Members Only Need Apply

World's Fair 28/8/26 - showing the number of Back End fairs held at the same time.

MIDLAND SECTION.

A MEETING of the COMMITTEE of this Section will be held at the GRANT HALL, WEST BROMWICH, on WEDNESDAY, JULY 3, 1946, at 11 a.m. prompt. Applications for membership of this Section will be considered from the following:—J. L. Goodman, E. Crisp, B. Goodman (Subscribing), Nellie L. Fletcher, A. F. Macree. The applicant together with proposer and seconder must attend at 12 noon.
Will the following please attend at 2 p.m.: J. Charlton, Bernard Hill, G. Tweddle.
The following applicants for pre-war positions should attend at 3 p.m., when their cases will be considered:—
PAT COLLINS: Atherstone, Ashby de la Zouch, Bedworth, Burslem Carnival, Birmingham, Burslem (June), Bromsgrove, Brownhills Carnival, Bilston Bloxwich, Blackheath, Brierley Hill, Burton-on-Trent, Birmingham Carnival, Bordesley, Coventry, Cannock, Chastown, Cradley, Darlaston, Dudley, Evesham, Fazeley, Hinckley, Hanley Park, Hay Mills, Handsworth Park, Hednesford, Kidderminster, Kenilworth, Kingstanding, Lye, Lickey Hills, Leicester, Lichfield, Leamington, Longton, Llangollen, Newport, Northfield, Newcastle (Staffs.), Norton Canes, Netherton, Oldbury, Oswestry, Oakengates, Polesworth, Rugeley, Rubery Fete, Redditch, Stafford, Stirchley, Stafford Carnival, Shifnal, Smethwick, Stratford, Stourbridge, Shrewsbury, Tipton, Tamworth, Uttoxeter, Wrexham, Walsall, Wolverhampton, Wednesbury, West Bromwich, Worcester, Willenhall, Warwick, Loughborough.
J. CHARLTON: Leek.
H. WARWICK: Coventry Carnival.
E. N. BIRD: West Bromwich, Smethwick, Tipton, Tamworth, Bilston, Darlaston, Oldbury, Wednesbury, Brierley Hill, Cannock, Hednesford.
J. HUMPHREYS: Newcastle (Staffs.), Longton, West Bromwich, Smethwick, Hanley, Stafford, Darlaston, Oakengates, Cannock, Hednesford, Netherton.
E. FURBROUGH: Coventry, Leicester, Kenilworth, Birmingham, West Bromwich, Bedworth, Hinckley.
G. GIBSON: Bromsgrove, Kenilworth, Hanley, Newcastle (Staffs.)
W. LENNARDS: Stratford-on-Avon.
E. LEE: Ellesmere, Market Drayton, Whitchurch, Wem.
F. SMITH: Broadway, Chipping Campden, Bidford, Moreton-in-Marsh, Studley, Alcester, Stratford-on-Avon, Evesham, Pershore, Willersley.
HIBBLE & MELLORS, LTD.: Coventry.
R. EDWARDS: Broadway, Willersley, Pershore, Honeybourne, Breforton Club.
C. HICKMAN: Longton, Oswestry, Shrewsbury, Coventry, Wolverhampton, Bedworth, Chester, Newport, Birmingham, Bromsgrove, Burslem, Stafford, Hanley, Bloxwich, Brierley Hill.
H. ELSBURY: Wolverhampton, Chester, Birmingham, Kidderminster, Hanley, N.
H. BAUMAN: Ashby de la Zouch, Birmingham, West Bromwich, Tipton, Smethwick, Cannock, Hednesford, Oldbury, Stafford, Walsall, Leicester, Netherton, Coventry, Wednesbury.
F. STEVENS: Brackley, Moreton-in-Marsh, Redditch, Studley, Alcester, Evesham, Stratford-on-Avon, Shipston.
Applicants for ex-Servicemen's Privileges and Hardship Cases should attend at 4 p.m. as follows:—W. H. Hill, Jnr.: R. Wrigley, G. Stokes, A. Rimell Shepherd, Albert Law.
Will Mr. G. Stokes and Mr. F. Connor, Jnr. please attend at 4-30 p.m.
T. Harris, Chairman; Norman H. Dixon, Secretary, 13, Bennett's Hill, Birmingham.

World's Fair - June 1946 - showmen re-apply for their Pre-War positions: Pat Collins' list makes interesting reading.

FAIRGROUND TRANSPORT

CHAPTER 16

The study of showmen's transport is a very specialised subject and there is a wide gulf between the contemporary layman's generalised appreciation of the size and glamour of preserved showmen's engines, and the detailed knowledge and expertise of those enthusiasts who have researched the work of various engine builders or the fleets of the showmen who used these engines.

At least the experts agree on one thing...that the Pat Collins' firm is "difficult"! If records were ever kept of Pat's transport, the records were destroyed along with the records of the Gondola Works, and the Amusement Depot, Bloxwich.

On the one hand we have to deal with "over-estimates" of how many engines were used by Pat Collins; on the other hand we have to admit that early records may be incomplete. (Licensing records do not cover showmen's steam road locomotives until after the First World War, and builder's records are either non-existent, not available, or have yet to be 'interpreted'). Added to these problems we have to admit that Pat sometimes traded in fairground equipment and engines may have passed through his hands. Sometimes these find themselves being described as part of his fleet, when they were not, and vice-versa!

Pat was not the first showman to use the steam road locomotive, or the first to use engines built to showmen's specifications, but his fleet was certainly eventually quite substantial, and the firm continued to use steam when many others had abandoned it. The engines that continued to be used after the Second World War ensured that a generation very much still alive today can associate the firm with the use of the steam engine.

Sometimes the engines were used very self-consciously, like the occasion when Burrell "No.1" was used to take part of the Sutton Park Big Dipper down to London in the autumn of 1950 to prepare for the launch of Battersea Pleasure Gardens as part of the 1951 "Festival of Britain". Legends tell of John Collins instructing the driver (Cockney Jack) to stage a "breakdown" in the centre of London "that will draw everyone's attention to the engine and the building of the Big Dipper". He did so!

Perhaps even more remarkable than the way in which steam was used for so long by the Pat Collins' firm, is the fact that six of his engines still survive today in preservation. Three of the survivors are Burrells - built by the Thetford based firm favoured by Pat and many other showmen: "The Griffin", "No.1", and "Wait and See". The other survivors are the Foster, "The Leader", a Fowler, "Dreadnought" and a McLaren, "Goliath".

The preservation movement itself is not beyond complicating matters further! - "Dreadnought" has also appeared under the names "Goliath" and "Vanguard" since being preserved, and showmen themselves liked to change the name of an engine if they felt so inclined; therefore enthusiasts tend to identify an engine by its builder and the builder's number. We have accordingly adopted this course and present our list, builder by builder. In the case of Burrell engines it is worth separating the engines built "new" for Pat Collins, and those that he acquired second-hand.

BURRELL'S

ROAD LOCOMOTIVES.

Either Single or Double Crank.
Compound and Spring Mounted.

As Supplied to the

LEADING AMUSEMENT CATERERS

For prices and full particulars apply to the Manufacturers—

Chas. Burrell & Sons,

LIMITED,

THETFORD, NORFOLK.

- 165 -

It is almost impossible to find photographs that illustrate fairground transport in the days when horses did most of the work. It is almost as difficult to find pictures of the part that the railways played in the long-haul movement of fairground equipment. We dreamed of finding a picture of one of Pat's engines shunting a plate truck onto a wagon in Bloxwich Goods Yard, and our wish almost came true when we found these pictures, showing Pat's engine, "Lord James" (Fowler 11846) at work at Burton-on-Trent. Having propelled a road truck onto the railway company's flat wagon, the railway staff make the load fast. Engines were often stripped of their canopies and accessories when the weight was likely to be recorded on a Weighbridge, prior to travelling by train with their loads.
(LMS Magazine, 1928)

ENGINE LIST

FOSTER ENGINES

3318	1907	"The Leader"	7hp. New to Collins. Probably simply called "Leader". Scrapped later twenties. Reg: DH 2481
3663	1909	"King of Showmen"	Returned to Fosters in 1913 and replaced by "Clara".
13052	1913	"Clara"	10hp. Delivered April 1913 to accompany the Motor Car Scenic. About 1922 sold to Brother John Collins who passed engines and ride on to his son Michael Albert, as a wedding present. Driver: Billy Reohorn. Reg: DH 2477
14405	1921	"William Henry"	re-named and renumbered as:
14446	1921	"The Leader"	10hp purchased 1927 10hp. New to H Whiting. Reg: DH 4593 Preserved by Bill Hunt.

BELOW: "The Leader" (Foster 14446, DH4593) in the yard at Bloxwich by the old Paintshed, in the 1950's.
(Collection of Rob Webster)

LEFT: Drivers could become as legendary as the engines they drove, as a result of their skill and their long service with Pat Collins. In this picture, Driver Billy Mills stands by "The Leader" an engine, to which he remained devoted even after its 'retirement' from active service with the fair.
(Collection of Peter Hough)

LEFT: Jim Morley was given an award for over fifty years' service with Pat Collins, and he poses in this picture with "The Leader", at the Bloxwich Yard in the mid 1950's.
(Collection of Stan Webb)

LEFT: The front nameplate has been removed from "The Leader" and has been placed on the radiator of Showtrac No.2. (KDH 141), seen here taking the engine from Bloxwich to the Griffin Foundry, Oldbury, to be preserved by Tom Hunt and his son Bill. It heads through Walsall towards Pleck on 29th August 1963.
(Collection of Stan Webb)

FOWLER ENGINES

7758	1897	"War Horse"	Purchased second hand 1903 from G. Twigdon. Sold by the end of 1909 to Mrs. Haines, Salisbury.
11846	1909	"Lord James"	Purchased 1919. Worked in the 1930s with the Flying Fleas. Finally scrapped 1953. Reg: DH 2484
12228	1911	"Showman"	Converted to Scenic Spec. with Thompson & Walton crane, worked with No. 4 Scenic, (Motors) Probably used by Young Pat. Sold 1933. Reg: HF 1151
14424	1916	"Dreadnought"	Worked with No. 2 Scenic (Dragons and Peacocks), and later with Mont Blanc and Dodgems as late as 1952. Reg: DH 2545. Survives in preservation, but now carries the name "Goliath", but not to be confused with the preserved McLaren.
14879	1917	"King Edward VIII"	
14880		"Princess Marina"	Ex J Coneley, ex Bernard Cole, originally called "Premier". Sometimes listed as a Pat Collins engine, but this is doubtful.
14886	1917		
14969	1918	"Reliance"	Purchased about 1928 from J H Royale, later sold to Jones Bros (Flint). Reg: CT 6894

In April 1925 Pat Collins was issued with a vehicle licence, registration number DH 4334 for a Fowler Road Locomotive. It is not clear which engine this might be. The registration is transferred to Hertfordshire in 1941, and cancelled in 1950. Similarly, in July 1926, another Fowler Road Locomotive was issued with the registration number DH 5270.

RIGHT: "Lord James" (Fowler 11846, DH 2484) attends "The Flying Fleas" at Sefton Park, Liverpool, 12 May 1937.
(Photo: W.P.Riley, from the collection of Rowland Scott)

- 169 -

ABOVE: "Lord James" (Fowler 11846), Driver Billy Mills standing on the right, in a post-war photograph.
(Collection of Peter Hough)

BELOW: "Dreadnought" (Fowler 14424) at the yard in Bloxwich. Note Clara's van, the paraffin tank and paintshed. 25th March 1952.
(Collection of Stan Webb)

RIGHT: "Dreadnought" (Fowler 14424) pausing to take water on its way to Worcester just before the Second World War, towing the Atlantic Airways (large swingboats). On the left is the back of Jim Morley!
(Collection of Peter Hough)

RIGHT: "The Leader" - in preservation, attending Bloxwich Carnival with the Wonderland Organ in June 1965. Standing by the rear wheel is the late Jack Shepherd of the Cannock Chase showland family. Note the engine's canopy is now supported by ornamental brass front struts, and looks much smarter than in its working days!
(Collection of Stan Webb)

BELOW: "The Leader" at work, craning the heavy platforms of the Waltzer into position. Johnny Cook is guiding the jib, photographed about 1950.
(Collection of Peter Hough)

BURRELL ENGINES

1. Purchased new from the Thetford Factory:

1777	1894	"Emperor"	10hp. Eventually sold to Charles Hart of Barking. (May have been the first engine to be built with dynamo extension to the smokebox)
1888	1896	"Empress"	10hp. Spent all her life with Pat Collins.
2713	1904	"Her Majesty"	8hp. New to Collins. Associated with hauling Flora Collins' living van, and licensed in her name in 1921. Reg: DH 2475
3183	1910	"Helpmate"	7hp. Spent all her life with Pat Collins. First used with Young Pat's Yachts. Last licensed 1938. Reg: HF 1147
3291	1911	"Emperor"	8hp. (Scenic engine) Originally fitted with experimental Reynold"s Chain drive to the dynamo. Sold 1922 to John Collins, passing to his son M.A. Collins. (Along with "Clara", this engine accompanied the Motor Car scenic. Reg: DH 2476
3447	1913	"Jack Whyatt"	Named after the manager of Collins' No. 2 Switchback. After the First World War sold to George Wilkie.
3865	1920	"No. 1"	8hp., built as standard showman's engine, later converted to scenic type. Purchased to power the Scenic Whales. When this ride ceased travelling she attended Collin's Noah's Ark, and then the Waltzer. In 1950 "No. 1" hauled Collins' Big Dipper from Sutton to Battersea Fun Fair. This engine was first preserved by S. J. Crawley, Turvey, Beds. Changed hands and now restored and exhibited at Thursford. Reg: DH 2507

Burrell "No.1" with road train, pausing for water at Minworth, 28/9/52, towing the platform truck, car truck, and scenery truck for the Waltzer on the way to Nottingham from Aston. Driver: Cockney Jack, Steersman: Tommy Mannion.
(Collection of Stan Webb)

ABOVE: Burrell "No.1" the "Pride of the Midlands", with Drivers, Cockney Jack Harvey, and Jim Morley, photographed at Wolverhampton in 1948.
(Collection of Peter Hough)

BELOW: By 1951, when this picture was taken, "Pat Collins' Amusements on Tour" had been replaced with "Pat Collins' presenting Fun Fair" on the canopy. "No.1's" crane is seen at work on the pull down after Bloxwich Wakes.
(Collection of Stan Webb)

ABOVE: Nearside and offside views of "Emperor", Burrell 3291, when new in 1911, showing the Hans Renold chain from the dynamo to the flywheel - a suggested antidote to breaking leather belts when dealing with the starting load on the new electric scenics.

RIGHT: "Emperor" in later years, when owned by Michael Albert Collins.
(Photos from Collections of Bernard Morley & Jim Boulton)

BELOW: "His Majesty", Burrell 2713, on its side following an accident at Shrewsbury in 1929.
(Collection of Harry Mills)

- 174 -

2. Purchased Second-hand

1999	1897	"Victoria"	Purchased 1915. 8hp. New to Isaac Neal. Sold 1923 to Alf Ball, then George Beach. Scrapped in 1952. Sometimes included in lists of Pat Collins engines, but very doubtful. *
2081	1898		Purchased 1918. 8hp. Owned by various non-fairground companies before 1918. Sold 1920.
2170	1898	"Empress"	Purchased 1910. 8hp. New to A Twigdon. Sold for commercial use to Noah Judd. Sometimes included in the lists of Pat Collins engines but very doubtful.
2463	1902	"Shamrock II"	Purchased 1932. 8hp. New to H Caris. Finally sold to James White. Reg J 6803
2650	1904	"Independent"	Purchased 1907. 8hp. New to Relph & Pedley. Pat Collins renamed her "Mark Twain" Involved in accident in Blackheath. Sold to John McGuiric, Ireland. Reg: DH 2479

BELOW: "Independent" (Burrell 2650), seen here at Congleton in 1906, while owned by Relph & Pedley. It was sold to Pat Collins during the following year.
(Collection of Rowland Scott)

* NOTE: Although no proof exists that Pat owned the Burrell "Victoria", it's purchase does seem to coincide with Bob Neal's "defection" to Pat Collins, with whom he stayed for over thirty years.

- 175 -

2709	1904	"Mabon"	Purchased 1916. 8hp. New to James Dooner. Scrapped at Bloxwich about 1950. Reg: HF 1149
2733	1905	"Lily of the Valley"	Purchased 1913 . 8ho. New to Harris Brothers. Came to Walsall in 1907 for Smith Brothers (Millers). Doubtful if ever owned by Pat Collins.
2788	1906	"Alfred the Great"	Purchased 1914. 8hp. New to Alfred Ball. Rebuild in 1922 for Pat Collins to Scenic specification and used with No. 3 Scenic (Dragons). Later used with Dodgems. Reg; DH 2542 Remains of the engine thought to have been destroyed in fire at Bloxwich Yard. Some parts cannibalised to rebuild "The Griffin".
2801	1906	"The Major"	Purchased 1907. 8hp. New to Mrs Weir. Used in the 1930's for hauling Billy Weston's Ark (Driven by Dick Studt), later used with the Dodgems. Replaced in 1946 by Collins' first diesel "Showtrac", to which Burrell nameplates were later transferred. Engine was stored at Bloxwich until damaged by fire in the early 1950"s. Reg: DH 2733

LEFT: The original "Emperor", Burrell 1777 of 1894, seen here at Newport, Salop, in 1900.
(Collection of Rowland Scott)

BURRELLS GALORE:

RIGHT: "Mascot" (2988 of 1908) used by Pat at the time of the First World War, but seen here in 1938, when owned by Wm.Starr & Sons.
Collection of Rowland Scott)

RIGHT: "The Prince" (3038 of 1909) seen here in 1933 when used by Reuben Holdsworth, three years before being purchased by Pat Collins.
(Collection of Rowland Scott)

BELOW: "Lord Curzon" (4021 of 1925) in the yard at Bloxwich. Note the new fire station in the course of construction. The wall in the background still exists and bears the initials of the managers whose lorries are parked on the left.
(Collection of Rob Webster)

2804	1906	"The Griffin"	Purchased 1946. 8hp. Built as "The White Rose of York" for Alf Payne. Various owners until acquired by the Pat Collins firm. Renamed "The Griffin" as a reference to Tom Hunt"s Griffin Foundry. Now preserved by Bill Hunt. Reg: DH 2542
2988	1908	"The Mascot"	Purchased 1914. 8hp. New to John Proctor. Converted by Pat Collins to Scenic Specification. Sold in 1918 to Harniess Brothers.
3038	1909	"The Prince"	Purchased 1936. 8hp. New to Relph & Pedley then Rueben Holdsworth. Scrapped. Reg: BN 4883
3352	1911	"Faugha-a-Bella"	Purchased 1914. 8hp. New to Moore Brothers. Converted from contractor's type engine to Showman's spec. by Pat Collins. Possible used by Young Pat 1924. It was driving the Three-abreast at Sefton Park 1937. Reg: DH 2480
3910	1921	"Wait And See"	Purchased 1923. 7hp. New to Crowther & Johnson. Reg: DH 3544 Now preserved by Bill Hunt.
4021	1925	"Lord Curzon"	Purchased 1937. 8hp. New to Harry Hall. Brought into the Pat Collins empire by Walsall John - Harry Hall's brother-in-law. While in store at Bloxwich, damaged by fire during the early fifties. Reg: CH 4829

An unidentified Burrell was licenced in February 1921, Reg: DH 2502. This may have been "Empress" (Burrell 1888 of 1896), in which case the records suggest that this engine was scrapped in 1933.

"The Griffin"

- 178 -

RIGHT: The Griffin, Burrell 2804 of 1906, providing power for Bill Hunt's Wonderland Organ at Melton Mowbray Steam Fair on 28th May 1966. Note that the Bandmaster has now been restored and the frontage extended.
(Stan Webb)

McCLAREN ENGINES

1141	1909	"Electric"	
1438	1917	"The Whale"	10hp. Ex War Department. Assisted on haulage of Whale Scenic hauling the two trucks carrying the eight whales. Never had full showman's fittings. Later used for spares. Reg: DH 3455
1599	1917	"Samson"	10hp. Ex War Department. First named "No 2". Hauled the Scenic Whales. Sold 1943 to J Watts, Mddx. Scrapped 1948. Reg: DH 2483
1623	1917	"Goliath"	10hp. Ex War Department. First named "No 1" until the arrival of the Burrell. Travelled Joby Farrell's Dragon & Peacocks. Later accompanied the Dodgems - last used by Collins 1954. Reg: 2482 Now preserved by Frank Lythgoe.

The three 1917 Mclarens were purchased at a War Department Auction in 1919 at Avonmouth, where Joe Ashmore did the bidding so that others did not know that Pat Collins wanted them. Bill Morris collected "Goliath" and did the conversion work, and it was then driven by Bill Cornell. Later it was driven by Billy Reohorn and then Jim Morley.

SAVAGE ENGINES

"Little Samson" type 4hp Tractor of 1912
Traction Centre Engine No. 847 "The Wonder" of 1909 powered the No. 3 Scenic. (This ride was electrified in 1923).
Licensed in 1929 as DH 2478, but apparently derelict by 1933 in Sutton Park.
More information on the Savage Engines can be found in the Register included in David Braithwaite's book: "Savage of Kings Lynn".

BROWN & MAY ENGINE

"Little Helpmate"   Acquired about 1922, sold about 1928.
Reg: DH 3029

THE McLARENS

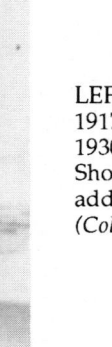

LEFT: "The Whale", 1438 of 1917, photographed in July 1930. Used only as a tractor, Showman's fittings never added.
(Collection of Rowland Scott)

LEFT: "Samson", 1599 of 1917 at Burnley Cattle Market, next to the Wall of Death about 1930.
(Collection of Peter Hough)

BELOW: "Goliath" 1623 of 1917 at Brickkiln Street, Wolverhampton about 1950.
(Collection of Rob Webster)

ABOVE: "The Little Helpmate" - a Brown & May engine used by Pat Collins during the 1920's, although he was not usually able to make much use of small engines. On the right, with his arms folded is Bill Mullett (Clara's brother). Little Joe Mullett is in front of him, and Maud Mullet on the extreme right.
(*Collection of Peter Hough*)

Young Pat's Engines

Fowler:
12228	1911	"The Showman II"	Ex Monte Williams

Burrell:
3183	1910	"Helpmate:	(HF 1147) See above.

ALCHIN

296	1926		3 ton steam wagon

FODEN STEAM WAGONS

1356		Reg M1604
4058	1924	Reg M5602
4178		Reg M5702
5224	1929	Reg M7293
5816	1927	Reg M8174
5820		Reg HA 345
9916		Reg HA 3207

Plus two Fodens licensed at Walsall - see below.

T GREEN & SONS

Horse-drawn generating sets:

1736	1893	1758	1898
1751	1894	1759	1898

NB: An engine was present at Pat's September Fair of 1892 according to the report of the event. What was it?

Miscellaneous Vehicles identified from the licencing records:

Ford Lorry	Reg: DH 2505	(Registered 2/21)
Foden Goods Wagon	Reg: DH 2585	(" 5/21, scr. 1933)
Foden Steam Wagon	Reg: DH 2673	(" 9/21, scr. 1935)
Austin 20hp. Car	Reg: DH 2370	(" 9/20, scr. 1935)
Unidentified Vehicle	Reg: DH 2432	(" 12/20)
FWD Motor Lorry (In Flora's name)	Reg: DH 3320	(" 3/23. scr. 1935)
Maudslay	Reg: DH 6573	(" 5/28)
Ford Motor Lorry	Reg: DH 5237	(" 6/26)
Berliet	Reg: DH 5408	(" 10/26)
FWD Lorry	Reg: DH 4629	(" 10/25)
Berliet Car	Reg: DH 5061	(" 4/26, scr. 1937)
New Hudson Motorcycle *	Reg: DH 1721	(" 9/19)
Syddlesy Deasor Motor Van **	Reg: DH 1944	(" 2/20, scr. 1933)
AEC Motor Lorry	Reg: DH 2839	(" 1/22, scr. 1935)
"Moon" Motor Car	Reg: DH 3044	(" 6/22, sold 1923)
Maudslay Motor Lorry	Reg: DH 3158	(" 9/22)
Sunbeam Motor Car	Reg: DH 3226	(" 1/23, sold 1925)
Austin Motor Car	Reg: DH 3343	(" 4/23, scr. 1933)
Ford Car	Reg: DH 3089	(" 7/22, scr. 1933)

This accounts for vehicles licenced at Walsall, but Pat Collins may have bought vehicles licenced elsewhere. In some instances the address is given as the Gondola Works, Shaw Street, in other cases it is Limetree House, Bloxwich.

*Licenced in the name of Patrick Ross Collins, and transferred to Walter Hobbs a year later.

**The body of this van is described as "grey, with owner's name on side".)

Post War Engines

The Pat Collins firm was unusual in that it continued to use engines well into the Post-War era - under the management of Clara Collins and Walsall John. The six engines continuing in use into the 1950's being

Burrell "No. 1"	"The Griffin"	"Dreadnought"
"The Major"	"Goliath"	"The Leader"

"Mabon" and "Lord Curzon" also survived in the early post-War years.
All these engines distinguished themselves in various ways, and were sometimes used to provide publicity for the fair.
In 1948 "No. 1" and "The Griffin" left the Birmingham Onion Fair at 3.30 p.m. and drove to Hull, 140 miles away, by the following evening, hauling the organ and No. 1 Scenic.
"No. 1" made the historic trip to Battersea Pleasure Gardens with the Big Dipper from Sutton Park in 1951.
"The Leader" was the last engine to be used when it pulled "The Waltzer" to Nottingham Goose Fair in 1957.

Motor Vehicles in Post-War use

K? 3881	Scammell chain-driven tractor
WV 1663	Foden four wheeler: No. 1. Carried the Dodgems
NDH 8	AEC Matador four wheeler
JTO 313	ERF eight wheeler No. 2. "Zo'e" carried the Dodgems
KDH 141	Scammell Showtrac No. 2 "The Leader"
LDH 253	Scammell Showtrac No. 1 "The Major"
MDH 37	Scammell Pioneer six wheel tractor (Registered 19/7/48)
MDH 77	Scammell Pioneer six wheel tractor (Registered 10/8/48)
MDH 181	Crossley ex. W.D. lorry
MDH 193	Crossley ex. W.D. lorry
MDH 895	Austin lorry (registered 5/7/49)

In September 1946 the firm registered a Tillings Stevens vehicle (KDH 139) and a Crossley (KDH 189). In June 1948 R Monte registered an ex WD AEC/Dodge, using the Bloxwich Yard as his address (KDH 119).

RIGHT: "Goliath" as it is today, presented by Frank Lythgoe at the Bishop's Castle Steam Rally 1990.
(Ned Williams)

BELOW: "Goliath" as a working engine, draws off the Aston fairground on 28th September 1952, as the Onion Fair is pulled down. Note: Alf Cartwright's Snack Bar.
(Collection of Stan Webb)

THE SHOWTRACS

Pat Collins, like other showmen, had not been slow to harness new sources of power to the work of moving and energising the fairground. In the 1890's, and during this century, he had invested in steam power. After the First World War, the first petrol engined lorries appeared, although Pat remained a very loyal user of steam.

Scammell Motors, of Watford, had supplied a few chain-driven diesel tractors to showmen before the Second World War, but, following the War, they decided to build a diesel tractor that would fulfil all the showman's requirements. In other words, it could do the work of the showman's engine, pulling loads, shunting them on the fairground, craning items into place during the build-up, and generating power when the fair was open. They called their vehicle, the "Showtrac", and an agent, Sidney Harrison, was given the job, in 1945, of acquiring orders from showmen.

Pat, of course, had died in 1943, leaving his successors to "keep the flag flying". Mr Harrison found orders for twelve vehicles, two of which were ordered by the Pat Collins firm. Presumably the decision was made by Clara, John Collins, and the Trustees of the estate. The two post-war Showtracs, and the other post-war vehicles, are therefore to be seen as acquisitions in the Pat Collins tradition, and in his name. We include them here because they became such a well-known feature of Pat's travelling fair in the 1950's and 1960's.

Delivery of the Showtracs was underway by 1946, but the ones delivered first were not completed to full Showtrac specification. The Pat Collins firm had the honour of taking delivery of the first fully completed Showtrac. Scammell Chassis No.6210 was sold to the Pat Collins firm in 1946, and was licenced by John Collins in the September of that year, receiving the registration number KDH 141. It was not given a fleet number or name, and it seems that it was delivered to John at the Crystal Palace Ground. Whether it went into use immediately or not is uncertain, as the vehicle then appeared at the Commercial Vehicle Show at Olympia, bearing the Pat Collins name.

When it did eventually begin to work for the firm, it joined "The Leader", and was assigned to transporting the new Waltzer, and was driven by Johnny Ryan. The name was "transferred" from the Foster engine it eventually replaced, and, because the second showtrac had entered service first, this vehicle became "No.2".

The firm's second Showtrac (Scammell 6358) was purchased in 1947, and was licenced by John Collins in the September, receiving the registration number LDH 253. It was collected from Watford by Frank Allen, who also drove it on the first occasion the firm put it to use, on a journey from Willenhall to Brierley Hill, carrying most of the old Lakin Waltzer in three trucks with a total length of 147.ft. Cockney Jack, driving Burrell "No.1" hauled the rest.

When Frank Allen left the firm, Jack Harvey became the driver of "The Major". The Lakin Waltzer was replaced by a Supercar Dodgem track in 1957, and from then on Jack Harvey was associated with both driving the Showtrac, and managing the Dodgem track. Jack Harvey had a great love for the steam engines, and he transferred the nameplate from "The Major", Burrell 2801, to the radiator of the Showtrac - with Clara Collins' approval. "The Major" received the fleet number: 1.

"The Major" became very well known, and appears to have been more frequently photographed than "The Leader". An eight-wheel ERF eventually took over the transport of the Dodgems, named "Zo'e"...after Frank Harvey's daughter. "The Major" was retired to Barry Island around 1976, where it is still occasionally used to generate power, or move equipment within the amusement park.

"The Leader" had been modified in 1955 by fitting a rear crane which utilized the vehicle's winch. This was very useful when building and pulling down the Waltzer; "The Leader" also travelled the Big Ark on some occasions. About 1966 it was withdrawn to Barry Island, and was eventually sold to Alfred "Pepper" Biddall, of Middlesex. He, and his son, are currently restoring it.

BELOW: Scammell Showtrac advertisement from World's Fair, 11/1/47, acknowledging John Collins for providing the vehicle.

```
The Scammell Showtrac

          WILL BE ON VIEW AT
     ::    OLYMPIA    ::
     (at back of Messrs. Butlins Moon Rocket).
        January 20 - 25
   SCAMMELL LORRIES LTD., WATFORD.
            Telephone: WATFORD 5231.
   Sole Distributors:
   SIDNEY HARRISON LTD., BURY ST. EDMUNDS.
            Telephone: BURY ST. EDMUNDS 207.
   With acknowledgments to CYRIL B. MILLS, Esq. for Location
        and JOHN COLLINS, Esq. for Showtrac
```

THE SHOWTRACS

The Showtracs

RIGHT: No.2. at Darlaston in 1958 with Johnnie Cook's Waltzer (Lister Lighting engine on the left)
(Collection of Mick Archer)

RIGHT: No.2. at Nottingham Goose Fair 1958 using the crane to assist in building the Waltzer.
(Collection of Peter Hough)

BELOW: No.1. bearing the nameplate, "The Major", leaving Wolverhampton Falkland Street on 5/4/59, with the car truck and net truck for the Dodgems. On the right is Scammell MDH 77. *(Collection of Fred Richardson)*

ABOVE LEFT: The ERF, JT)313, "Zoë" acquired to provide transport for the Dodgems, and named after Jack Harvey's daughter.

ABOVE RIGHT: The AEC Matador used to move equipment from Barry Island to the Back End fairs.

(Both pictures from the Collection of Fred Richardson)

LEFT: Foden four-wheeler "No.1" with the Dodgem load, seen at Aston in 1952. Jack Harvey eventually shortened the vehicle and fitted two generators.
(Rod Spooner)

LEFT: Scammell LDH77 with Speedway loads, seen at Aston in 1952. Manager Willie Weston on the footboard.
(Rod Spooner)

SCAMMELLS AT WORK

RIGHT: Pat Collins' older Scammell, used with Wattie's "Big Ark", driven by Billy Lowndes, seen at Aston in 1952.
(Rod Spooner)

RIGHT: One of the Scammell "Pioneers" in the yard at Bloxwich about 1952.
(Collection of Rob Webster)

BELOW: A variety of transport seen at Wolverhampton about 1950. MDH 895, stands alongside Burrell "No.1". Note the "gaff lad's" dormitory provided in the van on the right.
(Collection of Rob Webster)

- 187 -

LEFT: The box truck used by the No.1.Waltzer, seen at the Onion Fair 1961. Mick Archer has chalked up the next destination.
(Fred Richardson)

LEFT: The variety of sign-writing and coach painting on the trucks is evident in these photographs, taken about 1960.

(Collection of Fred Richardson)

BELOW: Two trucks and the paybox used with Frank Harvey's Dodgems, seen at Wolverhampton 5/4/59.
(Collection of Fred Richardson)

- 188 -

THE FAIRS

CHAPTER 17

Introduction

By the beginning of this century Pat Collins' fairs covered a vast area which could not be served by one fair moving around from place to place. In fact Pat Collins' fairs were in several places at the same time and the acquisition of a motor car made the personal supervision of the business, by the Guvnor, a little easier; his annual mileage was considerable! The organisation of so many fairs in itself would have been fairly complex, though no doubt the telephone and the telegram made things ever so slightly easier, and were welcome inventions.

Not all fairs occurred at the same time each year. The feasts of Easter and Whitsun were 'moveable'; others were defined in terms such as 'the first Monday after Michaelmas', or 'the first weekend in October'. The showman's year was planned to take account of all these things, as well as the requirements of local Councils, Carnival Committees and other special events.

It would be unwise to be too dogmatic about times and places. "Runs" or "Circuits" were scheduled and studying the "Ground to Let" advertisements in World's Fair can become a fascinating study in its own right! It is one of those esoteric subjects beloved by fairground enthusiasts, and early magazines they produced lovingly feature lists of gaffs and the equipment that appeared at them, partly compiled from memory and partly compiled from information gleaned from newspapers; but rides and shows often changed their name, and even the records that do exist can be the cause of further confusion.

Once the fair dates were fixed, ground space was advertised 'to let'. Tenants would apply to the office. Most tenants would provide round stalls eg Hooplas, named after the game introduced in 1908; or sidestalls ("sidestuff"). The showmen also called these attractions 'joints' and used different descriptions in describing them to the laymen ("flatties"); eg "Shooter" for Shooting Gallery, Coconut 'Sheets' and not 'shies', etc. If it was a large fair tenants with riding machines would be accepted, though at many fairs Pat expected to use his own machines. Tenants who could put on "shows" were also accepted.

The tenants were generally very well looked-after by Pat, and most of them travelled regularly with him for years. Tenant and lessee had mutual need of each other, and many, particularly those from established showland families would have been regarded as 'equals'. From this study we venture to say that you cannot 'become a showman'...... you have to be 'born one' and the inherited mantle of 'showman' seems more important than the size of attraction. For instance, the owner of a modest 'juvenile' (children's ride) might end up wealthier than a riding master (machine owner) down on his luck, and could well be a more esteemed showland figure.

These complexities need to be borne in mind when looking at the lists of attractions at each fair.

Pat was fond of saying..."It pays to advertise", and his fairs were well advertised by notices in the local press and by bill-posting. This was organised by the office, and for many years his bills and posters were printed by Willsons of Leicester. The fair also advertised itself by its arrival on site.

Ground managers were important. Quite often they were 'civilian', returning to their permanent homes. There were of course exceptions, like Herbert Barnard, in a dual role with an attraction he presented as part of the fair. It was the job of ground managers to liaise with local authorities, railway companies, horse, transport and fuel contractors, and anyone who might be inconvenienced by the arrival of the fair. Most of them were also "surveyors" who would mark out the ground with pegs and tapes, indicating the positions of all the attractions. This was a very skilled job, and one at which Pat himself was a master. If the Guvnor arrived while surveying was in progress, he would probably take his coat off, leave his gold watch by his stick, and take over the job. One of the skills was imagining how the patrons could be 'steered' by the fair's layout to spend their money in the appropriate places, as well as making imaginative use of the space available.

The ground manager might have to supervise the drawing on, as the attractions arrived, and keep a watchful eye on the "building up" by the managers and their men. Each ride might have a manager and foreman, and a workforce skilled in its assembly. The engine driver's work was not finished upon arrival. Most rides could only be built up with the assistance of the engine, craning components into place, or shunting trucks into position to be unloaded. After that the engines would have to take up positions from which their generators could supply power to light and drive the machines.

Most of Pat's fairs were planned and built up in the same way, with the riding machines in the centre, the stalls and sidestuff around them, and with the shows across the "top" of the ground, but every site had its own idiosyncracies, awkward corners, obtrusive street furniture, narrow access, or sloping ground. The latter was a nightmare, and much packing had to be used to make rides level. In the "good old days" this packing would have to be painted to match the ride. Living vans, water supplies, deliveries of "swag" (prizes) had to be organised - and everything had to be ready by opening time. Pat, Flora and Clara all knew the value of personal supervision and used their presence on the tober (the completed fair) to keep everyone on their toes. Pat would hand out instant dismissal if an employee was found to be at fault, but was equally fond of "reinstatement" after a suitable lapse of time and sufficient cursing and swearing. Drivers and managers seemed prepared to "go through fire" for the Guvnor, and Pat superbly played the role of 'benign' autocrat!

Once the fairs were open, it seems that the menfolk disappeared for lengthy discussion and liquid refreshment, until returning to the fair for the busy period - from ten o'clock until midnight, in Pat's day. (Most fairs now close at 10pm). There was always more work to be done, and a non stop stream of visitors, ranging from newspaper "scribes", to tradesmen offering their wares and services, came and went. The sacred music concerts had to be arranged, and the next round of repairs, transport and supplies had to be sorted out. In the days of horse-drawn transport the job was colossal, and even when the steam road locomotive arrived the showmen were heavily dependent on rail transport for many tasks. Very little was left to chance. Pat had his own favoured brand of coal, from South Wales, and this was delivered to Bloxwich, and taken out to the fairgrounds. At places like Chester he would have a wagon-load of coal brought to the local railway goods yard. It is not surprising that the larger fairs often had two ground managers.

We have not yet mentioned the problems of collecting income from this complicated rambling business. Managers had to collect rents from the tenants, and the money from each riding machine had to be collected. Sometimes car-loads of cash made their way back to Limetree House, before the money could be banked. Handling the money was an area in which there could be many abuses, and once again, part of Pat's success was the tight rein he exercised. It was a world of many complex cash transactions. Ride managers had to be able to pay staff from the takings, and many local lads found casual labour (paid for in copper) in return for assisting in pulling down the rides late at night. Fairgrounds must have been designed to give accountants nightmares or nervous breakdowns, yet Pat kept it all under his control. Some details are given in Appendix Two, under Testimonies.

BELOW: Pat's engines sometimes bore the legend, "Amusements on Tour" - which makes it all sound simple. As can be seen in this chapter, it was a vast complex business! In this picture "The Griffin" (Burrell 2804), hauls a Dodgem load along the Kidderminster - Wolverhampton road, near the Stewponey, in September 1953. On the extreme left a Wolsley brings up the rear with Walter Hobb s' living van.
(Collection of Stan Webb)

A book about such an important showman would be incomplete if it did not attempt to give some indication of how fairs were organised, equipment circulated, towns visited, rides, shows, and personalities changed. The World's Fair newspaper did not commence until 1904, and The Era newspaper was concerned primarily with the world of showbusiness and legitimate theatre, so details of Pat's organisation in the 19thC are as a result cautiously recorded.

By the early 1900's, it is clear that Pat could talk of four distinct "runs" of his own fairs.
By 1907 World's Fair was advertising "runs" in batches, and tenants were invited to book space on the following runs:-

Welsh Run:
Longton-Oswestry-Cefn-Llangollen-Shrewsbury and other towns to Chester
Midland Counties Run:
Dudley-Quarry Bank-Cradley Heath-Stourbridge, Brierley Hill.
Grand Easter Fairs:
Coventry,Wolverhampton,Birkenhead,Liverpool,London
May Fairs:
Birmingham-Leicester-Smethwick-Wednesbury-Darlaston-West Bromwich
Flower Shows - in June and July.
Worcester Races.

From this listing it is not possible to see what fairs were occurring concurrently, except at Easter. In later years the World's Fair reports individual fairs in more detail and it is possible to see which of the firm's riding machines were attached to each run, giving a much better picture of the complexity of the firm's operations.

Many people who worked on these fairs have assured us that the three or four fairs existed as separate entities, and that someone on the No.1.run would have little idea of what was going on elsewhere until fairs amalgamated at big events, or machines were called away to fill a gap somewhere else. Even so, we have been told of trucks being loaded, engines raising steam, and drivers standing by - all waiting for a telegram from the office to reveal their next destination! Changes of plan, the unexpected and improvisation were all part of daily life in the Pat Collins' empire.

Details of the 1948 and 1949 runs have been amalgamated, to give some idea of what might be going on as the three or four fairs went about their business.
The runs were worked out from World's Fair reports for 1948 and 1949, based on research by Cyril Rollins. It is not necessarily complete but is reproduced to give an idea of how things worked. By taking two consecutive years in the 1940s we have to be aware that this presents a picture of the empire at a time of decline! Since the 1930s the machine positions at the Lancashire fairs had been transferred, the Cheshire fairs were being presented by M.A.Collins, and the firm no longer headed towards the Mersey, etc.

Since readers will want to know something about the visits of Pat Collins' fairs to their own home town, and what kind of attractions were presented, it is hoped that the following geographical survey will give a general picture, even though it does not list every Gaff, or record everything presented.

By looking at Space to Let adverts and reports of fairs it is possible to produce an outline of the runs of Pat Collins' fairs - this table based on 1948 and 1949 gives some idea of where the fairs went.

	No1	No.2	No.3	No.4
Jan	Newcastle	Wellington		
Feb		Longton		Lichfield
Mar	Cannock	Oswestry	Dudley	Hanley
		Llangollen		
	Tipton	Corwen	Cradley Heath	
	Wolverhampton	Walsall	Lickey Hills	Coventry
Apr	Darlaston	Shrewsbury	Brierley Hill	Ashby
	Stafford	Wrexham	Oldbury	Wigston
May	Chester	Oakengates	Wednesbury	Leicester
	Brownhills	Oswestry		
Whit	Wolverhampton	Lichfield Bower	Lickey Hills	Walsall
	Birmingham	Hinckley	Birmingham	Birmingham
	Newport	Bedworth		Rugby
Jun	West Bromwich	Hednesford	Netherton	Blackheath
	Bromsgrove	Burslem	Shifnal	Knebworth
	Stafford	Tamworth	Tipton	Leamington
Jul	Hanley	Walsall	Lickey Hills	Bilston
			Chasetown	Shrewsbury
Aug	Bloxwich	Hinckley	Dudley	
	Darlaston			
	Oldbury	Bedworth	Pensnett	Donnington
Sep	Wednesbury	Leicester	Droitwich	Oakengates
		Blackheath	Dudley	
	Willenhall	Newcastle	Worcester	
	Brierley Hill	Ashby Statutes	Polesworth	Uttoxeter
			Atherstone	
	B'ham Onion	B'ham Onion	Tamworth	B'ham Onion
Oct	Wednesfield	Cannock		Northfield
	Goose Fair			
	Hull			
	Ilkeston	Ilkeston	Netherton	Hednesford
	B'ham Carnival	B'ham Carnival		Wigston
Nov	West Bromwich	Brownhills	Brierley Hill	Loughborough
	Tipton			
Dec	Willenhall	Hanley	Dudley	
	Wolverhampton			

- 191 -

BIRMINGHAM FAIRS

To folk unfamiliar with the West Midlands, it may seem strange that Birmingham and the Black Country could be two such separate and distinct urban areas. They do not look too far apart on the map! Pat Collins had chosen to make his home and his headquarters in the Black Country, but a trip to Birmingham then was as much a trip to 'foreign parts' as would be a trip to any other far-flung part of the world. But the fact that Britain's "Second City" was rather close to home meant that Pat inevitably strayed into it, and being Pat, he became associated with its best known fairs.

Fairs had been held at Ascensiontide and Michaelmas in Birmingham for several centuries. They were 'horse' fairs, and the Michaelmas fair had also become an 'onion' fair. Shortly before Pat Collins' arrival in the West Midlands, in the process of changing from trading fairs to pleasure fairs, they had been moved from the City Centre to a piece of vacant land at Aston, known as the Old Pleck. This was not a voluntary move: it was deliberate policy of the Council, who had voted in 1875, by a majority of 32 to 18 to ban all fairs from all roads and land belonging to the City. It was argued that fairs had outlived their usefulness, interfered with traffic and were "demoralising and vulgar".

According to Pat's own reckoning on the number of times he had attended the Onion Fair, he must have been present as the first event took place in Aston in 1876, when he was only seventeen and was still based in Chester. Presumably it was after he moved to the Midlands in 1882 that he was old enough and sufficiently confident to become involved with some of the problems associated with the fairs at Aston. When he took on the lease of the Old Pleck ground, about 1890, he had to deal with the gangs who made the lives of the showmen a misery with their protection rackets and threat of disruptive violence.

Pat encouraged the showmen to challenge the gangs collectively and putting the gangs to rout became part of the Pat Collins legend. At the Onion Fair in 1935, Pat told the story to C.H.Lea, the World's Fair correspondent, in these words:

"When I took the Old Pleck on a 25 year lease I was mad. On the eve of the first opening I went to the Police and asked for protection, but the Superintendent simply said, "God help you!". But later in the day he sent 25 men to be stationed around the ground.

One of the gangsters told me one of his friends had died and each showman would have to give a half crown contribution to his memory. I told the man to clear off the ground. He went away muttering curses, and I sent word around to stand firm.

At night two members of the gang came along and twitched my hat over my eyes. My fist shot out and down went the man. His friend was thunderstruck- in more ways than one, when he received a punch which made him sag at the knees. I gave the tip to the Police and the gang were run off the ground. They never gave any trouble again"

This account was fairly modest, and gave some credit to the Police for their eventual co-operation. Other accounts, perhaps not focussing on the particular year that Pat took out the lease on the ground, suggest that the battles with the gangs lasted over several seasons. It certainly contained all the drama needed to become a legend, and the names of the gangs themselves make good reading: The Black Bands, the Stool Boys, the Peaky Blinders. Sitting in the air raid shelter at Limetree House at the beginning of the Second World War, Pat was able to re-tell the stories for his grandchildren and great grand-children. One version described the leader of a gang agreeing a kind of "cease-fire" between gangsters and showmen while he and Pat fought a duel to settle things. The gang leader, admits that he has honourably been defeated by Pat's blows, and calls the war to an end!

Whatever happened, Pat established order, and the fairs in Aston prospered. Pat's acquisition of the ground at Aston, first at the Old Pleck and then the Serpentine, gave him the freedom to develop the fairs as his own, and on a large scale. Three times a year the level ash-covered surface of the Serpentine hosted his fairs. The Great Whit Fair was held on the Thursday, Friday and Saturday following the Bank Holiday. This enabled the equipment to be brought to Birmingham from the Whit fairs at Walsall and Wolverhampton and elsewhere. The Onion Fair was held at the end of September, and machines could gather from the Statute Fairs at Ashby and Atherstone, and several Black Country Wakes. Other showmen added to the fair, and Pat's "closest" tenants - his family and friends all became regular features of the Fair. Rides could even be brought up to Aston from the permanent amusement parks (Barry, Yarmouth, and the Crystal Palace), and would then use the Onion Fair as a jumping off point for their travels during the "Back End". Finally, in November, there was another fair at Aston, held to coincide with the Birmingham Carnival, or University Rag Week.

It seems probable that when the ground at Aston was first acquired it was as a joint venture by Pat and his brother John. They were also joint lessees at the Whit Fair at Wolverhampton in the early days, and for many years John was a member of the Midland Section of the Showmen's Guild, as well as the North West. There is a temptation to see Pat's rise to greatness in isolation, though as the lives and achievements of other showmen are unravelled, it is possible to get a better understanding of the parts they played in each others destinies.

Pat entertained Brummies at Sutton Park, and from time to time at the Lickeys, and, occasionally at other locations such as Handsworth, Northfield, Edgbaston Reservoir, Stirchley, Kings Norton etc. He owned halls at Monument Lane and Walford Road, and was sometimes known to put on a fair at Bingley Hall Birmingham (now demolished to make way for the International Convention Centre). Despite all this, Pat never entirely vanquished the "opposition" in Birmingham, as he did in the Black Country, and the

City remained the home of other important showmen.

Returning to Aston, let us look at the Fairs and see the volume of equipment Pat and his tenants assembled on various occasions. One of the earliest comprehensive accounts we have found of the Onion Fair is the description printed in The Era newspaper of 8 October 1904. It is interesting to see that shows rather than machines are given the most attention and regarded as being the major attraction of the fairground...but this is undoubtedly because the Era was the paper for aspiring Thespians. Flora Collins provided one of the two Bioscopes present that year, the "Superb Electrograph". The other was George Kemp's show. There were two Circuses: R.Baker's and Buffalo Bill's (the father of Richard Kayes who later presented Kayes' Circus at many Onion Shows). John Cordwell presented his Fine Art Show.

This was the period of "P Collins Ltd" and The Era informs us that the limited company presented four machines: the No.1 and No.2 racing Cockerels (Messrs Whyatt and Summerhayes), the No.1 Rolling Gondolas (W.Mullett), and the Four-Abreast (W.Bastable). Young Pat presented his Twin Tugs...presumably the early Savage steam yachts, and Brother John presented his Yachts, Motor Bicycles, and Newmarket Gallopers. Charles Farrell presented his "Farmyard" and Juvenile Flying Machine. Three other local machines were Mrs Shepherd's Ventian Gondolas, George Russell's Three-Abreast and Tom Jervis' Steam Swings. Joe Caddick came along with his photographic studio, and shooting galleries were provided by George Ford and William Dobson. Stalls were

ABOVE: Pat's fair on the "Reservoir Ground" of Aston in 1910. This appears to be a transitional phase between the expiry of Pat's lease on land at the Old Pleck, and the establishment of his ground at the Serpentine, at about this time. In the hazy background it is just possible to see the Nos. 1 & 2 Wonderland Shows standing next to each other, (one presenting a circus). Attractions include Pat's Motors and Platform Gallopers, Brother John's Motors, Yachts and Four-Abreast. Wm.Davies' Motors and Yachts, Russell's Three-Abreast.
(Collection of Bill Hunt)

presented by Messrs Cordwell, Cooper, Birch, Chaplin etc...the ground was managed by Mr Jeffries and Mr Slava. It is interesting to note that during 1904, Brother John, Pat, Flora and Charlie Farrell were also presenting machines at a fair at Kings Norton at the same time.

At the Onion Fair in 1907, the World's Fair report listed machines first and put the shows in second place. Pat presented the following: the No.1.Motors (Clara Mullett), the No.2.Motors (Jack Whyatt), the No.3.Motors (Young Pat), the Cockerels (W.Summerheys), the Wheely Whirly or "Japanese Sensation", ie. the Razzle Dazzle (Major Tyler), the Helter Skelter (John Hayes), the Royal Steam Yachts (Walter Hobbs) and the Four-Abreast (W.Davies). Brother John Collins presented three machines, his Four-Abreast, his Steam Yachts, and his Razzle Dazzle, and, for good measure, a Three-Abreast Galloper was presented by George Russell.

That was just the list of machines - then came the shows: Flora Collins presented the new Wonderland, showing films as well as presenting artistes like Little Titch. Sagar's Bioscope also attended, as well as Mander's Menagerie and several other shows. John Hayes, another local veteran showman, as well as

- 193 -

managing Pat's slip, was also presenting his own swingboats. There were many sidestalls presented by Pat's regular tenants, and Joe Caddick's Photographic Booth. In 1907 it was reported that there were no accidents and no drunkenness. Three railway companies had run 48 excursion trains to Birmingham, bringing 20,000 people to the fair!

1910 is regarded as the year that Pat finally settled on the Serpentine Ground, although how many grounds had been used at one time or another in the Aston area is not clear. The same year is supposed to be the occasion that Pat assembled 21 engines in a line across the site.

Harry Wilding produced a World's Fair report of the 1921 Onion Fair, giving a picture of the situation after the First World War: *"I know of very few places where the advantage of good space is so ample as at Aston. As usual, each lengthy side is occupied by stalls, shooting concerns and throwing games. The shows are placed at the end of the ground, and the centre is kept for riding machines - the whole presenting a wonderful charm of life and golden glitter"*. Harry Wilding poured superlatives into every description of the Birmingham fairs for the next decade. (see Ch.5)

Public transport brought people to the Onion Fair from a very wide area, making it a West Midlands equivalent to the Goose Fair, although Nottingham's Fair was better known nationally. Many "new" rides and shows were seen at the Onion Fair as if for the first time, even if they had reached the fair via local events where they had received little publicity. "The Swish" and "Over the Falls", for example, made grand entrances at the Onion Fair, after travelling for some time. Occasionally the pages of World's Fair records an innovation at the Onion Fair, which is recorded nowhere else! For example, in 1923, the Collins' latest American riding sensation was "The Sheik". After the Onion Fair it seems to have vanished back into the desert!

In 1929, Jack Todd, brought the first "Wall of death" to Brum at that year's Onion Fair. It took the fair by storm, and far eclipsed another innovation, the "Atlantic Rollers", specially brought to Birmingham from Great Yarmouth.

The 1930's saw the Onion Fair grow..and grow...it was always "bigger and better than ever" according to reports. When C.H.Lea called at Aston in 1934 he found Pat dealing with the arrival of the loads as his managers Pat Tyler and Bill Croydon were marking out the ground. Pat told him it was to be the equal of 'five fairs in one', all to be supervised by Pat himself - a man by then in his mid-seventies.

When Pat and C.H.Lea met again at the 1935 Onion Fair, Pat admitted that he had not been well. However, C.H.Lea wrote, *"The old time fire which made him the greatest of modern showmen is still to be discerned in his eyes and in his speech"* The rides in 1935 included The Racing Cars on their 105ft x 5ft track; and the Flying Fleas, both rides presented by Claire Collins; the Waltzer (Clara Collins) ; the Scenic (Ted Sherwood); the Dodgems (D.Shipley); Second Dodgems (J.Ryan); the Yachts (Captain Kelly);

the Jungle Grand National (Young Pat); the Airways (Baby Pat); Young Pat's Yachts (Mollie Collins); the Noah's Ark W.Weston); the Gallopers (Mrs Bird); the Ghost Train (W.Dutton). Walsall John was presenting his Speedway and a Waltzer, and his Wall of Death. Grandson, J.J.Collins and Norah presented their Skid. From the other side of the family came J.Collins' Speedway, and A.Collins' Waltzer. Outside the family a number of other showmen were represented: two Cakewalks (Harvey & Richards); two more Arks (Drakeley's and Frank Wilsons); Green's Caterpillar, two more Dodgems (Drakeley's and Wilsons); Wilson's Ghost train; Jervis's Ocean Waves and Jack'n Jill slide; Eddy Monte's Mono Rail, and Barnard's and Shepherd's swings.

The 1935 list of shows is just as impressive: Humphrey's Illusion Show; White's Cabaret; Dot Rayner's Fleas; Shufflebottom's Wild West Show, there were two Boxing Booths, Hughes' and Hickman's; Kaye's Circus; Tom Norman's presentation of "The Great Carno", J.Stockwell's and James Styles' freak shows. If they had time the punters could meet Colourado (the negro who was turning white), Shadola (the human skeleton) and Tatania, (the beautiful 29 stone giantess), and Karo (the Eskimo Midget), not forgetting Senor Senorita (the man/woman) and Princess Lena (the living doll). Mr Gardiner brought Wee Jimmy, the miniature racehorse along, but you'll be sad to know that Billy the Pig didn't manage to appear at the Onion Fair in 1935...he was ill! This bewildering mass of names may startle the reader unfamiliar with fairground sideshows, but they all "come to life", even in the sophisticated 1990's, to anyone who cares to read the detailed pages of the 1930's World's Fair. In those days the Onion Fair was obviously a great social occasion, followed by even bigger events at Nottingham and then at Hull.

The 1935 Onion Fair was laid out by Billy McCarthy and Bill Croydon, and G.Strickland was asked to show C.H.Lea around, so that he could report to readers. Another correspondent of the paper, "P.A.T" was presenting his own show, and he also described the fair in his report: *"The huge fair with its tens of thousands of multi-coloured lights, last Saturday night, looked a veritable paradise, and the ground was literally packed right up till 12 midnight. John Collins' Wall of death was drawing great crowds - with the inimitable Frank Hodgson as the coaxing frontsman. Mildred and Rob Lee riding the Wall...... Kayes' Circus was here again, as at Whit, and continuously displayed "House Full" signs. Young Billy Kayes, the youthful rider and comedy man on the rings was partnered by Sammy Freeman - what a circus family the Kayes must be..."* and so on...and so on...weaving an endless tapestry of fairground names and giving glimpses of vanished experiences... of people long departed and, interestingly, some still alive in the 1990's to tell the tale.

It is tempting to review what was brought to the Onion Fair year by year...the Thirties was a time of endless seeking of new rides and experiences..and each year Pat himself seemed to attract greater attention

ABOVE: A wonderful mid 1930's view of the Onion Fair. In the left foreground are the Yachts, presented as the "Atlantic Fliers". In the centre is Willie Weston's Noah's Ark, slightly concealing the Airways. Beyond are a set of Chairs and a Dodgem Track.
(Collection of Jack Harvey)

from the World's fair correspondents who regarded him as a Patriarchal elder statesman of the fairground. If you were invited into Pat's court, you were expected to respectfully listen to what the "King of Showmen" wished to say. It was in 1936 that Pat told his 'life story' to C.H.Lea, while at a fair at Handsworth Park in July, and the story was published in the Onion Fair report of that year. (See Chapter 1).

In 1936 Gilbert Dixon showed Mr Lea around the ground. He saw Pat's new attraction "The Whirlwind" (actually a new ride that Walsall John had brought up to Aston from Barry Island), and Walsall John's new Loop-o-Plane, brought up from Yarmouth via Oxford St.Giles Fair. As always some rides and shows were duplicated...and even triplicated. There were three boxing booths... Hughes', Woods', Hickman's. Todd's Wall of death, and Walsall John's Globe of Death. At least three Arks: Noah's (Mollie Collins), Over the Sticks (Harry Weston); Wild Stampede (Willy Weston) as well as Wilson's machine.

The quantity of equipment assembled at the Onion Fairs meant that a vast armada of transport was present, and in pre-War days this also meant a vast number of engines. Sometimes these were assembled in a line across the fairground, making a very impressive sight, but this added to problems with the water supply, and therefore more often they were dispersed around the ground.

After the Second World War the abandonment of steam was dramatic. Pat Collins' firm still retained half a dozen engines, and the Onion Fair was still somewhere that they could be seen together. In 1949 there were six engines present, four of which were kept in steam. As late as 1951, Burrell No.1. was being driven by Cockney Jack Harvey from Aston into the centre of Birmingham to advertise the Fair on Saturday afternoon. It was decorated with onions and advertised the Fact that Randolph Turpin was making an appearance at Hickman's Boxing Booth, having just returned from the USA and his fight with Sugar Ray Robinson. As well as No.1. the other Pat Collins' engines still appearing at Aston in the 1950's were "Goliath", "The Griffin" and "The Leader".

One of the great surprises of the Post-War period was the re-emergence of the No.1.Scenic. It was brought out of the yard at Bloxwich for the 1946 Onion Fair, and was left built-up at Aston for the Carnival Fair six weeks later. It was at the Onion Fair again in 1948, before making a spectacular final trip to Hull, after which it "retired" to Crystal Palace.

The details of the 1949 Onion fair show how pre-War engines and equipment were blended with the new Post-War image of the fairground. The No.1.Scenic and its organ had 'retired' to Sutton Park after its 1948 epic journey to Hull, but an organ could still be heard at the front of Tom Norman's Palladium Show, and there was still a fifty-year-old trumpet organ accompanying the Gallopers (presented by Jones Brothers).

ABOVE: Many people remember the entrance to the Serpentine Ground, and associate an evening visit to the fair with coloured lights plus the sounds and smells of the fair. This picture was taken in 1959 or 1960.
(Collection of Arthur Jones)

Everywhere else the gramophone and loudspeaker had won the day. There were still some very traditional old fashioned rides, including Harry Richard's Cakewalk, and a Lighthouse slip, although Billy Williams' Big Wheel now provided the vertical excitement to the fair's landscape. The rides provided by Pat Collins included three sets of Dodgems, an Ark, the Moonrocket, Figure of Eight, Loop-a-Plane, the New Looper, Ghost Train, Speedway Ark, Waltzer, and Brooklyn's Speedway, and John's "Ducks". Two older rides presented by Collins were the Three-Abreast and the Yachts.

That same year, other showmen added: Chair-o-Plane (Joby Farrell); Skid (Harry Hall); Airways (Morley); Dodgems and Ark (Frank Wilson); Caterpillar (J.J.Collins and Norah); Waltzer (J.P.Collins); Adult Swings (J.Shepherd). Juvenile rides were by Albert Rogers, G.Tweddle, Jimmy Williams, Jimmy Ryan, T.Crick, Mrs Chadwick and Mr.Hart. As well as several shows and the Boxing Booth; Kayes' Circus was still making an appearance shortly before its post-war demise. Clara Collins was in overall charge, and the World's fair correspondent Jack Mellor was shown around by manager Lionel Barnett. Jack used the pen-name "Wanderer"..and he was indeed a "wanderer"; his base was in Wolverhampton so the name had a double jokiness!. The Onion Fair had become a meeting place for the small band of fairground enthusiasts who were beginning to share their mutual interest, and Jack Mellor interceded with Cockney Jack to allow the enthusiasts onto the footplate of Burrell No.1.

The Onion Fair was such a successful gathering that it had its own momentum, and continued to be an impressive array of machines and shows even as the Pat Collins' empire declined. The description of the Onion Fair held just after Clara's death in 1962 shows how well the event survived.

Even when the Pat Collins equipment was reduced to three machines, augmented by John's equipment from the amusement parks, it was still possible to put on a big Onion Fair. The last one was held in 1968. After which the land was sold to Aston Villa Football Club to become a car park. A few years' later an Asda Supermarket was built on the site, which dashed the hopes of those who wanted to see the fair at Aston revived. With more interest now in traditional fairs...a new Onion Fair may yet rise from the ashes (Asda has also now been re-sited).

We cannot leave Birmingham without some mention of the fairs held by Pat Collins on other sites.

Monument Lane
This was a site where Pat Collins purchased the ground towards the end of the last century. It could have been used as Winter Quarters and was considered a suitable site for holding a Christmas Fair. Although the site was surrounded by a wall, the local residents complained about the noise during the Christmas Fair in 1906; consequently the following Christmas, Pat found he had trouble obtaining a Music Licence. The Police did not oppose his application and though Pat pleaded with the Magistrates that the music would come from his £2,000 Marenghi organ and that engine whistles would be controlled, they refused his application. It seems that the fair went

> **BIRMINGHAM "BLACKPOOL" WEEK CALLING!**
>
> from the EDGBASTON RESERVOIR.
>
> One of the greatest "gaffs" in the country is being held here
>
> **AUGUST 5th, to 12th.**
>
> **SPACES TO LET for Roundabouts, Dodgems, Automatics, Round Games, Stalls, etc.**
>
> Last year, between 300,000 to 400,000 people passed through the gates, paying 1/- each, and they were all spenders. Over ten million population to draw from, within a few miles. Ask anyone who was there last year for their verdict. This year will be better.
>
> I "tipped" Coventry Carnival as one of the best one day gaffs. This came home in spite of the rain.
>
> *Don't be too late, but BOOK NOW for the " BIRMINGHAM "BLACKPOOL" WEEK, and be sure of a "Winter's Keep."*
>
> Applications to:
> **P. COLLINS, Amusement Depot, BLOXWICH.**

ahead but without music, and then Pat expressed his desire to sell the ground.

It is not clear whether this ground became the site of Collins' "Palais de Danse". The latter generally seemed to come under the control of Young Pat, and an occasional circus was also presented there. Unlike the Walford Road premises, there is no record of it accommodating fairground equipment. An interesting note is that Young Pat advertised from the Palaise de Danse address that he intended to open a brand new Amusement Park in Birmingham. Later the same month World's Fair carried a news item to the effect that Young Pat was not likely to achieve his aim during 1936. The report admitted that rumours suggested the site might be Edgbaston Reservoir...Perry Barr Greyhound Track...or the site of the British Industries Fair at Castle Bromwich....speculation certainly covered a wide area. The mystery was not cleared up and nothing more has yet been found out about it

Edgbaston Reservoir
This was built to store water for the Birmingham Canal Navigation (BCN).

On its southern shore was a site used by showmen. Between the Wars, Pat Collins held a fair at the Reservoir for what became known as "Blackpool Weeks". It is possible, as described above, that Young Pat saw this as a potential permanent site for a small amusement park.

In 1933 the "Blackpool Weeks" hit the headlines, when the Police seized over three hundred automatic "gaming" machines. Seventeen showmen were summoned for "using a tent for the purpose of unlawful gaming therein". It was the old problem that had been encountered when Hoop-La was introduced in 1908, but it was even more difficult to plead that automatics were a test of the punter's skill. All the defendants pleaded guilty, and the summonses were dismissed on the payment of twenty shillings costs in each case, and the promise not to open in Birmingham again!

In the years immediately preceding the Second World War an unidentified showman does appear to have operated on the site on a permanent basis, but this closed at the outbreak of War. At the end of the War, the site was taken over by Butlins. Pat Collins' association with the site seems therefore to have been brief, and this is probably another example of Birmingham being regarded as the territory of other showmen.

The Lickey Hills
This large area of open space and greenery in south Birmingham offered a welcome escape from the confines of town and city. Trams to the Lickeys carried many thousands out to Rednal and the freedom of the hills. Tea rooms and permanent "amusements" developed to accompany the simple delights of the countryside. There were several 'rival' sites used by showmen, and other fairground families like the Jervises and Fletchers are more indelibly linked with the Lickeys.

However, Pat Collins acquired a lease on land there in the early 1920s, and it was apparently laid out by the brother of Herbert Barnard, one of Pat's managers. (It has been suggested that the Barnards were in fact the owners of the site). This small site formed part of a run that tenants could join by visiting the Lickey Hills after the larger Easter Fairs at Wolverhampton, Walsall or Coventry. It was also a jumping off point for rides or attractions that wished to move into Birmingham. The Lickeys was also a stop on the No.3. run that started in Dudley, and was therefore part of Young Pat's run for a time. The scene is described well by "P.A.T", the World's Fair correspondent who visited there in April 1936:

"Lickey is still only a small ground, but the hills are becoming the Hampstead Heath of the Midlands. The Guvnor is the one and only Alderman Collins who has just opened his Easter gaffs. I found Gilbert Dixon in charge at Lickey, where Billy Weston was presenting "Over the Sticks" and Joby Farrell presented a Cakewalk. The latter needs to be pensioned off and Joby should be given a newer machine. I also came across Timmy Kayes presenting his lion cubs. John Collins' Globe of death was there and was going on to do a fortnight at Stirchley."

Kingstanding
The name of this Birmingham suburb dates back to 1642, and the "King" it refers to is Charles I. Pat held his fair not far from the hill where the Royalist army had "stood", and his first use of the site was about 1932...just as the new suburb was developing. For several years the fair made a spring and autumn appearance at the site, at the corner of Kings Road and Shady Lane, and the latter event became a destination for some of the rides assembled for the Onion Fair. Perhaps because of this, the fair at Kingstanding

was quite large.

For example, in 1938, the fair included the Airways (Dennis Shipley); Dodgems (Will Mullett); Jungle Speedway (W.Hobbs); and the ageing Cakewalk (Joby Farrell). Shows included Jack Parry's, and Hickman's. Boxing Booths, Kayes' Circus and Skid Skinner's Wall of death (Baby John Collins). Bill Croydon was ground manager. Ironically, the spread of suburban housing which had made this fair worthwhile, eventually consumed the ground itself, and this was probably the last Collins' fair on that ground.

Other locations
At the beginning of this century it appears that Charlie Farrell took several rides and stalls to a small fair at Kings Norton, following the Onion Fair. Pat also regularly used Handsworth Park, and appeared at places like Northfield and Stirchley.

Indoor Fairs at Bingley Hall, Birmingham and Walford Road, Sparkbrook

Birmingham's Bingley Hall was often used to present circuses for a season that might run from Christmas well into the New Year (eg 1931). Sometimes these were accompanied by fairground rides, presumably as tenants of the organiser of the circus, and sometimes they were followed by fairs by a lessee, no doubt keen to find an indoor venue to earn some money while the weather was bad.

If unable to appear at Bingley Hall, Pat sometimes held his own "Great Circus and Fair" at the Walford Road Rink in Sparkbrook. For example, in November 1920 he opened for three months at Walford Road to rival "Wilkins Great Victory Circus" which occupied Bingley Hall.

It might be wondered what kind of machine could be built up inside such a hall? However, the Christmas fair held there in 1927 apparently included the No.1.Scenic, the Chair-o-Planes, Cakewalk and Over the Falls, as well as a freak show.

COVENTRY

The present-day County of the West Midlands consists of three separate urban industrial areas: Birmingham, The Black Country, and..Coventry.

Some Coventry fairs have significant associations with local events, eg the Lady Godiva pageants; and some of the more usual trading fairs grew into pleasure fairs such as the Whitsun "Pot" fair, also known as 'The Great Fair'. By the late 1850's these were established on Pool Meadow, by Hales Street.

Pat Collins held at least two fairs of his own in Coventry: the Easter Fair, and the Christmas Fair, and may have attended the Whitsun Fairs as a tenant, as far back as the late 1880's. When interviewed locally in 1895, Walter Hobbs, Pat's Brother-in-Law gave the impression that the Whitsun visit to the town was the result of travelling from Kings Lynn Mart down to London and then via Coventry back to the Midlands.

The Great Fair ceased to be held on Pool Meadow in 1930, when it was re-located at Barras Heath, until the War caused another move.

Pat's Easter fair, which can be traced back to the 1890's, was held on various grounds, until moving to the Corporation's Pool Meadow ground at the turn of the century. His earliest Christmas fair on that site, for which the advertising has survived was 1901. Just as the Great Fair had to move in 1930, Pat also had to

LEFT: The Great Carmo appeared at Yarmouth in 1935 and was then presented by Tom Norman's "Palladium" Show at the Onion Fair, before going onto Nottingham and Hull. (World's Fair)

move his Easter fair. It first went to Gulson Road and then to the Hearsall Common site.

The Christmas fairs ceased many years ago, and Easter is now the only time that Anthony Harris takes Pat Collins' fair into Coventry. The Whitsun fair, controlled by the Corporation is attended by other showmen. Coventry has always been host to a variety of showmen as it is accessible from several "territories".

When World's Fair reported on the Christmas 1935 fair, they mentioned that Herbert Barnard was in charge - as he had been for thirty years. Herbert Barnard managed various grounds for Pat, and presented his own set of swings.

Sometimes the weather was indifferent, and in 1935 also it seems that Hickman's Boxing Booth was built up, but then remained closed as the boxers failed to materialise! Norah Kayes was made of sterner stuff, and was observed parading outside her father's circus, despite having just spent five weeks in a Wolverhampton Hospital after falling from the Trapeze while in Cannock. The 1935 fair consisted of The Waltzer (Clara); Over the Sticks (Billy Weston); Wall of Death (John Collins Jnr ie Brother John's Grandson); Bill Meakin's Mono-railway (Eddy Monte); and the Dodgems (Dennis Shipley). As well as Hickman's closed Boxing Booth, and Kayes' Circus, Pat Kilbride was presenting his Illusion Show, Swings and striker by Herbert Barnard, Stalls by Tommy Roberts, Joe Corrigan, Frank Sherwood, Harry Jones, Jim Humphries, etc..

Pat Collins' other association with Coventry was in relation to a Carnival Fair, originally held to raise local hospital funds. It grew out of an "extra day" attached to the Great Fair, but became a separate one-day event which was held in the Memorial Park up until 1990.

THE BLACK COUNTRY FAIRS.

Pat Collins' arrival in the Black Country of the early 1880's, is described in Chapter 1. Up until that time shows were presented and fairs held in a generally disorganised manner. A travelling show simply opened for business on any ground it could find as it made its way through the area, and the proprietors of stalls and simple rides turned up at established fairs and Wakes and grabbed whatever places were going.

Pat's arrival coincided with the growing powers of Local Government, and when the new advanced technology of larger riding machines made such a haphazard state of affairs unacceptable. Dates and sites had to be arranged, someone had to take charge, and in return for organising the fair that person was able to let ground to "tenants". A showman who made progress into the expensive business of purchasing large riding machines and became a "Riding Master" needed the assurance that suitable ground and fairs were available on which to present them. This is what happened to Pat. As he acquired equipment he took the initiative and became the organiser of the fairs themselves, maybe paying for the privilege, in order to be able to let the ground to tenants to complete a good mixed fair. Alternatively, he could have purchased or leased land himself, and not have to worry about tendering for the lease of a regular fair. Adopting the policy of acquiring leases and purchasing land himself was a major factor leading to the rise of Pat, to become - "King of Showmen"

By the turn of the century, Pat's name was associated with almost every regular fair or Wake in the Black Country. There were some events that he never seemed to bother about, and left to other showmen. For example, the Sedgley Wake was left to the Davies! Even at Pelsall, so close to his headquarters, Pat appeared to leave the fair to someone else. Other events were presumably so minor that it was not considered worth building up a riding machine on the site, and these were left to fade away, or were frequented by a handful of swings, hand-turned roundabouts and a few stalls.

Occasionally the Black Country was invaded by "opposition" ...if a site could be found anywhere to open. For example, in April 1935 N.B.Davies, of Stoke, found ground available on the Birmingham New Road, on the outskirts of Wolverhampton, and built up his own Jungle Speedway, one other ride and a few stalls. Apparently business was poor. Later in the same year James Patrick Collins pulled down at Bridgnorth in November and chanced his luck in Wolverhampton for a few days, building up his Jungle Speedway Ark in North Street within a few yards of the Market Patch. Some local folk associated the fair with Pat because of the town centre location.

Pat's Black Country fairs had a special quality because of the kind of grounds he established. They were the antithesis of the grass sites enjoyed by rural showmen. The World's Fair correspondent, "JBT" had watched Pat arrive in the Black Country and become established. His reports of the early 1930's often provide interesting comments on the grounds. For example, having reported good business at Tipton in July 1935, he states, "I can go back as far as the 1887 Wakes when I sold gingerbread and ice-cream, and Caddick's, Antils's and Stockton's were familiar visitors. The ground is somewhat smaller now than then, and is controlled and owned by Alderman Collins. It was at one time a big marl hole, and was filled up with ashes, that's why it is so dry and dusty at times, but it drains well when it rains"

All over the Black Country, and outside its borders Pat bought marl holes, colliery banks and tips. The sites were levelled and graded with a clinker ash surface, and were then ready to host his fairs. Sometimes they could be let to travelling circuses, markets etc. Sometimes they provided winter quarters for his tenants. But most important of all they gave freedom of movement to Pat, and a guaranteed place to build up his riding machines without harassment from the local authority. On such dusty and dirty pitches it is a cause of great wonder that the rides could look so clean and bright always.

ABOVE: Wolverhampton Fair on the old Market Patch - now beneath the new Civic Centre! On the right is a Razzle Dazzle belonging to Pat or Brother John. In the centre is Wm.Davies' Four-Abreast and on the left are Gondolas - thought to be the ex John Murphy set (R31) sold in 1909.
(Postcard in Collection of Alex Chatwin)

Wolverhampton

Three major annual fairs were presented here; one at Christmas and / or New Year, one at Easter and one at Whitsun. They were held on the site of the retail market in the square overlooked by St Peter's Church, and to some extent they did interrupt the conduct of the market. Pat was the lessee of these fairs by the 1890's, and at least in the case of the Easter fair, was joint lessee with Brother John.

One of the earliest local descriptions of the fair paints a picture of Wolverhampton on a fine Whit Bank Holiday Monday, in May 1893. Even at that time many thousands of people had left the town on Daylong railway excursions, but their absence was matched by thousands pouring into the town... on foot... on the trams and ...in horse-drawn vehicles. Many folks were making for the races at Dunstall, but others made for the fair on the market patch. The Wolverhampton Chronicle's correspondent ("One of the Crowd") described what he saw:

..."*Steam was up as I passed through to business at nine in the morning, and from what I could hear of shrill whistles and of a thousand pipes, it was not down at midnight. The roundabouts were patronised by little children in the morning, and by big children at night...*

It is interesting to note the improvements that have been effected in roundabouts in late years. Don't you remember those fiery untamed gee-gees that a score or more of little boys used to push round ? There was very little danger from speed in those days...Then steam was introduced, and roundabouts became the rage of the fair. Velocipedes came into vogue - those boneshakers that developed into the beautiful bicycles of today - and for some years they took the places of horses, but the equine species have never wholly been knocked out, and never will be. The "Sea on Land" was next introduced, then mechanical galloping horses, then switchback cars, "Alpine Climbers", as they were called. The latest is the "Gondola" which however, is worked on the sampe principle as the Switchback. The present day roundabout is a gorgeous costly instrument of pleasure , decorated with much gold and varied colours. The machinery is of the best, and the musical organ large, if not always melodious. There are two of these whirligigs, in the fair which are illuminated at night with the electric light, beside which the gas and oil flames look extremely bilious.

There are scores of swingboats...they are very popular notwithstanding the fact that they have been productive of so many deaths and broken limbs. As to the machine which is known as "Roley-Poley", I am at a loss what to say. It is a queer invention and I would not care to mount it after a good meal. And what a roaring trade was done all day! I was told that some concerns would take no less than £100 during the hours they were running"

The "Roley-Poley" was most probably the "Razzle Dazzle". The writer went on to describe stalls selling Italian ice-cream and "Hokey-Pokey", and the "Besom Yard Gypsies" selling their wares, the toy stalls, and the photograph booths, where you could buy an "instant" portrait - produced by a new process, patented by the proprietor.

It is also interesting to note that the Rector of St Peter's, Rev.Jeffcock, used his new "Institute" which overlooks the square, to host the showmen to a meal on Sunday afternoon - the first time such an event had been organised.

Unfortunately, it appears the local paper never printed

ABOVE: Another view of Wolverhampton's Fair from the steps of St Peter's Church (note the Wholesale Market on the right). This early 1930's view is dominated by the presence of the No.1.Scenic.
(Collection of Jim Boulton)

BELOW: Pat pays a visit to the Wolverhampton Whit Fair in 1925, and he is seen here by the Platform Galloper - note the packing used to create extra steps onto the machine, to take account of the falling ground. On the left is an ice cream barrow and an Avery Weighing Machine. Beyond the round stall are the Chairs and Steam Yachts.
(Collection of John Ray, via Philip Eisenhoffer)

such a detailed picture of the fair again. Many searches have been made in the newspaper archives in an endeavour to read descriptions of the coming of the Bioscopes and Scenic Railways, but nothing has yet come to light. This is a pity because Wolverhampton's Easter fair must have been the scene of the first opening of some of those attractions

Ten years later, the great "Wonderland Show" which had first opened at Wrexham in March 1907, causing quite a stir, came to Wolverhampton two months later but the press made no comment. Perhaps the town was already familiar with the Bioscope...after all such shows had been around for almost a decade and Wolverhampton being a large town was frequently visited by travelling shows of all kinds.

World's Fair assured its readers that Wonderland was present in 1907 along with William Davies' Racers and Roosters; John Collins' Air Ship & Razzle dazzle. but it appears that many of Pat's machines were at Coventry at the time. The difficulty in providing a number of large Easter fairs simultaneously was solved by leasing space to others, and in the early 1900's William Davies often provided a machine at Wolverhampton while Pat attended Coventry. The practice continues today, and while Anthony Harris moves to Coventry to put on a Pat Collins Fair, his Easter Fair at Wolverhampton is usually presented by Stanworth's equipment, brought down from Stoke!

Whitsun 1908 in Wolverhampton was described in some detail by World's Fair:

"Again the fine organ of Pat Collins is the outside attraction at his large cinematographic show, and the fit up of the concern, together with his attendants, attired in black frock coats and silk hats, offer a completeness so neat and artistic, that, from a monetary point of view also, success is at once ensured. Beside he has his full equipment, with his racing motor cars, cockerels, horses, aeroplanes, looping the loop etc.

John Collins has his Electric Jumping Horses, Motor Cars and Airship, and there are William Davies' Horses, and Caddick's American Studio. In North Street (at the foot of the square) is Holland's Palace of Light" - pitched for its first time in Wolverhampton."

1908 was probably the zenith of the Bioscope, and it is interesting to see that two of the most famous shows came to Wolverhampton at the same time. Five or six such shows were known to line up at the really large fairs! In 1911, Wolverhampton's Easter fair hosted the opening of Pat's first purpose built electric scenic railway - the "Jungle Motors" (R15). Building the large scenics on the slope of the Market Patch called for the use of much packing material to keep the machines level.

A typical Wolverhampton fair in the inter-War years would still be dominated by the scenic railway. For example, in 1927 at Easter, this was the Joby Farrell machine, the Peacocks and Dragons (R15a) accompanied by the Three Abreast (Harry Weston Jnr), the Yachts (Pat Tyler), Over the Falls (George Roberts), the Swish (Jim Bailey), Jack Parry's three novelty shows, and Davies' famous model colliery.

Almost a decade later, Whit 1936, the Dragons and Peacocks were still at work, along with newer rides: Arks, a Waltzer and the Dodgems. Jack Parry was still to be found, but his show now presented "Big Chief Red Snake". There were two boxing booths - Hickman's and Hughes', Joe Gardner's Animal Freaks, and Tom Norman's Show - said to be on its first visit to the town as part of Pat's fair. Apparently the Scenic, freshly repainted from top to bottom, was busier than the newer rides, and Max Miller, who was appearing at the local theatre at the time, made a "star appearance" at the fair,

The Whitsun 1937 Fair was the last to be held on the Market Patch, and for Christmas 1937/New Year 1938, Pat Collins' fair was opened on the Brickkiln Street Patch, which became its home until the new Retail Market was built and the Ring Road transformed that part of the town. The fair then moved to Stafford Street and to Falkland Street, in the 1960's, but never with the success enjoyed on the two Market sites. Even at Brickkiln Street the fair faced the problem of being partly surrounded by housing - generating complaints of noise etc,. The Express & Star of 6 June 1938 printed the headline, "Noisy 'mikes' keep children awake", although there was little substance to the story. it is a reminder that, in an urban area like the Black Country, Pat's fairgrounds were often surrounded by housing.

Willenhall

Another Black Country town in which Pat acquired his own ground was Willenhall. The site was a large rectangular stretch of land alongside the Walsall Road, overlooked by the parish church of St Giles. It provided winter quarters for several families, and it is still possible to meet showmen who can say, "I was born on the Wakes' Ground at Willenhall". Two annual fairs were held on the ground - the Wakes itself in September, and a Spring fair, usually two weeks' before Easter. The latter was an opportunity to check, repair and repaint the equipment before moving onto larger Easter Fairs.

"Humpshire" - the little lock-making town of Willenhall, never greatly appeared in any of World's Fair accounts of Pat's travels, until the 1930's when the paper had its own Black Country correspondent - "JBT", who in 1936 told his readers:

"At Willenhall in 1896 my wife and I were parading and standing for the shooting - my wife stood for the knife-throwing by the late William Shufflebottom, known as Texas Bill. My wife was then a young smart-looking lass, and Willenhall folk used to gasp when they saw the knives whizzing at her...the show was a double wagon walk up, with organ, drums, etc..." In the summer of 1936 he found a retired showman still living quietly on the ground. Years later the ground was still used by retired showfolk, and the last of these had to be persuaded to join the retired showpeople at Goscote before the ground could be purchased by the local Council.

"JBT" returned to Willenhall in the September of 1936 to report on the Wakes - "Wet as usual!". He found a ground managed by Billy McCarthy, on which stood the No.1.Scenic (Ted Sherwood), the Waltzer (Clara Collins), the Ark (Mollie Collins), the Dodgems (Johnny Ryan), the Yachts (Admiral Kelly), the Ghost Train (W.Mullett) and the Loop o Plane (W.Dutton), plus the regular stall holders. From this list we can see that the Willenhall Wake was quite a substantial fair, reminding us that the Wakes formed a major part of the No.1.circuit - where the most money was to be made!

On the Sunday night a Sacred Music Concert was held on the Scenic's organ, at which Bill Croydon acted as MC., before the fair moved on to Brierley Hill. In 1936 Pat and Clara drove over from Bloxwich to attend the concert and to hand the money collected to the Willenhall Nursing Association.

Willenhall played another little part in the Pat Collins' story in September 1947, when Frank Allen brought the new Scammell "Showtrac" to Willenhall to carry a large part of the Waltzer to Brierley Hill - its first work for the firm.

The Wakes' Ground was eventually compulsorily purchased by the Council who wanted to build a new Fire Station. As it turned out, part of the ground became a football pitch and the Fire Station was built elsewhere. The town end of the ground was turned into a lorry park, and in the early 1980's Henry Bacon successfully gained the right to hold an annual pre-Easter fair on the lorry park. Latterly, Anthony Harris tried reviving the Wakes' fair itself, but it was not successful.

Brierley Hill

The number of Wakes all unfolding in the Black Country at almost the same time during the Autumn meant that the fair on the No.1.circuit could not be at them all. In the case of Brierley Hill, the fair was important enough to be on the No.1.circuit and the fair came directly from Willenhall, and later moved on to the Onion Fair. Brierley Hill regularly enjoyed the best rides and shows.

The ground on which Pat's fair was held was a typical Black Country pitch and was adjacent to the Brierley Hill Alliance Football Ground. Once again Asda has followed in the footsteps of Pat Collins, and their supermarket and car park are on the site today. The football pitch was used to play a particularly important local "Derby" during Wakes' Week, and both the football match and the fair are associated with regular wet weather.

Blackheath

Blackheath, in the south of the Black Country, also celebrated its annual Wake in September. The fair, on the No.2.Circuit, usually took up residence in the Market Place, but this could be augmented when required. In 1909 we have a record of the New Wonderland Show being built up at Blackheath. As well as providing Sacred Music on the Organ, the Sunday Concert appears to have used the Bioscope equipment to deliver "a sermon in pictures - the Life of Christ". That year it was accompanied by motor car scenic and the Racing Bicycles.

Writing about his childhood in Blackheath in the 1920's, Clarry Siviter has described the fair coming to his home town:

"Pat Collins' fair came to Blackheath every Autumn on a piece of ground at the back of the Market Hall. As kids we would watch the engines pulling the amusements into position, and would be scared stiff by the size of the monsters. The empty wagons were put on the land at the side of the Salvation Army, and we used to have a wonderful time playing on them.

We longed for the opening night, which was usually Friday, and we would meet at the bottom of the entry clutching our pennies. Saturday nights were the best. Crowds of people were out for a good time, balls banging at the coconut shies, the bell clanging on the "Try Your Strength" machine, rattles and hooters mingling with the cries from the showmen inviting us into their sidestalls.

I always looked for a young man who had a different show every year. To attract attention he would come to the front of the show and play a side drum (he was very good) while a scantily dressed girl did a little dance. Then he told us what we would see inside. One year he told us we were going to see something really special: the girl was going to show us her little bare behind! We made sure we were right at the front and the little show soon filled up. At the end of the show the man said, "This is the moment you have all been waiting for. The lady will now show you her bare behind". The curtains opened, and there stood the girl in a smashing dress, with her hands behind her back. She brought them forward to show us that she was holding a Teddy Bear...- that was her 'bear behind'!

Blackheath folk also used to go to the fair at Oldbury - it was bigger than our own fair. We could'nt afford to go on the bus as we needed the few pennies we had, to spend at the fair, but part of the fun was walking there and back in the crowd. To join in that walking is something I will never forget - all the laughter and singing"

In 1937 the Blackheath fair moved from its old patch near the market place to new ground at Bell End - at the foot of the Rowley Hills, nearer to Old Hill than Blackheath. More recently this gaff has been known as "Rowley Regis" and it was on this ground in 1983, that Anthony Harris completed the negotiations that made him the sole proprietor of Pat Collins' Fun Fairs.

An interesting side note is that Old Hill did not usually play host to Pat Collins' fair, it was one of the towns left to Mr Davies.

Dudley

The autumn fair at Dudley often coincided with the fair at Blackheath, but the town also enjoyed an annual Spring Fair, these were held on the "White Nobs Fairground" close to Trindle Road. The ground was cramped and far from level. It seems that the fair was held there simply by tradition - the Hayes family had held their fairs on the site before Pat Collins came to the area, and they continued to winter there. A run of fairs started from Dudley each Spring, taking in the smaller communities of the south west of the Black Country, and this formed the basis of the No.3.Circuit. This circuit sometimes ended with a third visit to Dudley as late as the end of November.

Dudley fairs did not receive much attention in World's Fair until they had a Black Country correspondent in the 1930's. "JBT" reported in March 1936 that huge posters were to be seen in Dudley announcing the two week fair opening on 6th March. He noticed that work was starting on the construction of Dudley Zoo, and this led him to add "Mr Collins is a very old and esteemed lessee under the Earls of Dudley, and the present Earl has had many a jolly time on Collins' rides"

But the fair at Dudley had its moments of glory. For example, in 1929, the Wall of death joined the Pat Collins firm at Dudley and became the "talk of the town" before moving on to greater fame at the Back End of that year. On that occasion Pat had put on a fair to accompany an ambitious September Carnival organised in Dudley.

The No.1.Scenic was well-known and well appreciated in Dudley, and after its withdrawal in 1937, the reports of the March 1938 fair were strongly lamenting the absence of the organ, and the omnipresence of "panatrope music". In later years the fair was built up on ground that is now a car park - opposite the Bus Garage

Netherton

We have not found any reports of the fair at Netherton in the pages of World's Fair, or of Stourbridge for that matter. The run was usually organised so that the fair could visit such towns twice a year, the second visit being associated with a "Wakes' Week".

The ground alongside the Halesowen Road, in Netherton, was a popular one. A friendly publican provided a fresh water supply for the travellers, as well as other liquid refreshment in the evenings, and in return Pat Collins paid the pub's water rates.

Cradley Heath

In June 1936, "JBT" reported seeing the same fair at Cradley Heath which had started out from Dudley in March. In fact "JBT" himself had a show there, and found himself next to Kayes' Circus where he learned that Norah Kayes and John Collins had just announced their engagement (J.J.Collins...Young Pat's son). Billy McCarthy was in charge of the fair and the attractions were: Over the Sticks (H.Weston), the Dodgems (George Monte), Cakewalk (Harry Richards), Barnard's Swings, Pat Kilbride's show, Kayes' Circus, and a one-week appearance from Tom Norman! There were sidestalls by Billy Bagnall, Tommy Tweddle, Charlie Deeks, etc.

This comparatively modest fair, with Harry Weston's Ark and the Dodgems as the major items of equipment also visited places like Netherton (June), the Lickey Hills (Easter), Quarry Bank and Stourbridge.

The fairground in Cradley Heath was the Porter's Field, now an industrial estate.

Darlaston

The World's Fair correspondent "JBT" gives us an insight into the location of Darlaston Wakes' fair when he reports on his visit to the ground in August 1933. Apparently, Pat Collins had used three different grounds in the previous 50 years, the first of which had been the Green. The second was a rather awkward site by the old tramsheds, but then Pat had been able to purchase land by St Catherine's Cross. Of this ground, "JBT" reports:

"The ground is an ideal one, easy of access for the public, and quite easy for show transport, and the ground even when not occupied by the Wakes is always well looked-after. When Mr P.Collins bought this land to preserve the Wakes, he also arranged a local caretaker, so the land is always tidy. Moreover, there is a good water supply to hand. The approach to the ground is from the main Walsall-Bilston Road. The approach is always decorated in the Collins' style with bunting, and is well arranged with electric bulbs of all shades, presenting a very pleasant appearance."

Its place in the calendar meant that it usually immediately followed the Bloxwich Wakes, and therefore occupied the August Bank Holiday weekend, and many attractions could move directly from Bloxwich to Darlaston.

Great Bridge

For many years Pat Collins used a site between Mill Street and Lewis Street, at the Dudley Port end of Great Bridge, for a Wakes' fair, but the site was "lost" when it was built upon during the early 1930's. It was one of the local sites sometimes used by "opposition" such as Drakeley's, and was sometimes used as a market. In 1931 the fair moved back to a site in "New Town" on the road from Great Bridge to Greet's Green.

Black Country folk display great skill in making subtle distinctions between individual settlements and communities that the outsider would regard as all part of the same place. The move led "JBT" to ask World's Fair readers if they realised that the Great Bridge Wakes had only once ever been held in Great Bridge itself, (ie. about half way between the two sites described above)

"JBT" was also able to take readers back to the "old days" before Pat Collins' arrival, when there had been so many small very localised "Wakes" held all over

RIGHT: Transport and living vans crowd the corner of Darlaston Fairground on 25/9/48 - the fair having moved here from Bloxwich Gala.
(Collection of Kevin Scrivens)

the Black Country. Thus it was that the move to New Town was a return to a site used in the mid nineteenth century for races and athletics known as the New Town Wakes.

Oldbury

The fairground in Oldbury nestled between pharmaceutical manufacturers Cuxson Gerrard and the foundry and engineering works of Hunt Brothers (Oldbury) Ltd; both these firms remain, but the fairground, still a colourful place, has long been re-developed and its tenants include both new and high tech firms and warehousing.

There were two access points one from Bromford Road with a fairly steep incline down to the flat ground, and the other opening was in Fountain Lane where the land was flat and more suitable as a vehicular entrance. Pat Collins' visited the site twice yearly, with a traditional fair around Easter time and again at the end of August/early September for the Wakes.

World's Fair correspondent described a 1907 event thus:

"This well-known Black Country Wakes commenced Friday 30th August and continued until 4th September, on the old Wakes' Ground, now in the sole possession of Pat Collins. It was a very large gathering of travellers and everyone seemed to be having a good time. At Collins' Great Show the special attraction was the Driscoll & Bowker fight - splendidly reproduced on the Bioscope.

Old faces I recognised included Messrs Cordwell, Chaplain, Stokes, Brown and Wright. The shows present were Mrs Collins' Organ Front Wonderland, the Westwood Giants, and Professor Leonard's Miniature Menagerie. Rides were provided by Pat Collins & Sons Racing Motors, the Farmyard Roosters, the Wheely Whirly, the Steam Yachts and Helter Skelter. The fair was under the management of Mr H.C.Humphries"

Oldbury Wake was in the news in 1926 when there was an alarming outbreak of fire. In the early hours of the morning the fire started in a small show belonging to a Mr Howard. It spread quickly into Jack Parry's 'Reptile House' but not before sixteen pythons, four crocodiles and three alligators had been roasted alive. (Two monkeys were rescued). The alarm was sounded by one of the occupants of a nearby caravan. Women evacuated their families to the homes of people living near the ground, or took refuge in the nearby Harmonic Inn.

The menfolk instituted emergency procedures, called the Police and Fire Brigade and started removing vans and demolishing shows to isolate the fire which had really taken hold and was fast moving towards the "Over the Falls" attraction. Mr Hawkins, the Manager, assisted by Messrs Dutton and Swann, created a gap around the fire and men were supplying buckets of water as fast as they could.

When the Oldbury Fire Brigade arrived the fireman found great difficulty in organising a water supply for their hoses, as the fire was at the extreme end of the ground. It was over three hundred yards to the nearest hydrant, and when reached the hydrant itself was blocked! A pump was rushed round to the canal, but the canal was so muddy and weed-filled that it was feared the hose would become blocked. Eventually two hoses were brought into action and the fire was extinguished. By this time the police had arrived, followed by Bill Croydon, the Ground Manager, summoned from his home in Wednesbury.

Jack Parry had lost over £1,000 worth of equipment and animals, and at least four other small shows had been destroyed. The cause of the fire could not be discovered, but the Oldbury Weekly News assured its readers that showmen regularly checked their equipment after the fair closed for the evening, and no-one present could remember ever having encountered a similar fire. Showmen rallied round to help their colleagues, and, when the Onion Fair opened at Aston two weeks later Jack Parry's Show and Frank Howard's Novelties were both back in business.

In 1939 the visit of the Wakes to Oldbury coincided

with the outbreak of the War. The fair had been open two days, Friday and Saturday, when on Sunday September 3rd news was heard on the wireless that War had been declared. The fair was pulled down, and most of the showmen returned to the yard at Bloxwich to find out what would happen next.

Oldbury was also the location of an oft-repeated story about Pat and the way in which drivers would unofficially supply power to the tenants in return for some favour. The story describes Pat's arrival at Oldbury one evening, the fairground was a blaze of light and sound. Pat looked round then issued a command that all his engines be shut down immediately. As he expected, the fair is plunged into darkness, and most of his tenants lights go off too! In the ensuing gloom the noise of the tenant's own petrol generators can be heard.... struggling into life... and some lights come back on. The drivers express amazement that anyone could have tapped into the Guvnor's power cables, but Pat curses and swears and threatens everybody with dismissal...then he ordered his engines be opened up again...and the show went on.

Tipton

The No.1.Circuit fair visited Tipton twice yearly, and the No.3.Circuit fair put in an appearance during the summer to support the Carnival. The fair accompanying the Carnival was therefore under the jurisdiction of Young Pat during the time when he took over the No.3.run. His Dragon Scenic was the main riding machine at such events, and in 1931, for example, the only other machine present was "Over the Sticks". Hickman's Boxing Show and Proctor's Circus added some substance to the fair, and, as well as stalls, there were Barnard's swings. "JBT" who reporting for World's Fair recalled the times when 14 sets of swings could be found at a Tipton fair.

The Carnival Fair was certainly a "poor relation" and in 1935, Jubilee year, no machines could be spared for Tipton at all, until Harry Weston arrived with "Over the Sticks" on the last day! Fortunately, the two visits of the No.1.fair provided Tipton patrons with all that was the best in Pat Collins' empire.

The Wakes Ground was off Queens Road, and a Health Centre now stands on the site. In 1990 Anthony Harris agreed to help Tipton Civic Society place a plaque on the building to commemorate the Wakes and Pat Collins.

West Bromwich

A Wake was held here almost at the end of the season, usually at the beginning of November. The equipment on the No.1.Circuit could stand at West Bromwich before moving to Tipton and then "home" to the yard at Bloxwich. H.M.Jay wrote a long description of West Bromwich Wake, and the report appeared in World's Fair of 7 November 1931.

"On the day that we were building up we had a visit from Professor Parney,* (rain) but he did no serious damage, just laid the dust a little and left a few puddles, but a few carts of ash soon put this in order. From Friday to Monday no better weather could be desired. However, about midnight on Monday a terrific gale arose, accompanied by a deluge of rain that continued for the whole of Tuesday. Fortunately, the ground which was formerly the West Bromwich Albion Football Ground, has a fairly hard surface.

Thousands of people were attracted to the fair, but they were a very stubborn class, so much so that the great majority of them stuck their hands deep down in their trouser pockets and refused to take them out. It was difficult to know the reasn why...perhaps Simon's Parrot* could throw some light on this serious problem. (*A regular column in World's Fair for the exchange of gossip)

No...we did not take a lot of money, but we had a lot of fun. In fact we ran a "sweep" to see who should go into the workhouse first. The gale considerably damaged many of the tenants' joints, tilts being ripped to ribbons, and much woodwork broken. None of us opened at all on Tuesday and we left West Bromwich sadder, but certainly not wiser, men and women.

The lessee, Alderman Collins supplied the Golden Dragons & Peacocks (Joby Farrell), a Dodgem (Albert Badger), the Whoopee (Billy Mullett), Helter Skelter (Joe Delaney), Cakewalk (Harry Swain) and the Yachts (Baby Pat). Shows included Paulo's Circus, and Headley's show. Tenants included George Studt, Mrs Chaplain, John Hall, Jim Humphreys, Tommy Roberts, Joe Fletcher etc. there were enough sheets to cover an army under canvas"

When a World's Fair reporter visited the site in November 1935 he found plenty of stuff on the ground, much of it moving on to another gaff that year at Loughborough. He found the No.1.Scenic (Ted Sherwood), the Waltzer (Clara), the Dodgems (Johnny Ryan), the Yachts (Walter Kelly) and the Airways (Baby Pat). Shows were presented by Jimmy Styles, Chas Hickman, Kayes' Circus, John Collins' Wall of Death and Dot Raynor's Flea Circus

Wednesbury

Pat Collins' fair was usually held on ground by Mounts Road, and was held at the beginning of May. It appears to have been provided by the fair on the No.3.Circuit, which opened first in Dudley in March. A second fair was held in the Autumn following the fair in Oldbury.

In the Autumn of 1929 the World's Fair correspondent spoke to Joby Farrell, who was in charge of the Scenic at Wednesbury, and found him very knowledgeable about the fairs of the Black Country. Along with Joby's machine, there was a Three Abreast (Mrs Bird), the Yachts (Walter Kelly), the Chair o Planes (Walter Hobbs), plus the Lion Show and Hickman's Boxing Booth. Mr Goodes' refreshment vans came in for a special mention as they were so clean and bright.

```
╔══════════════════════════════════════════════════════════════╗
║         COME TO BLOXWICH — WAKES WEEK                        ║
║                    AND SEE                                    ║
║         PAT COLLINS' GRAND FETE & GALA                       ║
║              (WAKES GROUND, BLOXWICH)                         ║
║           Sat. Mon. & Tues., Aug. 13, 15 & 16.                ║
║                THE SHOW OF ALL SHOWS.                         ║
╚══════════════════════════════════════════════════════════════╝
```

NEW RIDES, SHOWS, THRILLS, NOVELTIES &c., &c.

A PAGEANT OF FUN.

GRAND ILLUMINATIONS.

A Real Gala Land.

Admission to the Ground 2d. each day.

6 BIG STAGE ACTS
2 PERFORMANCES DAILY
at 3-30 & 7-30.

ON THE STAGE
The 4 ASTOUNDERZ
2 Ladies, 2 Gents. Mid-Air Gymnasts.

JAY ROD One Wheel Wonder Comedy Cyclist.

LES BOURTETTES Comedy Gymnasts and Eccentrics.

PETRA & BABTEA Novel Lifting & Bending Speciality.

PROFESSOR ALEXANDER'S Royal **Punch & Judy Show**

THE 3 GLISSONS Unique Balancing and Contortion Act.

THE GREATEST VARIETY SHOW ever seen in the District. Engaged by Mr. Pat Collins at a big expense.

GRAND BENEFIT
Tuesday, August 16th,
In aid of the Walsall General Hospital.

Grand ORGAN RECITAL
Sunday, Aug. 14th at 8 p.m.
In aid of the King George V. Memorial Bloxwich Playing Field Fund.

Admission by Programme 2d.

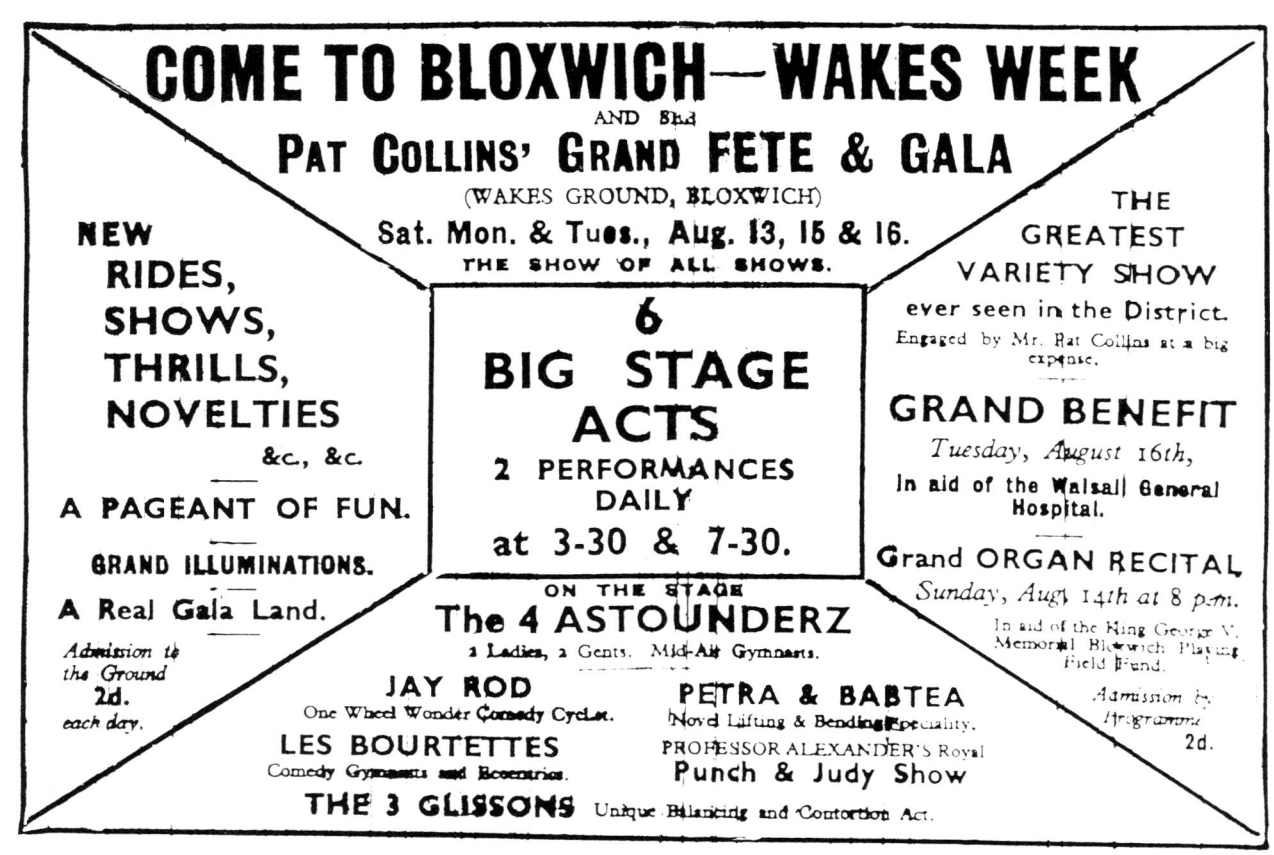

BLOXWICH

A great deal of attention has already been given to the Bloxwich Wake as it played a central part in the life story of this great showman. He attended the Bloxwich Wake from the first year he made the Black Country his home...in 1882. At that time it was still held on The Green, and Pat's "base" was in Walsall. But from then on the fair in Bloxwich, and Pat's life, were on a collision course.

The Bloxwich Wake was held on the third Monday in August, and the Darlaston Wake was held a week later. There were over twenty "Wakes" held by different communities in the immediate area at slightly different times. By the 1890's there were many who wished to abolish the events altogether because they were associated with too much drinking, rowdyism, and enjoyment.

The new concept of an August Bank Holiday led many to hope that the Wakes would be replaced by this single holiday. Employers hoped there would be an end to the confusion and absenteeism surrounding the many different Wakes happening at different times. Local Councils went to the Home Secretary with a "Consolidation of Wakes and Fairs Scheme" in 1897, and the local paper wondered if 1897 would be the last of the Wakes in Bloxwich, and elsewhere. The showman, no doubt, hoped otherwise. The Wakes, all within a short distance of each other, spread from late Summer to late Autumn, and made it worthwhile investing in large riding machines which could be moved around the network of towns and villages that made up the Black Country.

By 1898 the Bloxwich Wake was fighting for its life. Official opposition to it was stronger than ever. It was held on land at the corner of Blakenall and Church Street, and, again, the local paper thought it might be the last. The Bioscope had been present (Eddison's Cinematograph, but presented by whom ?) and Pat presented his Gondolas, roundabouts and menagerie. There were more stalls than ever and the event was well supported.

As the Summer of 1899 approached everyone watched the situation with interest as, at last, it seemed the Wake had been abolished. But Pat was not beaten. On 12 August an advertisement appeared in the Walsall Observer announcing: "Collins' Grand Fete and Gala - to be held 'in commemoration of the Bloxwich Wakes' " Pat had leased a large field, Tenter's Croft, near the Pinfold, and conveniently close to the tram terminus. The "Fete and Gala" was different in that customers had to pay for admission to the ground, but once inside could enjoy a large range of free entertainment - jugglers, clowns, high wire acts, etc. as well as pay for the rides, which included the Gondolas, the Mountain Ponies, and the "Electric Jumpers", ie the mechanical Gallopers. Wall's Cinematograph Show was there, as well as Purchase's menagerie.

The crowds flocked to the "Fete & Gala" in larger numbers than ever. So much for abolishing the Wake! Pat had undertaken much fly-posting over a wide area, and must have been pleased with the result. A reporter from the Walsall Free Press was dismissive of the rides, they were the "usual business"...but he went on to say: "There were the usual conglomeration of fat women and other monstrosities, live alligators, snakes, peep shows and boxing booths. But preeminently in the fair stood Purchase's Menagerie which is certainly well worth a visit, where the intrepid lion tamer Beaumont is engaged, and who goes through some outstanding performances with the animals, notably entering the den with the untamed Wallace - son of the original Wallace of Wombell's time...If the numerous scars exhibited by the tamer are any criterion of the stories he told me, then he has had many severe encounters with the animals under his charge" The final chapter of this story was that a lioness gave birth to cubs on the Tuesday, and the new enlarged lion family moved on to appear on its own pitch at Rushall for a couple of days.

Thus a new tradition was established. From then on, Pat Collins always held his "Fete & Gala" at Bloxwich in the middle of August every year - on the field by the Pinfold. If the Council had been instrumental in banning his Wake it is ironic to note that Pat leased the field from a Councillor - Alderman Lindop. Punters continued to pay admission to the Gala, and the tradition of providing a wealth of free entertainment became firmly established. By the turn of the century this included not just the clowns, jugglers, pole and wire acts, but also balloon ascents, parachute drops and firework displays. The advertisements every year list the attractions in detail and would form the basis of a detailed history of the Gala alone.

The "Wonderland Show" was brought to Bloxwich in 1907, and this brought with it the establishment of another tradition - the Sacred Music Concert on the Marenghi organ on the Sunday when the Gala was otherwise closed. Pat also introduced a "benefit night" on the final evening of the Wake. In 1907 that was held on the Wednesday, adding an additional night to the fair's usual run. but some years later it reverted to Tuesday night. The first occasion raised over £63 for the local Hospital Fund. Sometimes this money was taken from the admissions, sometimes from what was spent on the rides and stalls. If the latter was the case, it was quite well known for Pat to "twist the arm" of a tenant, if not satisfied with the contributions being handed over!

The Galas continued to be held throughout the First World War. As well as running Hospital Benefit Night, Pat also ran a "benefit hour" every day during the 1918 Gala to try and raise money for a £500 fund being established to help local boys who had fought and become prisoners of war.

Meanwhile, Pat was "closing in" on Bloxwich. In 1911 he had been able to purchase the field on which his Gala was held. Between the field and the southern end of Bloxwich High Street was Limetree House. In fact one entrance to the field was via a track alongside the house. Several notable folk had lived in the house, including Alderman Ingram, one of the "Fathers" of Walsall Council. In the years before the First World War it was occupied by Richard Thomas. Sometime during the War, Pat obtained the Lease on Limetree House, and he and Flora moved from Chester House, by the Gondola Works, to Bloxwich.

In 1918 some of the land at Shaw Street was sold and the headquarters of Pat's organisation began its gradual move out to Bloxwich, which was not really completed until 1933. In 1926 Pat purchased Limetree House, and it remained his permanent home until his death there in 1943.

The land behind Limetree House became the site of the Gala, winter quarters, and, eventually a vast sprawling yard where retired fairground equipment "faded away". Returning to our story of the "Gala" it soon became known as the "Wake" again, and the field from 1920 onwards was called the "Wakes Ground"...(technically something it had never previously been).

In 1922 the Walsall Observer interviewed Pat to mark his 40th attendance at Bloxwich Wake. Pat recalled:

"When I first attended Bloxwich Wake as a showman, the fair was pitched on the Common, the site of the present Bloxwich Park. Those were strenuous days, when more often than not, the use of fists was the only possible argument. Wakes Week was invariably synonymous with great rowdyism. Rival factions would meet on the Common and, stripped to the flesh, would fight for hours until they were almost unrecognisable. A Wake without dozens of fights would in those days have been no Wake at all. When the rowdies had fought themselves to a standstill, their only remaining sport was to try and take it out on the showmen. The man who could not fight, soon went to the wall.

...Roundabouts in those days were quite primitive affairs, originally pushed round by hand...The advent of steam made great changes. Lighted by the old style naptha lamps, the merry-go-rounds, with their new engines, went at a speed that had never before been known. Prominent among the other attractions was the Ghost Show...parts of this show are still preserved at the Gondola Works...and Boxing booths were very popular. It was in these that the rowdy element more often than not met their match".

In 1899 the reporter had been rather impressed with Beaumont and the Lions at Purchase's Menagerie. Later, in the 1920's Pat was travelling his own Menagerie, usually described as Mrs Collins' show. The lion tamer was Albert Williams, known to the world as Macomo. The inter-war years also featured a number of artistes who came to Bloxwich year after year, such as Professor Cadman, and his Punch & Judy show, and Professor Bert Powsey who specialised in making a high dive into a small tank of water four feet deep. In the 1930's artistes who appeared at amusement parks during the summer would be brought to Bloxwich for the Wake, and then perhaps appear in the Midlands again when the Onion Fair was on.

In 1932 the lion in Mrs Collins' Menagerie escaped, while wintering in Bloxwich, and made his way to a house in Church Street. The lion went in through the back door and made his way to the front room. The man of the house made a quick exit .... while his wife thoughtfully shut the door to the room. The lion was later 'captured' and returned to his quarters! When Flora Collins died in April 1933, it seemed that the Menagerie was going to be closed down. However, when Bloxwich folk made their way to the Gala in 1933 they were able to watch the lion...in new employment...running around inside a "Globe of death" ...dodging a trick cyclist! Or perhaps it was the cyclist trying to dodge the lion?

The quest for something new throughout the 1930's brought many strange "acts" to the Wakes. In 1939 the star of the show was a Swiss Giant, Violo Myllerinne, who at the age of 22, was 9.ft.10 inches tall.

The Second World War more effectively interrupted the life of the Wakes than its predecessor, and after the War, the spell had been broken. Clara maintained the links with Bloxwich, and was President of the local Carnival Committee, and later Walsall John occupied the same position for a while. The Wake - or annual fair in Bloxwich on the Collins' ground, continued until 1970, when the ground was sold to Asda for the construction of a supermarket. John left Limetree House for Blackpool, and the house was retained as an office for a time. The sale of the ground and the eventual demolition of the house to provide a car park in front of the new supermarket brought to an end the long association of the Collins' family with Bloxwich.

The locals in Bloxwich still resent the demolition of Limetree House and often express the opinion that it should have become an old persons home as John Collins had wished.

In August 1971, the Fair was held on its new site... at the junction of Goscote Lane and Harden Road, under the management of Anthony Harris. It was advertised as "The Biggest Wakes ever to visit this area", but the rain turned the site into a sea of mud, which added to the local feeling that the "real" Bloxwich Wake was dead and gone forever. The fair was repeated for a year or two on the Goscote Lane site, but today Anthony Harris presents a Pat Collins Fun fair annually in Bloxwich, in the Memorial Park in June. However, there is little to link this today with what had once been such a significant event in the Pat Collins' calendar.

WALSALL

Fairs in Walsall have a history going back to the days when trading fairs were established by Charter. A Grant in 1220 established a September fair, and another in 1339 created a June Fair. The dates were altered in 1417, and again by Royal Charter in 1627. From then on, one fair took place in February, and the other fair, an "Onion Fair" continued to be held in late September.

In Chapter 2 the effects of the passing of the Walsall Corporation Act of 1890 were related, when the Council took on the responsibility for the licencing of fairs. By that time Pat had been appearing at local fairs - pleasure fairs rather than the traditional trade fairs, for several years, and had acquired his first machines and was largely in control of the events. The Council decided to create a fairground on land at Midland Road, and in September 1891 Pat was the lessee of that fair. A "battle" followed in 1892 (see Chapter 2) but after that, peace returned and Pat staged the fairs at Midland Road.

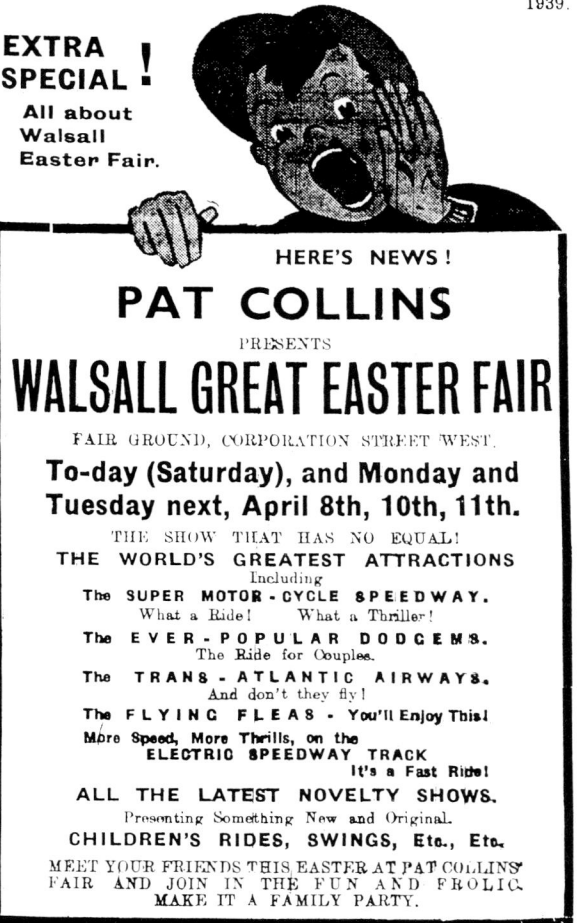

1939.

EXTRA SPECIAL !
All about Walsall Easter Fair.

HERE'S NEWS !

PAT COLLINS
PRESENTS
WALSALL GREAT EASTER FAIR
FAIR GROUND, CORPORATION STREET WEST.
To-day (Saturday), and Monday and Tuesday next, April 8th, 10th, 11th.
THE SHOW THAT HAS NO EQUAL!
THE WORLD'S GREATEST ATTRACTIONS
Including
The **SUPER MOTOR - CYCLE SPEEDWAY.**
What a Ride!   What a Thriller!
The **EVER - POPULAR DODGEMS.**
The Ride for Couples.
The **TRANS - ATLANTIC AIRWAYS.**
And don't they fly!
The **FLYING FLEAS - You'll Enjoy This!**
More Speed, More Thrills, on the
ELECTRIC SPEEDWAY TRACK
It's a Fast Ride!
ALL THE LATEST NOVELTY SHOWS.
Presenting Something New and Original.
CHILDREN'S RIDES, SWINGS, Etc., Etc.
MEET YOUR FRIENDS THIS EASTER AT PAT COLLINS' FAIR AND JOIN IN THE FUN AND FROLIC. MAKE IT A FAMILY PARTY.

The scene in September 1893 was described by the Walsall Free Press.....

"The glamour of Midland Road on Monday night was as garish, as false, as fascinating as gas and electricity could produce...There was a menagerie, there was a circus, "open to all classes at one penny". There was a superbly fat woman. There was a counterfeit "French Casino" to which ladies and boys were not invited, and doctors admitted free. There were notable pugalists. There was the indispensable Ghost. There were pictures of the "Rowdy Dowdy Girls" only thought to be suitable for "Men of the World", and all sorts of freak shows. Spectacular folly, extended into exaggerated grotesqueness, is always successful. Walsall Fair was a grand display.

The merry-go-rounds were of startling proportions, imposing, many coloured, ornamented with all kinds of artfully contrived embellishments. Gilt and red paint and plaster figures were sickening in their obtrusive presence. There was a switchback apparatus, big and strong, sadly in need of paint. I never before thought silence could be so sweet as I did when I turned and left Midland Road behind me"

The reader is left to wonder what the dilapidated switchback was? According to the advertisements Pat was presenting his Venetian Gondolas in Walsall for the first time. His machines were usually beautifully turned out. Perhaps the writer was exploiting poetic licence, or perhaps the Midland Road ground was dirty and dusty - like many other Black Country fairgrounds. (It was called Midland Road because it ran alongside the sidings and engine shed of the Midland Railway).

Walsall, like Wolverhampton, was on the edge of the Black Country, with which both towns sometimes disassociated themselves! Both were large towns by Black Country standards, with long pre-industrial histories. Both therefore deserved large Easter Fairs, as well as fairs at other times of the year. In Walsall, a midsummer fair became popular in association with the Hospital Fund-raising Carnival. A fair at the end of September was not such a good idea, as that was the height of the Wakes' season, leading into the big Back End fairs. One could conclude that, although Pat made Walsall his headquarters, the Walsall fairs were never a major part of his operations.

In 1917, there was some kind of dispute with the Council ...again... and Pat did not hold the fair at Midland Road at Easter. It moved to private land made available by a Mr Boyes at the New Mills, Pleck. After the First World War a new fairground was provided at Corporation Street West. Fairs on this ground were also held on August Bank Holiday, to which some of the equipment could move from the Bloxwich Wake.

Like other grounds leased by Pat Collins, the Corporation Street site provided space for circuses etc. to come to Walsall, and, on at least one occasion Pat himself used it for this kind of event. For example, at Christmas 1934, he found he was not able to put on his usual fair at Wolverhampton. He decided to open at the Corporation Street site with Kayes' Circus, augmented with some animals from Jack Parry's travelling show. There was no pantomime on in Walsall that Christmas and the local paper commented on the fact that Walsall people were making their way to Wolverhampton to see Randolph Sutton at the Grand, while Wolverhampton folk were flooding into Walsall to see the circus and the fair! Pat Tyler was in charge of the fair, which included the Gallopers, Dodgems, Juvenile roundabouts and swings.

Dick Kayes and his family provided the equestrian, acrobatic and trapeze acts in the circus, as well as a lion act, and Jack Parry's contribution was very popular as people were permitted to handle, or approach at very close quarters, a number of unusual animals. These were looked after by David Russell, a West Indian snake-keeper who travelled with Parry's show. Some "exotic" human interest was added by the African "Ashanti" with his fire-eating demonstrations.

The fair at Corporation Street assumed greater local importance as it became known that Pat was about to become Mayor of Walsall. The ox-roasting was attended by Pat on the Monday evening and was turned into a great fund-raising event for charity, followed on the Tuesday evening by a "benefit" for a local hospital charity - a success these events had not enjoyed since the withdrawal of the Wonderland Organ in 1937. At the Easter fair in 1939, Pat was able to attend in his Mayoral robes, and was able to enjoy despatching and watching his Civic party on an 'accelerated' ride on one of the machines.

The Corporation Street site continued to be used well into the Second World War. At the Easter of 1940, an enlarged Blackout Fair was opened, providing space for the Dodgems, motor-cycle Speedway Ark, and even the Atlantic Airways beneath the blackout. The Walsall Observer reported that while visiting this fair they met Swami, the Indian knife-thrower, touring with Pat Collins, who was not at all happy at having to work nights as well on War work, in a Midland wheel-making factory.

Although the Corporation Road ground continued to be used after the War, the site is now occupied by an industrial estate, (one of the roads is called Fairground Way) and when Pat Collins' fair is presented at Walsall at Easter in the 1990's it has to open in Reedswood Park. In recent years Anthony Harris has presented Pat Collins' fair at Coventry at Easter and therefore Messrs Stanworth stand in for him at Walsall.

Cannock Chase

The mining communities of Cannock Chase must have attracted Pat, because they had much in common with other towns that were firmly on his map, yet Pat appears to have only paid marginal attention to the Chase. Perhaps the communities were too small compared with the Black Country towns he frequented, and therefore he was prepared to leave them to other showmen, such as the Shepherds of Cannock, the Jervis' of Sankey's Corner, and William Davies - the showman who threaded his way in and out of Pat's territory serving communities Pat chose to ignore!

In the end Pat seems to have sent his fairs to the larger towns of Cannock and Hednesford.

When "P.A.T" filed a long report on the Cannock Wake for the World's Fair of 22 October 1938, he expressed the opinion that you had to come to Cannock to find out what a "Wake" was really like. He felt that the Wakes in the Black Country had simply become normal pleasure fairs, but out on the Chase, the arrival of the fair still coincided with community celebrations and rituals, one of which concerned the "Cannock Cake"...apparently cooked to a secret recipe and served in every home on the Monday of Wakes' Week. Showmen were offered the cake, something to drink and beef sandwiches.

Reports of the fair at Hednesford are few and far between, but we learn that the October fair at Hednesford often "clashed" with a more remunerative fair in Smethwick, so, in 1928 for example, while Clara Mullett took the No.1.Scenic to the latter, Joby Farrell took the Proud Peacocks to Hednesford, along with Mrs Bird's Three Abreast and a set of Yachts. In a later year we learn that an Institute was being built in the centre of the fairground!

After the War, the Pat Collins' fair regularly attended the Chasetown Wakes.

OUT INTO SHROPSHIRE

Newport

This country town in Shropshire is remote from the industry and grimy hustle and bustle of the Black Country, but it stands on the axis stretching from Chester to the Black Country, and therefore found itself on Pat Collins' path as he travelled the roads that stretched from Birkenhead to Birmingham and from Llangollen to Longton! Newport had two "traditional" fairs, one on 28 May, and the other at Christmas - the "Gawby" fair.

These fairs had virtually faded away by the 1880's, and Pat took it upon himself to revive them. By 1910 the May fair had become quite a major three-day event, filling the main stretch fo the High Street. The location was its downfall: in 1939 the A41 was designated a "Trunk Road" and the fair could not block one of the Nation's main road transport arteries!

At the Newport Fair in May 1895, 36-years old Pat Collins was interviewed in depth by the Reporter from the Newport Advertiser, and this is quoted extensively in Chapter 3 because it provides an insight into the state of Pat's empire at that time. However, it is worth repeating here that Pat claimed he had been coming to Newport Fair since 1875, when he was sixteen. It is likely therefore that Pat became acquainted with such fairs while he worked out of Chester with his father, and in the 1880's as he began his own empire-building it was just as logical to "capture" these fairs as it was to "conquer" the Wakes of the Black Country.

One early report of Pat presenting the May fair in Newport dates from 1886 - earlier than any report we have from a Black Country paper. Commenting briefly on the fair of that year the Advertiser said that Pat had presented his new set of Hobby Horses, some Waltzing cars (?) and Caddeck's Photography Studio. Newport became an outpost of the No.1.circuit and thus enjoyed all the big rides and major shows, even if it meant lengthy journeys to and from the surrounding gaffs. One of the means by which the visit was extended from one day to three days was the introduction of the Wonderland Show, and its organ, and the promotion of a Sacred Music Concert to raise funds for a local hospital. Some years this was not presented if Wonderland had to be pulled down to quickly reach its next destination!

Newport was not entirely remote from the same events that could affect the well-being of a showman from the Black Country. For example, the depression of the early 1920's, and the coal strikes affected takings at the Black Country Wakes. Out at Newport, the Advertiser reported: "In recognition of local unemployment, Pat ordered no increase in prices on Saturday night". The paper admitted that the fair was still a dazzling show despite the depression, and congratulated Pat's managers for their conduct of the fair; Messrs Bailey, Fletcher and Parry. The star attractions had been the magnificent new Scenic Railway, and the "brave coloured lion tamer" on Mrs Collins' show...(Albert again!).

Two years later the No.1.Scenic again stole the show and was greeted as a new ride as the punters now travelled in "Whales". 1924 was also the first visit to Newport of the popular "Over the Falls" and a show featuring snake charmers. After this the fair seems to have been taken for granted by the local paper and no further descriptions of it are printed. Perhaps a hint of its eventual demise is forecast in 1933 when we learn that no fair was held as a result of some dispute concerning the occupation of the High Street, but apparently Pat erected a stall there to "maintain" his rights.

Today, the Pat Collins fair does still venture out into Shropshire, to take part in the Street Fair at Shifnal, a few miles from Newport.

Oakengates

Another Shropshire town where the name Pat Collins is still remembered . Mining and industry made Oakengates seem familiar to a Black Country showman, and the ground that Pat leased - Owen's Field, was partly surrounded by spoil heaps. The field was another place that could be used for Winter quarters for folk associated with the No.2.run. That fair provided the Spring Fair in Oakengates, but the Wakes, in late August/early September, was usually part of the No.4.run, which came to Oakengates from Donnington.

A typical fair at Oakengates Wakes was to be found at the ground in 1931. It was described as a "Galaxy of Amusements", but it had to be a fairly modest "Galaxy" of three riding machines, as the No.1. and No.2. fairs tended to absorb the best attractions as they began their assault on the Back End. The rides were the Steeplechasers (H.Weston Jnr); the Cakewalk (H.Swain); and the Chair-o-Planes (Jack Harrison). The only show was Bailey's Circus, and stalls and juveniles were provided by John Hall, George Studt, Jack Humphreys etc., plus Jim Shepherd's Swings and Joe Fletcher's Automatics, a fairly small fair by Pat Collins' standards.

On ground between Owen's Field, and the main road into Oakengates, Pat was able to build another of his cinemas - The Grosvenor - which opened in November 1923. He sold the cinema in 1926, so there was no link between the cinema and the showmen, although they were "neighbours".

Shrewsbury

Pat was known to visit Shrewsbury sometimes twice a year, and used two sites, but he is particularly associated with the fair on the Quays. Sometimes the "Welsh Run" embraced Shrewsbury to provide a fair in the Spring, sometimes the machines from the No.1. run could be sent, if the Shrewsbury fair did not conflict with Easter commitments. The attractions assembled in March 1930 provided an interesting mix: The No.1.Scenic (Clara Mullett); the Swish (Matey Weston); the Yachts (Young Margaret Collins); the

ABOVE: The fair at Chester Races, May 1959. The Odeon Waltzers second front has been freshly painted and is standing next to Walter Shaw's Space Rockets.
(Collection of Fred Richardson)

Chairs (Walter Hobbs); the Lion Show (Wm Dutton); and the Wall of death (Jack Todd).

The second visit each year came in August at the time of the Carnival and Flower Show, but coincided with a time when Pat's attention was focussed on providing a fair on his home ground - the Bloxwich Wakes.

Ludlow

In 1914, in an expansionist mood, Pat organised a fair at Ludlow, but the continuance of such an expansion may have been curtailed by the First World War.

Chester

In April 1991 the front page of World's Fair ran the story that Pat Collins' Fun Fairs had just concluded a 10-year agreement with Chester City Council for the use of the Little Roodee Car park every May, coinciding with the Chester Races. In this way, Anthony Harris has preserved yet another tradition, for the Pat Collins' Fair has attended Chester Races for nearly a century. To Pat it was a significant port of call, as it was his birthplace, and for many years his sister, Maggie Collins, had used the yard in Union Street as her base.

When the Sacred Music Concerts and Benefit Nights started in 1907, Chester Royal Infirmary was another of the hospitals to gain from Pat's public benefaction. The concerts began again when the organ travelled as part of the Whale Island Scenic. In 1920, Chester had been the first town to receive one of Pat's new purpose-built cinemas.

Yet, for all this, it is still difficult to know just how strong was Pat's link with Chester, and vice-versa. In the 1959 Biography it was stated that Pat was made a Freeman of the City of Chester, but that was not so.

In Chester itself the local paper seems to have taken little interest in Pat, although they did comment fully on Pat's death. They described his rise from "poor boy to become one of the greatest and most successful showmen in the World" and did go on to say, "Mr Collins had a deep affection for Chester, and despite many business calls, invariably paid at least one visit to the City during Race Week...the annual visit of his fair to Little Rooddee was one of the attractions of Race Week".

Pat did occasionally present fairs at Chester at other times of the year - for example, Christmas and New Year Fairs on the Cattle Market, but it is the fair by the river that everyone remembers.

Because the Chester Races Fair was regarded as an important feature of the Collins' calendar, it sometimes gathered rides and attractions from more than one "run". Sometimes the fair that had been out to Llangollen and Corwen, and back to Wrexham by April, provided attractions that could go on to Chester. At the same time the No.1. fair could be making its way up to Chester via Stafford. (Even after the Second World War, Stafford fair provided a gathering point from which to go to Chester). These movements had to be planned to take into account the timing of Easter, and the decision concerning the allocation of major rides to the Easter Fair.

For example, in 1928, the No.1.Scenic, Clara's Whale Island, had been on the Welsh run, including a snow-laden appearance at Oswestry, before dashing up to

Blackburn for Easter, which was early enough that year for the ride to re-appear at Wrexham. Here it was joined by the Swish (Walsall John); the Yachts (George Bailey); Over the Falls (Walter Hobbs,Jnr); Stockwell's three Freak Shows, Chas.Relph's show, Jack Parry's show and Bert Hughes' Boxing Booth, plus stalls from Wright & Rogers, Fossetts and John Hall, etc. Flora Collins' wagon "The White Lady" was also regarded as a star of the show.

As "The White Lady" and the other attractions, moved on to Chester, they were joined by the new Miniature Brooklyn Motors (Bill Mullett), the Grand National Hurdle Racers (H.Weston) and the Chair-o-Plane (Billy Dutton). Jimmy Styles and Jimmy Headly provided more shows, and Hickman's replaced Hughes' Boxing Booth. On other occasions the Chester fair was augmented by rides from other branches of the Collins' family, or even the Welsh "opposition", Messrs Simon & Greatorix.

The Fair in 1930 was a memorable one. The Whale Island and the Lion Show were among the attractions, but the advertisements made much of the fact that both the Wall of Death and the Globe of death were going to be present - "First time Together in England". In fact, Pat had run into trouble using the term "Wall of Death" and therefore the attractions were advertised as "The Death Defiers in the Dome of Satan and the Globe of Terror".

On Monday 19 April Jack Todd and 15 year old Jimmy Styles went up on the Wall for a practice run before the fair opened. Jimmy sat on the petrol tank. All went well until the engine faltered. Jimmy fell from the bike, and Jack Todd fell after him as he tried to grab him. The machine fell on top of the pair of them, and Jimmy was knocked-out. They were taken by ambulance to Chester Royal Infirmary and spent the evening in hospital while a "Benefit" was being held at the fair for the hospital! A substitute took Jack's place on the Wall, ..the story of the accident quickly spread..and crowds flocked to see it.

Jack Todd returned to the Wall when it had moved on to a fair in Montgomery, but one legend added to the story is that the hospital sent Pat a hefty bill for Jack's treatment, and this led to the funds raised at the Sacred Music Concert being directed elsewhere for a year or two afterwards! In 1930 the concert took place in Pat's absence, and the Lord Mayor had to read a long letter from Pat extolling the virtues of charity. When the Mayor paid tribute to Pat's generosity, it was left to Young Pat to briefly reply.

When the fair returned in 1931, the Globe of Death was missing, but the Wall was being traversed by a Baby Austin, allegedly capable of 70mph. The other attractions were the Whale Island, Over the Sticks, Ghost Train, Lion Show and "Radio Cars".

Wrexham

The fair here was usually held in April, and its place within the organisation of Pat's runs depended on the date of easter. The No.1. could take in Wrexham on its way to Chester Races, or the No.2. run could include Wrexham as it travelled towns on the Welsh border and towns of the Upper Dee Valley.

Wrexham had strong associations for the Collins' as it was Flora's home town. Both Flora and Pat supported the local hospital charity there. In fairground history Wrexham earns a mention as the place where the Collins' opened their new Wonderland Show and the magnificent Marenghi organ in April 1907. Wonderland was joined by Relph and pedley's Show and Joby Farrell's "Coliseum of Moving Pictures"...suggesting that the fair at Wrexham drew in enough punters to support three Bioscopes! Also prsent were: the Motor Car Racers, a Helter Skelter, Whirling the Whirl, Young Pat's Flying Yachts, Charlie Farrell's Jumping Horses, John Collins' Razzle Dazzle, and J.Caddeck's Photo Studio. Stalls were by Cordwell, Wright and Fossetts.

The following year, 1908, "Wonderland" was at Wrexham again, and Relph & Pedley's show was again present, and, according to World's Fair, they were also now presenting Whirling the Whirl. Other shows were Harris's Miniature Zoo and the Westwood Twins on their 1908 tour of Pat's fairs. The rides were: the No.1.Motors (George Bailey and Clara Mullett); the No.2.Motors (Jack Whyatt); Pat'c Cockerels (Bill Mullett) and Pat's Yachts (W.Hobbs); plus sideshows. While the 1908 fair was running, Wrexham Carnival Committee held a supper for Pat and Flora and their employees, over seventy of them, to express their thanks to Pat for raising money for the Wrexham Infirmary. Presumably Pat had instituted Sacred Music Concerts on the Wonderland Organ the previous year for the benefit of the hospital.

World's Fair give us another glimpse of Wrexham Fair in April 1920, the "best for six years - fine weather and a rattling good fair" which included: the Scenic Railway (Clara Mullett); Gondolas (Joby Farrell); Four-Abreast (H.Weston), Flora Collins' Beast Show featuring Macomo the black lion tamer, Collins' Yachts and Shows by J.Caddeck, Dot Rayner, H.Hughes, with Stalls by Wright, Fossett, Payne, Chadwick and Cordwell.

Some things did not change very much. When the World's Fair reported on the Wrexham fair of April 1936, their correspondent started his report by saying "I saw the same tenants who have been there for thirty years - the Wrights, the Rogers, the Deeks, Bert Hughes and his splendid boxing saloon, and Russell's arcade. They were joined by Rayner's Illusion Show, James Styles, and Joe Gardner with Billy the Pig. Rides included Pat Collins' Airways, Skid, Over the Sticks, Dodgems and new Loop o Plane".

OUT INTO WALES

The Welsh Run may have been in some way connected with Pat's sister, Maggie Collins, or even Johanna and her husband Job Davies, though whatever the case, as early as 1907 Pat advertised the run in the "Ground to Let" columns of World's Fair, as if the fairs were his own. The run embraced fairs at Oswestry, Llangollen, Cefn Mawr, and Corwen, returned to Wrexham, sometimes Shrewsbury and "other towns to Chester".

In March 1920, a World's Fair report tells us that Mr.Hobbs steered Pat Collins' machine into place with great skill at Corwen, on ground which was a sea of mud. The machine was the Three Abreast. A stallholder, Mr Wright, was also turning people's attention to transport matters with his impressive new Foden tractor. A successful picture show was presented by John Cadman.

The same report mentions the fair at Llangollen where Joby Farrell was presenting Pat's Gondolas along with Mr Fossett's shooter and R.Cordwell's throwing game. Hickman's novelty show and Ted Jervis' popular Glide also earn a mention. What is interesting is that it does not seem to be the same list of attractions as those at Corwen. Nor does it match the fair that was at Wrexham a few weeks' later (see above) apart from the Gondolas. These are the puzzling links encountered when trying to reconstruct the organisation of runs so far in time after the events.

Corwen was as far west into Wales that Pat ventured, and reports of the fair at Corwen often mention the "opposition". Sometimes they have just left, sometimes they move in as Pat leaves. On one occasion they were built up when Pat arrived, and the two fairs opened, one on each side of the road! (See Chapter 5 and the events of 1925 - and Pat's comments on coming to Corwen about 1870). Corwen was also associated with bad weather.

There is evidence here also of Pat trying to expand his empire at the fringe. In this case we find one example in 1927, of a fair being organised at Mold.

An entirely different assault on Wales were Pat's trips to Cardiff. According to Father Greville, of the Friendship Circle of Showland Friends, Pat held two indoor fairs in Cardiff. In 1908 or 1909 he is said to have used the St Andrew's Hall, Queen Street (later the Olympia Cinema) and a year or two later he is said to have used the skating rink in Westgate Street. If this is true, perhaps the White Brothers were inspired to counter-invade the Midlands in bidding for part of the Evesham Mop Fair!

HEADING FOR THE NORTH WEST

Pat and Flora Collins settled in Walsall in 1882, but for several years he continued to describe himself as a "Roundabout Proprietor of Chester". He became a Midlander gradually, and never entirely turned his back on Cheshire and South Lancashire. Perhaps he and his brother John had travelled this area with their father or their Aunts. On at least one occasion Pat claimed that his father had opposed the idea of his children setting up on their own. To what extent they worked together, and what grounds each took from the days of travelling with their father, will probably never become clear, but Pat sometimes ventured north-westwards, and John sometimes ventured towards the Midlands.

In Cheshire they strayed into each others territory. In 1914 it is interesting to note that both John and Pat visited Northwich. Pat opened there towards the end of February, and John opened in May!

Crewe

This is the kind of town Pat may have visited with his father, and as fairs became more regulated during the 1880's he may have set out to include Crewe in his empire. Describing the Flag Lane Ground in March 1907, the World's Fair reported that Pat was presenting a "wonderful carnival of roundabouts and sideshows. Many visitors appreciated a ride on the Royal Motors, the Steeplechasers and the Helter Skelter, and enjoyed the shows and stalls".

In 1908 we learn that Pat was raising money for the local hospital in Crewe, repeating the pattern established elsewhere. "Wonderland" was being presented by Walter Kelly. A Mr Gordon was the operator, and a Mr Albert Horton was the Musical Director. This is one of the few insights ever given into the staffing of the Bioscope Show.

Merseyside

Merseyside, in particular Liverpool is strongly associated with the empire created by Brother John Collins, but there were fairs which the brothers organised jointly, and there were some in which Pat alone was the lessee.

Pat's presence in Liverpool was often in response to special occasions. For example, in 1904 and 1907, Pat and John joined forces to present large six-day fairs for the August Bank Holiday "Pageant Week". (In 1904 this had been associated with a royal visit). Both fairs enjoyed great success, and the 1907 event saw the Wonderland Show standing next to Bostock & Wombell's Menagerie. The Wonderland Show included a "singing picture" called "Hannah won't you open that door?", using the Gaumont "Chronophone" sound system.

Another important event in Merseyside was the opening of the Mersey Tunnel in the summer of 1934 - another excuse for a Royal Visit. Fairs were held by a number of showmen in parks on both sides of the river. Pat and Young Pat were on ground in Sefton Park, Liverpool, and in Central Park Birkenhead. The first motorist through the tunnel was a World's Fair advertiser, A.L.Bieber, and the Pat Collins' firm had some fun trying to take an engine through the tunnel.

The 1937 Coronation brought Pat back to Sefton Park, for eight days over two weekends. This also was a great success, and Walsall John did well with a show presenting replicas of the Crown Jewels. Jack Todd returned to the scene with his own Wall of death, and travelled for the rest of the 1937 season with Pat Collins, down to the Black Country, to the Onion Fair etc...These major 1930's fairs are described in more detail in Chapter 7.

On the southern shore of the Mersey estuary, Pat Collins had a long and undocumented association with Birkenhead and the New Brighton area of Wallasey going back at least to the 1890's. For a time

Young Pat was the lessee of various fairs in the Wirral. Generally, it appears that the firm withdrew from this area by the 1930's. Once Birkenhead had enjoyed Christmas fairs, organised by Pat, but the last of these seems to have taken place in 1930. The Borough Road Ground was then used for building a new library

THE NORTH WEST

Bolton
The fair here was held to coincide with the New year, and this sometimes led to a hasty pull-down after a Christmas engagement to despatch a machine to Bolton where it had to be built up quicklyin time for the opening. One year, Pat asked his fellow showmen to unite in asking Bolton Corporation to delay the opening of the Bolton fair for one day to make matters easier. Sometimes the Christmas Fair at Queens Road, Manchester, held by Pat's nephew, Michael Albert Collins, was a stopping off point for the machines making for Bolton.

As at the other Lancashire fairs, Pat was usually anxious to present the latest or most popular attractions at Bolton. In 1909 this meant sending the Cakewalk and Haunted House. Twenty years later it was a matter of sending The Whale Island; The Swish; Over the Falls and the Lion Show.

Oldham
Pat Collins had positions for two riding machines at Oldham's fair on the Tommy field, and often this meant taking the rides that had appeared at Ashton on to Oldham. (See George Reohorn's testimony).

Hyde
Pat Collins had positions for two riding machines at Hyde.

Ashton Under Lyne
A manufacturing town with a population of over 50,000, Ashton held its annual Wakes fair in the market place every August. Pat Collins usually sent two riding machines. These were not always the rides that enthusiasts expected. For example, in 1933 "Cyclist" was surprised to find the No.1.Scenic (Clara Mullett) and the Dodgems (J.Ryan). He had expected to see the Four-abreast, but reported to World's Fair readers that it's replacement - the Scenic, now carrying Dragons and Peacocks rather than Whales, looked "direct from the makers".

BELOW: Oldham Wakes on the Tommy Field in 1913. The view is dominated by Pat's Gordon Bennett Motors, then travelled as a Scenic Railway by Young Pat. On the right are William Mitchell's Motors.
Collection of Kevin Scrivens)

Blackburn

Pat held two positions at the Easter Fair at Blackburn until 1933, and of course this fair coincided with major events nearer home, sometimes limiting what could be sent. In an interview on 18/8/90, Baby Pat recalled taking a machine to Blackburn: "It was always a lot of trouble as you had to have the traction engines on one side of the road, and the rides on the other. You were not allowed to run the cables overhead - they had to go under a grid that ran across the road. It was always a lot of fuss to get the cables through."

Burnley

This northern town was visited by Pat Collins where the fair was held at the end of June and the town has a history of fairs extending back to the end of the 13thC. For many years Brother John had three ride positions at Burnley and Pat had two, between them accounting for five out of the seven rides that occupied the Cattle Market. In the years between the Wars, one of these positions was habitually occupied by the No.1.Scenic, and the other by a variety of rides - often the firm's latest attraction. For example, the Swish and Over the Falls were sent to Burnley when they were new. One year the Wall of death appeared, ridden by Speedy Williams (Eddy Monte).

In 1927 Pat took the No.1.Scenic, Cakewalk and Over the Falls to Blackburn, and for some reason the Cakewalk and Over the Falls went on to Chorley during the following week.

Pat last travelled to Burnley in 1933, when "Lord James" took a small Ark. On eposition went to Green's, the other to Shaws'. The Lancashire Collins still attend today.

Nelson

The northernmost point reched in Lancashire by Pat Collins appears to be a trip to Nelson in July 1914!

HEADING NORTH EAST

Nottingham

One of the best known fairs in Britain must surely be the Nottingham Goose Fair; the Charter for which was granted in 1284 by Edward I. It is a three day event, opening every year on the first Thursday in October, and closing on the Saturday night.

The fair is organised by the Corporation, and therefore Pat Collins attended the Goose Fair as their tenant. Many articles and books have been written about this famous fair, including "Victorian Nottingham" (Iliffe & Baguley) and "The Great Nottingham Goose Fair" (Peter Wilkes).

In the 1890's as riding machines became more crowd pulling than shows, Pat Collins established himself as a significant riding master at the Goose Fair, alongside other top "machine men". His importance by 1895 can be measured by the space given to an interview with him featured in the local paper (see Chapter 3), where Pat and Brother John's rides dominate many early Goose Fair photographs.

In 1927 the Goose Fair was held in the City's central "Market Square" for the last time, and Pat led the opposition to the proposed removal of the fair to the Forest site, off the Mansfield Road, then regarded as an "out of town" location. However, once the move was forced upon the showmen, he led them in making the best of it, and very soon demonstrated that the increased space available at the Forest site was an opportunity to make the fair even more impressive.

At the new site in 1928, Pat had the latest "Radio Cars", the Swish and Over the Falls, as well as established attractions like the Three Abreast, Helter Skelter, and two Scenics, plus the LionShow and "Hit the Deck". The following year he brought both the Globe and the Wall of Death.

Despite the space available at the Forest, occasionally Pat could not be accommodated! In 1935 he wanted to take a Big Brooklyn Race Track, but there was insufficient room. In its absence it was announced that Pat would be presenting "The Monster", a new ride built by Messrs Lang Wheels. The machine really belonged to Fred Gray, but was built up in the Pat Collins position. Pat did present an Ark, and a Glide, and it was noticeable that the fair was becoming dominated by Arks, Waltzers and Dodgems, with only two Scenics present.

Pat's No.1.Scenic made its last appearance at Nottingham in 1937, when it was accompanied by John's Loop-o-Plane, Young Pat's Big Wheel, the Flying Fleas, Ghost Train and Dodgems. In 1938 the last Goose Fair was held before the Second World War. Pat re-affirmed his committment "always to bring something new" to the Goose fair, although he was very dependent upon Walsall John to make this promise possible. In 1938 they brought the Moon Rocket, and John's Ro-Lo Fun House, plus other attractions.

Fairs were held in Nottingham during the War, but they were now the "proper" Goose Fairs. When the renowned Goose Fair did open again - in 1946 - Pat Collins was dead, but the firm continued to regard the fair as an important part of the calendar. Positions at the fair are still leased by the Pat Collins Funfair, to this day.

Bulwell Wakes

On the outskirts of Nottingham is Bulwell, and a fair was held there in October or November. Not to be outdone by the Goose Fair, the event at Bulwell was staged on two, or sometimes three sites. It seems that each site was granted to a different lessee. In 1907 we learn that Arthur Twigdon ran one site, Relph and Pedley ran another, and Pat Collins ran the third. He presented his Racing Cockerels and Helter Skelter and the Wonderland Show. Such was the growing popularity of Bioscopes at the time, that Pat let part of his site to James Crighton ...for another Bioscope!

Another year, 1914, Messrs Hall and Proctor were his fellow lessees. Similar collaborations happened at other events which were on the fringes of Pat's territory, eg. being joint lessee with Arthur Twigdon at a

Leicester event. In this year when the Great War commenced, Pat took his Teddy Bears to Bulwell and let space to Mander's Menagerie and Braham's "Temple of Mystery".

Hull Fair

Immediately after the Goose Fair an even larger fair is held in Hull. The three major Autumn fairs for many years were the Birmingham Onion Fair, the Goose Fair and Hull Fair, and each was larger than its predecessor. The larger the fair, the greater the rivalry between showmen. Thus, at Hull, the Pat Collins' firm could sometimes present the rides not accommodated at Nottingham...such as the Water Dodgems in 1932, and the Brooklyn Race Track in 1935. (See the Hull Fair advertisement placed in the local paper by Pat Collins, reproduced in Chapter 7). Pat's Rolling Gondolas are said to have been present in Hull as far back as 1898, but it is not clear when he first attended.

VENICE IN NOTTINGHAM.
P. COLLIN'S IMPROVED PATENTS.
The Latest! The Best! Quite up to Date!
The only Two Machines of their kind in the World.
THE VENETIAN BOAT GONDOLAS AND THE GRAND GALA GONDOLAS.
Direct from Venice.
The Boats on these Machines are faithful Reproductions of the Gondolas used by the Dogges of Venice in their GRAND PROCESSION as immortalised by Shakespeare and Byron. The Costly, Artistic Carvings, and the Magnificent Paintings, executed by the most eminent Italian artists, excel all ever seen in this way, and are worth a Fortune in themselves. The Machines are fitted with Indiarubber Tyres, gliding noiselessly along, like Sailing on one of Italy's Silvery Lagoons.
ALSO CHANNEL TUNNEL RAILWAY.
Greatest novelty ever introduced into Nottingham. Most enjoyable and amusing feature of the Fair, and its greatest attraction.
IF YOU FAIL TO SEE COLLIN'S SPECIALITIES YOU DO NOT SEE THE FAIR. 6692
— 1899 —

ABOVE: Advertisement for "Venice in Nottingham" and the Channel Tunnel Railway - both taken to the Goose Fair by Pat in 1899.

BELOW: Nottingham Goose Fair, October 1910. It is interesting to have a three-quarters view of the Wonderland Show, in which the canvas auditorium can be seen in relation to the elaborate frontage seen by the patrons. Although Pat was known to present a Helter Skelter at Nottingham the tower on the right is not thought to be his.
(Nottingham Libraries)

Yorkshire

Britain's largest county was not usually associated with the name of Pat Collins, but that is not to say that Pat never set foot in it. Once again, we are handicapped by our limited knowledge of Pat's early travels. In his 1895 Newport Advertiser interview (See Chapter 3) he casually includes both Lancashire and Yorkshire in his list of "destinations".

In August 1892 a "Ground to Let" advertisement in The Era proclaims that the old fairground in Rotherham has been built on, but a new ground has been established "just across the river", and the joint lessees are J.W.Bostock and Pat Collins. Later it seems that Brother John Collins ran this fair and the one in Sheffield.

In June 1907 Pat presented the Racing Cockerels at Halifax Fair, and in 1907 they are said to have appeared at Wakefield. The latter is also supposed to have been visited by the Ostriches in 1900. Dewsbury was visited by the Racing Cockerels in 1906.

HEADING SOUTH WEST

When Pat tried to expand south-west-wards from Birmingham and the Black Country, he found himself heading into territory associated with other showmen, such as Frank Wilson of Redditch; Tom Clarke of Kidderminster; George Strickland of Alcester, etc. Some other families had been important in the area when fairs consisted of perhaps one riding machine, swings, sheets and a few stalls, and some of them, such as the Stricklands, seem to become associated with Pat. However, at one time or another, Pat Collins' fair visited such places as Bromsgrove, Redditch, Droitwich, Kidderminster, and Evesham. Although not a major figure in the history of Stratford Mop fair, or the famous Oxford St Giles fair, a Pat Collins' ride has been known to appear at such events.

At Bromsgrove the fair was established by Charter, and took place towards the end of June. The Horse Fair that took place at the same time had declined by the early 1930's, and Pat's fair seemed to vary in size, depending on the firm's other commitments. For example, in 1932 seven riding machines and several shows attended, but in the following year only three machines appeared - the No.1.Scenic, the Dodgems, and Over the Sticks, plus the Rowliers motor-cycling in their Globe of death.... with the lions!

One fair of which Pat was the lessee for a number of years was held to coincide with Worcester Races, late June - early July. A selected mix of machines and attractions were assembled for this event. In 1934 the attractions included the Joby Farrell Scenic, the Noahs Ark, Dodgems, Swish, Yachts, Yo Yo, and Ghost Train. Even Harry Strickland was persuaded to build up a set of Gallopers that had been packed away for years. Shows included the Globe of death (The Rowliers) and the Empire Circus.

The following year Worcester fair was visited by Fr Greville, who sent his observations to World's Fair, under the name "Priest Reader". He found all Pat Collins' equipment in 'first class condition'. The attractions included the Airways, Noah's Ark, Dodgems, Yachts and Chair-o-Planes. It was the year that

BELOW: Pat's name on an arcade in the early 1960's - it may have been travelled by Barry Island Pat. Providing a variety of "indoor" amusements grew out of experience with the Black-out Fair, and with the early saloons of "Automatics".
(Collection of Fred Richardson

"Wee Jimmy" the World's Smallest Race Horse, and Billy the Pig were travelling with the fair, as well as Dot Rayners' Flea Circus and Price's "Continental Show". Fr Greville took note of the presence of three engines, "Alfred the Great", "Dreadnought" and "Lord James".

The Evesham Mop Fair played its part in the story of Pat Collins by providing Pat with a perverse reason for calling his Barry Island Amusement Park 'Evesham Park' - see Chapter 13). Pat was proud to announce in 1921 that he had acquired the lease for Evesham Mop, but in subsequent years it appears that he was only granted certain sites, rather than the entire fair. At some stage in the 1920's he must have found himself outbid by the White brothers from South Wales. On at least one occasion, an appearance at Evesham played a part in the strategic planning of a machine's itinerary. For example, in 1923, "Over the Falls" used Evesham as a jumping off point for an appearance at Stratford Mop.

TOWARDS THE EAST Travelling East from Walsall, Pat attended fairs in the Staffordshire towns of Lichfield and Burton on Trent. He crossed the Trent into Derbyshire to visit Ashby de la Zouch, and during the climatic Back End run his machines called at Ilkeston. Travelling south-eastwards, Pat visited places like Tamworth, Nuneaton, and sometimes Polesworth and Atherstone, in Warwickshire. In May and October Pat Collins visited the distant town of Leicester.

Lichfield

The Cathedral City of Lichfield held two fairs, historically connected with each other, and respectably 'Chartered'. They were accompanied by rituals that remain as part of local Civic and community life. The late 19thC arrival of the 'pleasure fair' is usually seen as something which has been 'tacked on' and as a result scant attention has been paid to the fair in the local paper - the Lichfield Mercury.

From the point of view of historians, fairs are significant in themselves indicating the extent and development of the leisure industry in our society. For example the Shrovetide fair is important because it marks the opening of the season. In Longton and Lichfield the Collins' empire had to emerge from a short period of hibernation. Often these occasions were notable for the bad weather, for instance, the Black Country Wakes' Week was often associated with rainfall, but at Lichfield the Shrovetide Fair could face frost, snow and icy winds.

However, in 1905, the fair was used to launch the new organ-fronted Bioscope. The Lichfield Mercury was not impressed! It stated *"Pat Collins supplied the usual roundabouts shows etc. in the Market Square"*...the Era, on the other hand was more forthcoming saying *"Pat Collins Ltd filled the Market Square to repletion. The chief attraction was an entirely new Cinematograph Exhibition - certainly the best ever seen in the district"*

In 1905 the Market Square was filled with the Bioscope, the Cockerels and stalls. With the space available the Shrovetide Fair was always modest, but the Bower Fair filled the City with fairground attractions by opening on at least three sites, and was usually accompanied by trading stalls. It was one of Pat's important Whitsun Fairs, which now takes place on the Spring Bank Holiday.

Possibly one reason for the City's apparent lack of interest in the Shrovetide Fair was that Pat tended to open on the Saturday, Monday and Shrove Tuesday. In other words, the Civic ceremony which included the Declaration of the opening of the fair actually coincided with the fair's final day! The pleasure fair and the Civic ceremony were brought closer together after the War, when the pleasure fair resumed after a five year absence. From then on, the Proclamation has always been read from the steps of a riding machine.

In 1973 even when the affairs of the Pat Collins' empire was at a low ebb, it was still possible to fill Lichfield with attractions on three separate sites at the Bower Fair. On the Greenhill site the attractions included Jack Harvey's Dodgems, and Ronnie Weston's Big Wheel and Mini Octopus, supported by a few juveniles and sidestuff. In the Market Square Lol Bishton's Cakewalk provided an old-fashioned fairground ride, along with the sounds of the Bruder organ. It was joined by Billy Bagnall's Dodgems and John Humphries' Arcade etc. The Dam Street Car Park sited Elias Harris's Skid and Hurricane Jets, Billy Bagnall's Waltzer and Anthony Harris' Juveniles (one of which - the "Vintagers", was new that year).

RIGHT: Pat, who listed "motoring" as one of his interests in "Who's Who", demonstrates his steering skill at the "Roller-On" game at one of his fairs in the mid 1920's. The fair has always woven fantasies around that symbol of technology and affluence: the motor car. *(Collection of John Ray)*

Burton on Trent.

On the border of Staffordshire and Derbyshire lies the town of Burton on Trent - famous for brewing, and ...probably...the number of railway level crossings within its limits! At one stage the town enjoyed four chartered fairs, but the only one to survive into modern times has been the Statutes Fair, with a Charter going back to the time of King John.

Burton Statutes Fair was originally a trading and hiring fair held following the Eve of St Modwen (October 29), but this was altered at some stage to the first Monday after Michaelmas. In the story of Pat Collins, its significance was that it usually fell between the end of the Onion Fair and the opening of the Goose Fair. In other words, after the hectic pull down at Birmingham on the Saturday night, and the dispersal to various destinations in the early hours of Sunday morning, some of the attractions could make for Burton for a one day stand before rushing on to Nottingham!

The phrenetic activity surrounding the coming and going of a fair provided the people of Burton with non-stop entertainment, while it was there. For example, in 1903, and again in 1907, the Bostock & Wombell Menagerie came to Burton for a one night

LEFT: Burton on Trent 1952. John Collins' new Rotor, built by the local firm: Orton and Spooner.
(Collection of Arthur Jones)

BELOW: The Rotor being pulled down at Burton, 1952.
(Collection of Arthur Jones)

stand of two shows on the Saturday before the Statutes Fair. According to the paper, the Burton Daily Mail, the crowds turned out on the Sunday to watch the Menagerie depart, and to await the arrival of the fair. Some of the fairground equipment arrived by train from Birmingham and had to be carted into the square. Then three showmen's engines arrived with their road trains, followed some time later by horse-drawn equipment belonging to the stall-holders, who also brought their living vans. The climax was the arrival of four or five horse-drawn carriages bringing the important figures of the fair. Amidst all the arrivals, the fair had to be built up to be able to open on Monday. On Tuesday morning the departure was every bit as hectic.

The paper gave more space to all this than to a description of the fair itself, but we do learn in 1907 that, "Collins' Motor Cars were overloaded by 10.pm, and there were many disappointed patrons unable to obtain a ride on this, or Weir's Gallopers".

The fair eventually grew to a three-day event (Saturday, Monday and Tuesday) although this must have been awkward when the Saturday clashed with the Onion Fair, and they had to open in Burton from Monday to Wednesday.

The year that the fair suddenly received a great deal of attention in the local press was 1929, when Victor Davey from Rotherham was collecting fares on Monday September 30th and was fatally injured in an accident on the Dragon Scenic. The Burton Daily Mail tells the story:

"Davey was stepping from one car to another when his foot slipped. He overbalanced and fell between two cars, one of which was derailed in consequence. There were few passengers in the cars at the time, but considerable alarm was caused, and a large crowd quickly assembled. The machine was stopped immediately and Davey was extricated. He was found to be terribly injured about the head and body, a car having passed over him. He was taken to Burton Infirmary in a critical condition. An unfortunate feature of the accident is that Davey had only been employed on the work that day".

Twenty three year old Victor Davey died in hospital the following Saturday and a Coroner's Inquest took place on Monday 7th October. The ride's foreman, James Harris, had to give evidence, and some of his off-hand replies put showmen in a rather bad light, and the Inquest was therefore featured in the press in great detail. Harris claimed he knew nothing about the accident because he was not there at the time. It looked bad that young Flora Collins, Pat's grand-daughter had been left in charge from her position in the paybox.

Harris said that there was one money-taker to each car, and therefore there was no need for a money taker to step from one dragon car to the next. He admitted that when money-takers left the machine, one taker would cover for another's absence. He had no idea how fast the ride revolved, and when asked how many times it revolved for each ride he replied "We have no special number - we make hay when the sun shines". His lack of concern for the ride or Davey's death seemed inappropriate. The pathologist added that his examination of Davey revealed that he had TB (Tuberculosis) and would not have lived long. The Coroner's Court returned a verdict of Accidental Death.

With attention focused on the Fair, the Burton Daily Mail ran a front page illustrated story on the day after Davey's accident...not about the accident, but about the Globe of Death. One of their reasons for the interest in this attraction was, of course, that it was manufactured in Burton on Trent - by Orton & Spooner. The photograph showed the mesh orb, and its French riders.

That was not all! A 70 year old black worker on the fair was attacked by a drunken visitor. Elias Harris came to his defence. Both Elias and the drunkard were arrested and taken to court, but only the latter was fined. To cap it all, there was a minor accident on the Auto Skooters. Not a good year...but it did not stop the fair going to Burton again.

The "local interest" concerning Burton's association with fairground business, via the rides and equipment manufactured by Orton & Spooner could be exploited by the fair when necessary. For example, in 1931, when Young Pat was in charge of bringing Pat Collins' Fair to Burton, he was encountering hostility from the local business community as the fair clashed with "Shopping Week". Young Pat responded in two ways, firstly he gave a lengthy interview to the Burton Daily Mail, and secondly he had large placards attached to each machine saying "This machine was made by Orton & Spooner of Burton".

BELOW: The fattest man, the ugliest woman, the shortest, the tallest, etc. etc., were all regularly presented at Pat Collins' Fairs until such shows faded away in the 1950's. After the patron had visited the show he was often invited to buy photographs of what he had just seen. This picture was purchased at Brierley Hill fair by Roy Mullender.

Young Pat told the Mail that over £150,000 had been spent with the local firm in the forty years he had been travelling, and a third of that figure had been spent by Pat Collins since 1921, he went on to say that he estimated 200 people travelled with the fair and they spent over £500 during their stay in the town. "Brewing beer is the staple industry of Burton on Trent, and I don't think you can accuse us of neglecting this famous industry, and nor do the thousands of patrons we attract into the town during our stay" said Young Pat...this was a risky line to take as newspapers often linked fairs with drunkenness and disorder, so he quickly turned the reporter's attention to the lion that he had brought along to Burton.!

Bill Croydon the Ground Manager, provided the paper with a list of attractions to be seen in Burton in 1931: These included the Dodgems (Young Pat); a new ride called The Whooper, and a Ghost Train (Baby John); The Hurdle Racers (W.Weston); a Noah's Ark (Bill Mullett); Cakewalk (H.Swain); the Yachts (Walter Kelly) and the Lion Show featuring Captain Clarke. Elias Harris was presenting the Wall of Death "on a more pretentious scale than before"; Joe Chadwick had his "Crazy House" and Jack Headley presented three shows. Even Young Pat presented a show - the Guillotine Illusion, managed by W.Wright. Among the tenants presenting shooters, sheets and stalls we find John Hall, Richard Deeks, Billy Williams, Tommy Roberts, Billy Bagnall and Mrs Chadwick. The newspaper article, based on the interview with Young Pat, and the paper's own observations, was greeted as being 'remarkably fair - good publicity for Pat Collins, and Burton's industries'.

Ashby Statutes

The annual Autumn fair at Ashby de la Zouch was another fixture that had to be accommodated within the movement of the rides at Pat's busiest time of year, usually just before the Onion Fair. For a while Pat was the joint lessee of this fair with Fred Cox.

Leicester

The large fair at Leicester was held towards the end of the Back End, and there was also a popular May fair. At the latter in 1933, the World's Fair commented on the excellent combination of the atmosphere of the old time fair and all the latest attractions - the No.1.scenic with the organ freshly re-tuned, the Gallopers, Yachts and Cakewalk, alongside the latest Caterpillar ride (Greens) and the Noahs Ark, Globe of Death etc. A dozen engines were said to have been present. On at least one occasion Pat organised a Grand Circus and Christmas Fair at the Granby Hall in Leicester. In Chapter 5 we have described how this was advertised as the "Showman's Answer to the Talkies!"

Ilkeston

At one time Pat had been the sole lessee of the fair held in Ilkeston in October, but later he appears to have been content to be a tenant of the Corporation, and it made a useful port of call for rides returning from the Hull fair. For example, in 1928, three machines came directly to Ilkeston from Hull: Walsall John's Over the Falls (Jack Berry); Auto-Scooters (Baby Pat); Cakewalk (Baby John). They were joined by the Hurdle Racers (Mrs Bird's Three Abreast) and a set of Yachts, and the fair was crowned with Clara Mullett's Whale Island.

HEADING SOUTH EAST

The No.3. Fair generally ended up in East Warwickshire in late Summer and early Autumn, taking the Pat Collins flag into areas associated with other showmen. The fair sometimes visited Atherstone, Polesworth and Nuneaton. Travelling further afield, into Leicestershire, it was possible to visit Hinckley and even Lutterworth. A report in 1934 describes the whole fair moving from Nuneaton to Lutterworth and then back to Hinckley at the end of August. At Hinckley there were the remnants of a traditional horse fair held in the street on the last Monday in the month, but the fair had to be built up on the outskirts of the town.

Although these fairs did not do very good business, there were four riding machines present and a number of shows, as well as numerous stalls. Perhaps these fairs attracted tenants hoping to travel north again, up the A5, in anticipation of moving into the Onion Fair later in September

THE POTTERIES

Pat had two sisters-in-law who came from the Davies family of Stoke on Trent. William Davies Snr was a showman who had travelled in North and South Staffordshire before the 1880's, and the advent of the "modern" fair, and riding masters who established themselves as lessees. By the beginning of this century, William Davies came southwards to be a tenant of Pat Collins.

Pat himself was established as a lessee in some of the principal fairs of the Potteries, an industrial area of the type much favoured by him. By the end of the last century, the miners and workers in heavy industry were 'good spenders' at the fairground, and responded wholeheartedly to the fairground's blend of technical sophistication and "vulgar" pleasure. In some cases the traditional Wakes of the Potteries, eg at Hanley, nicely dovetailed into the Collins' calendar, so that money could be made in North Staffordshire during the summer before returning the No.1.attractions to the Black Country for the Back End. Thus the major Pat Collins' attractions always made their way to Hanley Park in June or July, and appeared alongside the Flower Shows, Dog Shows and Military Tattoos.

From time to time there was trouble with local authorities, and fairs previously held in the Market Place were pushed into parks, as in Hanley. But in other places Pat purchased his own ground - as at Burslem. At Longton, the fair on Shrove Tuesday provided an annual chilly opening to the travelling season, quite a contrast to the conditions sometimes enjoyed in high summer.

World's Fair, dated 12 August 1933, describes Summer in the Potteries thus:

"Hanley and Stoke Wakes, held on the fairground at Regents Road, Hanley commenced on August 4th, and continued until August 9th. The weather proved to be just what Bank Holiday weather ought to be - continuous sunshine. And, well, even in the Potteries it is possible to be merry and bright while the sun is shining. Approximately 100,000 people left the Potteries on Saturday for the seaside, but the remaining 250,000 came, en-masse, to the gigantic fair provided by Alderman Collins. Even though the people round here are feeling the pinch of bad trade, there were very few who had not managed to save something "for the Wakes".

The ground was arranged to everyone's advantage, was well illuminated at the entrances, and kept tidy by Tom Kemp and his staff. The principal attractions included the lessee's (Alderman Collins) Dragon and Peacock Railway (Miss Mullett in charge), the Dodgems (Dennis Shipley); Over the Sticks (H.Weston Snr); Ghost Train (A.Collins); Cakewalk (H.Swain). Amongst the regular tenants were Wright & Rogers and Mrs Chadwick, Mrs Swann with her Panam etc., Messrs Deeks, Fossett, Hall, Humphreys, Cordwell and Williams. Shows included Proctor & Paulo's Circus. Whorley Freaks, and Hickman's Boxing Booth. D.Goode provided a refreshment stall and there were the usual sellers of birds, balloons, and other fairground novelties"

These hot sunny days in August at the Hanley Wakes contrasted greatly with the rain or snow often encountered at Longton Shrovetide Fair. Although this was often the fair regarded as 'opening' the travelling season, for one of the "runs" there were occasions when Pat Collins presented a fair in the Potteries, for a week or two ...in January! This was held on ground 'Adjoining Betty Plant's Toffee Factory' (Morley Street/Slippery Lane) and was often quite a large fair.

BELOW: The journey from fair to fair in the days of steam meant planning the trip with a view to finding places to stop for water. In this instance "Goliath" (McLaren 1623) pauses at Minworth on Sunday 28 September 1952, driven by Cockney Jack. The train consists of the principal truck, plate truck and box truck. (The car truck was towed by another vehicle). Young "cowboys" pause in their game to watch the engine replenish her tanks from a hydrant.
(Collection of Stan Webb)

- 223 -

LEFT: In 1937 Wolverhampton's fair moved to the patch at Brickkiln Street. On this site "Goliath" and "No.1" stand side by side to make clear the comparative size of the huge McLaren and the Burrell. (Both preserved). On the right Harry Richards stands by the cab of the lorry.
(Collection of Roy Webster)

LEFT: Folks don't seem to know whether they should stare at the camera or "Collins' Latest Yo Yo Ride" of 1933 vintage. Note the loudspeakers and the cartoon - inspired decorations of the rounding boards.
(Collection of Joe Chadwick)

Lottie Weston's Panam supplied Brandy Snap to many Black Country fair-goers. (Lottie was the wife of Harry Weston, Jnr. who managed Pat's Three-Abreast).
(Collection of Flora Williams)

- 224 -

WHO'S WHO

APPENDIX 1

In this Appendix to the main text we set out to provide biographies of the principal characters in the story of Pat's life. Although some of this information is repeated from previous chapters it has been done so that the lives of these people can be appreciated in their own right.

PART ONE - THE FAMILY

Johanna Collins (1847-1907)

Born 1847, first child of John and Norah Collins - oldest sister of Pat. Married Job Davies (1836-1888), and travelled from Chester and Wellington with swings and stalls. Died 5th January 1907. Her daughter, Sarah Ann (1874-1906), married Charles Farrell (1868-1915), which established the links between the Collins and the Farrells.

In later life, Pat Collins told World's Fair that he first travelled to the Welsh Fairs of the Dee Valley with his brother-in-law, describing Job Davies as "the great Welsh showman". We are not certain that Job Davies was related to the Staffordshire Davies', the family that Brother John's wife, Selina, came from.

Margaret Collins (1853-1925)

Second daughter of John and Norah Collins, "Aunty Maggie" travelled Cheshire and North Wales in her own right, and presented her own set of gallopers, swingboats and sidestuff. Margaret advertised "ground to let" on her Chester-based "North Wales" run in The Era at the turn of the century, but it is not clear which part of Wales she travelled. It may have been the Flintshire, Denbighshire area.

RIGHT: Aunty Johanna with her three grandchildren on the right: Joby, Margaret and Hannah Farrell, whose mother died at the age of 32 during childbirth.
(Collection of Sally Muldowney)

She had "retired" by 1920, and suffered ill health. She moved from her base at Union Street, Chester, to Pant Asaph, near Holywell, where she died on 10th September 1925.

On her death, the Chester Chronicle said,
"Born and bred in Boughton, Miss Collins attended St. Wedburgh's Day School, and then went to a convent in Shrewsbury. Miss Collins was a robust type, and she used her vigour by going about and doing good. Miss Collins could, if she had wished, have lived in luxury, but she preferred a humble abode. She toured the country in her caravan, and was a friend to all young people. She was a real saint, whose motto was 'Blessed are the pure in spirit'

- 225 -

LEFT: Aunt Maggie - the saintly woman of Chester whose language on occasions caused men to recoil in horror!
(Collection of Sally Muldowney)

World's Fair added: *"The late Miss Collins, whilst one of what is known as the weaker sex, was actually the opposite, for in her younger days no man could have taken greater responsibilities or worked harder than she did. Her one weakness, if it can be called that, was charity. It is many years since we first met the deceased, and she has always stood out in our memory as one who was fearless, but just"*

Her Three-Abreast was purchased by Slaters of Carlisle in 1932, and was travelled by them for five years. It is later thought to have appeared at Seaton Carew. To what extent Maggie created the run that became Pat's North Wales Run is not clear, but it is clear that Margaret Collins was the lessee of fairs such as the Chester Races in the early years of this century. Aunty Maggie was also a figure that the family turned to when in need of help. Although her brothers operated larger fairs in urban areas, and tended to regard her fairs as "tea parties", it was Aunty Maggie who was consistently financially successful. She was also very generous to her brothers and nephews in her will.

John Collins (5 April 1857 - 24 January 1929)

John, referred to in this book as Brother John, was only two years older than Pat. The story tells that he was born on Fair Day at Denbigh, while the family was in the process of settling at Chester, and while his father travelled to the fairs of North Cheshire. John and Pat appear to have followed in their father's footsteps, helping to travel and operate their father's rides before starting out on their own. In the early 1880's he married Selina Davies, the daughter of William Davies, Snr, of Stoke on Trent, possibly the second Collins' connection to this established North Staffordshire travelling family who already travelled as far south as the Black Country and Birmingham. (See comment on Job Davies, above).

The extent to which the careers of Brother John and Pat are inter-linked is very difficult to establish. 'The Era' newspaper of the 1890's talks of the P & J Collins Syndicate. They were joint owners of some property and joint-lessees of some fairs, they built up alongside each other at events like Nottingham Goose Fair, and were also "tenants" to each others' fairs. They both took part in founding the Showmen's Guild, and were its steadfast supporters thereafter. John was also a supporter of World's Fair.

Eventually, John established his base in Liverpool, and it was in Liverpool that Pat joined his brother in presenting the large fairs that were put on to mark important occasions, Victory in 1919, the completion of the Mersey Tunnel, Coronations, Royal Visits, etc.

John had three sons and three daughters. The sons entered the business, and were working on their own account by the time John died at the beginning of 1929. Sons John and James Patrick presented the rides that appeared at some of Pat's fairs during the 1930's - adding to the complexity of recognising which Collins is which when reading contemporary reports of these fairs in World's Fair. At some fairs there were three 'John Collins' present! (i.e. Walsall John, Young Pat's John, sometimes called Baby John, and brother John's son, John).

There was a strong family resemblance between John and Pat, and, as described in Chapter 5, Pat was very distressed by his brother's death. Biographical work on John Collins has been presented elsewhere in this book, and readers interested in the John Collins' side of the family can refer to the article in World's Fair of 9th April 1977.

Flora Collins, nee Ross (1861 - 1933)

Flora MacDonald Ross was born on 2nd June 1861, the fourth and youngest daughter of a jeweller and watch-maker of Wrexham. She was born in Church Street, at the shop occupied by her father, James Ross. The shop was later occupied by T.W.Dronfield, and in the 1870's James Ross had moved to premises at 31 Hope Street. It is said that Flora used to visit the Church Street premises whenever the fair came to Wrexham, because that was where she had spent her childhood. James Ross (born 1822) came from Scotland, and had married Mary Morris (born 1833). Of Flora's three sisters, we have been able to identify Catherine, three years older than Flora, and Annie, who was seven years older and who trained to be a milliner.

After her death, World's Fair wrote: *"Wrexham to her always had its native charm, brimful of memories of her early days, and recalling the time when her lover, a young travelling showman in the person of Patrick Collins, sought and found her"*.

Flora married Pat Collins in Liverpool, on 20th July 1880, when she was nineteen and he was twenty one. Because she was not born into Showland, but adopted it by marriage, the story is often told as if she had been swept off her feet by a dashing young showman, and was plucked from an environment or upbringing on which she had to turn her back. However, one or two clues suggest that Flora's association with Showland should not be regarded as quite so drastic or unusual. It would appear, for example, that one of her older sisters, Annie, had also married into Showland, by becoming Mrs Walter Hobbs Snr. (One reason for Flora wishing to be buried at Wrexham was to be buried alongside her sister Annie, who had died on 28th March 1930, five years before her husband Walter).

The truth is that we know little about Flora, other than the fact that she and Pat married in Liverpool in 1880, and two years later they had arrived in Walsall and decided to 'settle' in Shaw's Leisure. We know that Young Pat came along in 1886, and that sometime in the 1890's the family home became 'Chester House' in Algernon Street, a few yards from the Gondola Works – the centre of the growing empire.

During the 1900's we came across the first records of equipment being purchased or owned by Mrs Collins, but there is no real way of knowing whether anything should be read into this in terms of imagining that their businesses had separate and independent financial lives of their own. So little is written about Flora in her lifetime, that we have to look, once again, at the words printed after her death by World's Fair... *"Often in their more prosperous moments, leaving her husband to manage and control his own business, she would venture to embark on her own, managing and controlling her own shows"*

Thus the Bioscope was often described as Mrs Collins' show, and later the Lion Show and Menagerie are intermittently described as hers. What is quite clear, however is that Flora Collins played a very active part in fairground life, and she became a respected figure in Showland as a result of her own virtues - not simply because she was Pat Collins' wife. Many references to Flora stress her ladylike virtues, and link these qualities with a lifestyle that was in no way remote from the day to day work of the fair. She appears to have enjoyed travelling, and her van was always given a commanding position in the fair. From the van door she would

ABOVE: The Young Flora Collins; a picture used by Young Pat when inserting an "In Memoriam" notice in World's Fair.
(Collection of Sally Muldowney)

BELOW: "The White Lady", photographed at Chester in 1909. Flora's Orton & Spooner living van.
(Collection of Kevin Scrivens)

reprimand her grand-daughters and their contemporaries if they dared to leave the ground without being properly dressed including their gloves! Equally, she was not afraid to take command at the front of the Lion Show, where she was sometimes seen with a huge black brooch shaped as the head of a lion – with eyes made of diamonds.

She showed great charity and kindness to anyone who faced hardship, and she had other qualities that were worthy of a "Queen" of Showland. Quoting World's Fair, again, *"Her carriage and deportment were splendid, and she had the earnest desire that her sex should not lower the tone of the fairground... She had a personality and persuasiveness that were irresistible. In the early days, when ground was wanted and difficult to get, she would meet officials and talk them into what she wanted. She grew as her husband grew, and carried their more prosperous days with dignity".*

Flora travelled in her living van, "The White Lady", until the early 1930's, and enjoyed reasonable health until the Autumn of 1932. She died on 9th April 1933 and her funeral is described in Chapter 7. Her son, Young Pat, paid for the memorial on her grave at Wrexham, and its wording, apparently written after Pat's death, ten years later, has often led to some confusion – hence some folk believed that Pat was buried with Flora at Wrexham. The problem today is that there are few people alive who can remember Flora, compared to the number that remember Clara, Pat's second wife. We hope that we have done our best to give both Flora and Clara their rightful places in the story.

Patrick Ross Collins: "Young Pat" (1886 - 1966)

Pat and Flora's son, Patrick, was born in Chester, on 7th March 1886. As he grew up, his parents prospered and rose in the fairground world. He was sent to Ratcliffe College to complete his education, and was, no doubt, expected to follow in his parents' footsteps into Showland. It seems his education gave him a taste for writing letters, as he later engaged in a great deal of correspondence with World's Fair.

Young Pat's 'Coming of Age' has often been associated with the inauguration of the Wonderland Organ and Bioscope. Sometimes it is said that Pat and Flora gave the show to Young Pat as a 21st birthday present, and in recognition of his forthcoming marriage. It has not been possible to verify this, and the facts suggest that he took over the second Wonderland after his marriage.

'The Era' newspaper, of 16th March 1907, did carry a very full report of Young Pat's coming of age, and described a banquet held in his honour at the Royal Hotel, Oswestry, on the night of his birthday. A hundred guests were entertained, dined, toasted, and danced the night away in fine style. The highlight of the evening was the presentation of an illuminated Testimonial to Young Pat. This project was led by Ernest Leech, John Tinney, Walter Kelly, George Bailey, and Little Titch (Bob Jones). On the evening itself Mr J.Gordon made the presentation speech and Little Titch handed over the Testimonial.

Young Pat made a speech, and then, amidst much cheering, Pat rose to make a speech saying that it was the happiest and proudest moment of his life. He then handed his son a gold watch, upon which was his monogram.... inscribed in diamonds! Pat claimed that he had bought the watch sixteen years previously in anticipation of this event, indicating once again that his prosperity was substantial even by the early 1890's. Young Pat received over one hundred other valuable presents, including cheques from his Mother, a mounted five-pound jubilee piece from his 'adopted sister' Clara, and some silver-backed toilet brushes from Miss Fossett.

Miss Eliza Fossett married Young Pat on 22nd January 1908 at St.Wedburgh's Church, Chester. It was briefly described by World's Fair as a quiet wedding attended by only a few relatives, and Pat was noticeable by his absence! Apart from telling us that Eliza was the daughter of John Fossett, and supplying cameo photographs of the pair, 'The Era' adds nothing to the story. Why so much attention, and ceremony, was attached to Young Pat's 21st and why his marriage received so little, is

LEFT: Young Pat as a young man, as seen in The Era's report of his 21st birthday.
(Collection of Molly Seldon)

RIGHT: Young Pat as a father with his four children, Margaret, Flora, Pat and John.
(Collection of Molly Seldon)

not clear! Eliza later added "Molly" to her name, and died on 11th August 1973, aged 86. She shares a grave with her daughter, Margaret, in Wrexham.

Equally unclear is the extent to which Pat and his son worked together. Although he may not have been given the Wonderland Show as a present, there are references to Young Pat and his wife running the show during 1907 and 1908. In 1907 the rounding boards of the Cockerels, and one of the Shows, bore the legend, "P. Collins and Son". Around 1910 the lease of the Palace grounds at New Brighton was obtained by Pat Collins, and along with the theatres and cinemas in New Brighton, we are left to wonder to what extent everything was owned by Pat, but supervised by Young Pat, or to what extent Young Pat operated independently.

Young Pat's first child, Margaret, was born towards the end of 1908, followed by "Baby Pat" in 1910, "Baby John" in 1912, and Flora in 1913. For a few years, the family had a permanent home in New Brighton, but then, in 1914, the lease on the ground at New Brighton was won by George Wilkie - and then won back by Pat in 1920! In between regarding New Brighton as 'home', there were periods of intensive travelling, and therefore it is very difficult to chart the progress of Young Pat. For example, on losing the ground at New Brighton in 1914, Young Pat seemed to throw himself into establishing his own run of fairs, opening in Welshpool.

Even in the early 1920's, when holding the New Brighton lease for the second time, Young Pat was busy standing in for his father at the opening of the three cinemas (Chester 1920, Bloxwich 1922 and Oakengates 1923). His son, Baby Pat, explained that Flora took him down to Bloxwich and he grew up with Limetree House as his home, until sent away to Ratcliffe College. Generally, the grandchildren worked for Pat and they entered the business on completing their education, rather than working for their father.

At the end of 1921, Young Pat had been elected as the New Brighton Ward representative on Wallasey Council, but the loss of the lease on the New Brighton Amusement Park, for the second time, seems to have ushered him back to the Midlands Section of the Showmen's Guild telling the section in June 1925 "I have come back to Showland". Young Pat and Eliza, usually known as Molly, moved into the household at Limetree house.

Young Pat had a gift for stirring up acrimonious quarrels in the correspondence columns of World's Fair. Sometimes these arguments centred on matters like, "What was the best showfront ever built?" (His mother's ex Wall & Hammerseley Show, according to Young Pat!). On another occasion Young Pat told readers that he had invented the Noah's Ark, seen at Wembley in 1930). Sometimes the arguments were more personal, and in mid 1927, a writer using the initials "G.E.S." suggested that young Pat's progress in Showland was purely a result of being Pat's son. Young Pat's response was one of the few auto-biographical statements he appears to have made:

"I left school at 13 & 1/2, married at 19, and by the age of 32 had purchased ten machines, including three electric scenic railways, two sets of jumpers, two large joy wheels, a set of yachts, two sets of Gondolas and a helter skelter. I had also opened fresh places and fresh

```
         COLWYN BAY
     AMUSEMENTS PARK
        (Adjoining L.M. & S. Railway Station).

      8   F  E   8
          I  R
          G  U
   A long ride, a fast ride and a thrilling ride.
            AEROPLANES
   Miniature planes which fly under their own power. Great for the Children—
              makes them "Air Minded."
              FARMYARD
           Amusing and Instructive.
          JUNGLE STAMPEDE
           Fastest ride in the Universe.
             NOAH'S ARK
                or
         TOM THUMB'S MENAGERIE
      Educational and intensely interesting for young and old.
        MINIATURE BROOKLANDS
            Racing Midget Petrol Cars.
              COLLINS'
       World-renowned DODGING CARS
         The only Cars of their kind in the World.
           A THRILLING and POPULAR Ride.
      Colwyn Bay Amusements Park
         (Adjoining L.M. & S. Railway Station).
```

ABOVE: Advertising for Young Pat's Amusement Park at Colwyn Bay, appearing in *"Town Talk"*, a local paper, at Easter 1935.

positions for myself in all parts of Lancashire, Yorkshire, Cheshire and South Wales. My managers were Marco Roberts, Albert Taylor, Billy Taylor, Bruce Bleese, Harry Humphries, Jimmy Burton, Jim Crew, Harry and Billy Harris, Alan Bosco, Dicky Bird, etc..

...I believe it is the general impression that I have had a crutch to lean on throughout my career, but my income tax returns disprove this.

...I am proud to say that I have recently been taken into partnership by my Dad – and that those who know Pat Collins for the shrewd businessman he is, will be aware that he would not take a man into partnership with him unless he believed him to be capable of the position – whoever he may be".

How useful it would be to travel back in time and ask Young Pat to explain much of this statement. If he was two years out on his marriage date, what are we to make of his list of machines and positions? It all adds to the mystery surrounding the true nature of Young Pat's progress.

If, as he states, the end of the 1920's was a (second) period of entering into partnership with his father, we can find evidence of this in the projects to which his name was attached at that time. For example, the Palaise de Danse at Monument Road (refurbished in 1929) appears to be under Young Pat's supervision. When Pat moved into the Barry Island site at the beginning of 1930, it is Young Pat who seems to be in charge of letting space to tenants. There was also a period when Pat seems to have given his son the No.2.run - the run that began in Dudley in March, travelled down through the south-west of the Black Country and out to places like the Lickey Hills. Thus fairs on this run are sometimes described as Young Pat's fairs, and his Dragon Scenic travelled once more, having once 'settled' at New Brighton.

But the early 1930's also seem to be a time of Young Pat striking out on his own again. In particular he acquired land next to the railway at Colwyn Bay, in North Wales, and developed his own amusement park on that site. This opened at easter, the beginning of the 1935 season, and was something of a novelty on that stretch of the Welsh coast. There are two personal matters that also would appear to have had an effect on the course of Young Pat's life. In the mid 1930's his marriage to Molly (Eliza) was over, and his mother, Flora, had died in 1933. He may also have had other personal reasons for breaking away from the Midlands, and wishing to start afresh in Colwyn Bay.

Molly appears to have stayed in Bloxwich, and their children all entered the business during the mid 1930's. World's Fair continued to describe rides such as "The Airways" at Pat's fairs as being presented by Patrick Ross Collins – but this is probably a reference to Baby Pat; it is barely conceivable that it was Young Pat's machine. But even historians can easily become confused when fathers and sons have the same name, especially since Young Pat did not entirely cut himself off from his father's fair, or from other activities in the Midlands.

For example, in 1937, Young Pat bought the first Eli Big Wheel to travel in Britain. Although possibly intended for use in Colwyn Bay, it travelled extensively with Pat's fairs. However, apart from the arrival of the Big Wheel, most other references to Patrick Ross Collins' activities in the Midlands from the mid 1930's onwards are references to Young Pat's son. Another example of this concerns the Grand Theatre, in Walsall. This ancient theatre, almost next to the entrance to Walsall Station, in Park street, had survived a chequered career as theatre and cinema, but was regarded as redundant by ABC when they opened the Savoy at the top of Park street on the 3rd October 1938. For a few weeks the Grand languished, but then Baby Pat acquired the lease from ABC and, with the help of his manager, Fred Albert, set about reviving live theatre. The venture was short-lived, as the theatre was destroyed by fire in June 1939.

When Young Pat joined forces with his father in presenting the 1938 Royal Visit Fairs in Liverpool, he was interviewed by Frederick Bowman of the World's Fair, who was told that Young Pat had created Ice-skating facilities at Coventry, Newport (Mon), Wolverhampton and Coventry. We have no further details of these.

Young Pat himself is thought to have been interested in providing the fairs that were part of the Wartime "Holidays at Home" scheme, whereby Birmingham Corporation were looking for someone to present fairs in the Birmingham parks. It has been suggested that Young Pat could have acquired this contract, but that his father was reluctant to support the venture and supply riding machines. Pat was more concerned with his "Black Out Fair" which he travelled in the Black Country. The contract went to Bob Wilson, who was to become an important Midlands showman.

Young Pat was definitely back in the West Midlands during the War, and was photographed for the front page of World's Fair (3/2/40) in Army uniform as "Gunner Patrick Collins", when he was entertaining the Lord Mayor of Birmingham at the Palais de Danse to raise funds for wounded soldiers. True to form, two years later he is on the front page again (6/2/43) as "ex-Gunner Collins" and back in Colwyn Bay.

Young Pat's Amusement Park at Colwyn Bay was eventually sold to Arthur Barnard who had joined him before the War with an Arcade. Today the site has disappeared under the North Wales Coast Road. Young Pat died on 24th February 1966, and was buried on the Great Orme, Llandudno. His death appears to have caused no comment in World's Fair, or in the local papers... perhaps the Biography of Young Pat waits to be written!

Clara Mullett (1880 - 1962)

Clara was born on the fairground at Bradford on 17th June 1880, the daughter of William Mullett, Snr. When the Mullett children were orphaned, they were adopted by Pat Collins, and Clara and her brother William grew up on Pat Collins' fairs, and as part of his extended household. Clara became extremely knowledgeable and competent in all matters relating to the business, from the working of machines and engines, to the management of the finances of the fair. When Pat acquired his first purpose-built Scenic in 1911 (R15 The Jungle Motors), Clara managed it, and the Foster engine 13052 was named after her, when it was delivered in 1913.

In 1921 the machine was replaced with the new Orton and Spooner Scenic, and Clara became manager of this machine. When the Whale cars were put on the machine in the following year, it began its long career as "Clara Mullett's Whale Island", and travelled extensively as the firm's No.1.ride, for over a decade. Many reports commented on how well it was always turned out. The machine, and Clara Mullett herself, became well known to pre-War generations of fairground enthusiasts.

Clara was both a senior manager and the Guvnor's secretary within the organisation of the fair and she could collect the takings from managers and rents from tenants etc., and because we know she eventually became Pat's second wife, it would seem natural to wonder what the relationship was like between Clara and Flora. Joe Ashmore can very accurately recall working for Pat during the early 1920's, and remembers driving Flora and Clara to Wolverhampton Station to catch the train to London to attend an important Showmen's ball, and the two ladies seemed to get on very well together. Most people who can remember both Flora and Clara do recall them as two very different kinds of women.

In Chapter 7 we described Pat and Clara's wedding which took place, quietly, on 11th January 1935, (two years' after Flora's death). It would be wrong to imagine that Pat's second marriage was not significant in the future destiny of his fairground empire, but embarking on a second marriage as a widower or widow, seems fairly common in Showland. Whether they had married or not, Clara would naturally have been Pat's companion in the aftermath of Flora's death. The consequences for the fair, of the second marriage, became more manifest after Pat's death in 1943. Rather than simply passing to Young Pat, and his children, as people must have expected, the fair had to be administered by the Estate's trustees. This left Clara, in her sixties, with the travelling fair to operate during rather difficult times, and the Amusement Parks in the hands of Walsall John.

Clara became a prominent public figure during Pat's term of office as Mayor of Walsall (1938-39), and performed the role of Mayoress with the same humour and dignity that Pat brought to the role of Mayor. In December 1938, the Express & Star published a rather naive interview with Clara focusing on the "Mayoress At Home in a Caravan" – as it put it in the headline. The reporter had been sent to the Wolverhampton Christmas Fair to meet Clara in her van, where Clara's "housekeeper", Mrs M Slade, was dispensing cups of tea. He began to report thus: *"In the comfort of the Mayor's Parlour at Walsall Town Hall, or the plain economic severity of a small caravan, Mrs Collins, Mayoress of Walsall, and the wife of Pat Collins, the Well-known showman, is equally at home"*.

The phrase "plain and economic severity of a small caravan" was simply journalistic nonsense, and the accompanying photograph showed Clara enjoying her cup of tea in the 12.ft x 6.ft living room of her van in luxurious surroundings! Thus the novelty of a Mayor and Mayoress from the World of Showland tended to confound local journalists.

When their year as Mayor and Mayoress ended, it coincided with the beginning of World War Two and the fair then continued its existence "blacked out". Clara nursed Pat as his health deteriorated during the last year or two of his life, mainly spent away from the public gaze, at Limetree House.

When peace returned, two years' after Pat's death, Clara found herself still in charge of a large organisation. The travelling fair alone consisted of three or four sections, and the 'empire' did not really begin to contract until the 1950's. Clara also continued many of the charitable initiatives undertaken by Pat, ranging from the work of the Bloxwich Carnival Committee to the putting of half crowns on the window sill of Limetree House, for those in need.

To many, she was "Aunt Clara", and to Walsall John's children she was a "grand-motherly" figure, in the same way that Flora had been to Young Pat's children. But Clara, 'the kind old lady' still knew how to run a fair, and, while chain-smoking Players' cigarettes, liked to discuss the technicalities of machines and fairground transport. Jack and Clara Harvey knew her well during this period, and she would join Frank in the Paybox of the Dodgems and tell him to "Chop 'em" if she thought the ride was too long!

On 28th May 1959, Clara was presented with a Biography of Pat Collins, at a special event held at the T.P.Riley School in Bloxwich, to mark the centenary of Pat's birth. She was too overwhelmed to speak on this occasion – and an opportunity was lost of hearing Clara's own account of her life, but Walsall John said a few words on her behalf.

Clara died on 7th September 1962, and her funeral on 11th September was a huge affair. The Express & Star's headline was, "Fairground Folk Bid Their Queen Farewell". Over two hundred mourners came to St Peter's Church, Bloxwich, and hundreds of local people lined the High street to see the funeral cortege make its way from Limetree House, to the church. The list of mourners and their floral tributes published in World's Fair on 22 September 1962 reads like a Who's Who of the Collins' family and Showland empire.

She was buried in Bloxwich Cemetery, alongside Pat. World's Fair reported *"Fr. Walshe conducted the burial service, and as the coffin was lowered to its last resting place there were few dry eyes among the assembled mourners, for all were aware that their beloved "Clara" and "Pat" had been reunited".*

"This Grand Old Lady of Showland was one of the most colourful personalities in the business, with a profound knowledge of the fairground and its people...She will be remembered best as 'Clara Mullett', a name that was used with affection by all who knew her...and the famous Scenic Railway bearing the name of Pat Collins was always alluded to as 'Clara Mullett's Machine'.

Small in stature, but big in heart, Mrs Collins loved to pause for a chat with her old friends, and although she moved with the times, she always retained an affection for the days of steam and the gilded carved work of the old roundabouts. To this day there is a showman's engine standing in the yard at Bloxwich – a memorial to the good old days".

Clara died in the presence of Jack and Clara Harvey, and her last words were also the last words of Pat – "Keep the Flag Flying". Ironically, a few weeks' after her death, the remains of the Scenic were burnt while the site was being cleared at the Crystal Palace, Sutton Park. Whatever brave words were spoken and written at the time of Clara's death about the Pat Collins empire enduring forever, and going from strength to strength, the truth is that Clara's death marked the end of an era, and the travelling side of the business was not going to see a revival for some years.

LEFT: At the end of October 1938, Pat and Clara were photographed with their favourite dog at Limetree House for a feature on "The Next Mayor" for the Walsall Observer. Pat had always kept dogs at Limetree House and it was not unknown for Alsations to be used to bring up the lion cubs born in the shows. Animal life at Limetree House included chickens, a cow, and a long-lived parrot who could say, "Here comes the Guvnor!" when not swearing and cursing.
(Walsall Local History Centre)

Mollie Collins, also known as Eliza, Young Pat's wife.
(Collection of Joe Chadwick)

ABOVE: Baby Pat, or "Boy" Pat - Young Pat's son, as a young man. Always a favourite of his grandfather, Baby Pat managed rides like the Airways before the Second World War. Just as the book was going to press, on 9 October 1991, we learned that Baby Pat, in his 81st year, had passed away, and was to be buried at Wrexham, alongside his mother, Mollie, and his grandmother, Flora Collins.

(Collection of Joe Chadwick)

BELOW: Miss Clara Mullett, cigarette in hand, checks the arrival of the loads as the trucks draw onto the ground. Although manager of the firm's No.1.machine, and always given the best equipment, engines etc., she cannot have imagined that one day it would be her task to "Keep the Flag Flying".

Esther Davies

No survey of the immediate Collins' household would be complete without some mention of Esther Davies, known to most people as "Hetty". Hetty was born on 11th May 1882, in Wrexham. Her mother was Sarah Davies, but her father's name was not recorded at the time of registration. She became Pat's "adopted daughter" and her name is duly recorded in many of the descriptions of the events' in the Collins' family history, from Young Pat's twenty first birthday party in 1907, through to Pat and Clara's wedding in 1935, and Pat's funeral eight years' later.

Pat was "The Guvnor" even to his immediate family, and particularly in his relationship with Hetty, who he appears to have "summoned" when required. For example, in his year as Mayor, Hetty took part in preparing the ceremonial robes and dressing Pat for important occasions. She lived life in the shadows, although she was well known by the many who passed through Limetree House; Hetty died in 1959, and was buried in Bloxwich Cemetery.

ABOVE: Walsall John and Claire
(Collection of Vanessa Forte)

Walsall John

Pat Collins' adopted son, John, was born on 26th June 1906, and his position within the Collins' family has sometimes been shrouded in mystery in the sense that people have wished to take us aside and put forward their own theories about his identity. Sometimes we have been told he was Pat's illegitimate son, sometimes we have been told that Clara Mullett was his mother. Because such stories are circulated, it seems worthwhile setting out what we have come to regard as the probable truth.

We know from John's Birth Certificate that he was born in Neath, and his mother registered herself as Johannah Collins on the Certificate. Johannah and Nellie Collins were the daughters of another Pat Collins, sometimes known as 'Wrexham Pat', who was a cousin of Pat. (A son of Pat's father's brother... slipping back into the family's Irish ancestry). Wrexham Pat died when he was about thirty, and his daughters were "adopted" by Pat, in much the same way that the Mullett children were taken under Pat's wing. No father's name is recorded on Walsall John's certificate, but according to information given to us, it is likely that his father was Young Pat (then only twenty years' old), and a second cousin to Johannah. When John was brought into the Collins' household it seems that he was looked after by his Aunty Nellie, until she married Nathanial Charlton.

Like other Collinses, Walsall John was sent to Ratcliffe College, and made his way into the family business. As a young teenager he was travelling with the fair, under the watchful eye of Clara Mullett. George Reohorn travelled the fairs with his father for a month in 1918, and he and John being about the same age "knocked about together". At Oldham, Clara gave John a pound so that he and George could have a day out at Manchester's Belle Vue. This was during the summer holiday period, and when John was probably still at Ratcliffe. (See George Reohorn's recollections).

Just as the legends surrounding Pat's childhood tell of a rejection of formal schooling and a desire to be educated on the fairground, John seems to have followed a similar path. He left Ratcliffe as early as possible and while still in his teens he ran sidestalls for his father, and acquainted himself with the many aspects of life on the fairground. He was interested in the steam engines and showed mechanical and inventive skills. He was also able to develop pugalistic skills in the boxing booth - an interest in boxing was something else he shared with Pat.

Quite at what stage John started working for himself rather than for the Guvnor is not clear, and it is likely he gradually started doing the former while continuing in the latter role for many years. Even if a ride was his own, his relationship with Pat was that of tenant to landlord. Certainly by the mid 1920's, in his own early twenties, he was becoming associated with presenting new novelty rides, and when Pat Collins acquired the lease at Yarmouth Pleasure Beach, for the 1929 season, John, in his twenty third year, was nominally 'in charge'.

Possibly Pat's acquisition of Yarmouth Pleasure Beach, gave a particular focus to John's restless quest for novelties and new ride sensations, in the sense that it provided somewhere to put them, try them out, and market them in the case where Pat or John were acting as agents or importers of foreign equipment. In Paris, John saw the German-built roller coaster of Hugo Hans, he purchased it and brought it back to Britain. It was erected at Gt Yarmouth for the 1932 season.

At the end of the 1932 season, Walsall John married Claire Hall, the daughter of Harry Hall, an important showman from Derby. The Derby Telegraph published a picture the following day, but it was left to the Derby Advertiser, a weekly paper, to fill in the details and publish a photo-montage of the couple in close-up superimposed on a view of the congregation inside St. Mary's Church, Derby.

The name of the bride is given as Clara Kathryn Hall, although we have always found her to be called Claire. Harry Hall, "known for miles around Derby", gave his daughter away, and Violet Hall and Maisie Proctor were bridesmaids. There were six hundred guests invited to this event in which two showland families were brought together, and a lavish reception was provided at the Derby Assembly Rooms. The Best man was John's schoolfriend and colleague, Jack Barry.

The Derby Advertiser explained to its readers that John Collins was "An amusement caterer operating English fairs in France, Germany, and Central Europe – He owns the largest Scenic Railway in the World, which is at Great Yarmouth". As a final touch, we are told that the couple were off on a honeymoon that would take them to Egypt, Monte Carlo, Paris and Hamburg. This would suggest that John was about to buy the Pyramids, import them to France, and have them rebuilt as a Scenic Railway in Germany!

In later life John used most of his wanderings to mix business with pleasure, and his children recall continental holidays that centred around visits to major European amusements parks. Returning from these trips John travelled First Class, but sent his children Third Class; they were all reunited at their journey's end.... this was in the Guvnor's tradition of not spoiling the children!

On 28th January 1933, the World's Fair printed a profile of John's progress, giving us a clear picture of the story:
"....full of energy and ambition, Johnny is happy only when he is managing to pull off a good deal, and is up to his eyes in work. In addition to his attractions at Bingley Hall, Birmingham where he holds the reins, he has had his attractive new ride "The Yo Yo", at Olympia.

Always in search of new attractions, he is very much a globe trotter. It is his proud boast that he discovers a novelty each year, and it is a fact that he has managed to do that trick for the past nine years.
He manages the Amusement Park at Great Yarmouth, which has the largest ride in England as its main attraction. This is the wonderful Scenic Railway which was purchased from Herr Hugo Haase last year. This season will see "The Yo Yo" ride at Yarmouth and Barry Island, and it will be seen at the principal fairs" (In fact, it was one of the two rides John presented at Kings Lynn a few weeks' later).

"He has an able aide-de-camp in Jack Berry, who has been with the Collins' family for ten years, and who was

ABOVE: Walsall John takes three of his children to the Battersea Pleasure Gardens in 1951. L-R: John, Vanessa and Patrick, Walsall John. The name of the bear has not been recorded.
(Collection of Vanessa Forte)

at Ratcliffe College with John. John recently got married, and like most showmen, finds an able partner in his wife".

Thus it would seem that John was presenting his own novelty rides about 1924, when he was only eighteen, and even at the time this profile was written his restless energy was well known.

John and Claire bought a house in Great Yarmouth, and although they must have spent a great deal of time travelling, they did enter into the community life of the town, and the day to day running of the Amusement Park. One photograph exists of John and Claire joining their staff in presenting a large carnival float on behalf of the Pleasure Beach.

The arrival of the Scenic Railway at Yarmouth in 1932 was also significant in the sense that it represented something that became John's "specialism". It seems that Pat was never full of fatherly encouragement when it came to his sons' endeavours, and in particular he poured scorn on the practicality of making money from large scenic railways. John triumphantly proved him wrong! Sometimes, in bringing a new ride into the country, John was then able to act as an agent in importing and assembling further examples. For instance, he was able to do this with the "Loop a Plane" in 1936, and again at the Empire Exhibition in Glasgow in 1938 when he built his really large Big Dipper.

John and Claire's first daughter, Anne, was born at Yarmouth on 24th May 1934, and the World's Fair commented on the fact that she enjoyed the sea air. (Her own memory is that the sea air did nothing but give her bronchitis!). The very early 1930's were a time when Pat, Young Pat, and Young John, were all very much "in the business", individually and collectively, and at occasions like the Autumn Onion Fair all three were present.

It was circumstances outside his own control that brought John closer to the command of the empire, and ultimately gave him the responsibility for "Keeping the Flag Flying". First came Flora's death, and in 1935, Pat's second marriage to Clara. Young Pat's own first marriage came to an end during the same year, and he had moved away from the Midlands and settled at Colwyn Bay. All these three events led to Walsall John becoming Pat's "right hand man", particularly in running the amusement parks and the travelling fair during the hectic round of Back End fairs. Somewhere along the line the mantle of "Young Guvnor" seemed to shift from Young Pat to Walsall John.

Towards the end of the 1930's it seems that John's home shifted to Barry, but after War broke out the family joined the household at Limetree House in Bloxwich – to enjoy the use of Pat's famous air-raid shelter. In 1940 they moved to Sutton Coldfield, first to Blackroot Road and then to Four Winds in Halloughton Road. Meanwhile Pat sold the lease on the Barry Island site to John, and thus it was not part of Pat's estate when he died.

The ex-Glasgow Exhibition Big Dipper had been built up in Liege in 1939, and then had been hurriedly "evacuated" when the War broke out. Legends tell of "the last boat out of Belgium" etc! After building it up at Barry Island, John had to concern himself with running the Black-out Fair, and like many other showmen, John became involved in providing Wartime transport for munitions, and other work for the Government. It is difficult to know to what extent the War interrupted his progress as a showman on an international scale. He became involved in part ownership of a roller coaster in San Francisco just before the War.

Although Great Yarmouth Pleasure Beach remained part of the Collins' empire until the 1950's, John himself seems to have shifted the centre of his universe well and truly to Sutton, and the next three children were born there: Vanessa (1940), John (1943) and Patrick (1945). It is possible that the removal of the miniature railway from Great Yarmouth and its subsequent incorporation into the revival of the railway at Sutton Park is explained by John's greater association with the Midlands from the mid 1930's onwards. It seems to logically follow the building of the Scenic Railway at Sutton in 1937.

When Pat died in 1943 and the empire had to be administered on behalf of his estate, it was also logical that Clara should go on running the travelling fairs and that John oversaw the management of Great Yarmouth, the Crystal Palace, and his own Park at Barry Island. The two worlds overlapped, as always, when the rides came out of the amusement parks at the end of the summer and toured the Back End fairs. Thus John was well-known to the travelling fair folk as well as the staff of the parks. He was known as Walsall John, or, in recognition of his restless energy, "The Bustle" or "The Bustler".

John inherited many Collins' characteristics, and perhaps displayed them in an exaggerated manner. He could be charming, and generous, he could also be practically involved in solving problems, but most of all he "bustled" – always searching for something "new" and a success that would be greater than the last one. When it came to showmanship he possessed a certain brilliance – a worthy prince to follow the "King of Showmen", but there was also a certain tragic dimension to his destiny.

John was quite happy to "diversify". For example, during the War he purchased a covered market in Erdington. After the War he opened a hotel near Kenilworth on the lines of a "Motel". He used the term "Auto Villas". Sometimes he lost interest in new ventures very quickly, and like Pat, his financial fortunes must have risen and fallen alarmingly. His association with the Big Dipper was highly symbolic! His life was like a ride on a roller coaster. Yet even his globe-trotting was perhaps just a modern equivalent of the many miles that Pat must have travelled in his time.

In 1951, John was involved in the creation of the Amusement Park at Battersea, to mark the Festival of Britain. The Big Dipper was taken down at Sutton Park in the Autumn of 1950, and was moved south. One trip made spectacular use of the engine, Burrell "No. 1". John can also be remembered for his part in preserving the post-War use of the showman's engine on his fairs, and he seems to have liked to buy vintage rides such as the steam yachts. He and Clara seem to have understood the historic value of the showman's engine, and the organ and scenic that survived at Sutton Park.

With the Big Dipper's departure to Battersea, John

also seemed to turn his back on Sutton Park. His marriage to Claire came to an end, and he married Kay Collyer. A daughter Jane, was born on 23rd April 1952. Apparently unabated, his globe-trotting continued... he was involved in building the "World's fair" in Brussels in 1958, a roller Coaster at the Lunar Park at Rome, and then one in Montreal. Back in England he had developed the Parks at Seaburn, and Seaton Carew, which opened in 1950.

Clara died in September 1962, and four years later John became the "residual legatee" of the estate of Pat Collins - on 5th April 1966, after Young Pat's death. Almost twenty years after Pat's death everything finally belonged to John; by this time he was sixty years' old, and the pace of his amazing existence had slowed down. In the same year his sons took over the control of the Barry Island Amusement Park. Just as Pat had sold the lease to John in about 1940, Walsall John relinquished the lease to the next generation.

The following years saw many of the assets of the old "empire" stripped, leading to the demise of the Onion Fair for example. In 1970, the ground at the back of Limetree House was sold to the Asda Supermarket enterprise, and it was only a short time before the future of Limetree House itself was threatened. John, by then, was living in Blackpool.

By 1971, Limetree House was still an "office", but John was apparently offering it to the Council in Walsall in the hope that it might become an old folks' home. Nothing came of this plan and it was eventually demolished, after a period of semi-dereliction, to provide space for a car park in front of the supermarket.

John died in Blackpool in August 1977. The funeral, in Blackpool, was a quiet family affair. His son, Barry Island John, told World's Fair that this was what his father would have wanted, "Because he knew that everyone would be busy with the season – that's the kind of man he was".

Walsall John's life was all "bustle", and full of alarming ups and downs. As the World's fair had observed way back in 1932, he was at his best when his energy and inventiveness were vested in his work. Because he was "The Guvnor" during the period of the post-War decline of the travelling fair, the decline in his own well-being and the decline of the business seem linked in a rather tragic way. Looking at it today, we can see that he did play a significant part in "Keeping the Flag Flying", and that even if Pat himself had lived to be a hundred and fifty he could probably not have maintained the empire as it was at the end of the 1930's into the rather different world of the 1990's.

It can also be seen in the account of Pat's life, that he returned to the day-to-day realities of the travelling fair when his batteries needed re-charging. For all his globe-trotting and sometimes extravagant life-style, it seems that John also shared this habit of "returning to the fair" when times were bad. He might suddenly appear from nowhere in his private aircraft, or draw up in a large American car at the fairground. It seemed to represent some kind of spiritual homeland to his restless soul, just as it did to Pat.

Pat Collins' Grandchildren

a) Young Pat's Children

Young Pat married Eliza Fossett (also known as Molly) in January 1908, and their first child, Margaret, was born towards the end of that year. On 27th November 1930, Margaret married Elias Harris, creating the link between the Collins' and Harris' families that forms the background to Anthony Harris's accession as Proprietor of Pat Collins' fairs today. Margaret died on 10th January 1934, after an operation in Walsall General Hospital, and is buried at Wrexham.

On 13th May 1910, a son was born, and in true showland tradition was given his father's name, Patrick Ross Collins. To distinguish him from his father, we have called him Baby Pat, or Boy Pat. He was born in New Brighton, but he grew up around Walsall, and went to live with his Grandmother, Flora, until going off to Ratcliffe college in 1918. When he left school in 1925 he went straight into working on his Grandfather's fairgrounds. Thus he can remember the last two Goose Fairs held in the Market Place in Nottingham, when he worked on the Dragons and the Slip.

When the Goose Fair moved to the Forest site he took the Dodgems for a couple of years and when Spinners appeared he took one to Nottingham to put them on the Slip's former position. He recalls, *"We couldn't take the money fast enough – there must have been ten of us taking money on it!"*

In the 1930's he travelled a set of steam yachts for a couple of years (1932 - 1934), and later The Airways.

Another son, John James, was born on 31st March 1912, and his early life followed the same kind of pattern as Baby Pat's. To distinguish him from other Johns, he was sometimes known as Baby John, and to some folks as Goggles John, simply because he wore glasses. Like Baby Pat he was initiated into the realities of fairground life after

ABOVE: Patrick Ross Collins, the "Young Guv'nor" stands on the platform of the Three-Abreast, holding his son, "Boy Pat" just before the First World War - the days of the penny ticket.

(Collection of Joe Chadwick)

leaving Ratcliffe College. Baby Pat recalled seeing John in the Paybox of the Catwalk, at the cold Shrovetide fair at Longton – the scene was undescribably bleak!

On 8th January 1937, Baby John married Norah Kayes, the twenty year old daughter of Richard Kayes who presented Kayes' Circus. After their marriage, John and Nora obtained a Wall of Death and successfully travelled it for several years. Norah recalls, "John told me that he had decided not to have just one rider - he would have three - all girls - and they would all ride at the same time. The girls were called "The Blonde Bombshells" and it was fabulous. People used to gasp at the way the girls zipped up onto the wall, and they looked so good in white crash helmets, white blouses, white breeches and white boots. John paid them to have their hair bleached. They were led by a tiny girl called "Pepper"..... she was "Pepper by name and pepper by nature"..... and they rode those large Indian bikes for us for about two years – up until the War"

In fact John and Norah ended up with two Walls of Death, John presenting the blonde Bombshells and Norah presenting a show featuring Skid Skinner and his wife Alva. Both shows appeared with Pat Collins' fairs, and John and Norah also took them off on their own travels.

John was a tank-driving instructor with the Army during the Second World War, until invalided out with a badly ulcerated leg. He and Norah had bought a set of Dodgems from Young Pat, and while John was recovering, Norah ran the Dodgems on a permanent site somewhere in the Birmingham area. She was helped by showland servicemen who used their leave to help run the Dodgems, but the task was still a considerable strain.

After the War, John and Norah sold the Dodgem and bought a Caterpillar from J.P.Collins, who had bought it the previous year from F.Jervis of Buckley. They travelled with the Caterpillar, and then took it to Barry Island for a couple of years. Norah sat in the Paybox, and John, or his foreman, drove it.

Norah continues the story: "We sold the Caterpillar to some men from Margate, and bought a Skid. We didn't do very well with the Skid, and wondered if we should take it to Barry Island. Walsall John suggested that we took it to Seaton Carew – a place that was so far north we didn't even know where it was! Walsall John said that Seaton Carew had opened the previous year and that it had been succeessful.

So off we went to Seaton Carew, but our first season was a washout, I wanted to return to the Midlands, but John thought we should stay and see if the second season *improved. It did improve, and during our third season Walsall John's manager left, and my husband was asked to take over the park. At the end of the season we bought it from Walsall John."*

Walsall John had also developed some amusements at Seaburn, and these were acquired by Norah and John's sons, John and Pat. Baby John died in 1979. Norah Collins, and Ann Collins (Walsall John's first daughter) are the only two members of the Collins' family alive today who can give a first hand account of Pat's life at Limetree House in the early years of the War. Norah's account provides us with an interesting insight when Pat talked of her two sons as his "Grandchildren". They were really his "Great Grandchildren" but Pat appeared to forget his own sons when he thought of family relationships!

Another daughter was born to Young Pat and his wife on 25th October 1913, and "Young Flora" also worked for her Grandfather. At the age of sixteen in the Autumn of 1929, she was looking after one of the machines at Burton Statutes Fair when one of the gaff lads was fatally injured when he slipped between cars.

Flora married Lord Randall Eddy Monte, and during the 1930's they travelled various rides such as a Monorail on Pat's fairs. After the War, Eddy Monte established a well-known Wall of death, a popular feature of the Post-War fair. The death of their nineteen year old son Michael, in October 1959, led to their gradual loss of interest in the travelling fair.

Flora Monte died in 1985 and Eddy Monte died three years later. They are buried close to Pat's grave in Bloxwich.

b) Walsall John's Children

Walsall John's first daughter, Ann, was born in 1934, and the first years of her life were spent in Yarmouth. She remembers Pat at the very end of his life but John's other children were born too late to know him. Vanessa, John and Patrick grew up with the Crystal Palace Amusement Park and then Barry Island, as their first encounters with the empire that had been built by Pat Collins. Today, it is Walsall John's youngest son, Patrick, who is the Proprietor of the Barry Island site, and he has been joined in the business by his son – Patrick!

BELOW: Baby John, or "J.J" Collins, presents the Blonde Bombshells on his Wall of death in 1938. The show appeared at a number of Pat Collins' fairs.
(Collection of Norah Collins)

The Lancashire Collins

A separate book could be written on the showland dynasty established by Pat's brother, John Collins. However, you will note that some information about this side of the family has been included on our family tree, in order to make it more comprehensive, and because links can be made between these two sides of the family. As indicated previously, Pat and his brother John, may have worked together at various times, eg as joint Lessees of some fairs, and as tenants to each other. Thus John's machines came to the Midlands, and Pat took his machines to fairs in Liverpool.

After John's death there was a period when his three sons operated as Collins' Brothers of Liverpool, and then they went their separate ways. The youngest son, James Patrick (1889 - 1966), is particularly associated with bringing his rides to the Midlands, sometimes as a tenant of his Uncle, sometimes taking leases on fairs on the fringes of his uncle's territory, eg. at Bridgnorth, and sometimes even within Pat's territory, eg at Wolverhampton.

After the second World War, during the period when the equipment on Pat Collins fairs could less and less be provided by the firm itself, J.P.Collins' Waltzer filled the gap. It was an elegant machine, built by Lakin & Co. in 1933 for Thurstons, and was managed by J.P's son, Kevin Collins. 'J.P.' retired, but Kevin continued to present the Waltzer. For several years the machine was built up for a summer season at Dudley Zoo, and then joined Pat's fairs for the Back End. It appeared for the last time when it stood for two seasons at Barmouth in the mid 1970's, and then went into store. It was destroyed by fire in October 1990, while stored near Cannock, and a valuable example of an early Waltzer was lost forever.

As well as J.P's Waltzer, a Moonrocket (or "Airways") also appeared on a number of Pat's fairs, managed by J.P's other son, Brian. While moving from Bromsgrove to Worcester, the Saurer tractor associated with this ride was destroyed by fire, and was temporarily replaced with Pat Collins' engine "The Leader" (driver Dick Studt). The ride was broken up in 1952 and for twenty years, 1959 to 1979, Brian was associated with the rides provided at Alton Towers. All three children of J.P.Collins still live and work in the West Midlands, but are not now associated with the travelling fair.

WHO'S WHO: In the following pages we have listed many of the people mentioned in this book - but probably only a tiny fraction of those associated with Pat Collins and his fairs. Many photographs have come to light where it is now impossible to identify the subjects. Conversely, we can read page after page of names in World's Fair and have no idea what the people looked like. Future generations will want to see their ancestors, so....after reading this book go and label your photographs!

BELOW: J.P.Collins' Waltzer, seen at Oldham Wakes in June 1948. This machine travelled extensively with Pat Collins' fairs during the post-war years.
(Collection of Kevin Scrivens)

BELOW: Pictures like this, taken in the 1920's, may feature your grand-parents, but if found unlabelled leave us wondering who everybody was (In this case it has been suggested to us that the lady with the dog is Fanny Barnard). The machine is the ex-Gordon Bennett Motors.
(Collection of John Ward)

ABOVE: This group of men are thought to be standing on the ex-Tuby Scenic Motors (R30) at the Wembley Exhibition in 1924. (Gavioli 110 key organ in the background). From left to right the three men are - Albert Badger, Harry Weston Jnr, and Matey Weston. The uniformed men are money-takers.
(Collection of John Williams)

WHO'S WHO - PART TWO

It is impossible to list everyone who worked for or was associated with Pat. But as they say in newspaper reports and public notices..."Please forgive omissions". We give dates of death or birth wherever possible as this may aid further research.

Arranged in alphabetical order of SURNAME:

HARRY ALCOCK:
Ground Agent. Ex-Policeman who was ground agent/manager during the forties and fifties. Played a large part in collecting information for 1959 Biography of Pat Collins.

FRANKY ALLEN:
Born 1920. Ride manager, managed the Big Waltzer in the Post War era. Joined the Fair about 1936, working for Charlie Hayes. Wartime experience with heavy transport enabled him to collect the first Showtrac, and use it, along with Burrell "Number One" to move the Waltzer from Willenhall to Brierley Hill. Eventually left the firm to set up on his own - with a shooting gallery.

ALBERT BADGER
Worked for Matey Weston and later managed the dodgems.

CHRISTINE BAILEY:
Born 1914, a native of Walsall. Her weight at birth was 16.lb., and her weight was to be her destiny! Christine grew to a height of 6 feet, and weight of 29 stone. She entered show business at the age of 17, and travelled in America, before returning to Britain in 1934, to trave as the Giantess, Titania, with James Styles' Show, appearing at many of Pat Collins' fairs. She established her home in Pelsall, and one feature of her appearance at Black Country fairs was that there were always people in the audience who knew her.

GEORGE BAILEY:
Ground Manager. One time associated with the Welsh Border Run. Died 12.2.34 after thirty years with Pat Collins.

BILLY BAGNALL:
Born 1897. First appeared at the Crystal Palace about 1922 with a coconut shy, and travelled stalls and sheets in 1920's and 30's with Pat Collins. In 1948 he became Manager of the Amusement Park at Crystal Palace, and remained in that position until the closure in September 1962. He then "retired" to his own Amusement Park at Chasewater. He was a respected showman, and was President of the Showmen's Guild in 1961. Died 14.8.74.

HERBERT BARNARD:
Ground manager and presenter of a set of Swing Boats, built in 1892, which travelled forty five years and looked "as good as new". A good example of a showman working for Pat, and in his own right. Herbert Barnard owned ground such as that at Lickey Hills, on which Pat's fair stood.

ARTHUR BARNARD:
Son of Herbert Barnard, born 23.5.02. Went to Young Pat's Amusement Park in Colwyn Bay with an arcade, before the War, and eventually bought the entire park from Young Pat.

LIONEL BARNETT:
Ground agent/site manager. Started work for Pat Collins in 1920 and worked his way up, becoming the last of the old ground managers, still working in the mid sixties

C.C.BARTRAM:
A well known showman, born in the USA on 13.7.1873. He managed the Barry Island site for several years before the Second World War, and died 24.6.40.

MARY ANN BEVAN:
"The Ugliest Woman on Earth", born Plaistow 20.12.1874. Became progressively uglier after her husband's death in 1914, and took to travelling as a "freak show" for various showmen, and did several tours of the USA for Barnum & Bailey. Was occasionally presented at the Onion Fair.

LOTTIE BIRD:
1873-1943. Manager of Pat Collins' "Three Abreast" gallopers, after her husband's death. Pat paid for Mrs Bird's son, Arthur, to go to Boarding School. Arthur later worked with his mother and drove the engine "Wait and See". After Arthur's marriage, in 1933, to Nellie, the couple ran shooting galleries as Pat's tenants.

JAMES BOYS:
Proprietor of the New Mills, at the Pleck, Walsall. Friend and political supporter of Pat Collins. When Pat had to move the Walsall Fair from Midland Road, James Boyes was able to make space available at New Mills at Easter 1917. Mr Boyes was also instrumental in chauffering voters to the polls when Pat stood for Parliament.

ELSIE MAY BRADBURY and LILY BRADBURY:
Elsie started to work for Flora Collins as a maid in Flora's living van, "The Victory" when she was eight and left when she was 21 when Flora died in 1933. Elsie and Lily's Mother, CAROLINE BRADBURY, did the laundry for Limetree House. Lily worked for Pat and Clara as a cleaner and later travelled with them. She then went to work for John and Claire Collins at "Four Winds", Sutton Coldfield, and looked after their four children. When John and Claire travelled in "The Victory", Lily travelled in "Twixt Major" and prepared their meals.

ABOVE: Herbert Barnard and his wife Esther by the wheel of the family's Foster, also named "Esther" (11416, purchased in 1924). Arthur is at the wheel, and Fanny Barnard (who married Willie Weston) is next to her mother.
(Collection of Ann Andrews)

RIGHT: A picture taken on 6 October 1956 at the Goose Fair. Clara Collins in her living van. In the foreground (left to right): Harry Alcock, Bob Neal, and Jim Morley holding the cup presented to him to mark fifty years service with Pat Collins.
(Collection of Peter Hough)

RIGHT: Ted Sherwood, Clara's foreman, who managed the No.1.Scenic after her marriage, and then the Dodgems, is on the left, and Tommy Draper is believed to be the centre figure; unknown figure on the right. They are sitting on the steps of the Big Ark, converted to an Autodrome.
(Collection of Peter Hough)

TOM BEW:
"Cockney Brew"...recorded as manager of the Lion Show - 1927.

HARRY BROWN:
Steersman on the engines and general handyman at Bloxwich Yard. His wife, was housekeeper after the death of Esther Davies (Hetty).

JOE CADDICK:
Born 1847, died 1.1.26. Travelled a Photographic Booth/Studio at the end of last century and beginning of this one. In 1889/1890, he used his literary skills to promote the cause of the Showmen's Guild. Joe was said to have been the purchaser of the first showman's wagon built by Orton & Spooner. His son, JOE Junior, ran a sidestall, "Gee Whizz" on Pat's fairs during the 1920's.

ALF CARTWRIGHT:
Had the catering concession at Collins' fairs for many years, a concession inherited from his father. Also ran a cafe in Wednesbury

DANNY CARTWRIGHT:
Born and bred in Bloxwich, and represented the area on Walsall Council for 43 years. Left school at 10 to become a baker's assistant. Had a very varied career, from confectionery work to mining; became Pat Collins' Manager at the Crystal Palace in 1935 and Mayor of Walsall in May 1957. Died 6 June 1963, aged 77. Great ally and companion of Pat on the Council, though not of the same political persuasion; more radical and very much more vocal in local politics.

SID CARVER:
Ride manager, managed the Airways.

MARGARET CHADWICK:
nee Farrell: A grandaughter of Joanna Collins, who married Joe Chadwick. Joe died young and Margaret continued to travel sidestalls and juvenile rides with the No.1.Pat Collins fairs. Margaret had two children: Joe and Eileen. Eileen married Johnny Cook.

CAPTAIN CLARK:
One of the lion-tamers associated with the Collins' Lion Show, said to have left the business to run a newsagents shop in Leamore.

JOHNNY COOK:
1917-1974. Married Eileen Chadwick in 1946, and for several years they travelled in the Lancashire Section, then returned to the Midlands where he took over as driver of No.1.Showtrac, and managed the Waltzer, until it was withdrawn to Barry Island.

GEORGE CORBETT Snr & Jnr:
George Corbett Snr worked for Pat Collins for fifty years. Worked on Mrs Bird's Three Abreast and later managed them. His son was born 1918 and worked on the fair from 1932/33 onwards. After the War he helped bring the No.1.scenic out of store and build it up at the Crystal Palace.

JOHN and ROSINA CORDWELL:
Travelled as tenants of Pat, from early this century onwards. John Cordwell died 30 June 1943.

JACK COUPLAND:
Engine driver, sometime driver of the "Dreadnought".

BILLY CROSS:
Engine driver, remembered as being rather short - and had to stand on a box to drive the engine.

BILL CROYDON:
A popular and respected ground manager with Pat Collins' fairs for a number of years. Often hosted the Sacred Music Concerts. Died 26.1.47. One of his sons, Clifford Croydon, managed John's small Waltzer after the War.

HARRY CULLIS:
Born 14.6.1856. Veteran showman who presented a show of gymnastics or boxing booth on Pat's fairs from the 1900's onwards.

ESTHER DAVIES:
"Hetty" - adopted into the Limetree household where she eventually became housekeeper.

RICHARD DEEKS:
1863 - 1933. A well known showman who travelled extensively, but frequently as a tenant of Pat Collins

RICHARD HENRY DELANEY:
known as "Joe". Born 21.12.1866. Mentioned as early as 1892, when presenting a shooting gallery at the Walsall September fair described in Chapter 2. Joined Pat's firm early this century, completing forty years' service. Just before the First World War he was managing the Yachts, and after the War he was made manager of the Crystal Palace site, Sutton Park in the period when the park was reconstructed, 1919 onwards. He died at the Crystal Palace on 27.12.34. Mrs. Minnie Delaney stayed at Sutton until 1940. She died in 1956.

GILBERT DIXON:
A ground manager for Pat Collins during the 1930's was the son of Bob Dixon who had been one of the founder members of the Showmen's Guild.

GEORGE DUDSON:
Pat's electrician, based at Bloxwich Yard.

WILLIAM DUTTON:
Manager of several rides including the Ghost Train, pre-War. Flora's nephew.

FLORA and EDITH EASTWOOD:
Maids/Secretaries to Pat Collins. Daughters of Bill Eastwood, a showman. When Pat heard that Bill's wife was expecting another child in 1915 he said he would give Mrs Eastwood £5 and a basket of newly laundered baby clothes if it was a girl, and she was called Flora, after his wife. Flora's older sisters, Edith

TOP LEFT: Joby Farrell sits with Baby Pat on one of the cars on the Scenic Railway that he managed for Pat for many years. (The Farrells family were adopted by Pat when their mother died in 1906). When the Scenic was scrapped Joby managed other "vintage" machines for Pat until he acquired his own Chair-o-planes.
(Collection of Sally Muldowney)

TOP RIGHT: Richard Kayes, proprietor of Kayes' Circus, that travelled with Pat's fair in the 1930's and Albert Williams, "Maccomo", the lion tamer.
(Collection of Norah Collins)

BOTTOM LEFT: R.H."Joe" Delaney, who joined Pat in the early 1890's and became manager of the Crystal Palace Amusement Park after the First World War, and presented his own shooting gallery.
(Collection of Brian Ball)

and Elizabeth were both "in service" for Pat Collins, and in her late teens, Flora worked for Pat for about five years, as a maid in "The White Lady" living van. Pat was seldom there and Flora's job was simply to be there, and to give and take messages to folk who came to the van.

BILL EDGINTON:
Engine driver.

JOBY FARRELL:
Son of Charles Farrell and Sarah Ann Davies; ancestry linking Farrell, Davies and Collinses. Joby managed a scenic Dragons & Peacocks, for Pat for about 30 years, before fulfilling his own ambition to own his own ride. He purchased a set of Chairoplanes, which he presented as a tenant at Pat's fair until his death. Joby married Margaret Murphy and had three children: Sally, Charlie and Joby. Charlie travelled a big wheel al over the country which is still travelled today by JOHN CRICK.

JOE FLETCHER:
Travelled an "Automatics" Saloon with Pat between the Wars. His son, JIMMY, married ESTELLE COLLINS daughter of James Patrick, and they established a permanent arcade at the Lickey Hills.

HARRY & CHARLOTTE FOSSETT:
Regular sidestall tenants of Pat Collins.

JIM GARDNER:
The showman associated with presenting Billy the Pig, and Wee Jimmy, the world's smallest racehorse, at Pat's fairs in the 1930's.

NORMAN GOODWIN:
Ground agent/site manager, had also managed lion show.

JOHN GWINETT:
Born 1913, started work in the yard at Bloxwich about 1926 and later drove lorries for the ride managers.

JAMES HALL, JOHN HALL:
James Hall was a lifelong tenant of Pat Collins, with a coconut shy. His son, John, born 1903, first joined Pat about 1928 - as a tenant at Chester Races, with rifle range. He later joined what he called "Young Pat's Run", visiting places like Matlock, Buxton, Hay Mills and some Warwickshire towns.

DICK HARRIS:
Ride manager. Managed the steam yachts in the mid 20's and the Swish (1928).

ELIAS HARRIS Snr:
Died March 1934 while travelling a sidestall with Pat Collins fair. Married to Amelia Harris; sons: Moe, Elias Jnr, Walter, and Tom; daughter - Millie.

ELIAS HARRIS:
Born 5.3.05. Died 25.9.81. Married Margaret Collins, Pat's granddaughter.

Later, after Margaret's death, Elias travelled in Southern England and married Evelyn Baker. Their son, Anthony Harris is now the proprietor of Pat Collins' Fair.

GERTIE HARRISON:
Secretary in the Bloxwich office, had worked for Pat Collins from about 1919 to the mid sixties.

JACK HARVEY Snr:
"Cockney Jack". 1900 - 1955. Engine driver, particularly associated with driving Burrell "Number One".

JACK HARVEY JNR:
Son of Cockney Jack. Born 1922. As soon as he left school, went to Limetree House to ask for a job on the fair, and eventually became Ted Sherwood's foreman on the Dodgems. When he came back to the fair after the War he became Manager of the Dodgems, and did not retire until 1985. After moving the Dodgems it was Jack's job to go back with the Showtrac to move Clara's van, and Young Jack had been the last man to drive Burrell "Number One" on a journey from Wolverhampton to Chester, because his father was ill at the time. Married Clara McGill

JACK HAYES:
One time a ride manager, but later known as a carpenter at the Bloxwich Yard. His father, also Jack Hayes, ("Deaf'un"), had been a Dudley-based showman before Pat established himself in the Black Country.

BILLY "WATTIE" HAYES:
Ride Manager, managed the Speedway Ark.

CHARLIE HAYES:
Wattie's son, managed the Brooklyn Track before the War, and helped dismantle it to make the Black-Out fair! Managed the new "Odeon" fronted Waltzer, just after the Second World War, until it was taken over by Frank Allen.

CHARLIE HICKMAN:
His Boxing Booth was a frequent feature of Pat Collins' fairs during the 1930's. Charlie Hickman was born 3 December 1910, and was named after his father. Charlie died on 14 September 1938, when his son, also Charlie, was only two years old. His widow, Lydia Hickman, carried on the business for a number of years.

ALFRED HITCHCOCK:
Must have appeared somewhere.

WALTER HOBBS Snr:
Died 7.1.1935. Manager of the Steam Yachts in mid 1900's, and over the years managed a variety of rides for Pat Collins. It appears that Walter was married to one of Flora Collins' sisters, Annie.

RIGHT: The only person identified in this picture is Billy "Lump Coal" Reohorn, standing on the extreme right, dressed very much as an engine driver was expected to dress. They are standing in front of what is thought to be an early "Looping-the-Loop" ride.
(Collection of the late George Reohorn)

RIGHT: Frank Allen photographed by the No.1. Showtrac.
(Collection of Frank Allen)

RIGHT: On 3 November 1975 Joe Proverbs celebrated 52 years' service with the Pat Collins' firm, having started in 1923 when he left school. For years he and Gertie Harrison ran the office, Joe dealing with the tenants' bookings, publicity and general administration. Joe is in the centre of the picture to the left of Anthony Harris.

WALTER HOBBS Jnr:
A pre-War manager of the Dodgems, and post-War manager of the Three Abreast gallopers at Crystal Palace until his death in 1947. Married Amelia Jones. He had worked for the firm since Bioscope Days, it was said that he started on the No.2.Wonderland.

BERT HUGHES:
Presenter of one of the Boxing Booths that appeared at Pat Collins' fairs before the War.

BILL IRELAND:
One of Pat Collins' engineering staff, if not, at some stage, Pat's "Chief Engineer" or foreman.

TOM JERRISON:
An early manager of the steam yachts.

FANNY JONES:
Housekeeper at Limetree House.

KARO:
A dwarf who travelled with James Styles' Freak Show, along with Titania, the Giantess (see Christine Bailey, above).

THE KAYES FAMILY:
RICHARD Kayes, a son of the famous Buffalo BILL Kayes, ran a Circus that travelled with some of Pat's fairs during the 1930's and 1940's. His daughter, NORAH, married BABY JOHN COLLINS, son of YOUNG PAT. One of her brothers, TIMMY Kayes, looked after a shooting gallery at The Crystal Palace until the ground closed. He died 8.9.1966.

PAT KILBRIDE:
Presented shows such as "Secrets of Life in the Chinese Underworld".1936.

LITTLE TITCH:
Real name, BOB JONES, toured with Pat Collins' Fair during the first decade of this century, as a "show".

CAPTAIN GEORGE LAURENCE:
Born 1873. Joined Lord GEORGE SANGER as an "elephant boy" when he was 16, and three years later joined Pat at New Brighton as a lion tamer, travelled with TOM BEW, and was badly mauled at Willenhall in 1896.

JIM LEWIS:
Engine Driver. Started work in the fairground with Leiskies Big Wheel in 1906. Became FLORA COLLINS' Stepman on the Wonderland Show and ERNEST LONG'S assistant, (Long being the driver of Collins' "Leader"). Jim learnt to be a driver and drove for Collins' and many other major showmen, retiring in 1946. He also, at one time, produced a weekly column in "World's Fair", and later was a well-known figure at steam rallies.

PADDY McGILL:
A tenant with his own sidestalls on Pat's fairs in the 1930's, but who took responsibility for clearing up the sites as the fair left. His daughter, CLARA, married JACK HARVEY. Paddy's wife, also CLARA, was the daughter of Bill Mullett, Clara Mullett's brother.

BILLY MILLS: Snr.
Engine driver. Came originally from Leeds. Drove the "Emperor" and "Lord James". One of his best recorded runs was from Russell Square, London, to Tipton, a journey of just over 120 miles, in fourteen hours, pulling one of the scenic rides. The journey must have included at least six coal and water stops. After working for Pat Collins for several years he transferred to Brother John Collins, then another showman, until returning to Pat. Billy was one of the drivers who survived into the final period of engine use in the Post-War period, and, as senior driver, drove "The Leader" until its withdrawal. He lived into his nineties, and during his retirement he continued to motor-cycle over to the Griffin Foundry to "tinker" with the engines as they began their life in preservation.

BILLY MILLS Jnr:
"Young" Billy, born 1916. Started work for Pat Collins on the No.1.Scenic (Clara Mullett) and later worked on the Joby Farrell scenic, Johnny Ryan's Dodgems, and Matey Weston's Small Ark until he joined Frank Sherwood on the first Waltzer. Married Nora Chadwick, and after the War they travelled their own sidestuff on the No.1.circuit.

HARRY MILLS:
Born 1920, brother of Young Billy Mills. Joined the fair as a panatrope boy, worked on various rides. After the War, he was Clara's driver for about nine years.

JOEY MITCHELL:
Engine driver. Drove "Samson" at some stage.

JIM MORLEY:
Engine driver. Born 1883. Died Feb,1971. Joined Pat Collins in 1906 and retired when 78. In 1956 he received a cup to mark 50 years with the Pat Collins firm, and claimed to be the only driver to receive a pension from the firm.

WILLIAM MULLETT:
Clara's brother. Married 15/5/1897. Managed rides for Pat Collins, until settling at Barry Island.

BOB NEAL:
Engine driver. Bob was the son of Israel Neal, a showman who travelled his own set of Gallopers, a set of swings and several stalls. Bob drove Burrell 1999 "Victoria" for his father, and when this engine was sold to Pat Collins in 1915, Bob came with the engine and thus began his long career as one of Pat's drivers. "Victoria" was sold again in 1923, and Bob worked on Pat's other engines.

ABOVE: Gertie Harrison, who joined the firm in 1922, worked for fifty years in the office at Bloxwich until she retired at the age of 72.

ABOVE: Joe Delaney on the steps of his living wagon. *(Collection of Brian Bull)*

BELOW: Managers and Men - pose on the Orton & Spooner "Jungle Scenic Motors" of 1911. A number of such photographs exist but it is now almost impossible to identify the people we can see, although there are several distinct styles of dress - possibly reflecting their status. On the extreme left is Joe Delaney in cloth cap. The gentleman second from the left in bowler hat, appears in other photographs and may have been a Ground Manager. Two of the men on the right wear the caps favoured by engine drivers. The cars on this ride were replaced with Dragons during the First World War. The ride opened in Wolverhampton in 1911 and the "Car" on the left bears a "DA" (Wolverhampton) number plate! *(Collection of Brian Bull)*.

- 249 -

TOM NORMAN:
Well known travelling showman and "auctioneer" of showmen's tackle. Known as "The Silver King". He died 24.8.1930, aged 70 but his son, also named Tom, revived the show, and frequently travelled with Pat during the 1930's and 1940's. His "Palladium Show" and organ, became a popular feature of the Onion Fair.

JACK PARRY:
A showman who had presented shows at Pat Collins' fairs for many years, including "Big Chief Red Snake" (Rex Ward), and various reptile shows. Settled in Walsall during World War Two, and became an ambulance driver.

HARRY PASSEY:
B.26.12.01 - D.17.12.57. Ride manager. Looked after the Dragon Scenic when it finally came to rest at Crystal Palace after the War. Married Lily Peplow (1930), sister of John Peplow - one of the men who worked for him.

MAURICE PENDLE:
Engine driver.

A.H.PROVERBS:
1891 - 1936: worked for Pat Collins for 27 years as Pat's Booking Manager for the cinemas and theatres as well as the fairground.

J.J.PROVERBS:
Musical Director at the Cinema-de-Luxe in Chester, when it opened in 1920. Moved to the Grosvenor, Oakengates, when that cinema opened in 1922

JOE PROVERBS:
1909 - 1980. Started work for Pat Collins in 1923. Eventually was in charge of the office at Bloxwich, and was Pat's secretary and chief administrator. Joe also took responsibility for the firm's publicity. His role became particularly important after the Second World War, when the fairs were directly under the control of the office. Joe was going to retire in 1974, after 52 years' service, but in fact stayed for a few years to help the office re-establish itself in the High Street, after the last of the land and property at the Pinfold was sold.

JOHN PURCHASE:
Replaced Tom Bew as manager of the Lion Show in 1927, thought to be connected with Purchase's Menagerie.

DOT RAYNER:
Presented a Flea Circus which often travelled with Pat Collins' fair before the War.

WILLIAM REOHORN:
"Lump Coal Billy": Engine driver, died 1945. First worked for Jacob Studt in the 1890's, and, at the beginnning of this century was a driver for Baker's of Southampton. Then drove for Captain Walter Payne's Bioscope Show until about 1909, when he came to the Midlands and joined Pat Collins as driver of "Flora" with the No.2.Wonderland Show. In 1913 the new Foster, "Clara", was purchased by Pat Collins and this became Billy's favourite engine. "Clara" attended the motorcar scenic, and when this ride was passed to M.A.Collins about 1922, Billy went with it. He returned to Pat Collins about 1930 to drive "Goliath".

ARTHUR ROWBOTTOM:
Accountant, Company Secretary and Office Manager in the post war period.

GEORGE ROBERTS:
Engine driver and sometimes ride manager, eg. managed Over the Falls in 1927.

ALBERT ROGERS:
Born 1913. In his teens started work with the family sidestall - Wright & Roger's Shooting Gallery - which travelled with Pat Collins' fairs for over half a century. Some parts of the stall dated back to the 1870's and were still in use, in their original form into the 1980's.

BILLY RUSSELL:
famous Black Country comedian and variety artist. Billy's father was a scenery painter at the Tivoli, New Brighton, when he met Pat Collins, and then became a fairground painter. Young Billy worked for Pat occasionally until his stage career "took off".

JOHNNY RYAN:
1893 - 1977. Came from Sheffield, and had worked for Farrar's before joining Pat Collins as an engine driver on "Dreadnought", with the Joby Farrell scenic. Became manager of an early Dodgem (with Lusse cars), and fetched the first Supercar Dodgem from Coventry about 1938. His sons, Johnny and Jimmy both entered the business.

F.T.SALVA:
Manager and Booking agent for Pat Collins, and for joint ventures by Pat and brother John, around the turn of the century.

WILLIAM SAVAGE:
B.11.12.1857 - D.24.4.1934. His father was related to Frederick Savage, of the Kings Lynn firm, and William joined the firm and became Chief Clerk. Relinquished his post to become secretary to Pat Collins at Walsall. Took part in Walsall's Liberal politics. Followed Rev.Horne as Secretary of the Showmen's Guild in July 1918, and in 1926 moved to London.

TED SHERWOOD:
"Dublin", Ride Manager, for years was Clara's foreman on the Whales and later managed the Dodgems. Ted's wife was one of Clara Mullett's sisters. Ted's sons, Frank and Billy, were also ride managers.

DENNIS SHIPLEY:
Pre-war manager of one of the Dodgems.

GEORGE STRICKLAND:
Sometime manager of the Crystal Palace Site, Sutton Park, and earlier a ride manager, as was his brother Shadrack, sons of Harry and Sadie Strickland.

DICK STUDT:
Engine driver.

JAMES R. STYLES:
Well known showman, presented a number of shows on Pat Collins fairs such as Titania, the Beautiful Giantess; Colourado, the negro turning white; Shadola, the human skeleton; Karo, the Eskimo midget; etc. A prolific writer and fairground publicist, and propagandist on behalf of the Guild.

GEORGE HENRY SUTTON;
"Tarzan". 1904 - 1976. A ride manager for Walsall John. Tarzan had first worked on Pat Collins's fairs as a lad, working on Walter Harris's coconut shy, but graduated to working for Pat until directed to War work during World War Two. Clara obtained his release papers and he worked on the Black-Out Fair after Pat's death. Eventually managed a small ark, rebuilt as a waltzer for John Collins. Tarzan had the same fierce loyalty to John that the previous generation had for Pat. He had skills in patching up rides and keeping them going that were appreciated in the Post-war era, and also drove one of the Showtracs.

GEORGE SUTTON Jnr:
"Young Tarzan", son, George, born in 1932. Started work on the fair as a "panatrope boy" in his mid teens, eventually becoming foreman on the Dodgems, managed by Walter Hobbs in the 1940's. Young Tarzan was taught about electrics and machines by Johnny and Jimmy Ryan, and he together with Albert Martin had the sad task of burning the remains of the Dragon Scenic at Sutton Park.

TOM TAYLOR:
Manager of one of the sets of Yachts, 1920's.

HARRY SWAIN:
Manager of the Cakewalk, mid twenties, and several other rides into the thirties.

CHARLES SWANN:
1871-1935. Was a tenant of Pat Collins for many years, and all his four children married into other families associated with Pat's fairs - the Weston's, Sherwood's, Deeks etc.

WILLIAM THOMAS:
Engine driver: Drove "Her Majesty" late 1920's/early 1930's. His brother, Fred Thomas, sometimes worked as Steersman and travelled as a general worker 1927, and spasmodically thereafter. He also built wooden model replicas of the engines and sold them to the managers and some of the Collinses.

JACK TODD:
Early Wall of death rider whose show was adopted as part of Pat's fairs late 1929.

PAT TYLER:
Ground manager, associated with pre-war Black Country Run. Left the fair at the outbreak of war, and is believed to have gone to work at Rubery Owen, Darlaston.

HARRY "MATEY" WESTON:
Ride manager - managed the Ark for Pat Collins for years. Had started work for Pat Collins about 1905. Before the arrival of the Ark, he had managed the Swish. Harry's wife was Rosa, and they had seven children, Harry,Jnr., Rose, Willie, Ivy, Albert, Alfie, and Flora.

HARRY WESTON Jnr:
1898 - 1985. A son of Matey Weston, manager of the Three Abreast from mid-twenties onwards. Married Lottie Swann.

WILLIE WESTON:
also known as Billy, another son of Matey Weston, manager of the other Ark. B.11.3.01. Married Fanny Barnard daughter of Herbert Barnard, on 27.4.26; had a talent for fairground painting.

THE WESTWOOD CHILDREN:
Travelled as a show with Pat Collins Fairs in 1908. The family had come to Britain from New Zealand, and two of the children were 'giants'.

JACK WHYATT:
Manager of the No.1.Motors before the First World War, and manager of the No.2. just after, later established as a showman travelling his own equipment in Lancashire.

WORLD'S FAIR CORRESPONDENTS:
Many of the reports of Pat's activities which appeared in World's Fair are anonymous, or the authors use initials such as "P.A.T", and "J.B.T". Often their comments suggest that they were interesting figures in their own right, with a wealth of knowledge that has now been lost. We have quoted extensively from JBT's "Black Country Bits" and from the work of CHARLES. H. LEA, a freelance journalist who died 23 May 1940. Another admirer of Pat Collins was HARRY WILDING. He was only four years older than Pat, and had a first hand view of Pat's progress, which he frequently suggested should be the subject of a book.

HORACE YATES:
Horace "Kiss me Daddy" Yates: driver of "The Darkie" - one of the powerful lorries used after the Second World War.

ABOVE: Billy Mills (engine driver) sits (third from left, top row) among the men photographed on the steps of "Molly's Ark", managed by Matey Weston. The men include "Snakey" Jock, and Tarzan (George Sutton). Late 1930.

Collection of Harry Mills)

BELOW: We have failed to identify people, or satisfactorily date this picture, but photographs of "Over the Falls" seem rare. This view of the pay box and steps does show the tubular scaffolding-like structure and painted canvas frontage.

(Collection of Harry Mills)

- 252 -

PERSONAL TESTIMONIES

APPENDIX 2

JOE ASHMORE

In an interview in November 1989, Joe Ashmore, who was born in 1902, talked about his life, and the time he began to work for Pat Collins... in 1918:

I've always had the ability to make money. As a child of eight I went to freshly ploughed fields to collect worms and sold them to a fishing shop at ...... a bucket. In my forties I was a millionaire. Yet I feel I owed it all to Pat Collins, and what he was able to teach me. He was a brilliant man.

My father was a friend of Pat Collins because my father ran a carting and transport business in the days of horse traffic. He bought and sold horses and the trailers and drays and carts, and one Sunday in 1918 Pat Collins came in to see him. Pat looked at me and said to my father:

"What does that lad do?"
"He shows pictures and drives cars"
"Well, why isn't he working for me?" replied Pat. "I've got fourteen cinemas and theatres, and I could make a man of him!" Then he turned to me and continued "Give your notice in, and report to me at the Gondola Works in Walsall on Monday morning at half past nine"

When I first arrived at the Gondola Works, Pat Collins was not there. My father had sent me over to Walsall in a pony and trap – with my suitcase with all my clothes in. I found two men in the yard removing a wheel from a traction engine. They were working the wheel off and it was wobbling so I put my hand up to steady it just as Pat Collins arrived.

"Come away you bloody young fool - that wheel could kill you", were the first words he spoke to me. I thought to myself that I had made a mistake in going there – I had never been spoken to like that before – ever! Then he politely asked how my Mother and Father were, and took me into the office to have a cup of tea while he made a couple of phone calls on an old wind-up telephone. Then he took me along to the Carpenter's Shop, where they were working on the organs. He showed me a Gavioli he had bought out of Belgium before the War, and they were rebuilding it. All the trumpets and whistles were highly polished, and he gave me the job of lacquering them, using a little saucer of lacquer and a piece of wadding. The other man was working on the mechanism that produced the music from the rolls, but I wasn't allowed to see how that was done!

Later Pat returned and announced that we were going up to Bloxwich. Petrol was rationed at the time but Pat had three cars - a Humber, a Sunbeam, and a Garratt. We drove up to Bloxwich, to Limetree House, and I was introduced to Fanny Jones, the Housekeeper. Pat said, "Find Joe a room, and treat him as if he were one of our own lads – he is the son of a great friend of mine". He washed his hands in a basin on the landing and told me to do the same and then he took me down to lunch – a lovely meal with a glass of beer with it, followed by a drop of sherry or brandy. I was also given a cigar. After all this, Pat said, "Now I will take you to where I want you to show the pictures".

As we walked from Limetree House, past the Pub and the shop, to the Electric Palace, my expectations were based on my experience at Smethwick Empire, so I imagined that Pat's cinema in Bloxwich would be as grand. As we walked through the entrance I realised it was nothing more than a tin shed. Once again I thought I had made a great mistake in coming to work for Pat Collins, but the cinema did have one great attraction – a big old gas engine to generate the electricity!

I was soon introduced to other parts of Pat's empire. We returned to Limetree House and jumped into the Garratt to go to Walford Road. Of course we had to wind it up to start it, and the car had no electrics – just two paraffin sidelights and carbon headlamps. On the journey I displayed my knowledge of cars by saying "Mr. Collins, you are slipping the clutch. You'll burn the cluth out". His response was, "OK, you drive the bloody thing!".

Thus we arrived at the Walford Road Skating Rink,

which Pat owned, and where he also showed pictures and put on boxing shows. We waited there for the Manager to give us the takings. We chucked the money under the back seat of the car – just the silver – the coppers were left for the managers. One of the managers, a Mrs. Strickland, gave me a cup of tea and a cake, and as we talked I realised they were nice people to be with.

When we set off in the car Pat opened the glove pocket and took out a knuckle duster and said, "Put that on those bloody great fists of yours. If we get stopped, let them have the money, but if you have to protect yourself, you're big enough to do so". Fortunately, my father had taught us how to protect ourselves as lads. At Limetree House we chucked the money under a big settee – to be taken back to the yard next morning to be banked. Strangely enough, the Collins' always seemed to be short of cash, although he had built up so many assets.

In the evening, we returned to the Electric Palace. In those days the films were very inflammable and Pat had a crafty way of approaching the projection room very quietly so that he could open the door quickly and find out what was going on inside. I followed him in and we found the operator puffing away. Actually this operator claimed he couldn't care less about Pat Collins because he had a good job as an electrician at the pit, which kept him out of the Army, but he went to pieces when he saw the gaffer. The fire blankets which were supposed to be wet, were as dry as cork, and the two fire buckets of sand were full of fag ends. I was instructed to take control of the machines immediately. I cant remember whether they were old Ernimanns or Gaumonts, but whatever they were, you could hear them a mile away!

I ran the show until the end and then reported to Pat in the 24 stone Manager's office (Mr Leach was his name). I knew Pat had cinemas in Darlaston, one in Warwick, several in the Potteries, and in the old tin shed at Dudley Port, perhaps all over the place. I also knew the state of this one in Bloxwich was a disgrace. I said, "Mr Collins, you'll have to spend some money. You'll have to get a new screen, or send for Malins in West Bromwich. They can drop the screen, open it out flat, put glue all over it, and throw silver sand over it, to make a first class screen". Pat told the Manager to get that organised.

The Theatre was a proper showman's outfit – there were wires hanging out everywhere, so I completely re-wired the place, cleaned the arc lamps and white washed the reflectors till I got a good clear picture. I felt very enthusiastic about it, and there was something exciting about working for Pat Collins – I could still be his slave today! I admired his ability to make quick decisions, often in a very far-sighted way.

My room in Limetree House was a little bedroom over the back kitchen, and Fanny Jones looked after me like a mother. Sometimes, I would get to bed about half past twelve, and then the phone would ring. It would be the "Young Guvnor", Pat's son, Patrick, who ran the Wallasey Pleasure Beach, and sat on Liverpool Council. He would be coming to Wolverhampton Station, and I had to take the Sunbeam over to pick him up. Pat's other son, John, lived with Clara Mullet. John was a bachelor, but Young Patrick had children – the boys were sent to Ratcliffe College, Leicester, to be brought up as gentlemen, and there were two daughters, but they were only youngsters at the time.

While working as an operator at Bloxwich, I was still earning money installing bells in shops. In fact, I reckon I did nearly all the wiring in Bloxwich. I still bought motor bikes and did them up. The dearest one cost me Fifteen pounds from a pawnshop. I worked on them in the old stables that the ragman let me use at the back of the Pub. When petrol came off rationing my father sold that machine for me for Ninety pounds. But the errands that I undertook for Pat made him value me as a driver, and he asked me to train an assistant to take over the operating. Eventually, he said, "You know my ways by now, I want you to drive me about".

As a result of this, I found myself visiting the fairgrounds, and I learnt to be a surveyor. I could check the ground, and knock the pegs in, and, using the tape, mark it all out. At night I would sometimes help by taking half the paybox, or if they were short of a taker, I could ride round on the cars and do that job. Sometimes I would sit on a traction engine and talk to the drivers. A driver might say, "I'm going to have a pint - so keep your eye on the water gauge". They would show me how to put on the injectors, and the water pumps, and how to fire the engine. After the pull-down I was allowed to steer the engines for the drivers, and while doing that I learnt to drive them.

At Sandbach Police Court, I was fined thirty shillings on September 28th, 1920, for driving at a speed in excess of five miles per hour, and my licence was endorsed for three years! But my real initiation as a driver came later. I was sent up to Mrs Collins' Lion Show at Stockport. After the pulling down, Jim Morley had taken the rail-born loads to the station but as he was a long time coming back, Pat sent me to look for him and the engine. I found him outside the pub and in no fit state to drive. Pat told me to drive the engine, a Burrell I think, back to the fairground. The loads were coupled up and I was appointed a fully fledged driver. Another driver came over to warn me about a steep gradient at Congleton, and then I was off!

On the steep grade a valve let me down, and I had to stop and ring the Yard Foreman for instructions. I was told to damp the fire down, draw the firebox, get the fire bars out, take the face off, without damaging the gasket, take the rod out and take it to a Blacksmith for straightening. I stayed in Congleton overnight and reassembled the engine the next morning. When I reached Cannock, I met a couple of regular drivers who had been sent out to meet me to take over the engine. But after all my troubles I was not going to let them do so. Having brought the engine so far I was determined to drive it right into the Wakes Ground at Bloxwich. This I triumphantly did... and everyone on the fairground cheered. My suit and shirt were covered in oil, but I felt the wonder of being a full-blown engine driver.

Working for Pat Collins gave me experience of many other things. For example, I went to sales and bid for things on his behalf. After the First World War there were sales at Castle Bromwich, on a site that had once been an aerodrome. They were selling some lorries, and we bought an AEC Mobile Army Workshop for £300. It had an Austin generating set in the back for driving its machines. We went to a big sale at Avonmouth Docks where traction engines and steam wagons were being sold, including some brand new McLarens. We bought five engines on that occasion, and, as usual they were all knocked down to me and I paid for them with Pat's cheque. Buying and working with this equipment taught me a lot.

An entirely different kind of experience came via the Boxing Booth. As another source of income I would sometimes act as a stooge to fight the boxers. I would walk past the booth and they would say, "Here's a lad from your home town who is going to fight Jim Slater". I would strip my shirt and braces and put the gloves on and fight three rounds with him, which would earn me a drink. Jim Slater had fought three championships and had a cauliflower ear. I had to be very careful not to bump it, but on one occasion I did catch it, and it really hurt him. He set about me, and I found myself fighting back. In fact, I put him on the floor, which totally surprised me, ...and everybody else.

Generally, I avoided the violence occasionally found on the fair. I did see the White Muffler Gang from Manchester invade the fair on one occasion, and sometimes there were fights if punters had had too much to drink. Of course, Pat could fight, and young Walsall John... he was dynamite... he could knock them down like ninepins. Boxing was an interest of Pat's, and he did have three "White Hopes" on the fair – Jim Slater of Hednesford, a Middleweight, Mark Longmore, of Walsall, a Lightweight, and John Bullsman (?) a college lad from Cambridge.

Events did come to pass that eventually led me to leave Pat Collins. A syndicate came to Walsall to consider buying all his theatres. The five gentlemen arrived on Sunday night, we took them to their hotel, and they met us at the Gondola Works the next day. I drove them from place to place. For example I took them to Darlaston where they went to the Council Offices to see if it would be possible to put a car park next to the Olympia Cinema. It took them all week to see everything, and on Saturday night a party was put on for them, after which Teddy Tompkins, the other driver and myself took them back to their hotel. When we arrived, one of the gentlemen said he was very pleased with the way they had been looked after, and gave me £30. Pat Collins said, "What's this for? I don't allow that. Give it back to them". I felt the money was well-earned and it broke my heart to give it back. Later that night Pat instructed me to take a Priest to Willenhall. "And don't accept anything!" he said. The Priest did give me a pound, and I accepted it.

The next morning, all this was still on my mind. Fanny Jones said "The Guvnor's waiting to see you". I thought of the new combination I had bought, and the fact that I had not been home for fourteen weeks. I found myself saying, "He can bloody well wait then – I'm finished!" So I packed my bags and rode home.

Pat Collins came round to my home on Tuesday night saying, "You've been with me long enough to know my ways. I want you to come and steam "The Leader" at Great Bridge fairground and take it back to the yard". I said, "Yes sir". I took "The Leader" to the yard, damped the fire down and handed it over to Bill Ireland, the Yard Foreman. I returned to Great Bridge by tram to retrieve my motorbike and went home again. I knew I had turned my back on the fair. I took a girl to the pictures that night, and by the next day my father was finding me jobs to do. My life then unfolded in other directions, and although I had turned my back on the fair, my path still crossed that of Pat Collins and I continued to respect his courage and his judgement. When he stood for Parliament, I sent three cars over to Walsall, and drove one myself, to take people to vote.

GEO REHORN

After talking to George Reohorn in February 1990, about his family and himself and about working for Pat Collins, the following notes were made:

My father was William Reohorn, known as Billy Reohorn, or often known as "Lump Coal Billy" because he was always able to get the best lumps of Welsh Steam Coal for his beloved engine, "The Clara". He drove this engine for Pat Collins. He was a marvellous driver, and as well as displaying great skill in driving and caring for his engine, he was skilled in using electrical gear, handling the wire rope that was used in erecting rides, and knew how to build the fair on the soft ground found on some "difficult" showgrounds.

His skill could partly be explained by his showman ancestry. His father, who ran a halfpenny rock stall in South Wales, was a cousin of Jacob Studt. The Studts had come from Bavaria, apparently coming to this country to evade military service. They established themselves as horse dealers in South Wales, and from there graduated into showmanship. My Dad was given his first job by Jacocb Studt and apparently could drive an engine when little more than a boy.

When he left South Wales Dad went to work for Bakers, in Southampton. There, about 1905, he met and married my Mother, Lily Rintell. She was a Lancashire lass from Horwich, who was a "parader" - one of the dancing girls who appeared on the stage in front of the Bioscope shows to attract the customers. I was born in 1906, by which time Dad was working for Captain Walter Payne, an American who had bought a Bioscope. Dad drove the engine that hauled the show from place to place and provided power for the organ and the projection equipment. It was the kind of Bioscope where the organ was placed in the centre of the stage, and the entrances were provided on either side. My parents lived in a caravan that travelled with the show, while Captain Payne stayed in hotels. However, my Mother stayed in Southampton when I was expected, and my Dad was in Reading when I was born.
About 1909, Dad came to the Midlands to work for Pat Collins as a driver on "The Flora", the engine used with Pat's No.2.Wonderland Show. His favourite engine, however, was to be "The Clara", supplied new to Pat Collins in 1913, by Fosters. (We have not been able to identify "Flora").

Meanwhile, my Mother had established a family home in Kings Hill, Wednesbury. Pat Collins wanted my Mother to join Dad on the fair to manage a ride, but she refused to give up a family home for the insecurity of life on the fair. Pat Collins was able to dismiss a manager at a moment's notice in some circumstances. My other Grandfather, my Mother's father, joined us in Wednesbury. He was a retired seaman who had been round the world several times and who could speak several languages. I always found his company interesting. Of course, Dad was often away. He travelled all over the place for Pat Collins - from the Onion Fair in Birmingham, to the Goose Fair at Nottingham, and even to Newcastle on Tyne. Although he could not read or write, you could show him a map of England and Wales and he could tell you the distance between any two towns!

At the age of twelve in 1918, I had the chance to see my Dad at work and learn about Pat Collins' Fair at first hand. I was given one month's holiday to travel with Dad. The trip began by catching the tram from Wednesbury to Dudley. The fair had been open on the side of the hill, but when we arrived we found the fair pulled down and the loaded trucks lined up ready to move off. Dad raised steam in "The Leader", because his beloved "Clara" had gone in for boiler repairs. We eventually set off but we broke down two or three times on the day's journey. We arrived at our destination in Hanley, in darkness. Showmen rarely travelled in darkness as the engines only had oil lights, and the other drivers 'took the mickey' out of Dad because "The Leader" had come in last.

I was sent for by Miss Clara Mullett, the manager of the ride. When I went into her caravan, I found Pat Collins also sitting there. They both put me through the third degree:

"How many times did you stop?"
"Two or three times"
"How many times did you stop at a Public House?"
"Once - to get something to eat."

And that was that. on the first day of the trip I had met "The Guvnor", as everybody called him, and encountered the kind of scrutiny with which he conducted his business. His control of the fairs was exercised through the managers of the rides, and the ground managers who set out the fairs and administered them. Pat Collins dealt only with the managers and drivers – the real "showmen". The others who worked on the fair were the "Flatties", often recruited from the Walsall area, but with whom Pat had relatively little contact.

After a week in Hanley, we set off for Oldham - to the Tommy Field, where the fair was erected on sets, on a slope, not on grass. This gave me an insight into my father's responsibilities. First of all he had to place "The Leader", then he had to supervise the building of a gantry on which the organ would be built. He had to go round with a spirit level to make sure it was all level. Then the organ had to be hauled into place with a wire rope. Four men were stationed at each wheel of the organ in case anything happened – and it did! The wire rope suddenly snapped. Fortunately, I had stood well back. If I had been in its way the rope would have cut me in two. The four men immediately pushed blocks behind the wheels, and another engine had to be summoned to complete hauling the organ into place.

Everywhere my Dad went he used the same lodgings year after year. In Oldham he lodged with my Irish Gran, my Mother's mother. While we were building The Whale, she came onto the Tober to tell us she had a lodger and could not put us up. One of the other lads said we could join them at their lodgings. The Landlady was an old woman who smoked a clay pipe and we had a hilarious week staying there because the lads would talk about her in her presence without her knowing what they were saying as they talked in back slang. While we were at Oldham, Miss Clara Mullett gave John Collins a pound and instructed him to take me to Belle Vue. We had a very full day out, saving just enough money to get us back to Oldham. John was Pat Collins' son, often known as "Walsall John", and we "knocked about" together. When the fair was open we rode all the rides – without having to pay, of course!

Our next week was spent at Ashton under Lyme. Between Oldham and Ashton there was one very steep gradient, and Dad had to take the trucks up one at a time. He drove and steered, and the crew of four men stood ready with the blocks. I walked up the footpath, praying that the huge steel driving wheels would not slip and cause my Dad to slip backwards, but we all reached the top satisfactorily.

In Ashton there was no problem with the lodgings. I remember getting up on the second morning we were there, the building-up was still in progress, but Dad had disappeared. The landlady said, "The Police came and collected him during the night". I walked down to the fairground to look for him. He eventually arrived but shrugged off the entire incident. Soneone had reported to the Police that he was a German spy! He suspected another driver – one with whom he was always at loggerheads. There was often great rivalry between drivers – particularly in the race to arrive first when moving from place to place.

At the end of that week we caught the train back home - my month's holiday had been a real education. When I left school the following year, I did not join the fair – instead I went to work at the Staffordshire Nut & Bolt Company in Darlaston Green.

My father had been so attached to "The Clara" and its ride – the Motor Car Scenic Railway and Gavioli Organ, that when the ride was transferred to Pat's brother John, about 1922, he had stayed with it. It then passed to John's son, Michael Albert Collins, but Dad still stayed with the "The Clara" up in Lancashire. He used to come home to Wednesbury every Saturday night by catching the Midnight mail train to Wolverhampton and walked the rest of the way! He had eventually returned to Pat Collins about 1930, and then drove "The Goliath" He was once offered a job driving a steam lorry for the Kings Hill firm of Samuel Platts, but he could not give up fairground life.

He was very particular about his engines, and he was always to be seen with a large piece of cotton waste in his hand, systematically wiping his charges down. He always wore a peaked cap, his "cheese-cutter", and dressed very smartly when the fair was open. He used to wax his moustache like "The Guvnor". At such times he was usually in charge of two engines, one to provide power for the organ and the ride, the other to provide power for the lights. He firmly believed that the diesel engine would never replace steam on the fair.

Dad was usually ready to help folks out, and if a stall holder had no power he would allow him to tap into his supply. He used to come home with boxes of French Nougat, and all sorts of wonderful things that had been given for such favours. Of course, tapping into the Guvnor's power supplies was very frowned upon but the sideshow stallholders often used to do it. Arriving at Oldbury one night, Pat was determined to find out how many sideshows were tapping into his power lines. He ordered a complete shutdown on the engines – and the entire fair was plunged into darkness, not a single sideshow was providing its own power! It was by checking such things that a showman could establish control of his fairs.

I remember that night John and I returned to the fair at Oldham. I went to the Paybox to thank Miss Clara Mullett for paying for my day out. I noticed that the Paybox contained a board with squares numbered from one to eight. The taker had to put the fare in the appropriate box, and in this way the manager of the ride could see that all the occupied cars on the ride were accounted for. This carefulness in handling money made Pat Collins seem a rather different figure to the generous social benefactor image that he cultivated in public. When I knew him he never carried any money upon his person. If he arrived in his chauffeur driven car at the fair, and wished to give someone a tip, he had to obtain the cash from his managers! He promised my father a pension of thirty shillings a week, but it never materialised. On the other hand, he made sure the men who worked for him, such as the drivers, were paid fairly and regularly.

As a social benefactor Pat would arrange Sunday concerts on the organ. My Dad would put on clean overalls and his best cap for these occasions, and smoke a cigar, but such 'voluntary' work was unpaid and occupied most of his 'day off'. But Dad always had a good-humoured attitude towards his work and his life revolved around the engine. His brothers, Harry and Tommy, were also traction engine drivers, and his friends, and rivals, were fellow drivers like Cockney Jack Harvey, Jim Morley and Billy Mills, who drove "The Emperor". Although the crew were lesser mortals, they too were often known and remembered by their nick-names, like Yorky, and Flash Harry, and Flop, who used to steer for Dad.

Although Wednesbury was our home, and the place to which he retired, I don't think Dad ever forgot his birthplace. I remember once going over to the yard at Bloxwich on a Sunday because a Frenchman was coming to tune the Gavioli organ. For my Dad he played "Land of My Fathers", and it brought tears to Dad's eyes.

"Lump Coal Billy" (William Reohorn) died in 1945, and, sadly his son George Reohorn, died in October 1990, some eight months after our interview.

JOHN PUGH

I well remember my brother taking me to a fairground one Wednesday afternoon in 1915 – while the War was on. I know it was a Wednesday because it was my brother's half day off from his job in a grocery shop. I was only about five and a half years' old, but I can remember looking through the entrance, a huge wooden gate that was only open enough to allow people to go in and out while the fair was closed to the public. It was winter and the fair must have opened for only a few hours each cold night. It must have been one of the fairs run in the Liverpool area by John Collins, and it was there that the fair bug got me, and I have been a fairground admirer ever since.

To mark the Peace Celebrations of 1918, a fair was held in Sefton Park, put on by Pat Collins, John Collins, and John's son, Michael Albert. I was very impressed by this huge gathering of engines, rides and living wagons, filling the whole field to capacity. I was told by someone that the boss was "Pat Collins", and I remember seeing him, with his bowler hat and gold watch chain, telling people what to do. I did not imagine that one day I would work for him, and even come to own a living wagon that he had once had built by Orton & Spooner.

Times were rather hard in Liverpool in the late 1920's. I wanted work, and I noticed an advert in World's Fair stating that Pat Collins wanted a showman's painter and signwriter. I immediately wrote for the job.

I arrived early on Monday morning, and met the depot foreman who told me his name was Sid Headley. He was a man born into showland, and he was the son of the late Jack Headley, who had also worked for Pat Collins. He said, "Have you ever done any showman's painting? Come with me and I'll show you the sort of work I need doing". He showed me some very old scroll work, and asked me if I could do that kind of thing. I said, "That's very high class work, but I could try and do something like it". "I doubt it", he said, "I've had several painters in the last few weeks and not one of them has been good enough for this job. I'll start you on condition that if I don't like your class of work by twelve o'clock, I'll give you your rail fare back to Liverpool!"

I felt a little uneasy, but decided that I would just have to try my best. He put me in a corner of the paint shop, so that I was not distracted by being among new people and left me to mix my own colours. No one bothered me and I was left to work on a piece of the old Scenic Dragon ride. By eleven o'clock I had made quite a bit of a flash for him to see, but I was not very happy, and was thinking about the journey home.

Then, in came Sid with Pat himself, and the first thing I heard was Sid saying, "Well, it looks as if we've got someone at last".

The Guvnor smiled and said, "You've got a job for life".

I've worked for many firms as a coachpainter, but working for Pat was the best. Being a man who liked my freedom, I later worked for myself – but showmen's painters generally do.

Pat used to come and tell us how, in his young days, he had slept in a belly-box under a trailer many a time, pointing to a trailer in the yard that had just been built. And he was always full of advice. One day he told me, "When you get down to your last threepenny piece, get it changed to halfpennies, so that you can rattle it". In other words, never let people know when you are broke.

Pat didn't like to see his workers idle, and I remember one wet and foggy day when Pat was in a bad mood. He saw an engine driver not doing anything, so Pat told him to raise steam, and that he would be told later what to do next. That was about 10 o'clock and by 4 o'clock it was growing dark, but the driver had a full head of steam! Pat came out of his house, and said to the driver, "What's all this for? I don't remember telling you to go anywhere".

On one occasion the Gallopers centre truck was on the way to a fair when it hit a bridge and was smashed very badly. The cheese wheel and centre drum were in a very bad mess. It was about 7 o'clock, and the Galloper was due to open the next day, so the centre truck was brought back to the yard at Bloxwich. The Yard Foreman went to the homes of the workmen, and they came in and worked all through the night. They completed the job and the centre truck was taken to the fairground, and the ride opened on time. It was all kept secret from Pat, and he never found out about it. He was not well at the time, and although I think Mrs Collins knew about it, she kept the secret for the sake of his health.

Pat could be full of fun, and he had a way of shouting at people, and then he would grin. He was known for sacking people, and then calling them back saying that he didn't want them to go. He would tell you to watch your step and then tip you half a crown. One morning the sun was shining and foreman Sid came into the workshop with a pound note in his hand, saying "The old Pot and Pan IS in a good mood - he's giving out pound notes as if they are handbills this morning!"

He was a true showman from the word go. I remember once a small circus had a fire while in Liverpool, and when Pat Collins heard the news, he sent them a brand new tent - and they opened on time. This was the kind of thing he would do.

I was working on a packing truck one day when he shouted over to me while he was talking to an engine driver. "I want you to go to Birmingham with this engine. You can steer an engine can't you?"

"No", I replied, "and I haven't got a licence".

"Don't let that worry you", he laughed, "I pay all the fines here" – so I did the job.

Another time he said, "Come here, my son. I want you and Jim to go over to Birmingham Police Sports Day with a Coconut stall". We had a good time – everything was free, so we did not have to handle any cash!

Pat had two Alsation dogs that had to do exactly what he wanted them to do. He would bend over and they had to jump over him, but one was better at it than the other. Of course the one that couldn't do it used to make Pat quite bad tempered but he trained it to do it in the end! He also had a parrot, which I think he bought in Liverpool about 1919. It was still alive when I last visited the office in 1975!

Pat had a very large fleet of engines, and I wouldn't say they were the best to be seen on the fairground, because they did more work than most others. Some of them were very noisy and were in need of painting, and I don't think any of them had pressed-on rubbers like we see today. The wheels had pieces of solid rubber from old wagons and these pieces could work loose and looked a very makeshift job. Some drivers would come and go, saying they were "going south", in search of better engines. Other drivers worked for Pat for most of their lives.

Pat owned an old cinema at the end of the High Street ("The Central" used by Pat as a cinema while the Grosvenor was being built to replace the Electric Palace), and it was full of old fair tackle. But one day the order came to clear the place out, because Pat had sold it. All the old organs, and other old things, had to be brought into the Bloxwich Yard and it was a shame to see such things being burnt, Pat never liked selling anything to other showmen, and that's why things were burned, or left to rot at the Crystal Palace. I wonder what he would have thought of me – his humble servant – later on to be the owner of his living wagon. I also have a small brush which he used to brush down with before going off to Guild meetings or other important places, with a flower in his buttonhole. I also have Aunt Clara's old cane chair that was in that wagon!

PETER HOUGH

The following was recorded after an Interview with Peter at Bloxwich.

The current controversy concerning winter quarters for showmen has been featured on a television programme. When I saw it, I said "There's only one man who could sort that out – Pat Collins – he'd soon have the Government sorted out if it was in his day. He'd really fight, he'd get on with it and make sure they got somewhere to quarter in..." He was President of the Showman's Guild for twenty years.

My father knew Pat Collins well, and his memories went back to before the First War. When the fair came to a town like Bloxwich in those days, all the amusements were delivered by rail – shunted into the sidings at the station. All the local farmers in the area put in so many horses to haul the fair tackle from the station to the fairground. But my Dad wasn't too keen on it. He felt it was a cruel job for the horses. Innocent looking loads could prove much heavier than they looked. But that's how it worked up until the war.

I was told, unofficially, that Pat Collins bought his first traction engine as a result of the railway company not delivering his stuff on time.

In his heyday, he had 28 engines all licensed at one time, and once they were all lined up at the Onion fair in Aston. The fair was laid out in a big circle and all 28 engines stood side by side across the diameter – all generating – they did it once, but never again, because they found it created problems when it came to supplying water to the engines.

The big scenic engines - 8hp engines – had a big crane on the back for lifting the cars on and off the tracks because a scenic car could weigh all of 20 cwt. The engines had two dynamos – the main generator and the small exciter.

The starting of a Scenic railway was so heavy a single operator could not do it. And once a Scenic railway had started, it never stopped all day. A crawler gear could be used to keep it creeping as people were loaded and unloaded. (The Scenics lasted into the early 1930's).

He never paid his men a lot of money, but they were utterly dedicated – they would go through fire for him. It was his 'influence'. They were never rewarded with money. Any of his men could have left and got a job anywhere else if they had wanted to, but there was a 'bond' between them.

One employee told me, "If you start on Pat Collins to tell him off, always make sure you know what you're talking about, otherwise he'll make mincemeat of you! And if you curse him get ready for a cursing back - better than what you can give him!"

During the building up time he could take his jacket off - with his gold watch in its pocket – and he would just hang it up somewhere – but it would still be there when he came back after setting things out. And don't forget all the villains in the world used to follow the fair around, but no one dared touch his watch. They respected him.

He was a great organiser – a magician at organising. He could set the fair out better than anyone else, even if he wasn't an 'educated' man.

One of the drivers, Billy Mills, told me that one night Pat came to the Fowler he was driving, "The Lord James" and he said "That engine's working bloody hard tonight – shut it off". And sure enough, the lighting on half the stalls went out. You could hear popping and banging as they tried to start their own generators. The Guvnor knew when an engine was overloaded, and he warned Billy never to do it again - but I'm sure he did, they all did! Some drivers even had to sell the coal and oil to make their money up – until Pat caught them, and they would be dismissed on the spot, unless they were really good drivers like Mills and Reohorn. He knew he couldn't replace men like them.

There were plenty of men who could push an engine about the country, but there were only a few in the elite who could drive them and keep them running - men who could have run the fair on their own, without any help!

Pat himself could set the fair out alright – striding around with his tape and a man to knock the stakes in the ground, and after setting out all the big machines he could set out the tenants – the little coconut sheets and the skittle alleys and the hamburger joints. Tenants looked up to him because he provided them with a living, and he looked after them because they were putting the bread and butter in his mouth, and keeping his show going. Rental from the side tenants was just as important as his income from the rides. The fair needed a balance of rides and all the stalls and novelties. Mind you, a tenant could not afford to fall out with Pat, because they wouldn't be able to find anywhere better to go to. Many of them stuck to him all their lives.

Laying out the site in Goscote in the 1930's was a good example of Pat's caring attitude. he even looked after his followers – the blokes who slept around the rides. When they died, he must have buried many of them – otherwise all that was in front of them was a pauper's grave. He never loosed them down.

ANTHONY HARRIS

At an interview on May 18th, 1990, at the Rowley Regis fair, the following interview was recorded.

People come to the fair and ask me, "Is this really still Pat Collins' fair?"...I tell them it is, and they say...."Are you Pat Collins?"...I usually say, "Yes, but my name is Anthony Harris".

I was born on 22nd April 1940, my Father was Elias Harris, and my mother was Evelyn Caroline Baker. She was the oldest daughter of Dan Baker, son of George Baker of Southampton – the largest haulage contractor in the South of England in his time. Somewhere in their history the Bakers' had been of fairground stock, but it is because I am the son of Elias Harris that I am running Pat Collins' fair, nearly half a century after Pat's death.

My father, Elias Harris, worked fairs in the south of England, while I was growing up. He ran a Wall of Death, and we travelled the London fairs, Southampton Common, the South Coast, and across into South Wales, to Neath, Llanelly and Carmarthen. Oxford, was about as far towards the Midlands that we ever travelled.

At the age of eight, I was a Wall of Death rider, and I've still got my little motor bike to this day. In the school holidays I used to be the first act! But, as I grew up, father saw the problems of finding staff to move the Wall of Death about and decided we would be better off with a roundabout. The Octopus was one of the first novelty rides and we decided to buy one. I remember the last time the Wall was built up - it was at Neath. I went up to ride on it on the last day, and it was then pulled down and packed away - sheeted up in the yard. If we ever suggested to father that he sold it, he would have none of such nonsense, but we didn't understand why.

We did not know that the Wall of Death had been a wedding present from Pat Collins to my father at the time of his first marriage to Margaret Collins. (This aspect of the story is discussed in Chapter 15). When Margaret died, Elias left the Midlands and the circuit of fairs that were associated with her family. He married my mother about 1936, and we grew up with no knowledge that my father had ever been married to anybody else.

Although we had no idea that father had been married before, we used to play in an old bus that father had used as a temporary home while working as an aviation fitter during the War. Our home was in Hook, in Hampshire, and as we played in the old bus we were aware of a picture that was hung in it. My cousin, Michael Monte, pointed out that the man in the picture looked like my father, but the woman certainly wasn't my mother. When the story was unfolded to us we understood why there was more of a family atmosphere around when working with the Collinses.

I was sent off to public school at Yately Manor, near Sandhurst, where I learnt to talk uppie-yuppie, and I left school about the same time as John and Pat, the sons of Walsall John, who was running Pat Collins' fairs at the time. We all returned to the fairground about the same time.

My father's return to the Midlands and re-association with the Collins' family had happened slowly. Once he had packed the Wall of Death away and entered the machine business with his Octopus, he had travelled mainly in the Eastern Counties, and for many years we had travelled with Stanley Thurston and Sons.

Meanwhile, we drifted nearer the Midlands. We used to visit Luton, then Bedford, and then, one year went to Northampton and eventually to Coventry. It must have been then that John Collins said to my father, "Why don't you come home?". And so it was that we joined Collins' fair at Birmingham Onion Fair. It was dusty and dirty, and compared to the grassy Eastern Counties sites, we thought it was terrible – but we took a lot of money, much more money than we were used to. So the next year we joined them at Bedworth and went on to Worcester and Birmingham again. The year after that we returned to the Midlands completely, except for June and July when we went to old haunts like Henley Regatta and Basingstoke Carnival. Aunt Clara was still alive at that time but John was really the Guvnor. However, he had so many other interests, including Battersea and Yarmouth, the fairs were administered by managers. So that's how I found myself in the Midlands, and back in 'the family', with John's sons, John and Pat.

Even before John's death (in 1977), the management

of the fair had been in quite a mess. Father had been asked to sort things out, but he also found it difficult to cope with, so I found myself playing a larger part in the management of the business as well as presenting our own machines.

Then came a time when John wanted to leave Barry Island and this involved selling his interest to Pat. In order to raise the money to buy that interest, Pat sold his share in the travelling fair to me. It took about eighteen months to sort everything out, but the deal finally resolved while the fair was here at Rowley Regis, and I took full financial control of the business in the Autumnn of 1983. No-one need have feared that I would change the name of the business... that was one of its greatest assets! Thus it became vested in me to "Keep the Flag Flying" in Pat Collins' dying words... and that's just what I intend to do.

We will never go back to running several fairs all at the same time on different sites, as Pat Collins had done before the War. However, I am making sure we expand on the sites we have got, and present a good show that is capable of being personally supervised. Things are getting better. We now need Local Authorities to realise that the fair is a good thing, and they should give us better amenities on the sites. For example, with proper power points we could get rid of the silly generators - we could go "green". With a proper current supply, the noise and fume levels would become minimal and the fair could enjoy a cleaner and quieter environment. I know that noise is part of the atmosphere, but that could be created without the sound of generators blasting us into the next century.

It was all because John Collins had asked my father to return to the Midlands, and assist in managing the fair, that has led to me assuming the mantle of Pat Collins' Fair – cemented by me being part of a trio with Pat and John. It is marriage and friendship that has created the fair that exists today. I have also maintained other traditions associated with Pat Collins, for example, I have followed his footsteps in the Showman's Guild, and even in terms of religion. My father became a Catholic to marry Margaret Collins, and mother became a Catholic to marry Elias! And we still maintain that Catholic link.

When I obtained control of Pat Collins' Fair in 1983, the only ride I gained was the Dodgems that had previously belonged to Barry Island Pat. All the other rides were ours anyway. What I had really gained were the foundations of the business ... the forty to forty five fairs a year.

Our transport is now in a distinctive green and cream livery. I think I inherited my ideas about fleet colours from my Baker side. My father had no concept of fleet colours at all. He painted equipment whatever colour happened to be in the tin, but I am a painter, and I like to think I have an eye for colour. We do all our own decorating and make a feature of the Pat Collins' name – we are even having "PC" put on the mud flaps. I know that the Black Country is greener than it was, but on a grey Black Country day I still think it is nice to see a bit of green, despite Pat Collins' once being associated with the traditional showman's colour of maroon.

I know that John Collins would have nothing green on the fair, and I had never seen grass painted blue until I saw his grass – he had a duck ride with blue grass and blue trees – it might have been turquoise, but it was still blue! He was obsessed with the idea that green was bad luck, I think my father painted his truck green, but I don't know if it was done mischievously or whether he wanted to demonstrate that he wasn't going to allow anyone else to dictate to him what colour he could use. Green has been lucky for me.

I married Christine Gabrielle Shaw in 1968. Christine is the daughter of Walter Shaw of the Lancashire Section. My wedding present was "The Skid" (we didn't have the Waltzer then, we only had the Octopus and the Jets). My three sons are Anthony Charles, Charles Patrick, and Michael Dan Spencer. They are all "Pat Collins mad", and I am sure they too, in their turn, will "Keep the Flag Flying".

THE PRESERVATION & RESTORATION HISTORY OF THE PAT COLLINS NO.2. WONDERLAND ORGAN

Bill Hunt.

This instrument was produced for Pat Collins in 1908, it formed the centre piece of the Bioscope Show, which was the most magnificent show ever to travel with the British Fairground.

The gold leaf was on all the carved work, rather as it is today on the organ, and the total built-up length was some 60 feet long and 30 feet high. The carved front of the Bioscope and the organ was by Orton & Spooner of Burton on Trent. The organ was one of three 104 key instruments produced by Marenghi, of Paris, who had left the Gavioli concern some years earlier to improve and build upon what had been done prior to his starting his own business. The other two organs which were very similar went to Thurstons and Kemps.

It is said that the Bandmaster on Pat Collins organ was bigger, this figures because Pat Collins always had to have something bigger and better than anyone else, indeed the showfront in total was better. There is a photograph taken about 1910 at the Nottingham Goose Fair which shows it off in its magnificence.

Very soon these big organs suffered from lack of maintenance, some of the pipes were very soon taken away from the top of the organ; these pipes, incidently had to be dismantled every time the organ was moved and it was not long before the big

Bioscope shows were taken over by the permanent cinema, certainly by the time of the First World War the fun was over and the organs were stored. Luckily the electric drive big roundabouts were on the increase with the motors underneath the cars rather than being driven from a centre engine, this meant that there was a void in the middle of the big roundabouts, and these big organs could be cut down and, in the 1920/21 era, it was put into the Pat Collins No.1. Scenic Railway, known as the Dragon and Peacock Scenic because the alternate cars were dragons and peacocks. The organ was sent up to fit into the ride for its first outing in the market place at Burton on Trent, the ride having been built by Orton and Spooner. Pat Collins had ordered a brand new Showmen's Scenic Burrell to drive the ride and it was known as No.1. for the whole of its life.

Of all the fairground organs in preservation today, No.2. Wonderland is one of the most famous, and perhaps as ornate as any with its very heavy gold leaf carvings... the six ladies in their rather scanty attire of course always attract attention... and the bandmaster, is particularly attractive because of the size; most fairground organ figures are considerably smaller.

With a weight of 10 tons and a length of 30 feet it does take quite a bit of handling to pull it around the country. We do this with a Scammell tractor unit which, at one time, was in the hands of Shell Mex & BP as an articulated tractor. However, we have restored it into the style of the fairground and I do think that it is an admirable addition to the organ and everyone seems to like the Scammell as much as the organ now.

In recent times we have of course added to the repertoire of music books and these are taken out to the rallies with the organ. They weigh a considerable amount and sometimes we have to leave some of the music behind.

Mechanical improvements to the organ have continued over the years in my ownership and each year we find some little job to do which makes it just that little bit better. Keeping it in tune, of course, is quite a job and I have a very good volunteer helper who does assist me in that direction; his ear is much better than mine!

I have had a connection with the Collins' firm for many many years, going back to my childhood, and it is with great pride that I keep the Pat Collins' name on the top of the organ. It is really part of our heritage and a tribute to the man who travelled it in its original condition.

Perhaps it would have been very nice to have retained the Bioscope showfront, but of course, Collins' abandoned that many, many years ago. I have often been asked why I didn't buy the Scenic Railway roundabout as well, but I don't know what on earth I would have done with it, it took up an enormous amount of room and it would have been a complete white elephant. Some years ago it was thought that I had in fact purchased it, and that I had stored it away from the public gaze. I have had to put the record straight and say that sadly, I saw it being burnt. Somebody may have liked to have had it, but it would have been far too much for me to handle.

I acquired The Leader in 1962 and although a certain amount of work was done to the engine prior to 1972 we only used her occasionally because the gears were so worn that it was really a shame to carry on the destruction of such a unique engine, because by then the remaining 9 engines in the Class had been broken up and I particularly wanted to save and preserve The Leader in its true form.

In 1972 I began a complete restoration which continued until 1979; new gears were fitted, the engine was completely and utterly rebuilt. I managed to acquire a very large ex-Pat Collins' dynamo, exactly similar to the one she carried most of her working life, it was a slow speed model and a perfect fit for the engine.

With such a rebuild it would have been a shame not to have given the engine a full test on at least one occasion, and the chance to do this occurred in 1981 at Stourpaine. Much talk had gone on about what various engines could do, and a certain amount of boasting between engine owners and showmen as to what could or could not be done by a traction engine, for by that time, many had forgotten just what it was like to have them on the fairground.

So, we coupled the engine to the James Noyse Gallopers at Stourpaine Bushes, a terrible day, typical Stourpaine mud with a line up of engines perhaps some 20 in number. No-one up to then had managed to drive both the lights and the ride and the organ of those Gallopers. The full running load is some 450 amps at 110 volts with a starting load, if one is clumsy, reaching perhaps 500 amps. We achieved this performance with the Leader for the whole of one Saturday evening, and it amazed everyone there. It was very hard work. The engine was really working... and we did prove that it could be done.

During the war years, my company Hunt Brothers (Oldbury) Ltd frequently did repairs to the traction engines to keep them running. Diesel oil and petrol were scarce and there was an allocation of coal for the Showmen to keep the engines running. After all they did not only haul rides to the grounds, but they generated as well.

Many times when the fair came to the Oldbury area, a traction engine would be found in our yard with the odd little job being done, few bolts here or there, or the re-machining of a bearing or a new bearing being fitted, just literally to 'keep the show on the road'.

After the War this practice continued with frequently bigger jobs being undertaken as the engines became worn out. In 1946 my Father acquired a large Burrell from another Showman. He always wanted to own a Showman's traction engine and here was his opportunity. Some of them were by then being scrapped, however, it was a good engine and Collins' were so short of motive power that they asked to purchase the engine. The engine was in fact, renamed by us, being called "The Griffin"... it had previously been "The White Rose of York", and it went on to do a considerable amount of work for Collins' until the mid-Fifties, when she was retired. I purchased this engine in 1962, having had first option on it for many many years, because we had shown a considerable interest in it even after it had been sold to the Collins' firm.

I had been introduced to the Fairground as a young boy during the War years. I suppose I must only have been about 7 or 8 years' old. From then on I climbed on and around the traction engines both when they were being used to generate electricity and hauling the loads. I got to know the drivers well and really the whole business of the Showmen's traction engine was a natural progression and it is for me as easy to climb an engine and to drive them as falling out of bed. It has just been a natural part of my life.

I was only 12 years old when I was told to look after a Showman's engine, generating. It was a big Fowler on Oldbury Fairground, the name of the engine – The Dreadnought – and my Father gave the driver half a dollar and told him to go to the pub and get a drink and to leave me to it. I was scared stiff, but I never let the Showmen down and from then on many a night I looked after the engines for them. I was also introduced to the roundabouts and managers, and taught how to ride on the boards of the Arks and collect the money. Occasionally I would be allowed to look after the Dodgems in the Paybox, but never when they were really busy, because the fairgrounds on Friday and Saturday nights shortly after the end of the war were absolutely packed with people in a way we never ever see today. Everyone was just getting a little bit of freedom following the war years, and really the travelling fair was cheap entertainment.

Mrs Martin

"I used to worship at St Peter's RC Church, High Street, Bloxwich. Pat Collins used to worship there regularly; he always sat on the left hand side, near the altar and had a cushion. When the plate was passed around for the first collection Pat would always put a one pound note on the plate. During the second collection he always put a ten shilling note on the plate."

Mr George Corbett

"Once when coming from Tipton with the Three Abreast my Dad and the men hit a bridge and smashed all the gearing...crowds of people gathered round...Pat Collins was talking as nice as pie to everyone...then, when he got the men on their own he sacked them all! Afterwards he came to see Dad and apologised and gave them all their jobs back".

Reg Corbett

"At a time when the pictures and the pubs were the only escapes from a life of hard work at the coal face or by the furnace...Pat Collins' fairground burned like a 'beacon of anticipation' for the Black Country people".

RIGHT: Almost half a century after Pat Collins' death his name lives on thanks to Anthony Harris' travelling fair, the preserved engines, and the Wonderland Organ. Long may they continue to stir people's memories of the "King of Showmen".

OTHER PUBLICATIONS AVAILABLE FROM URALIA PRESS

Black Country Folk at Werk
NED WILLIAMS
Local people give an illustrated account of their working lives - in their own words. Most traditional local industries represented.
96 pp A4 pbk.
£5.95. plus post and packing.

More Black Country Folk at Werk
NED WILLIAMS
A sequel to the above, looking at the Black Country through the eyes of workers in a variety of other occupations, including "show business" eg Billy Kayes tells us about Kayes' Circus, which travelled with Pat Collins.
96 pp A4 pbk
£5.95. plus post and packing.

Shop in the Black Country
NED WILLIAMS
Over 200 pictures, plus 25 in colour, of local shops - their design and their history, trade by trade, erea by era, from the 1880's to the 1980's, form corner shops to mighty multiples.
72 pp A4 pbk
£4.95. plus post and packing.

The Railway to Wombourn
NED WILLIAMS
A profusely illustrated account of the history of the GWR branch line from Oxley Junction to Kingswinford Junction, via Wombourn.
64 pp A4 pbk
£4.95. plus post and packing.

Wombourne What Was
MAY GRIFFITHS
Pictorial history of the village of Wombourne with informative captions.
96 pp A5 pbk
£3.99. plus post and packing.

Our Town - The Story of Willenhall
SAM and MARY CLAYTON
An illustrated account of what two local people found when they set out to discover the history of "their" town, famous for its lock manufacture.
64 pp A4 pbk
£4.50. plus post and packing.

Wolverhampton on Wheels
SIMON DEWEY & NED WILLIAMS
96 photographs and a full colour cover bring you all the excitement of Wolverhampton's transport history: trains, trams, trolleys, buses, motor cycles, cars and commercials from horse-drawn days to the present.
96 pp pbk.
£4.50. plus post and packing.

ALL BOOKS available BY POST from:
URALIA PRESS,
23 Westland Road, Wolverhampton. WV3 9NZ.
Add 10% for P & P

AFTER READING THIS BOOK
You may wish to pursue an interest in local history or the Fairground, or a Preservation Society, the following are therefore brought to your notice:

THE BLACK COUNTRY SOCIETY
is interested in all aspects of the region's past, present and future; holds monthly meetings, arranges visits and other events, and is currently planning a spectacular 25th Anniversary celebration in 1992. A quarterly journal is published "The Blackcountryman", Editor Stan Hill. Enquiries to Membership Secretary, Ron Julian, 97 Stream Road, Kingswinford, DY6 OHR.

THE FAIRGROUND ASSOCIATION OF GREAT BRITAIN
organises meetings and exhibitions in various parts of the country. Quarterly journal the "Fairground Mercury", Editor Graham Downie. Other publications include: Books on Gallopers, and Moon Rockets, and currently in preparation... a book on Hull Fair. Enquiries to Membership Secretary, Stephen Smith, 38 Stratford Ave, Newcastle-under-Lyme, Staffs. ST5 OJS

THE FAIRGROUND SOCIETY
contributes a column in the World's Fair, maintaining a useful contact network among fairground fans. Publishes a quarterly journal "Fairground Society Jottings". Enquiries to Mr & Mrs R. Tunnicliffe, Rutland Cottage Music Museum, Whaplode St Catherines, Spalding, Lincs. PE12 6SF.

THE FAIR ORGAN PRESERVATION SOCIETY
promotes and encourages all forms of interest in, and the preservation of, Fair Organs and Mechanical Musical Instruments. Quarterly journal "The Key Frame", regularly reported in World's Fair. Enquiries to Membership Secretary: Mr J M Page, 24 London Road, Pembroke Dock, Dyfed, SA72 6DU

THE FAIRGROUND HERITAGE TRUST
is actively preserving Britain's fairground heritage and hopes to establish a museum at Northampton. Details from Geoff Weedon, 34 Sacville Garden, Hove, Sussex, BN3 4GH.

FAIRGROUND MODELLING
Interested? Plans, kits and accessories are now widely available for fairground modellers in a variety of scales. Details of kits in 4mm scale can be obtained from Langley Models, 166 Three Bridges Road, Crawley, RH10 1LE. Details of suppliers in larger scales can be found in society journals.

FUNERAL OF ALD. PAT COLLINS.

The funeral took place at Bloxwich on Monday, December 13, of the late Alderman Pat Collins, who died on December 8, in his 85th year.

A special family service was held on Sunday evening at St. Patrick's Church, Walsall, and on Monday morning a solemn Requiem Mass was held, Father J. Hanrahan officiating.

After Mass a stirring address was given by Provost Yeo, who in the course of his address announced that Mr. Collins had been offered a Knighthood six years ago, but refused it, preferring to be known for the remainder of his life as just Pat Collins.

From the church the funeral made a special detour through Walsall, past the Town Hall and Council House, where he had served his town so well. Crowds of people lined the streets of Walsall and Bloxwich to pay tribute and last respects to one who had always been their benefactor and friend.

The hearse was met at the gates of Bloxwich Cemetery by the clergy and choir of St. Peter's Church, Bloxwich, who preceded the body to the vault where the interment took place with the solemn burial service being conducted by Father J. Hanrahan, of Bloxwich.

The bearers were Messrs. H. Weston, senr., Ted Sherwood, Frank Sherwood, Ike Bailey, Cpl. Joe Proverbs and P. Cosgrave.

The Mourners.

The mourners included:—Mrs. P. Collins, senr. (widow); Mr. P. R. Collins and Mr. John Collins (sons); Mrs. J. Collins (daughter-in-law), Mr. P. R. Collins, junr., and Mr. J. J. Collins (grandsons); Mrs. E. Monte (grand-daughter); Miss Hetty Davies, Mr. M. A. Collins and wife, Mr. J. P. Collins and wife, Miss Norah Collins, Mrs. McDermott, Mr. Michael Collins, junr. John Collins, junr., Mr. and Mrs. J Farrell, Charles, Sally and Jeby, Mrs. M. Chadwick, Norah and Eileen, Mr. E. Monte, Mr. Walter Hobbs, Mrs. H Studt, Mrs. N. Charlton, Mrs. P. R. Collins, Mrs. J. J. Collins, and Mrs. J. McCoughlin (nephews and nieces).

Among the hundreds who also attended the funeral we were able to obtain the following names, and we apologise for any names missing:—The Chief Constable of Walsall (Mr. Mark Watson); The Mayor of Walsall, Deputy Mayor and Town Clerk; The Mayor of Chester (Ald W. M. Jones); Ald. S. E. Edge, A. J. Stanley, E. H. Ingram, D. Cartwright, G. Tibbits; Councillors F. Bonner, Dr. E. P. Drabble, T. Partridge W. Kendrick, H. F. Truman, Mrs. A. McShane, A. E. Hurst, J. Venison, Mr. J. Cavanagh W. Atkins, J. R. Summers, C. G. Moore, S. Wiggin, B. Power J. Colebatch, and T. F. Mayo. The Borough Member was represented by Mr. T. E. Bennett.

Mr. L. K. Mason, representing the Chamber of Commerce; Mr. E. F. Sharpe, representing Walsall General Hospital; Mr. H. Coad, representing Messrs. Nicklin and Cotterill; Mr. J B Cooper (secretary and accountant to Mr. P. Collins); Mr. E. Steel; Mr. and Mrs. H. Chapman; Mr. John Ryan; Mr. S. Salisbury; Mr. and Mrs. J. Ryan; Madame Lilley and Husband; Mr. E. Harris; Mr. Pat Tyler; Mr. F. Fordick; Mr Jim Collier; Mr and Mrs. T Hughes Mr. J. Symonds, Mr. Jerrison (Burton-on-Trent); Messrs. Orton and Spooner; Mrs. Littletord; Mr. J. Shepherd; Mr. A. Hayes; Monte Goodman (Leeds); Mr and Mrs. Joe Saxon; D. Brooks; Mr. A. J. Rogers; Norah Rogers; Mr. A. J. Peters; C. Deeks, Mr. D. Shipley; Mr G Roberts; Mr. Frank Wilson; Mr J. Murphy (General Secretary, representing the Showmen's Guild); Mr. Frank Mellor; Mr and Mrs. Mrs. Geo. Roberts; Mr. J. Ingham, H. H. Hall, junr.; Mr. and Mrs. Jack Proctor; Mr. Jas. Whyatt; Mr. Jim Trayner; Mr. H. Barnard; Mr. T Cordwell; Mr. Wood (representing Lancashire Stallholders); Mr. A. Stout (representing Lancashire Section Showmen's Guild); Mr. L. Silcock; Mr. W Chadwick; Mr. W. Dutton.

Mr. John Peters, representing Yorkshire Section Showmen's Guild; Mrs. G. Lowe; Mr and Mrs. F. Sherwood; Mr Jack Barry; Mr. A. Jerrison; Mr. A. Webber; Mr. T. Kayes; Mrs. A. Fletcher, Mrs. Hollinder; Mr and Mrs. J. Cordwell; Mrs. Millership; Mr A. Buckland; Mr. E. Buckland; Mrs. J. Connor; Mr and Mrs. J. Hall; Mr. W Manders; Mr. G. Manders; Mr. G. Symonds Mr Andrews; Mr. H. Jones; Mrs E. Fossett; Mr. W. Owen; Mr. J. Shepherd; Mr Fred Connor senr.; Mr. and Mrs. G. Tweddle; Mr. Pat Tyler; Mr. P. Magill; Mr. H. Humphreys; Miss Harrison; Mr. W Croydon; Mr. F. Bibb; Mrs. Clough; Mr. Tuby; Mr. Jas Harris; Mr. H. Seff representing the A.C.A.; Mr W. Weston; Mrs. A. Badger; Mrs. L. Hickman; Mr and Mrs. D. Watson; Mr Chas. Evans, South Wales; Mr Ben Coles; Mr J Bibb; Mr. Birkett; Mr. and Mrs. Sam Birch; Mrs. J. Swan; Mr. Geo. Strickland; Mr. T. Roberts; Mr. and Mrs. A. Hedges; Mrs. W. Sherwood; Mr. Maurice Cohen; Mrs. R. Deeks; Mr H. Roper; Mr. and Mrs. Fred Hart, Mr. Victor Hart; Mr. C. Deakin; Mr. W. Lennards, Vice-President Showmen's Guild, Mr Lawson Trout, representing Mr Geo. Black; Mr T. E. Bennett, representing Sir George Schuster, M.P.; Mr. T. Harris, Chairman Midland Section Showmen's Guild; Mr. and Mrs. Ted Sherwood; Mr A. Cook; Mr. W. J. Morgan, representing J. R Bentley (Insurance) Ltd.

Floral Tributes.

Wreaths were sent by:—Mrs. P. Collins (wife); Son Patrick; Nora Collins; Hettie; John and Clara (son and daughter-in-law); John and Nora Collins; Enoch Hall; Michael and May; Mr. and Mrs. Harry Hall; Mr. and Mrs. J. C. Proctor. Niece Maggie Chadwick and family; Niece Flora and Jack McLoughlin; Nephew Job, Maggie and family; Grand-daughter Flora, Eddie, Molly and Michael; Nephew and Niece James and Bella; Daughter-in-law Mollie; P. R. Collins, junr.

Mr. and Mrs. H. Swain and family; The National Fire Service. "D" Division; Mr. and Mrs. R. Keeble; Mrs. J. Swann and family; Mr. and Mrs. Jim Shepherd; Mr. and Mrs. H. Weston, junr.; Midland Comforts Fund; Mrs. Weston; Mrs. Harris; Mr. and Mrs. C. West; Mr. and Mrs. J. Humphreys; Will, Amy and family; Capt. and Mrs. Clarke; Mr. and Mrs. F. Bibb; Mr. and Mrs. H. Chaplain and family; Mr. and Mrs. Horace Jones and W. Morris; Tenants, Kingston Hill Fair Ground; Mr. and Mrs. Tom Cordwell and family; Mr. and Mrs. A. McGill and family; Clara and Willie McGill and family; Bloxwich Branch of the British Legion; W. J. Webster, Willenhall; Mr. and Mrs. Tom Jones; Fred Kimberley; Walsall Constitutional Club; Mr. and Mrs. C. Hayes, junr.; Mr. and Mrs. C. Hayes, senr.; Mr. and Mrs. Buckland; Mrs. J. Lewis; Mr. and Mrs. Recco; Mr. and Mrs. Reaney; Mr. and Mrs. H. Paulo, junr.; Mr. and Mrs. George Tucker; W. H. Williams and Sarah May; Mr. and Mrs. J. Newsome; Mr. and Mrs. T. Southwood; Mrs. Crewe Addie; Mrs. Deeks; Mr. and Mrs. George Roberts; Mr. and Mrs. Charlton; Mr. Goode; A. Law; Danny Brooks; W. H. Roper and family; Mr. and Mrs. Tierney; Mr. and Mrs. Low; Mr. and Mrs. G. Corbett; A. Cook and family; W. Hall and family; Mr and Mrs. Shipley.

Mr. and Mrs. J. J. Caddick; Nellie Mullett; Mrs. McLoughlin and Annie Bibb; Lancashire Stallholders' Federation; Mr. and Mrs. Sam Clough; W. Weston and family; Mrs. Holden and family; Lancashire Section, Silcock Brothers; Mrs. L. Hickman and son; Mr. and Mrs. J. Wright; Mr. and Mrs. B. Hayes; F. Hart; T Roberts; Mrs. A. Fletcher and family; Mr. and Mrs. R. Wilson; Mr. and Mrs. A. B. Buckland, Buckingham; Mr. L. A. Hackett, Southport; George and Hannah White, Cosy Corner, Barry Island; Mr. W. Messham; Mr G. Messham; Mr. Ernie Leech, Crewe; Gilbert Dixon and family; Messrs. A. Deakin and Sons; Mr. and Mrs. Charles Johnson; Mrs. Wm. Pinder and family, Haltcastle.

Mr. and Mrs. J. Romain; Mr. and Mrs. Lewis; Alfred Denville, M.P.; Mr. and Mrs. J. Corrigan, senr.; Mr. and Mrs. Bob Lakin; W. E. Butlin; R. Kayes and son; Mr. and Mrs. Chadwick; Mr. and Mrs. Henry Thurston, Wellingborough; Bloxwich Depot and Office Staff; A. J. Peters, Worcester; Estelle and Frank Buckley; Mr. and Mrs. Arthur Barnard; Mr. and Mrs. Bert Hughes; Green Brothers, Preston; Mr. and Mrs. Jack Parry; Mr. and Mrs. T. Murphy; Derby, Notts and Lincs. Section of the Showmen's Guild; Yorkshire Section; Norman H. Dixon; President. Officials and Members of the Showmen's Guild; Chairman, Secretary and Members of the Western Section; Northern Section, Showmen's Guild; Mr. and Mrs. Cartwright, Wednesbury; Mr. and Mrs. W. Lennards; John Simons and family; Mr. and Mrs. Thomas Hughes; Mr. and Mrs. Elias Harris; Fanny Jones; Mrs. Bradbury's family; Mr. and Mrs. George Strickland; The Tenants, Sutton Coldfield; Mr. and Mrs. J. Ryan; John G. Cotterell; Solly Salisbury and family; H. J. Nicklin; The Mayor and Members of the Walsall Town Council; Mrs. Mullett and family, Barry Island; Fred Conner, junr.; Mr. and Mrs. Harry Seff; Mr. and Mrs. Mills and family; Reginald Tildesley; Mr. and Mrs. J. Saxon.

The Tenants, Pleasure Park, Barry Island; J. Ransome Bentley, Birmingham; Mr. and Mrs. H. Chapman; Mr. and Mrs. Twigdon; Mrs. Kate Jerrison; Miss Sarah and Richard Weir; Orton and Spooner families; Mr. and Mrs. Harris; Mr. and Mrs. Hedges and family; Mr. and Mrs. Sam Birch; Mr. and Mrs. W. Hill; Jack Barry; Mr. and Mrs. J. B. Cooper; Jim Collier; Mr. and Mrs. Frosdick; J. Day and son, Merthyr; Mrs. Sheldon; Frank Wilson; Mr. and Mrs. John Chipperfield; Wattee and Wife; Mr. and Miss Johnson; Mr. and Mrs. J. R. Minns; Mr. and Mrs. Wm. Wilson; Staff, Barry Island Pleasure Park; Mr. W. Lyons; Mr. and Mrs. Bernard Jones; Mr. J. Ryan, senr., Moreton; Mr. and Mrs. E. Steel and family; Caldmore Liberal Club; Bloxwich Allotment Society; A. Sargent; Mr. and Mrs. Charles Drakely and Minnie; Midland Section of the Showmen's Guild; Mr. and Mrs. A. Rogers and family; Mr. and Mrs. Frank Sherwood; Mr. and Mrs. W. Croydon and family; Billie and Nellie Ireland; Mr. and Mrs. Ted Sherwood and family; Mr. and Mrs. Herbert Bernard; Directors of John Hawley; Mr. and Mrs. Tom Dobson; Mr. and Mrs. J. Cordwell; Madame Lilley and husband; Mr. and Mrs. Ernest Humphreys; Nephew Walter Hobbs; Walsall Liberal Club; Sir George and Lady Schuster; The Liberals of Walsall; Gourock Ropeworks; Mr. and Mrs. Joe Proverbs; Mr. and Mrs. Albert Sedgwick; and Albert Sedgwick and Nellie. — W. Croydon.